# THE GOSPEL ACCORDING TO ST. MARK.

# THE GOSPEL ACCORDING TO

# ST. MARK

## WITH NOTES CRITICAL AND PRACTICAL

### BY THE REV. M. F. SADLER
LATE RECTOR OF HONITON AND PREBENDARY OF WELLS

WIPF & STOCK · Eugene, Oregon

Wipf and Stock Publishers
199 W 8th Ave, Suite 3
Eugene, OR 97401

The Gospel According to St. Mark
With Notes Critical and Practical
By Sadler, M. F.
ISBN 13: 978-1-62564-966-9
Publication date 6/12/2014
Previously published by G. Bell & Sons, 1884

# INTRODUCTION.

THE Church has never known but one St. Mark, the Evangelist and the companion of St. Peter and St. Paul. The first mention of him in the New Testament is in Acts xii. 12: [Peter] "came to the house of Mary, the mother of John, whose surname was Mark, where many were gathered together, praying." From this we gather that he was the son of a Christian lady of much consideration in the early Church of Jerusalem, whom we afterwards learn to have been the sister of Barnabas (Col. iv. 10). We next find him at Antioch in the company of Barnabas and Saul (xii. 25), and acting as their minister at the commencement of their first missionary journey, but leaving them for some reason not specified, and returning to Jerusalem (xiii. 13).

It was a reason, however, which Paul resented as unworthy of a special messenger of Christ, and he refused to have him as their minister on their next journey. Barnabas, however, took him and sailed to Cyprus. The whole passage runs: "And some days after Paul said unto Barnabas, Let us go again and visit our brethren in every city where we have preached the word of the Lord, and see how they do. And Barnabas determined to take with them John, whose surname was Mark. But Paul thought not good to take him with them, who departed from them from Pamphylia, and went not with them to the work. And the contention was so sharp between them, that they departed asunder one from the other: and so Barnabas took Mark, and sailed unto Cyprus" (xv. 36-39). I cannot forbear giving the reader the remarks of the late Professor Blunt (in his "Scriptural Coincidences") on this place: "A curious chain of consistent narrative may be traced throughout the whole of this passage. The cause of the contention between Paul and Barnabas has been already noticed by Dr. Paley. I need not therefore do more than call to my reader's mind . . . . the passage in the Epistle to the Colossians (iv. 10), where it is casually said that "Marcus was sister's son to Barnabas," a relationship most satisfactorily accounting for the otherwise extraordinary pertinacity with which Barnabas takes up Mark's cause in this dispute with Paul . . . . One circumstance more remains still to be noticed. Mark, it seems, in the former journey, "departed from them from Pamphylia, and went not with them to the work." How did this happen? The explanation, I think, is not difficult. Paul and Barnabas are appointed to go forth and preach. Accordingly they hasten to Seleucia, the nearest seaport to Antioch, where they were staying, and taking with them John Mark, "sailed to Cyprus" (xiii. 4). Since Barnabas was a Cypriote, it is probable that his nephew Mark was the same, or at any rate that he had friends and relations in that island. His mother, it is true, had a house in Jerusalem, where the disciples met, and where some of them perhaps lodged (xii. 12); but so had Mnason, who was nevertheless of Cyprus (xxi. 16). How reasonable, then, is it to suppose that in joining himself to Paul and Barnabas in the outset of their journey, he was partly influenced by a very innocent desire to visit his kindred, his connections, or perhaps his birthplace, and that having achieved this object, he landed with his two companions in Pamphylia, and so returned forthwith to Jerusalem. And this supposition, it may be added, is strengthened by the expression applied by St. Paul to Mark, that "he went not with them *to the work*," as if in the particular case the voyage to Cyprus did not deserve to be considered even the beginning of their labours, being more properly a visit of choice to kinsfolk and acquaintance, or to a place at least having strong local charms for Mark (p. 334-336).

It is satisfactory to find that this temporary estrangement was turned into attachment arising from the sense of Mark's value as a labourer in the same holy cause, for St. Paul writes to Timothy, "Take Mark and bring him with thee, for he is profitable to me for the ministry." He had before this been in the band of Paul's fellow-labourers, for in the Epistle to Philemon we read his name as sending his salutation to him (v. 23-24).

The last allusion to him makes him a companion of St. Peter. " The Church that is at Babylon [probably Rome], elected together with you, saluteth you, and so doth Marcus, my son." It is conjectured that St. Peter calls Mark his son, because he had been converted by him.

These are all the allusions to him in Scripture. It is clear that notwithstanding his first slight defection, he became afterwards so established in the faith, as to be a fellow-helper and close companion of the two leading Apostles.

Ecclesiastical records make him to have been the founder of the Church in Alexandria. Eusebius thus writes of it:—

"The same Mark, they also say, being the first that was sent to Egypt, proclaimed the Gospel there which he had written, and first established Churches at the city of Alexander." ("Eccles. Hist." bk. ii. ch. 16.)

The Holy Scripture tells us nothing whatsoever respecting the writing of his Gospel. There is no preface to it fixing its authorship, as in the case of St. Luke's Gospel, of the Acts, and of most of the Epistles; but if there be one single fact of the early Church more certain from the united concurrence of all Church history than any other, it is that the composition of his Gospel was occasioned by, and closely connected with, St. Mark's intimacy with St. Peter. Papias, Justin Martyr, Irenæus, Clement of Alexandria, Tertullian, Origen, and Eusebius, are alike in their testimony on this.

Papias was Bishop of Hierapolis in the time of Polycarp, *i.e.*, very early in the second century. He took pains in collecting reminiscences of our Lord and of His Apostles, and the following extract from his exposition of the oracles of the Lord, is preserved in Eusebius:—

"And John the Presbyter also said this, 'Mark, being the interpreter of Peter, wrote accurately all that he remembered, but not, however, in the order in which it was spoken or done by our Lord, for he neither heard nor followed our Lord, but, as before said, he was in company with Peter, who gave him such instruction as was necessary [or as rendered by Dr. Westcott, 'Who used to frame his instruction to meet the [immediate] wants of his hearers;' the sentence is ambiguous], but not to give a history of the Lord's discourses; so Mark has committed no error, writing (as he did) some things as he has recorded them (or remembered them). For he was carefully attentive to one thing, not to admit anything that he had heard, or to state anything falsely in these accounts.'" ("Eccles. Hist.," bk. iii. ch. 39.)

The reader will here observe that this very early writer notices the almost entire absence of our Lord's discourses in St. Mark's Gospel in the words, "but not to give a history of the Lord's discourses."

Justin Martyr's covert allusion to this Gospel is remarkable. It

## INTRODUCTION.

is to be remembered that the account of the Lord's giving the name Boanerges to the two sons of Zebedee is recorded in St. Mark only. Justin has occasion to mention this, and writes thus (Dial, ch. 106).

"And when it is said that He imposed on one of the Apostles the name Peter, and when this is recorded in his (Peter's) memoirs, with this other fact, that He named the two sons of Zebedee Boanerges, which means, 'sons of Thunder,' this is a sign," &c.

Justin's name for the Gospels is "Memoirs of the Apostles," so here having mentioned the Apostle Peter, he calls the Gospel of St. Mark, so particularly identified with him, "his" Memoirs.

Irenæus thus alludes to St. Peter's connection with this Gospel:—

"Matthew also issued a written Gospel among the Hebrews in their own dialect, while Peter and Paul were preaching at Rome, and laying the foundation of the Church. After their departure Mark, the disciple and interpreter of Peter, did also hand down to us in writing what had been preached by Peter." ("Adv. Hæres." iii. ch. 1.)

Clement of Alexandria is quoted by Eusebius as bearing the same testimony, which is thus cited by Eusebius from a lost work, the Hypotyposes, sixth book.

"So greatly, however, did the splendour of piety enlighten the minds of Peter's hearers, that it was not sufficient to hear but once, nor to receive the unwritten doctrine of the Gospel of God, but they persevered in every variety of entreaties, to solicit Mark as the companion of Peter, and whose Gospel we have, that he should leave them a monument of the doctrine thus orally communicated, in writing. Nor did they cease their solicitations until they had prevailed with the man, and thus become the means of [the composition of] that history which is called the Gospel according to Mark. They say also that the Apostle [Peter], having ascertained what was done by the Revelation of the Spirit, was delighted by the zealous ardour expressed by these men, and that the history obtained his authority for the purpose of being read in the Churches." ("Eccles. Hist." bk. ii. ch. 15.)

There is another passage from Clement quoted by Eusebius, in which he gives the same account of the occasion which induced Mark to put in writing what had been preached by Peter, though he somewhat modifies the statement respecting St. Peter's approval:—

"When Peter had proclaimed the Word publicly at Rome, and declared the Gospel under the influence of the Spirit, as there was a great number present, they requested Mark, which had followed him from afar, and remembered well what he had said, to reduce these things to writing, and that after composing the Gospel, he gave it to those who requested it of him, which, when Peter understood, he directly neither hindered nor encouraged it." ("Eccles. Hist." bk. vi. c. 14.)

Tertullian very shortly, but still more decisively affirms the connection between St. Mark's Gospel and St. Peter's preaching:—

"The same authority of the Apostolic Churches will afford evidence to the other Gospels also (besides St. Luke's) which we possess equally through their means—I mean the Gospels of John and Matthew—whilst that which Mark published may be affirmed to be Peter's, whose interpreter Mark was." ("Against Marcion," bk. iv. ch. 5.)

Similarly Origen:—

"The second is according to Mark, who composed it as Peter guided him" (ὑφηγήσατο αὐτῷ). (Eus. "Eccles. Hist." bk. vi. ch. 25.)

Lastly, Eusebius, in whose works so many of these extracts are preserved:—

"It is Mark indeed who writes these things. But it is Peter who testifies them concerning himself [particularly in the matter of his denial], for all the contents of Mark's Gospel are regarded as memoirs of Peter's discourses." ("Evangelical Demonstration.")

In glancing over the preceding statements the reader will notice that they all testify to the same fact, which is the entire dependence of St. Mark's Gospel on the preaching of St. Peter. Most of them teach that it was an accurate reproduction, and yet there is sufficient discrepancy between them to show that they were not all derived from the same source, as, for instance, from Papias. The differences in the above statements are principally upon the matter of the extent of St. Peter's superintendence, from that of Origen, who tells us that St. Peter "guided" St. Mark in his composition, to that of one of the statements of Clement, "which when Peter understood, he directly neither hindered nor encouraged it," but this latter seems to refer rather to the publication than to the writing.

The contents of the Gospel, I need hardly say, fully bear out the external evidence for the Petrine origin of this Gospel, for they present the extraordinary phenomenon of one who was certainly not an eye-witness of the acts of the Lord, describing them as if he had not only been an eye-witness, but a very observant one. I have made it my business, throughout the notes, to direct the reader's attention to the proofs that the writer must have derived his information respecting the scenes in the life of the Lord which he delineates from a constant companion and faithful and loving observer. It is a remarkable fact that St. Mark's real Gospel, *i.e.*, that which presents his peculiarities of close observance and faithfulness in minute detail, really commences with St. Peter's first entrance into close companionship with the Lord, *i.e.*, at chap. i. 18. Immediately following upon this, we find a very detailed description of a miracle of the casting out of an evil spirit in the synagogue, an account only found in Mark: then the going to Peter's house, and the healing of his wife's mother, present two or three slight touches true to nature which are not in St. Matthew, which I have noticed in the commentary. Then the sojourn in Peter's house is given with many details, which would not be preserved in a body of tradition, but which would abide in a loving memory, particularly that the Lord rose up early a great while before day, and went out to a solitary place to pray. Again, in the beginning of the next chapter we have the healing of the sick of the palsy, "borne of four," given with a fulness of incidental detail which is in extreme contrast with the somewhat bare and hurried notice of the same in St. Matthew.

To give more of such instances would only be to re-write what is in my notes. I would only mention that St. Mark, more than any other Evangelist, notices the looks and gestures of the Lord. Thus: He looked round about to see her that had done this thing; He beheld the rich young ruler, and loved him; He looked round about upon His disciples when He warned them of the danger of riches.

Whether, then, we look to the extraordinary unanimity in ecclesiastical records, or whether we look to the contents of this Gospel, nothing can be more certain than that it is based upon the teaching and preaching of St. Peter, and indeed reproduces it, so that we may adopt the words of Tertullian: "The Gospel which Mark published may be affirmed to be Peter's, whose interpreter Mark was," and of Origen, "Mark composed it as Peter guided him."

## THE RELATIONS OF ST. MARK TO ST. MATTHEW.

The great bulk of the Gospel of St. Mark is the reproduction of the same tradition respecting our Lord's life and acts which is to be found in St. Matthew. Very little is contained in St. Mark which is not to be found in St. Matthew. Not only the incidents, but the order of the incidents (except in chap. v.) is much the same. For instance, they both mention out of its proper order and apparently for the same purpose, the anointing at Bethany. They both omit the ministry at Jerusalem described by St. John. They both omit the ministry (in Peræa) described in Luke x.-xviii. 14. But though St. Mark reproduces so much that is to be found in St. Matthew, it is clear that he could not have copied it from St. Matthew's Gospel, as he reproduces it frequently in needlessly different words, sometimes with omissions of small matters which, if it had been his design to give us the incident in a perfect form, he would not have left out. Take, for instance, the Transfiguration. If St. Mark simply copied St. Matthew's Gospel, with additions and minute touches of detail to make a more perfect narrative, why should he omit the important fact that the Lord's face "did shine as the sun"? Why should he omit the words of the Father, " In Whom I am well pleased " ? Why should he omit the contents of the sixth and seventh verses of St. Matthew's account ? " And when the disciples heard it they fell on their face, and were sore afraid. And Jesus came and touched them, and said, Arise, and be not afraid."

Owing then to the great similarity of the matter common to both, and yet that there are such manifest indications that the one could not have borrowed from the other, the relations of St. Mark to St. Matthew have presented very great difficulties, and yet it seems to me that there need be little or no difficulty, for the oldest account of the origin of St. Mark's Gospel, that of Papias, which I have just quoted, directs us to as satisfactory a solution of the problem as at this distance of time and with our lack of historical materials we can well expect.

It is particularly mentioned by Papias that St. Peter gave Mark such instruction as was necessary, but *not to give a history* (or connected narrative) *of our Lord's discourses.*"[1] Now it is the characteristic of St. Mark's Gospel to be a Gospel of incidents, particularly miracles, but not of discourses or parables as St. Matthew's. St. Mark gives only four parables, while St. Matthew gives fourteen; and yet they both alike record that "without a parable spake he not unto them." The omission then of so many parables must have been intentional on the part of St. Mark or St. Peter. Then there is not a single line in St. Mark's Gospel of the sort of teaching which we have in the Sermon on the Mount, whereas in St. Luke's Gospel we have much of the teaching of that sermon reproduced. Take, again, the charge to the Apostles. In St. Matthew x. it occupies thirty-six verses. In St. Mark vi. 7, 11, it occupies four or five. Take, again, the denunciation of the Scribes and Pharisees. In St. Matthew it runs over a chapter of thirty-nine verses. In St. Mark it occupies but three verses of chap. xii. I need scarcely mention that St. John's Gospel is principally a gospel of discourses.

So that, compared with the other three Gospels, St. Mark's is so absolutely without didactic matter that it must have been intentionally omitted. To have given more could not have fallen in with the plan of St. Mark, or St. Peter. Now why was this? Evidently because in the body of tradition which St. Peter preached, which is virtually the same as St. Matthew's Gospel as we now have it, there was sufficient didactic instruction, and that given in as perfect a form as possible, whereas in that same body of tradition, the incidents of the Lord's life were not given in as graphic and full a manner as they might have been. The hearers of Peter had been particularly struck with this. The Apostle Peter in his teaching added nothing to the discourses of the Lord, as embodied in the tradition reproduced in St. Matthew (or in some collection of tradition answering to it, but now lost), whereas he did add very materially to the account of the incidents and miracles of the Lord's life. He added those details, those touches of nature which made his accounts that photographic representation, if one may reverently use the expression, which we have in this Gospel, as compared with that of St. Matthew. God, Who gives to each man his particular gift, one after this manner, another after that, may have given to St. Matthew, a retentive memory to repro-

---

[1] ὃς πρὸς τὰς χρείας ἐποιεῖτο τὰς διδασκαλίας, ἀλλ' οὐχ ὥσπερ σύνταξιν τῶν Κυριακῶν ποιούμενος λόγων.

duce faithfully parables and long discourses. He gave to St. Peter an eye observant of all the lesser details which add lifelike charm to a narrative. And these it was which the Roman Christians desired to have preserved, and so they begged St. Mark to reproduce the accounts of miracle and incident, and as the oldest historian tells us, "not to give a history of our Lord's discourses."

If the didactic teaching of the Lord is part of the everlasting Gospel, and it would be blasphemy to say that it is not, then St. Mark's is a subsidiary Gospel, not intended by the Inspiring Spirit to be a book by itself, but to be the companion, the inseparable companion of three others, two of which supply the more human, the last, St. John, the more divine and exalted discourses of the Word made flesh. In saying this we do not assert the inferiority of St. Mark's Gospel. On the ground which it covers we assert its superiority, but it does not cover all the necessary ground. St. Matthew and St. Luke give us in the matter of discourses, the human side of the Lord's didactic teaching, St. John the divine side.

I may be asked, then, whether I believe that St. Matthew's Gospel was in the hands of the Christians of Rome who entreated Mark to write what Peter had taught so graphically. I answer, that there is much probability that it was. St. Peter must have been acquainted with the full body of Palestinian tradition or original teaching respecting the Lord. It is impossible to suppose that in his instructions to his converts he did not preach the doctrine contained in the Sermon on the Mount and in the parables, such as "the field sown with wheat and tares," "the leaven," "the merchantman," which are not in St. Mark. He gives us through St. Mark one parable not found in St. Matthew. He of all men could not have been ignorant of the very striking parable of the labours in the vineyard, for it arose directly out of his own question, "What shall we have, therefore?" (Matt. xix. 27, &c.) He must have known and taught all this. And yet it is quite clear that he had never thought of putting any of his teaching into writing. Why was this? Was it because the teaching of the New Testament era was oral teaching, and so much so that throughout the Apostolical Epistles we have not one word of any written Gospel being in the hands of any Church of Christian converts? And yet do not such precepts as, "Let the word of Christ dwell in you richly in all wisdom," demand some written Gospel containing the sermons and parables of Christ?

## INTRODUCTION.

My own belief is that St. Matthew's Gospel was in the hands of St. Peter and his converts, that St. Peter preached its contents with additions of his own, not because it was the work of his brother Apostle, but because it comprehended the bulk of the tradition respecting the life, death, and teaching of Jesus; but, being a tradition, it could only represent the acts of the Lord in a somewhat formal and general way. But St. Peter's mode of describing the incidents of the Lord's life was so graphic and striking, that his converts desired a permanent record of *that* particular part of his instruction. This St. Mark accomplished, and St. Peter, according to some accounts, with some hesitation gave his approval.

I cannot think for a moment that St. Peter would have left his converts without any permament authoritative record of the Lord's life and teaching, but he may have hesitated, or at least not been forward to publish his own particular rendering of the principal things which the Lord did. Happily his natural backwardness was overruled by the Spirit of God, Who made St. Mark His instrument in handing down to us a more lifelike delineation of the principal acts of Christ.

What I have traced out is, I believe, the sole reason for the existence and form of this Gospel, but it is a worthy reason.

I cannot agree with those good men who think that this Gospel was written to exhibit the power of Christ, and for that purpose only—for if St. Matthew's Gospel or St. Luke's) was divested of all its didactic teaching, *i.e.*, all its record of the words of Christ—then the miracles and other acts of power, being by themselves, would come out in stronger relief, with quite as much emphasis as they do in St. Mark's. And far less can I believe that this Gospel was written with any controversial view, as some German critics have most absurdly imagined. I believe that nothing was further from the thought of the Evangelist than to uphold some imaginary Petrine or Pauline views. He was importuned to reproduce a certain phase of Apostolic delineation of miracles and incidents, and he did this, so that we see in his pages at times the very manner, the look, the gesture of the Lord.

# A COMMENTARY.

## ST. MARK.

### CHAP. I.

THE beginning of the gospel of Jesus Christ, ᵃ the Son of God;

ᵃ Matt. xiv. 33.
Luke i. 35.
John i. 34.

1. "[The] Son of God." These words retained by all principal Uncials except ℵ, by Vulgate and Syriac, and almost all cursives.

1. "The beginning of the gospel of Jesus Christ, the Son of God." The most probable meaning of this verse is that which connects it with the two following. "The beginning" of the Gospel, or good tidings of salvation, was the preaching of the Baptist, because it was good tidings to right-minded men that God was on the eve of fulfilling His ancient promise of sending His Son into the world as its Redeemer. That this should be the *beginning* of the New or Gospel state of things was in accordance with the declarations of God by the prophets Malachi and Isaiah; and so the Evangelist proceeds to say, "*As* it is written in the prophets." The prophets foretold that God would not send the Messiah into the world without having His coming announced, so that men should not be taken by surprise; but that He, before He actually was manifested, should be duly heralded by one who should stir the religious heart of the chosen people far more deeply and widely than any prophet who had gone before him. And so Malachi prophesies: "Behold, I send my messenger before my face;" and Isaiah foretells the sound of a "voice of one crying in the wilderness, prepare ye the way of the Lord." The Evangelist here combines two prophecies, as if they were one, as in reality they are;

B

2 As it is written in the prophets, ᵇBehold, I send my messenger before thy face, which shall prepare thy way before thee.

ᵇ Mal. iii. 1.
Matt. xi. 10.
Luke vii. 27.

2. "In the prophets." So A., E., F., G., H., K., M., &c., most Cursives, and some versions; but "in Esaias the prophet" is read in ℵ, B., D., L. 33, Vulg., Coptic, Syriac. (Schaaf.)

and he probably includes both under the name of the older and more important prophet.

"The gospel of Jesus Christ, the Son of God." The works which Christ undertook to perform for our salvation—the reconciliation of the world to God, and the exercise of His Mediatorship and Headship over the Church—could only be brought about by One Who shared our nature, and yet had in Himself the fulness of the Divine Nature; and so the Gospel is here called the Gospel of Jesus Christ, the Son of God. The Gospel of Jesus—of Him who was in very deed the Lord, the Saviour—of Christ, as One anointed with the Holy Ghost and with power, and the whole Divine Person was the "Son of God."

The two prophecies which the Evangelist combines and cites are unintelligible, unless they set forth the coming of a Divine Person amongst us. It will be well to show this by giving them with their context. The first is from Malachi iii. 1: "Behold, I will send my messenger, and he shall prepare the way before me, and the Lord whom ye seek shall suddenly come to his temple, even the messenger of the covenant, whom ye delight in. Behold he shall come, saith the Lord of Hosts. But who may abide the day of his coming, and who shall stand when he appeareth?" Now the Evangelist quotes this passage, not exactly, but freely, and his freedom is seen in his substituting "*thy* way" and "before *thee*" for "my way" and "before me." In making this alteration, he identifies the Divine Being Whose way is being prepared with the Lord Jesus. According to the prophet, St. John the Baptist was God's messenger, to prepare the way before God; according to the Evangelist, to prepare the way before Christ: so that he who is sent before the face of Christ is sent before the face of God; the way of the Lord which he prepares is the way of the Son of God.

The citation from Isaiah teaches precisely the same: "The voice of him that crieth in the wilderness, prepare ye the way of the Lord; make straight in the desert a highway for our God. Every

3 ᶜThe voice of one crying in the wilderness, Prepare ye the way of the Lord, make his paths straight.  ᶜ Is. xl. 3.
Matt. iii. 3.

4 ᵈJohn did baptize in the wilderness, and  Luke iii. 4.
John i. 15, 23.
ᵈ Matt. iii. 1.
Luke iii. 3.
John iii. 23.

---

4. "John did baptize," &c. "John came who baptized in the wilderness," &c., or, "John appeared who baptized," &c. The Greek word for "was" [ἐγένετο] lays more emphasis on the existing or appearing of John. ℵ, B., L., read article ὁ before "baptizing."

valley shall be exalted . . . and the glory of the Lord shall be revealed." Whose way is the Baptist sent to prepare? The way of Christ, but of Christ as the Lord, according to the words: "Thou, child, shalt be called the prophet of the Highest, for thou shalt go before the face of the Lord, to prepare his ways." Whose glory shall be revealed? St. John answers, "The Word was made flesh, and dwelt amongst us, and we beheld His glory, the glory as of the Only-begotten of the Father."

The gospel, then, of this Evangelist is the gospel of the Son of God in the highest sense which we can give to the word "Son," for the Son of God is the Lord Whom men sought—coming to His temple, according to one prophet, and "our God," Whose way is prepared and made straight, according to another.

Now these two prophecies are to the Catholic believer the keynote of all that follows. Every miracle and every action and every suffering of Jesus recorded in this evangelical narrative is to be looked upon in the light of these two prophecies. It is the Lord, the Messenger or Apostle sent by His Father to bring in the new and better covenant; it is "our God" Who, throughout this Gospel, casts out devils, cleanses the lepers, gives sight to the blind, feeds the multitude, and at last dies on the Cross for our sins.

Unless we remember this throughout, we lose the significance of the Gospel itself: for it is not the Gospel of a created teacher, or mere human Messiah, but of One Whose Person was such that prophecies like these of "the Lord coming to His temple," and of "our God having His way prepared," could fitly be spoken of Him only.

4. "John did baptize [or John was one baptizing] in the wilderness, and preach [or was one preaching] the baptism of repentance for the remission of sins." Having cited the prophetic utterances respecting the preparation for the Lord's coming, the Evangelist now names the person who prepares the way of the Lord, the place

preach the baptism of repentance || for the remission of sins.

| Or, *unto*.
* Matt. iii. 5.

5 * And there went out unto him all the land

where he exercised his ministry, and the nature of that ministry. The person was John the Baptist, whose parentage and birth out of the due course of nature is told us by St. Luke. The place where he preached and baptized was not Jerusalem, but the wilderness: so that men had to go out of the wicked city into a rugged and desolate tract, to hear his preaching and receive his baptism, betokening how men must spiritually go out of the world if they would truly receive Christ.

The manner of his preparation was to preach repentance, and proclaim the baptism of repentance for the remission of sins.

As the dispensation of the Baptist was not a permanent, but a transitory and preparatory one, so this repentance and this baptism were not final, but preparatory. Both the repentance and the baptism were without efficacy, unless the one led to the acceptance of Christ as the Saviour from sin, and the other led to the Baptism of Regeneration, whereby men were engrafted into His mystical Body, in order that they might partake of His Life.

In my notes on St. Matthew, I have dwelt on the very prominent position of repentance and baptism, in the New Dispensation, as compared with their place in the old.

In the new state of things, repentance has become "repentance unto life," and baptism is an essential part of the Gospel: for the Lord says, "He that believeth, and is baptized, shall be saved," and His servant speaks of our having been saved by the washing or bath of regeneration; and asserts its doctrine to be one of the first principles or foundations of the doctrine of Christ (Titus iii. 5, Heb. vi. 1, 2). The ministry of the Baptist made men more ready to receive these first truths of repentance and sacramental union with the Son of God.

The reality of the Baptist's work of preparation was not seen till Pentecost, when two thousand were in one day added to the Church. Even at Ephesus, St. Paul found men ready to receive Christ, because of their previous baptism by John (Acts xix. 3); and even Apollos preached Christ fervently, knowing only the baptism of John (Acts xviii. 24-28).

5. "And there went out to him all the land of Judæa, and they

CHAP. I.]  CONFESSING THEIR SINS.  5

of Judæa, and they of Jerusalem, and were all baptized of him in the river of Jordan, confessing their sins.

6 And John was ᶠ clothed with camel's hair, and with a girdle of a skin about his loins; and he did eat ᵍ locusts and wild honey;   ᶠ Matt. iii. 4.
   ᵍ Lev. xi. 22.

---

5. "And they of Jerusalem, and were all baptized of him." ℵ, B., D., L., some Cursives, Old Latin (a, b), Vulg., and many versions read, "And all they of Jerusalem, and were baptized;" A., later Uncials, and most Cursives read as in Rec. Text; Syriac, *Et baptizabat eos in Jordane flumine quum confiterentur peccata sua.*

6. "And with a girdle of a skin." Revisers, "And had a leathern girdle about his loins;" *zona pellicea*, Vulg.

of Jerusalem." St. Matthew adds, "And all the region round about Jordan." From this we gather how effectual was the preparation on the part of the Baptist. Never before in all their history were the souls of the chosen people so stirred. The most part went to a considerable distance to hear the preaching, and through a rugged country where there was little or no lodging or provisions for such multitudes. They went to hear preaching which reproved the wickedness of their lives, and to undergo the burden of shame in the confession of sins.

But was this an effectual stirring of the dry bones? If we judge by the comparative fewness of those who became the disciples of the Lord in His own lifetime, it was not; but we must not so judge, for amongst those who flocked to John were the first Apostles, the chosen instruments by whom Christ founded His Church. The coming of such as these to the Son of God, through the ministry of John, made amends for the falling away of thousands; and, besides this, we know not how much of the rapid increase of the Church, as described in the Acts of the Apostles, was owing to the memory of the ministry of John.

6. "And John was clothed with camel's hair, and with a girdle of a skin," &c. The garb and food of the holy ascetic were suitable to his preaching, as Bede writes: "The dress and food of John may also express of what kind was his inward walk. For he used a dress more austere than was usual, because he did not encourage the life of sinners by flattery, but chid them by the vigour of his rough rebuke; he had a girdle of a skin round his loins, for he was one who crucified his flesh with the affections and lusts." And, again, Quesnel says, "In times of greatest corruption, God generally gives

7 And preached, saying, ʰ There cometh one mightier than I after me, the latchet of whose shoes I am not worthy to stoop down and unloose.

8 ¹ I indeed have baptized you with water : but he shall baptize you ᵏ with the Holy Ghost.

ʰ Matt. iii. 11. John i. 27. Acts xiii. 25.
¹ Acts i. 5 & xi. 16. & xix. 4.
ᵏ Is. xliv. 3. Joel ii. 28. Acts ii. 4. & x. 45. & xi. 15, 16. 1 Cor. xii. 13.

7. "One mightier;" better, "he that is mightier."
8. "I indeed have baptized." Perhaps, "I baptized you with water, but He shall baptize you in the Holy Ghost." ὁ before ὕδατι omitted by Neutral Text.

---

extraordinary examples of self-denial and holy zeal for His glory and the salvation of others, to awaken sinners who are asleep in a state of carnal security to a lively sense of their danger, and confound the slothfulness of sensual men."

7. "And preached, saying, There cometh one mightier than I after me," &c. There were many more things which the Baptist preached, but that feature of it is here mentioned which consisted in his witness to the exalted nature of the Person of the Redeemer. It is to be borne in mind that St. John himself was of the very highest rank among his countrymen, for he was the son of one of the heads of the courses of the priests. As such he would have received his rank from God, Who ordained the Aaronic priesthood. It would have been an unworthy degradation of that which God had Himself exalted to describe the difference between Jesus and himself in such terms as these, unless Jesus was in very deed the only Son of God. For all men are equal in nature, as partaking of a common humanity; and it could only be because the Divine nature was inherent in Jesus of Nazareth, that John could say with truth that he was unworthy to render to Him the lowest menial service. We could not imagine such a man as the Baptist saying this of himself and Cæsar.

8. "I indeed have baptized you with [in] water." The contrast here is not between St. John's baptism as being in water and the Lord's baptism as not being so, but between John's baptism as being in water only, and Christ's baptism as not being in water only, but in water and the Holy Ghost accompanying the element, and using it as His visible instrument, whereby the man is born of water and of the Spirit into the kingdom of God. By John's baptism, no change of spiritual condition was brought about; but, in Christ's baptism, "by one Spirit we are all baptized into one

CHAP. I.]            JESUS BAPTIZED.                     7

9 ¹And it came to pass in those days, that Jesus came from Nazareth of Galilee, and was baptized of John in Jordan. ¹ Matt. iii. 13. Luke iii. 21.

10 ᵐ And straightway coming up out of the ᵐ Matt. iii. John i. 32.

---

body." Petter, a Puritan commentator on this Gospel, expresses well the true meaning: "Our Saviour Christ, giving commission to the Apostles to baptize, He doth promise the presence and assistance of His Spirit with them unto the world's end, thereby to make that outward sacrament which should be administered by them effectual to those that should receive it." Quesnel gives a short but admirable prayer, that we should retain the grace of Christian baptism: "Grant, O Jesus, that the Spirit with which Thou hast baptized me may awaken and enlighten me more and more, remaining continually in me, and animating all the actions of my life."

Not, of course, as if Christ imparts the Holy Spirit only in baptism. The Lord constantly, in answer to their prayers, pours upon men the Holy Spirit abundantly. By His Spirit He fills them with repentance and faith and love and peace and every Christian grace.

9. "And it came to pass in those days, that Jesus came from Nazareth of Galilee," &c. From this we learn that He dwelt at Nazareth till His baptism—*i.e.*, till He was above thirty years of age,—so that He was rightly called a Nazarene, His whole private life having been spent at Nazareth.

Respecting the reason for this humiliation on the part of Christ to receive the baptism of sinners, see my note on Matthew iii. 13. To what I have there said, it may be added that He received baptism as the Second Adam, the New Head of the race, denoting that all, no matter how seemingly enlightened or holy, must be washed from sin in Him. In this, as in all things, He was "made like unto His brethren." In this submission, though sinless Himself, He was first "numbered with the transgressors."

10. "And straightway coming up out of the water, he saw the heavens opened," &c. Each Evangelist notices that the appearance of the Spirit, and the opened heavens, and the voice of the Father, took place when He came up out of the water. "That the outpouring of the Spirit did not take place before the submersion, perfectly accords with the symbolical character of the action [see Rom.

water, he saw the heavens ‖ opened, and the Spirit like a dove descending upon him:

‖ *Or, cloven, or, rent.*

11 And there came a voice from heaven, saying, ⁿThou art my beloved Son, in whom I am well pleased.

ⁿ Ps. ii. 7.
Matt. iii. 17.
ch. ix. 7.

12 °And immediately the spirit driveth him into the wilderness.

° Matt. iv. 1.
Luke iv. 1.

---

10. "Opened." The marginal rendering, "cloven" or "rent," is a better translation. *Vidit quod fissi sunt cœli,* Syriac.

11. "In whom I am well pleased." ℵ, B., D., L., some Cursives, some Old Latin, Vulg., and Syriac, and some other versions read, "In thee I am well pleased;" A. and later Uncials and most Cursives read as in Authorized.

vi. 1-6], which is not, indeed, in itself applicable to John's baptism, but which the Saviour typically imparted to the action of His baptism. The one part of the action—the submersion—represents the negative aspect, viz., the taking away of the Old Man [Rom. vi. 4] ; in the other part—the emersion—the positive aspect, viz., the appearance of the New Man, is denoted; the communication of the Holy Ghost must, therefore, have been connected with the latter." (Olshausen.)

"He saw . . . the Spirit like a dove descending." The pronoun "He" no doubt refers here to our Lord. But John also saw the descent of the Spirit. It was the sign promised by God, by which he was to recognize the Messiah (John i. 32, 33).

11. "And there came a voice from heaven, saying, Thou art my beloved Son," &c. There is a difference between St. Matthew, on the one hand, and St. Mark and St. Luke on the other, in that the two latter make the Voice addressed to Christ, "Thou art my beloved Son;" whereas St. Matthew writes as if it were spoken of Christ, "This is my beloved Son." The sense is precisely the same. If we are obliged to choose, we must take St. Mark as giving most probably the more exact account; but it is not improbable that the Voice as heard by Christ was addressed to Him to strengthen and assure His human nature; whereas the Baptist heard it said *of* Christ, showing to him that This was the One Who came to baptize with the Spirit. Bede remarks : "The same voice has taught us, that we also, by the water of cleansing, and by the Spirit of sanctification, may be made the sons of God."

12. "And immediately the Spirit driveth him into the wilder-

13 And he was there in the wilderness forty days, tempted of Satan; and was with the wild beasts; ᵖ and   ᵖ Matt. iv. 11. the angels ministered unto him.

---

ness." Why are we here told that the spirit *driveth* the Lord into the wilderness? It seems to teach us that the human soul or spirit of the Son of God shrank from such nearness to Satan as to be tempted by him, and to receive into His holy Soul the cursed suggestions of the Evil One. This teaches us how reluctant we should be to go to places or company in which we know that we shall be tempted. The holy, sinless Jesus was driven into the place of danger; and we too often rush into it of ourselves.

13. "And he was there .... forty days, tempted of Satan." From St. Matthew alone we should rather gather that the devil came to Him at the end of the forty days; whereas from this Evangelist and from St. Luke we learn that the whole forty days was a season of temptation, and the three recorded temptations were the last assault. How does this enhance the humiliation of the Lord, that He should suffer Himself so long to be assailed by the Evil One!

"With the wild beasts." This is mentioned to show us that He was in the wildest and most unfrequented part of the desert—some tract absolutely untrodden by the feet of men.

"And the angels ministered unto him." This seems to imply that, in some way unknown to us, He was comforted by the presence of these ministering spirits even before they brought Him food at the termination of His long fast.

Bishop Hall (quoted by Ford) remarks well: "I have ever with me invisible friends and enemies. The consideration of mine enemies shall keep me from security, and make me fearful of doing aught to advantage them. The consideration of my spiritual friends shall comfort me against the terror of the other; shall remedy my solitariness; shall make me wary of doing aught indecently; grieving me rather that I have ever heretofore made them turn away their eyes for shame of that whereof I have not been ashamed; that I have no more enjoyed their society; that I have been no more affected with their presence. What, though I see them not? I believe them. I were no Christian, if my faith were not as sure as my sense."

14 ⁹ Now after that John was put in prison, Jesus came into Galilee, ʳ preaching the gospel of the kingdom of God.

15 And saying, ˢ The time is fulfilled, and ᵗ the kingdom of God is at hand: repent ye, and believe the gospel.

⁹ Matt. iv. 12.
ʳ Matt. iv. 23.
ˢ Dan. ix. 25. Gal. iv. 4. Eph. i. 10.
ᵗ Matt. iii. 2. & iv. 17.

14. "Preaching the gospel of the kingdom of God." "Of the kingdom" omitted by MSS. of Neutral Text, ℵ, B., L., a few Cursives, Coptic, &c.; retained by A., D., later Uncials, almost all Cursives, some Old Latin, Vulg. and Syriac, and some versions.

14. "Now after that John was put in prison, Jesus came into Galilee," &c. How is it said that He came into Galilee, when, apparently, He had only left Nazareth of Galilee to be baptized and tempted? We should rather have expected that it would have been said, "He returned." The answer is that, between His baptism and the imprisonment of John, He exercised a ministry in Jerusalem which is recorded only by St. John in his Gospel (ii. 13; iv. 3). We must interpose between verses 13 and 14 the whole of the events recorded in St. John, from chap. i. 19 to iv. 54—viz., the call of the first disciples, the miracle in Cana, the first cleansing of the temple, the interview with Nicodemus and with the woman of Samaria, and the miracle of the healing of the nobleman's son.

"Preaching the gospel of the kingdom of God." The words "of the kingdom" are not in the Neutral Text; but that the Lord's preaching could most properly be described as the preaching of the kingdom of God is certain from Matthew iv. 23, where the Gospel which He preached is called the Gospel of the kingdom of God (see my note on Matt. iv. 23).

15. "And saying, The time is fulfilled." The Lord means that the time of the Law is completed, as if He said: "Up to this time the Law was at work: from this time the kingdom of God will work, that is, a conversation according to the Gospel, which is with reason likened to the kingdom of God. For when you see a man clothed in flesh, living according to the Gospel, do you not say that he has the kingdom of God (Rom. xiv. 17), for the kingdom of God is not meat and drink, but righteousness and peace and joy in the Holy Ghost?" (Theophylact. in Catena Aurea.)

"Repent ye, and believe the gospel." Notice how both the Lord, and His forerunner, and St. Peter (Acts ii.), and St. Paul (Acts

CHAP. I.]     AS HE WALKED BY THE SEA.     11

16 ⁿNow as he walked by the sea of Galilee,   ⁿ Matt. iv. 18.
                                               Luke v. 4.

16. "Now as he walked." ℵ, B., D., L., some Cursives, Old Latin, Vulg. read, "And as He passed by," &c.; A., later Uncials, almost all Cursives, and Syriac read as in Authorized.

xxvi. 20) preach first of all repentance; and it must be so, for repentance being a sense of sin, and a turning from it, and a desire to be delivered from it, makes the soul realize the glad tidings of the Gospel respecting such deliverance. Faith itself is quickened and transformed from a dead notion to a living energy by repentance.

16. "Now as he walked by the sea of Galilee . . . they were fishers." For full remarks on this call of four Apostles, I must refer the reader to my notes on St. Matthew iv. 18, &c. The present observations will be necessarily supplementary. St. Matthew and St. Mark give almost verbatim the same account; St. Mark's real addition to the account being that James and John were the sons of one who had hired servants to help him in his occupation; and so they did not leave their father unprovided for when they went after the Lord. And as we read of no remonstrance or opposition on the part of Zebedee, whose wife was now probably a believer, we may conclude that it was with his permission, perhaps approval.

The important question is, Why should the Lord choose His foremost Apostles from among fishermen? The answer is twofold.

First, their calling had inured them to hardship, and had accustomed them to face sudden and extreme danger—the lake on which they exercised their craft being exposed to sudden and violent storms. Then such a calling, demanding a constant exercise of patience and watchfulness, and, above all, being a very precarious mode of living, would make them familiar with disappointment ("We have toiled all night, and have taken nothing"); so that they would not be discouraged by it; and when they came to experience such disappointment in their apostolate, would not throw it up in despair, but go on letting down the net of the Gospel till the Lord was pleased to reward them. Their worldly calling would be the best discipline for their spiritual work. They must be prepared to endure hardness, for they had no settled incomes; they must be ready to face death, for at any moment a storm of bloody persecution might arise; they must be patient, both towards Churches and souls; and they must be content at times with taking a few converts in their nets, where they might have expected abundant draughts. Then, in the next place, the Lord chose men who, owing to their

he saw Simon and Andrew his brother casting a net into the sea: for they were fishers.

17 And Jesus said unto them, Come ye after me, and I will make you to become fishers of men.

---

calling, must have been "unlearned and ignorant men," that His grace might be made perfect in their weakness. That the then known world should have been, in two or three centuries, subdued to the faith by such men, and by such as succeeded them, was, next to the Resurrection of Christ, the greatest miracle of Christianity. Calvin has some admirable remarks on this: " Christ selected persons not only destitute of learning, but inferior in capacity, that He might train, or rather renew, them by the power of His Spirit, so as to excel all the wise men of the world. He intended to humble in this manner the pride of the flesh, and to present in their persons a remarkable instance of spiritual grace, that we may learn to implore from heaven the light of faith, when we know that it cannot be acquired by our own exertions. When our Lord chose persons of this condition, it was not because He preferred ignorance to learning, as some fanatics do, who are delighted with their own ignorance, and fancy that, in proportion as they hate literature, they approach the nearest to the Apostles. He resolved at first, no doubt, to choose despised persons, in order to humble the pride of those who think that heaven is not open to the unlearned; but He afterwards gave to those fishers, as an associate in their office, Paul, who had been carefully educated from his childhood."

Again, we may add, in choosing such to be Apostles, Christ called religious men, for they had "justified God" by attaching themselves to the ministry of the Baptist, and yet not prejudiced Pharisees, who would have had a world of traditional interpretation to unlearn. And, above all, not superstitious men, men by no means ready to look for supernatural action from their Master, as we shall have many opportunities of observing—in fact, men slow of belief, rather than otherwise.

This was their second call. The first, in John i., was rather to companionship and friendship than to the ministry. Now He calls them to discipleship; and afterwards, out of the mass of the disciples, He chose them with others to be Apostles.

17. "And Jesus said unto them . . . fishers of men." As I re-

18 And straightway ˣ they forsook their nets, and followed him.  ˣ Matt. xix. 27. Luke v. 11.

19 ʸ And when he had gone a little farther ʸ Matt. iv. 21. thence, he saw James the *son* of Zebedee, and John his brother, who also were in the ship mending their nets.

20 And straightway he called them: and they left their father Zebedee in the ship with the hired servants, and went after him.

21 ᶻ And they went into Capernaum: and ᶻ Matt. iv. 13. Luke iv. 31. straightway on the sabbath day he entered into the synagogue, and taught.

22 ᵃ And they were astonished at his doctrine: ᵃ Matt. vii. 28. for he taught them as one that had authority, and not as the scribes.

---

19. "Thence" omitted by B., D., L., a few Cursives, some Old Latin, Syriac, &c.; retained by A , C., later Uncials, and almost all Cursives and Vulgate.

marked in St. Matthew, none but He Who could sway all hearts by His Divine power could promise from Himself, "I will make you fishers of men."

18. "And straightway they forsook their nets"—*i.e.*, they forsook their means of livelihood, and gave themselves up to the Apostolic life of poverty, depending henceforth upon nothing but the goodwill with which God inspired the faithful to support their pastors.

21, 22. "And they went into Capernaum . . . taught them as one that had authority." Inasmuch as exactly the same words occur in St. Matthew, as describing the effect of the Sermon on the Mount upon the people who heard it, we can, by noticing the peculiarly authoritative statements in that sermon, tell the nature of this authority also. It was plenary authority, not only to set aside all the traditional interpretations of the law, but to put a spiritual gloss upon that law, to add a spiritual meaning to it, so as to make it a new thing. It was authority to use such expressions as "ye have heard that it was said to them of old time . . . but *I* say unto you." It was authority to promise that the man who heard His sayings, and did them, should be like unto a man " who built his house upon a rock," and to foretell that a day should come

**14** I KNOW THEE WHO THOU ART. [St. Mark.

23 [b] And there was in their synagogue a man with an unclean spirit; and he cried out,

24 Saying, Let *us* alone; [c] what have we to do with thee, thou Jesus of Nazareth? art thou come to destroy us? I know thee who thou art, the Holy One of God.

[b] Luke iv. 33.
[c] Matt. viii. 29.

---

23. "And there was in their synagogue." MSS. of Neutral Text, ℵ, B., L., and two or three Cursives read, "And straightway there was in their synagogue," but it adds nothing to the sense, rather the contrary. A., C., D., later Uncials, Vulg., &c., omit.

24. " Let us alone ; " rather, " ah ! " a mere exclamation. Neutral Text omits word altogether, so also Vulgate and Syriac.

when He would sit as Supreme Judge, and say to those whom He condemned: "Depart from me, I never knew you." So that it was nothing less than the assumption of divine authority which astonished these dwellers in Galilee.

23. "And [straightway] there was in their synagogue a man with an unclean spirit, and he cried out." It is to be noticed that this miracle (which is common to St. Mark and St. Luke) is the first miracle recorded by St. Mark. This Evangelist seems to bring out more fully than the rest the Lord's power over the hosts of evil spirits.

"With an unclean spirit." Is the word "unclean" used here as synonymous with unholy? for we can hardly suppose that evil spirits have the same fleshly propensities as evil men. The Scriptures regard all opposition to God as unholiness, and so impurity; God alone being the Holy One, and so the fountain of all holiness, and all beings cut off from Him are unholy: or must we not rather suppose that some of those evil spirits had special power of acting on their victims through the lusts of the flesh?

24. "And he cried, Let us alone [or simply "ah!" but omitted by neutral text], what have we to do with thee," &c. The personality of the evil spirit seems to have overborne that of the man, for the words which follow are the expression of no mere human thought or human knowledge. They seem to have been uttered spontaneously. The Lord had said nothing, but the evil spirit could not endure His presence, and perhaps the searching look directed on His victim, and so, in anticipation of his being cast forth, he cried, "What have we to do with thee?" As if he said, "In what way have I offended Thee? Hast Thou not permitted us to enter into sinners, and dwell in them? Is the time of our judg-

25 And Jesus <sup>d</sup> rebuked him, saying, Hold thy peace, and come out of him. <sup>d</sup> ver. 34.

26 And when the unclean spirit <sup>e</sup> had torn him, <sup>e</sup> ch. ix. 20. and cried with a loud voice, he came out of him.

---

ment so nigh? Have we not yet some respite? a little time longer to continue out of prison?"

" I [or we] know thee who thou art, the Holy One of God." It is to be remembered that by far the most frequent application of the term Holy One is to God Himself, and it stands to reason that here it must be spoken in the highest Divine sense, for the unclean spirit uses it to deprecate the wrath of One Who had authority to judge the world of angels.

It has been asked, Why did the evil spirits confess Him to be the Holy One, or the Son of God? Such an avowal would seem to tend to make men believe on Him. And ingenious reasons have been given to show their craft in so doing; but may it not have been the cry of fear, mingled with despair? ["The devils believe and tremble," James ii.] Again, why did our Lord so energetically forbid these evil spirits to acknowledge His Divine Sonship? Because He would not receive the testimony of these enemies of God. Perhaps it is only holy angels and holy men who can so testify of Him as to advance His kingdom; or perhaps the time had not yet come for the full revelation of Himself as the Eternal Son. The times of all things relating to Redemption were ordered by God, and it would have been as harmful that the full confession of faith should have been anticipated, as that it should have been delayed.

26. "And when the unclean spirit had torn him." St. Luke, in relating this, tells us that the evil spirit "threw him in the midst, and hurt him not," so that we must understand this tearing rather of a severe paroxysm, which seemed to wrench every sinew, but which the Lord so ordered that he was not injured by it.

Quesnel has a most pertinent remark on this: "When the temptations of the flesh are most violent in one who resolves to surrender himself to God, they are sometimes the last efforts of the devil, and the signs of the approaching deliverance of that soul. It is then that a man ought to redouble his prayer, to cry to God with all the strength of faith, and to invoke his Deliverer with the greater earnestness."

27 And they were all amazed, insomuch that they questioned among themselves, saying, What thing is this? what new doctrine *is* this? for with authority commandeth he even the unclean spirits, and they do obey him.

28 And immediately his fame spread abroad throughout all the region round about Galilee.

f Matt. viii. 14.
Luke iv. 38.
29 *f* And forthwith, when they were come out of the synagogue, they entered into the house of Simon and Andrew, with James and John.

27. "What thing is this? what new doctrine is this? for with authority," &c. Revisers (following Neutral Text), read, "What is this? a new teaching! with authority he commandeth even the unclean spirits," &c. Some translate it, "A new doctrine with authority!" I do not think, however, the Galilean multitude were at all likely to rush about exclaiming, "A new doctrine with authority!" The most likely exclamation by far to escape them is that in the Authorized.

28. "Spread abroad." "Everywhere" is inserted after "abroad" in B., C., L., one or two Cursives, Old Latin (b, e), Coptic, but omitted by ℵ, A., D., later Uncials, all Cursives, some Old Latin, Vulg.

29. "They were come"—"they entered." B., and seven or eight Cursives read, "he was come"—"he entered."

"How strange and fearful must all this have seemed to those who were looking on! The sudden cry of horror of the evil spirit, his fear of vengeance, and confession of helplessness, Christ's word of power, commanding him to depart, and then the last effort of impotent fury—his violently shaking and tearing his victim, but without power to hurt him." No wonder that

27. "They were all amazed, insomuch that they questioned among themselves, saying, What new doctrine is this? for with authority . . . obey him." Seeing the teaching of the Lord enforced by so stupendous an act of authority over the powers of hell, they naturally exclaimed, "What thing is this? what new doctrine is this?" &c. The reader will remember how, when Sergius Paulus saw the power of the apostle exerted against an emissary of Satan, he is said to have been "astonished at the doctrine of the Lord" (Acts xiii. 12).

28. "And immediately the fame spread abroad," &c. It is to be noticed how St. Mark seems delighted to notice the popularity of the Lord, thus in this chapter, verses 32, 33, 37 ("All men seek for Thee"), 45.

29, 30. "And forthwith when they were come out of the synagogue,

# SIMON'S WIFE'S MOTHER.

30 But Simon's wife's mother lay sick of a fever, and anon they tell him of her.

31 And he came and took her by the hand, and lifted her up; and immediately the fever left her, and she ministered unto them.

32 ᵍ And at even, when the sun did set, they  ᵍ Matt. viii. 16. Luke iv. 40.

---

... anon they tell him of her." It is interesting to notice how the account of this miracle compared with that of the same in St. Matthew, shows the presence of an eye-witness, of course St. Peter. St. Mark notices how it occurred when they came out of the synagogue—how Andrew, James, and John accompanied them —how when He entered the house He did not immediately see the sick woman, but they tell Him of her. This is most natural. He was not likely to see the sick woman at first, as she must have been in some quiet chamber, but "they tell Him of her." And so our Evangelist says, He "came," *i.e.*, into her chamber. St. Matthew says, He touched her hand; but St. Mark, He took her by the hand, and lifted her up. He, no doubt, touched her hand first, and then grasped it, and lifted her up, knowing that by His previous touch, but a moment before, the fever had left her. SS. Matthew and Luke say that she arose and ministered unto them; but St. Mark does not mention that she arose, because she had not risen of herself, but the Lord had lifted her up. Anti-Roman commentators notice, and with reason, that the Lord chose as the first of the apostles a married man, and that after his election to follow the Lord he did not separate from his wife, but the Lord honours the family, by sometimes dwelling in their house. Again St. Paul implies that at times, at least, she accompanied St. Peter in his journeys (1 Corinth. ix. 5). It appears from a very touching account given by Clement of Alexandria, that they were living together when she was called to be one of Christ's martyrs. "They say, accordingly, that the blessed Peter, on seeing his wife led to death, rejoiced on account of her call and conveyance home, and called very encouragingly and comfortingly, addressing her by name, 'Remember thou the Lord.' Such," he adds, "was the marriage of the blessed, and their perfect disposition towards those dearest to them" (Miscellanies VII., chap. xi.).

32. "And at even, when the sun did set, they brought ...

brought unto him all that were diseased, and them that were possessed with devils.

33 And all the city was gathered together at the door.

34 And he healed many that were sick of divers diseases,

---

**34.** So ℵ, A., E, F., K., some other later Uncials, almost all Cursives, Old Latin, Vulg.; but B., C., G., L., M., some Cursives and versions read, "knew him to be the Christ."

possessed with devils." It being the Sabbath, it would have been held unlawful to carry the weight of their sick folk from all parts to the Lord to be healed. Notice how all that were brought to the Lord for the exercise of His merciful power upon them, are divided into two classes only—those that were diseased, and those that were possessed. The reader, if he has not remembered it already, will thank me for reminding him of the hymn of Mr. Twells [20 A. and M.]:—

"At even 'ere the sun was set,
　The sick, O Lord, around Thee lay;
Oh, in what divers pains they met,
　Oh, with what joy they went away!

O Saviour Christ, our woes dispel,
　For some are sick and some are sad;
And some have never loved Thee well,
　And some have lost the love they had.

Thy touch has still its ancient power,
　No word from Thee can fruitless fall;
Hear in this solemn evening hour,
　And in Thy mercy heal us all."

33. "And all the city was gathered together at the door." This verse also is peculiar to St. Mark. It is the reminiscence of one who was somewhat perplexed at the multitudes who were crowding in front of his house, and knew not how they were to be satisfied, or where it would all end.

34. "And he healed many that were sick . . . they knew him." Here we have, again, the recipients of the Lord's benevolent acting divided into those that were sick, and those possessed. May not the first be taken to signify all afflicted in body, and the latter all diseased in soul or spirit?

"Suffered not the devils to speak." Theophylact remarks that

CHAP. I.]  A GREAT WHILE BEFORE DAY.  19

and cast out many devils; and <sup>h</sup> suffered not the devils ‖ to speak, because they knew him.

35 And <sup>i</sup> in the morning, rising up a great while before day, he went out, and departed into a solitary place, and there prayed.

36 And Simon and they that were with him followed after him.

<sup>h</sup> ch. iii. 12.
Luke iv. 41.
See Acts xvi. 17, 18.
‖ Or, *to say that they knew him.*
<sup>i</sup> Luke iv. 42.

---

it was dangerous to receive witness from such spirits, "for if once they find persons to believe them, they mingle truth with falsehood."

"Because they knew him." The MSS. of neutral text add, "Knew him to be the Christ;" but surely this is a very inadequate gloss. Before this they confessed Him to be "the Holy One of God," afterwards (iii. 11) "the Son of God." They knew Him to be the Ruler and Judge of the unseen world of good and evil spirits.

35. "And in the morning, rising up a great while before day," &c. It is from St. Mark alone (doubtless through St. Peter) that we get this most precious knowledge of the Saviour's practice in regard of prayer. St. Matthew says nothing of it, St. Luke that He departed and went into a desert place, but does not mention that it was for prayer; St. Mark teaches us that "He rose up a great while before day," that He might enjoy uninterrupted communion with God. What a lesson does this teach us, that if we would pray well we must pray early! How often have Christians to choose between the indulgence of a little more sleep and the time of prayer cut short, and scant and hurried devotion, or between a little self-denial in sleep and the freshest and best hours of the day given to God, and God blessing the self-denial by answering the prayer.

But how is it that St. Mark alone mentions this? Because he wrote what St. Peter taught, and the Lord was lodging in St. Peter's house, so that the apostle had means of noticing how the Divine Inmate rose up very early, before any of the household was astir, that He might go to some unfrequented place, and there be alone with His Father. Quesnel remarks: "Prayer is so necessary to him who preaches and labours in the Church, that, far from dispensing with himself on this account, he ought to take a time for it out of that which belongs to rest and the other necessities of life, rather than be deficient therein."

36. "And Simon and they that were with him [probably Andrew,

37 And when they had found him, they said unto him, All *men* seek for thee.

^k Luke iv. 43. 38 And he said unto them, ^k Let us go into the next towns, that I may preach there also: for ^l therefore came I forth.

^l Is. lxi. 1. John xvi. 28. & xvii. 4.

---

38. "Let us go." א, B., C.*, L., Cursive 33, and some versions insert "elsewhere," but A., D., later Uncials, almost all Cursives, Vulg., Syriac, Old Latin, &c., omit the word.

James, and John]," &c. This also must have come direct from one who took part in this following of the Lord. But does it not seem presumptuous that they should go after Him to break upon His retirement? They acted so because they understood not then, as afterwards they did, the need of prayer and retirement for the minister of God; and so we read,

37. "When they had found him, they said unto him, All men seek for thee." But that was the very reason why the Lord had withdrawn Himself. As long as the people of the place were crowding about Him for the exercise of His power of healing, or perhaps in many cases out of mere wonder or curiosity, He was unable to do that which by this His example He teaches us to be as needful as active work. Very probably, however, He had been a considerable time alone before they overtook Him, and so the work of intercourse with His Father was then ended, for

38. "He said unto them, Let us go into the next towns, that I may preach there also." By this time considerable numbers had gathered together, and had followed close after Simon, and they that were with him; so we learn from St. Luke's account, "The people sought him, and came to him, and stayed him that he should not depart from them." They desired somewhat selfishly, though naturally, to keep such a teacher and healer to themselves. But

"He said unto them, Let us go into the next towns, that I may preach there also: for therefore came I forth." His great work was preaching—the proclamation of the truth of God. Miracles were performed by Him in order to arrest men's attention, and to make them ask, as they did, What new doctrine is this? But their souls were saved, not by seeing His miracles, or even by being healed by them, but by receiving His message.

"Therefore came I forth." Does this mean come forth from His

39 ᵐ And he preached in their synagogues throughout all Galilee, and cast out devils.

40 ⁿ And there came a leper to him, beseeching him, and kneeling down to him, and saying unto him, If thou wilt, thou canst make me clean.

ᵐ Matt. iv. 23.
Luke iv. 44.
ⁿ Matt. viii. 2.
Luke v. 12.

---

39. Revisers (following Neutral Text), render, "And he went into their synagogues throughout all Galilee, preaching and casting out devils." Vulg., *Et erat prædicans in synagogis eorum, et in omni Galilæa, et dæmonia ejiciens.*

40. "And kneeling down to him." So A., א, C., L., later Uncials, almost all Cursives, Vulg., and versions; omitted by B., D., G., and Old Latin.

retirement, or came forth from God? Undoubtedly the latter. To the thoroughly believing mind all "comings forth" from Nazareth, from Capernaum, from His family, from His private life, cannot be compared to the great "coming forth" from God. "For this end was I born, and for this cause came I into the world, that I should bear witness unto the truth" (John xviii. 37).

40. "And there came a leper to him, beseeching him," &c. Respecting the typical nature of the disease of leprosy, and its incurability by any art of man, I have written sufficiently in my notes on St. Matthew (viii. 2).

"Beseeching him, and kneeling down to him." St. Matthew says: "worshipped him." St. Luke: "who seeing Jesus, fell on his face." Was this deep reverential kneeling or prostration of the nature of Divine worship, or was it only that somewhat exaggerated humiliation before those invested with rank and power which has always prevailed in the East? Taking all circumstances into account, it must have been more than the latter. St. Chrysostom brings this out well: "Great was the understanding and the faith of him who so drew near. For he did not interrupt the teaching, nor break through the auditory, but awaited the proper time, and approaches Him when He is come down [Matt. viii. 1, 2]. And not at random, but with much earnestness; and on his knees he beseeches Him, and with genuine faith, and right opinion about Him. For neither did he say, 'If thou request it of God,' nor 'If thou pray,' but 'If thou wilt thou canst make me clean.' Nor did he say, 'Lord, cleanse me,' but leaves all to Him, and makes his recovery depend on Him, and testifies that all the authority is His. 'What, then,' saith one, 'if the leper's opinion was mistaken?' Then (on the part of Christ) it were meet to do away

41 And Jesus, moved with compassion, put forth *his* hand, and touched him, and saith unto him, I will; be thou clean.

---

41. "Be thou clean." Revisers, "Be thou made clean"—the same word as the leper uses.

with it, and to reprove and set it right. Did Christ, then, do so? By no means; but, quite on the contrary, He establishes and confirms what had been said. For this cause, you see, neither did He say, 'Be thou cleansed,' but 'I will: be thou made clean,' that the doctrine might no longer be a thing of the other's surmising, but of His own approval."

Be this so or not, it is quite clear that the man could not have spoken or acted otherwise, if he had believed that the Lord was a Divine Being; and the Lord answered him in terms which accepted the acknowledgment of Divine power. Chrysostom goes on to contrast with tnis the conduct of the Apostles, on the occasion of the healing of the impotent man. "Why look ye so earnestly on us, as though by our own power or holiness we had made this man to walk?" (Acts iii. 12). Not so the Lord here. He assumes all power unreservedly: "I will: be thou clean." If it be objected that it was very unlikely that this poor leper should have such faith, we can only answer that, on natural principles, it was not only unlikely, but impossible, but "faith is the gift of God."

41. "And Jesus, moved with compassion, put forth his hand, and touched him," &c. St. Mark alone specially notices that the Lord was moved with compassion. Must not this remark have come direct from Peter, who was struck with some evident outward mark of compassion in the Lord's Divine Countenance, or in some gesture of pity which He showed?

"Put forth his hand, and touched him." "Wherefore, when cleansing him by will and word, did He also add the touch of His hand? It seems to me for no other end but that He might signify by this also that He is not subject to the law, but is set over it; and that to the clean, henceforth, nothing is unclean. For this cause, we see Elisha did not so much as see Naaman; but though he perceived that he was offended at his not coming and touching him, yet, observing the strictness of the law, he abides at home, and sends him to Jordan to wash. Whereas the Lord, to signify that He heals not as a servant, but as absolute Master, doth also touch.

Chap. I.]  THE LEPROSY DEPARTED.  23

42 And as soon as he had spoken, immediately the leprosy departed from him, and he was cleansed.

43 And he straitly charged him, and forthwith sent him away;

---

42. "*And as soon as he had spoken*" omitted by א, B., D., L., a few Cursives, Old Latin, Coptic, and Syriac; retained by A., C., later Uncials, almost all Cursives, Vulg., and other versions.

43. "*Straitly charged him.*" This translation too weak—"sternly charged him." *Comminatus est ei*, Vulg.

"*Sent him away.*" Literally, "cast him out;" *statim ejecit illum*, Vulg.

for His hand became not unclean from the leprosy, but the leprous body was rendered clean by His holy hand" (Chrysostom on St. Matthew viii., &c.).

42. "And as soon as he had spoken, immediately the leprosy." The skin of the man, which a moment before had been one foul blotch or sore, was instantly restored to its natural state at the word of Christ. By using the words, "as soon as he had spoken," the Evangelist emphasizes the fact that it was by the word of Christ accompanying the touch; and the word was, "I will: be thou cleansed." The cure was not gradual, but instantaneous—to show that all was by the Lord's power. If it had been gradual, it might have been ascribed to some natural cause. So, in the spiritual world, the Lord can convert men, and cleanse them in a moment; and, in the Lord's Sacramental action on men, the inward grace comes by, and along with, the reception of the outward sign.

43. "And he straitly [or sternly] charged him, and forthwith," &c. "See thou say nothing to any man," &c. The words of the Lord, in forbidding this man to mention the cleansing, are very much stronger in St. Mark than in the other Evangelists. "Sent him away," should properly be rendered "cast him out;" and from this it has been conjectured that the man, being unclean, had unduly intruded into the synagogue; but it is very unlikely that he had come into a synagogue to be healed. Two explanations may be given—one (that which I have alluded to in my notes on St. Matthew), that the Lord foresaw the hindrance to His ministry which would result from the crowds which the fame of the miracle would attract, and sought to avoid it; another, that the Lord desired him to go at once, without saying a word about the matter, to the priests, to be examined and pronounced clean by them, and to tender them the Levitical offering. Otherwise, if the priests

44 And saith unto him, See thou say nothing to any man: but go thy way, shew thyself to the priest, and offer for thy cleansing those things ° which Moses commanded, for a testimony unto them.

45 ᵖ But he went out, and began to publish *it*

° Lev. xiv. 3, 4, 10. Luke v. 14.
ᵖ Luke v. 15.

---

had heard of the cleansing through other means, it is probable that out of opposition to the Lord, and from a desire to discredit His miracles, they might have refused to pronounce the man clean.

"But go thy way, shew thyself to the priest, and offer for thy cleansing those things which Moses commanded." The offering which Moses, by the Word of God, commanded to be offered when the leper was pronounced healed, are very remarkable indeed, and serve to show that (no doubt, for typical reasons) God made the greatest possible difference between this disease and all others. The account of these offerings is to be found in Leviticus xiv. The most noticeable of them seems to be strictly parallel to the offering of the two goats on the great day of atonement, and is thus described: "Then shall the priest command to take for him that is to be cleansed two birds, alive and clean, and cedar, and scarlet, and hyssop; and the priests shall command that one of the birds be killed in an earthen vessel, over running water. As for the living bird, he shall take it, and the cedar wood, and the scarlet, and the hyssop, and shall dip them and the living bird in the blood of the bird that was killed over the running water. And he shall sprinkle upon him that is to be cleansed seven times, and shall pronounce him clean, and shall let the living bird loose upon the open field."

"For a testimony unto them." Most probably "for a testimony that I have by My power healed a disease beyond all the skill of man to cure, so that they may acknowledge the power of God in Me, and may be led to accept Me." I have noticed in my Introduction to St. John's Gospel, that this sending of the leper to the priests is one of those incidents related in the Synoptics which seem to necessitate a previous ministry in Jerusalem. A prophet of Galilee, unknown in Jerusalem to the priests of the Temple, was not likely to send the lepers to the priests *for a testimony*, unless he had exercised a ministry of healing and teaching under the shadow of the Temple, which the priests had rejected.

45. "But he went out, and began to publish it much, and to

much, and to blaze abroad the matter, insomuch that Jesus could no more openly enter into the city, but was without in desert places: ᑫ and they came to him from ᛫ ch. ii. 13. every quarter.

<sup>45.</sup> "Into the city." Not the particular city, but any city, as we use the word "town" in opposition to "country."

blaze abroad," &c. St. Mark alone mentions that the man deliberately disobeyed the Word of the Lord. Our feelings would lead us to applaud, rather than to blame, the man's conduct; but the sequel shows that it was an hindrance to the Lord's work. Must we not gather from this that all and every preaching of Christ may not be in accordance with His Will? The preaching which, under pretence of honouring Christ, divides His Church, and, by its irreverence and fanaticism, brings discredit on religion, really hinders the work of Christ. It frustrates the intention of His own holy prayer, for the unity of His Church, offered just before His Passion (John xvii. 20, 21).

## CHAP. II.

AND again ᵃ he entered into Capernaum after *some* days; and it was noised that he was in the house. ᵃ Matt. ix. 1. Luke v. 18.

2 And straightway many were gathered together, insomuch that there was no room to receive *them*, no, not so much as about the door : and he preached the word unto them.

1. "And again he entered into Capernaum after some days; and it was," &c. Capernaum is called in St. Matthew "his own city," because, after leaving Nazareth, He dwelt there.

"That he was in the house." Probably the same house mentioned in i. 29-32, &c., which would be Simon Peter's.

2. "And straightway many were gathered together . . . preached the word unto them." The expression, "no room to receive them,

3 And they come unto him, bringing one sick of the palsy, which was borne of four.

4 And when they could not come nigh unto him for the press, they uncovered the roof where he was: and when they had broken it up, they let down the bed wherein the sick of the palsy lay.

---

4. "When they could not come nigh him." So A., C., D., later Uncials, almost all Cursives, Old Latin, Syriac, and some versions. "Bring him in," א, B., L., a few Cursives, Vulg., and some versions.

no, not so much as about the door," implies that our Lord was in such a place in the house that His words could be heard about the door. The most probable explanation which agrees with all the circumstances is that He was preaching in a large room with an open court before it, enclosed on all sides, and full of people, the ceiling of the room being close under the roof. The roof could be reached by an outside staircase, or from the roof of the neighbouring house.

3. "And they come unto him, bringing one sick of the palsy, which," &c. The remark, " which was borne of four," is peculiar to our Evangelist, and seems to show that the narrator, St. Peter, had watched the transaction.

4. " And when they could not come nigh unto him for the press," &c. St. Luke tells us that they made several ineffectual efforts to bring him into the presence of the Lord. "They sought means to bring him in, and to lay him before Him. And when they could not find by what way they might bring him in because of the multitude," &c. This shows their perseverance, and so the strength of their faith. If they had not had a very firm belief that Jesus was both able and willing to restore the poor sufferer to health and strength, they would have been daunted by the difficulties they met with.

"They uncovered the roof where he was: and when they had broken it up," &c.

"They let down the bed wherein," &c. All this, of course, must have been done with the permission of the owner of the house, the Lord Himself being conscious of what was going on. From St. Luke we learn that they broke through the tiling, and probably through a ceiling underneath it. It may be that they had brought

5 When Jesus saw their faith, he said unto the sick of the palsy, Son, thy sins be forgiven thee.

---

5. "Thy sins be forgiven thee," or, "Thy sins are forgiven thee." *Demittuntur tibi peccata* [*tua*], Vulg. [Codex Amiat. omitting *tua*].
"Thee," ℵ, B., D., G., L., a few Cursives. Old Latin [b, e, ff] omit "thee." A., later Uncials, most Cursives, some Old Latin retain it.

the sufferer from some distance, and that this was the only opportunity which they were likely to have of setting him before the Lord.

5. "When Jesus saw their faith, he said," &c. The question has been asked, Was it right thus to interrupt the spiritual teaching of the Lord? He was then, by His holy doctrine, healing men's souls; why should this be broken in upon, in order that he might heal a sick man's body? The answer is, that our Lord very distinctly stamped it with His approval. And, indeed, it presented in itself one of the best illustrations both of the nature and of the success of His teaching, and gave Him an opportunity of setting forth a far higher and more spiritual doctrine than hitherto. For all the Lord's teaching was designed by Him to bring about faith in Himself, as the personal Manifestation of the power and goodness of God His Father.

And here was a case in which that faith which He desired to work in men was exhibited in a very noble and instructive way. For these men exhibited the right sort of faith—a faith which would overcome difficulties,—in fact, a determined and persevering faith.

Quesnel hints that, in breaking through the roof, they used a sort of violence which illustrates the words of the Lord spoken on another occasion: "The kingdom of heaven suffereth violence, and the violent take it by force." "That is a holy and necessary violence which a man uses in order to approach Christ. Happy that person for whom pious souls use so many good endeavours that he is at last brought nigh to Christ. It is absolutely necessary to come nigh unto Him, some way or other, either by the door or by the roof."

5. "When Jesus saw their faith, he said unto the sick of the palsy," &c. How is it that the Lord is said to see *their* faith—*i.e.*, the faith of the bearers,—and then addresses Himself, not to them, but to the sick man? He speaks to the paralytic as if he had not

6 But there were certain of the scribes sitting there, and reasoning in their hearts,

---

only faith to be healed in body, but also religious faith—a sense of sin, which would make him accept and welcome words of pardon. Very probably the bearers had been (as, indeed, seems from the narrative in St. Luke) most forward and urgent in contriving means by which they might bring the paralytic into the presence of the Lord. Perhaps he himself had been somewhat discouraged at the difficulties, and was afraid of intruding into His presence whilst teaching, and they had made light of the difficulties, and overcame his scruples.

Whatever be the explanation, the fact is noticeable that the Lord recognizes at once the strength of their faith, and also the sense of sin in the man himself: for if the man had been utterly indifferent to such things as the sinfulness of his past sins, and the need of pardon, the Lord could not have thus accosted him. This we seem to learn from the Lord's words, as recorded in St. Matthew: "Son, be of good cheer."

"Thy sins be forgiven thee," or "are forgiven," making the declaration of absolution more distinct and authoritative. Here we have an advance on the teaching which accompanied the former miracles recorded by St. Mark. The Lord first applies His forgiving power to the man's soul before He restores health to his body. It seems that the man must have been in a fit spiritual state of mind to receive this absolution, not only from a sense of the evil of sin, but from some (perhaps undefined) sense of the power of such a Teacher and Worker of miracles to speak in God's name.

It is too much, however, to say, as some seem to do, that there must be some spiritual work in the souls of those who came to Christ before there could be healing for their bodies; but undoubtedly by thus putting forth the cure of the soul, the Lord seems to emphasize that as *the* purpose for which He did His mighty works.

6. "But there were certain of the scribes sitting there, and reasoning," &c. St. Luke mentions the presence of these men far more circumstantially: "As he was teaching, there were Pharisees and doctors of the law sitting by, which were come out of every

7 Why doth this *man* thus speak blasphemies? ᵇ who can forgive sins but God only?

ᵇ Job xiv. 4.
Is. xliii. 25.

8 And immediately ᶜ when Jesus perceived in

ᶜ Matt. ix. 4.

---

7. "Why does this man thus speak blasphemies?" So A., C., almost all later Uncials and Cursives, Syriac, and some versions; but ℵ, B., D., L., some Old Latin and Vulgate, "Why doth this man thus speak? He blasphemeth."

town of Galilee and Judea and Jerusalem." From this we gather that this was not a chance presence, as it were, but a gathering of His principal enemies from all quarters to observe His words, with the view of finding some cause of accusation against Him.

"Reasoning in their hearts." They seem not to have had time to consult together, and express aloud their condemnation.

"Why doth this man thus speak blasphemies? [or as Revisers, "Why doth this man thus speak? He blasphemeth."] It is to be noticed that blasphemy is committed against the supreme God in two ways: either by ascribing to God what is unworthy of Him, or by ascribing to His creatures what belongs solely to the Creator and Supreme Judge. They did not know that " what things so ever the Father doeth, these also doeth the Son likewise" (John v. 19).

"Who can forgive sins but God only?" This is perfectly true, but did not apply to the present case, or to any other case of such power exercised either by Christ or by those who are commissioned by Him. For the kingdom of God is one vast system of Mediatorship, in which God is the Sovereign, in Whom resides all authority, all power, all grace of forgiveness or strength. God only can forgive sins because He is the supreme Judge, but He has committed all judgment, *i.e.*, all remitting or retaining of sins, to His Son. He judges, but He judges in and through and by His Son. And as He has commissioned and sent His Son, so His Son has commissioned and sent His apostles; and they in their turn have commissioned and sent the ministers who have succeeded them. God only forgives, but He conveys forgiveness by whatsoever channels—ministerial or sacramental—He sees fit to employ. [See my note on St. Matthew ix. 3, 4.]

8. "And immediately when Jesus perceived in his spirit that they," &c. The Lord at once gives them a proof by His revealing to them the secret reasonings of their hearts, that He was far

his spirit that they so reasoned within themselves, he said unto them, Why reason ye these things in your hearts?

<sup>d</sup> Matt. ix. 5.   9 <sup>d</sup> Whether is it easier to say to the sick of the palsy, *Thy* sins be forgiven thee; or to say, Arise, and take up thy bed, and walk?

---

9. " Thy sins be forgiven thee." See as above, " Thy sins are forgiven thee."
"Walk." So A., B., C., later Uncials, almost all Cursives, Old Latin, Vulg., Coptic, Syriac, &c. ; but א, L. read, " go thy way."

nearer to God, far more closely and personally connected with Him than they had imagined. It is the prerogative of God alone to search the heart. " I, the Lord, search the hearts " (Jerem. xvii. 10). St. Paul speaks of Him as the God Who searcheth the hearts (Rom. viii. 27); and Christ, again, in His message to the Church of Thyatira, " I am He that searcheth the reins and hearts " (Rev. ii. 23).

9. " Whether is it easier to say . . . thy sins be forgiven thee; or to say . . . walk." The Lord not only noticed their thoughts against Himself, but the very line which their false reasoning took. They must have said within themselves, " To say thy sins are forgiven is easy enough, for no one can prove or disprove whether what is so said is ratified in heaven or not; but let Him do something by which He can show that He wields the authority of God." Perhaps they thought that to heal this man's disease would be beyond His power. Thus Theophylact [quoted in Catena Aurea] : " The Pharisees thought it more difficult to heal the body, as being more open to view ; but the soul more easy to cure, because the cure is invisible; so that they reasoned thus : ' Lo, He does not now cure the body, but heals the unseen soul; if He had had more power He would at once have cured the body, and not have fled for refuge to the unseen world.' The Saviour, therefore, showing that He can do both, says, ' Which is the easier ? ' as if he said, ' I, indeed, by the healing of the body, which is in reality more easy, but appears to you more difficult, will prove to you the healing of the soul, which is really the harder of the two.' "

10. " But that ye may know that the Son of man hath power on earth," &c. By using the words, " the Son of man hath power on earth," it seems to me that the Lord exercises this power, not as the

10 But that ye may know that the Son of man hath power on earth to forgive sins, (he saith to the sick of the palsy,)

11 I say unto thee, Arise, and take up thy bed, and go thy way into thine house.

12 And immediately he arose, took up the bed, and went forth before them all; insomuch that they were all amazed,

---

10. The order is uncertain. It may be, "The Son of man hath power to forgive sins on earth," or, "The Son of man on earth hath power," or as in Authorized.
12. "And immediately he arose." So A., all later Uncials, Syriac, Old Latin, Vulg.; but ℵ, B., C., L., read, "And he arose, and immediately took up," &c.

Eternal Word, but as the Mediator. He exercises the power as the Son of man, but it is not inherent in Him as the Son of man of Himself, but as the Son of man the Messiah, ordered, sent, commissioned by His Father—and "on earth;" He has all power in heaven and in earth. At the last day He will judge, and so absolve or condemn, not men only but angels; but, in the face of His enemies, it was sufficient to assert that He had this power on earth. The sphere, both of the absolution and the miracle, was on earth. In all probability there had been something in the man's sin which required that it should be put away by such means, before the Saviour could fitly restore him to health.

11. "I say unto thee, Arise, and take up thy bed, and go thy way," &c. Notice how, whilst he was without power, the Lord bids him arise. That he should do this there must have been an instantaneous feeling of restored strength accompanying the Lord's words, so that he did what he had not done perhaps for years before, he made the effort to arise, and he found that he had strength from the Saviour so to do.

"Take up thy bed." By this the Lord showed that the restoration was instantaneous and complete. Though the bed was but a mat, it would have been far too heavy for one not properly restored to strength to carry away.

12. "And immediately he arose, took up the bed," &c. Mark the prompt obedience. As the Saviour had joined the "taking up the bed" with the arising from it, so he did.

It is said in St. Mark, that "he immediately arose, took up the bed, and went forth before them all, insomuch that they were all amazed." St. Mark's account is, that of one who saw the whole

and glorified God, saying, We never saw it on this fashion.

<sup>e</sup> Matt. ix. 9.

13 ᵉ And he went forth again by the sea side; and all the multitude resorted unto him, and he taught them.

<sup>f</sup> Matt. ix. 9. Luke v. 27.
‖ Or, *at the place where the custom was received.*

14 ᶠ And as he passed by, he saw Levi the *son* of Alphæus sitting ‖ at the receipt of custom, and said unto him, Follow me. And he arose and followed him.

---

14. " He saw Levi the son of Alphæus." It is worth while noticing the fact that D. and the Old Latin read here, "James the son of Alphæus," a manifest blunder of a very gross kind; and yet such a blot as this is actually registered as a marginal reading in Westcott and Hort's Greek Text.

---

scene, and on whom the signs of astonishment in the faces of the bystanders had made an indelible impression.

"And glorified God, saying, We never saw it after this fashion." St. Matthew reports that they "glorified God which had given such power unto men." St. Luke that they were filled with fear, saying, "We have seen strange things to-day." St. Mark: "We never saw it after this fashion." Each Evangelist reports different exclamations on the part of the crowd; but is not this most natural, and a proof of the faithfulness of the narrative? Would a crowd of excited persons, filling the house and court—perhaps two or three hundred—have all uttered simultaneously the same exclamation? Would not some have referred all the power to God, would not others have exclaimed that they had seen nothing to compare to it; would not others have simply stared, and thought it strange; and would not the admiration of the most part have been mixed with fear at an exhibition of supernatural power so close to them?

13. "And he went forth again by the sea side; . . . and he taught them." The account of His teaching of multitudes by the sea-side is peculiar to St. Mark. It is no doubt mentioned because it was the occasion on which He fell in with St. Matthew, and called him.

14. "And as he passed by, he saw Levi the son of Alphæus sitting at the," &c. In SS. Mark and Luke this apostle is called Levi, in St. Matthew he is called Matthew, the name by which he has ever since been known in the Church. That he had the name of Matthew (given by the Lord) added to his first name is in

15 ᵍ And it came to pass, that, as Jesus sat at meat in his house, many publicans and sinners sat also to-    ᵍ Matt. ix. 10. gether with Jesus and his disciples: for there were many, and they followed him.

---

accordance with what is told us of nearly all the other apostles, the greater part having some additional name. Such were the names of Peter, Boanerges, Didymus, Thaddeus, Iscariot, Zelotes, Nathanael, &c. We have here the call of one in a very different state and worldly position to those who hitherto had left all to follow the Lord. He was, from his occupation, in all probability far richer, and yet far less respectable, for the name of publican was a byword of contempt, our Lord Himself at times using it as if those whom it designated were, on the whole, a disreputable class.

Respecting St. Matthew's previous history we are told nothing whatsoever; but when we remember that when the Lord called Peter, James, John, Andrew, and Philip, he called men who had been under the instruction and discipline of the Baptist, and so were not called by any means in a state of indifference or unpreparedness, so it very probably was with St. Matthew. From many hints and notices respecting the publicans, we are led to believe that there had been some special religious movement among them as a class. Our Lord speaks of all the people that heard John, *and the publicans*, justifying God by submitting to receive his baptism (Luke vii. 29). He speaks of the publicans and harlots entering into the kingdom of God before the Pharisees (Matt. xxi. 31). We are told that the publicans came to be baptized, and the Baptist seems to have addressed them as if they had come separately and in a body (Luke iii. 12, 13). With this agrees our Lord's choosing the Publican in His parable as a special example of contrition. From all this I think it is more than probable that Levi, or Matthew, had been a disciple of the Baptist, or had submitted to his baptism, that his heart had been some time worked upon by the Spirit of God, and that the Lord's call was the decisive crisis in his religious history.

15. "And it came to pass, that, as Jesus sat at meat," &c. In my Commentary on St. Matthew, I noticed how the Apostle at once threw himself heart and soul into the new state of things,

## 34   NOT THE RIGHTEOUS, BUT SINNERS.   [St. Mark.

16 And when the scribes and Pharisees saw him eat with publicans and sinners, they said unto his disciples, How is it that he eateth and drinketh with publicans and sinners?

17 When Jesus heard *it*, he saith unto them, [h] They that are whole have no need of the physician, but they that are sick: I came not to call the righteous, but sinners to repentance.

[h] Matt. ix. 12. 13. & xviii. 11.
Luke v. 31, 32. & xix. 10.
1 Tim. i. 15.

---

16. "Scribes and Pharisees." So A., C., later Uncials, almost all Cursives, Vulg., &c.; but "Scribes of the Pharisees" read by ℵ, B., L., &c.
17. "Sinners to repentance." "To repentance" omitted by A., Vulg., and Syriac, as well as by ℵ, B., D. It is consequently very probably spurious so far as this Gospel is concerned, but that it formed a part of our Lord's words is certain from Luke v. 32.

and made a feast, to which he invited his brother publicans, in order that they might hear and receive the words which had saved him.

Each Evangelist remarks that *many* of such sat down. St. Matthew, that many publicans and sinners came; St. Mark adds, "and they were many;" St. Luke, "there was a great company of publicans and of others." Quesnel (a Romanist) remarks on this: "Every sinner converted to Christ must endeavour to conduct his friends to Him. Fruitfulness is a certain proof of the reality of conversion."

16. "And when the scribes and Pharisees . . . with publicans and sinners." It is quite possible that this was said, not out of malice, but out of sheer ignorance respecting the way of getting at the hearts of sinners, or out of inability to understand that Divine grace can reach the souls of the most abandoned. All their system of religion was external and unreal, and so they could not enter into the mind of One Who would condescend to mix and converse with the lowest, if He could only win them to God.

17. "When Jesus heard it, he saith unto them, They that are whole," &c. I must refer the reader to my note in St. Matthew, respecting the universal application of this verse to those who have kept themselves, by God's grace, comparatively pure from sin, as well as to those who have plunged into uncleanness.

"They that are whole have no need," &c., as if He said, "Why are you surprised to see Me in the company of sinners? You know well My purpose in mixing with them; surely it is as unreasonable to wonder at it as to be surprised at seeing a physician in an hospital.

18 ¹And the disciples of John and of the Pharisees used to fast: and they come and say unto him, Why ¹ Matt. ix. 14. Luke v. 33.

---

18. "The disciples of John and of the Pharisees." Properly, "the disciples of John and the Pharisees." So ℵ, A., B., C., D., K., M., Vulg., and Syriac; but many of the later Uncials (E., F., G., H., L.) and the greater part of Cursives agree with Rec. Text.

"I came not to call the righteous," &c. It has been asked, how our Lord could call by implication any human beings righteous. We answer that He could not speak otherwise. It is true that none are *absolutely* righteous, sinless as God, or even as the angels, and yet numbers are, and all are capable of being, and intended by God to be, made righteous. That very Word of God which convinces all of sin, speaks in every page of some being righteous and others wicked, some good and others evil. For purposes of salvation, all are accounted sinners, that all may partake of the righteousness of Christ; and God can in very deed so convince those who have lived in all good conscience (as St. Paul had) of their sinfulness, that their repentance is deeper and humbler than that of those who have lived in wilful sin, and so such are in a condition to receive Christ as heartily, and rely upon Him as implicitly as the grossest sinners to whom God has granted repentance unto life.

It is needful, however, to put in a word of caution. The Lord mixed with the lowest sinners, to win them to repentance; but for those to do so who are neophytes, who have but lately turned to Him, and who have had little or no experience of some of the most insidious forms of temptation, is exceedingly perilous. I knew one who began very well, and seemed to be truly converted, who fell terribly, and made utter shipwreck of his Christian character by taking part in one of the best of works—the London Midnight Mission.

18. "And the disciples of John and of the Pharisees used to fast," &c. "The disciples of John"—how is it that they joined with those whom their Master had denounced as "a generation of vipers"? It has usually been put down to jealousy of the growing success of Christ whilst their master was shut up in prison; but was it not owing to the marked difference between the outward life of John and that of the Lord? Jesus had Himself drawn attention to this difference, when He said, "John came neither eating nor drinking—the Son of Man came eating and drinking. It is to be

do the disciples of John and of the Pharisees fast, but thy disciples fast not?

19 And Jesus said unto them, Can the children of the bridechamber fast, while the bridegroom is with them? as long as they have the bridegroom with them, they cannot fast.

---

remembered that these disciples of John were those in whom the chief mission of the Baptist was not fulfilled. They had not, as the Apostles, been drawn through his teaching to Christ. They would naturally rest on what was outward in the mission of John, hold it to be final, be offended at the liberty allowed by the new Teacher, and so join with the Pharisees in putting such a question to the Lord.

"And John's-disciples and the Pharisees were fasting." It has been supposed, with some probability, that the feast in Matthew's house was on some day set apart by the Pharisees as a fast day, though not one of the appointed fasts of the Jews.

"Thy disciples fast not." In this they accuse by implication the great Teacher of not being sufficiently ascetic in His teaching and discipline, forgetting that the disciples of the Lord had forsaken all to follow Him—a far greater sacrifice than fasting twice in the week, and retaining all their possessions.

19. "And Jesus said unto them, Can the children [sons] of the bridechamber," &c. This answer of the Lord is one of those places in the Synoptics which exhibit both the sentiments and the language of the fourth Gospel. The Baptist there (John iii. 29) speaks of Christ as the bridegroom, and himself as only the friend of the bridegroom; and the Lord may have here intended to remind these disciples of John that their master had borne this witness to Him.

Fasting is connected with sorrow and mourning. The time of Christ's visible presence was a time of deep joy to those who recognized Him; and so it would be incongruous, if not hypocritical, to make such a time a time of fasting. But the bright day of gladness was to be succeeded by the night of bereavement: "and then shall they fast."

This is not so much a command, or direction, or law, as a prophecy; and the later parts of the New Testament teach us how

CHAP. II.]     THEN SHALL THEY FAST.     37

20 But the days will come, when the bridegroom shall be taken away from them, and then shall they fast in those days.

21 No man also seweth a piece of ‖ new cloth on an old garment: else the new piece that filled it up taketh away from the old, and the rent is made worse.

‖ Or, *raw*, or, *unwrought*.

---

20. "In those days." So most later Uncials, Old Latin; but ℵ, A., B., C., D., K., L., some Cursives, Syriac, Vulg. [Cod. Amiat.], read, "In that day."
21. "Also." Probably should be omitted after ℵ, A., B., C., L., Vulg., &c.

literally and universally it was fulfilled. When the Bridegroom was taken away, the Church, in its earliest and best days, did indeed fast. Thus, when Paul and Barnabas were set apart to the work to which the Holy Ghost had called them, the word came to those who were "ministering to the Lord, and fasting" (Acts xiii. 2). St. Paul ordained elders, after prayer with fasting (xiv. 23). He speaks of himself as being "in fastings often" (2 Corinth. xi. 27). He speaks of ministers commending themselves to God, "in labours, in watchings, and in fastings" (2 Cor. vi. 5).

All branches of the Church Catholic have from very early times observed times of fasting, particularly the day of the Lord's Death, and His rest in the grave. The Church of England gives abundant opportunity to her children to fulfil this prophecy of the Lord: such as the forty days of Lent, the Ember days, the Vigils, and each Friday in the year. That her children but scantily observe such seasons in no way puts her in the wrong as regards her duty to her Lord.

21. "No man also seweth . . . rent is made worse." In my notes on St. Matthew, I have dwelt upon the great principle underlying these two parables or similitudes—viz., that the kingdom of God, or the polity and religion brought in by Jesus, cannot be a mere patch upon Judaism to make up some deficiency in the older religion; neither can its spirit be made to work under the dead forms of the old system. On the contrary, the new religion is a new and far more glorious garment, and is animated by a spirit which would utterly refuse to be restrained in such worn-out vessels as the Mosaic laws and ordinances. At present, the disciples were as raw, unwrought cloth, which must be made into its own garment,

**22** And no man putteth new wine into old bottles: else the new wine doth burst the bottles, and the wine is spilled, and the bottles will be marred: but new wine must be put into new bottles.

ᵏ Matt. xii. 1.
Luke vi. 1.
**23** ᵏ And it came to pass, that he went through

---

22. The text and translation of this verse in our Authorized is according to A., Vulg., and Syriac. The Revisers, following Neutral Text, render, "No man putteth new wine into old wine skins: else the wine will burst the skins, and the wine perisheth and the skins, but they put new wine into fresh wine skins."

and not added as a mere makeshift to another; they were as new wine, which must be enclosed in the new vessel preparing for them, as the old was quite powerless to hold them together, and preserve them. The persons who were now blaming the disciples for want of strictness, were anxious to impose upon them mere outward Pharisaical strictness; but this was both foolish and premature. The time would shortly come when these disciples would lead far stricter and more self-denying lives than those who were now calling them to account, but they would be animated in this new life by different principles and a different spirit.

An inference is drawn by many pious writers from these words of the Lord, which is quite legitimate, though I am not sure that it was in His mind. It is thus well expressed by Quesnel: "Men often spoil all for want of well considering the strength and ability of such souls as begin to turn to God. The indiscreet zeal of a pastor, who requires too much of a penitent at first, often makes him give over all, and renders him the worse. It is a temptation to some beginners to be desirous of following the most advanced Christians in everything. The devil seeks either to discourage them, or to puff them up. We must lay deep foundations of humility and the love of God before we can possibly raise the spiritual building. Love will furnish us with all materials, and humility will preserve them."

23. "And it came to pass ... to pluck the ears of corn." The narrative of this incident seems to be a fitting sequel to what had just occurred. In the former verses the Lord had defended His disciples against the charge of laxity in the matter of fasting. They were in no way bound to keep the Pharisaical fasts. Now He claims on behalf of His own a far greater liberty in the matter of

CHAP. II.] NOT LAWFUL ON THE SABBATH. 39

the corn fields on the sabbath day ; and his disciples began, as they went, ¹ to pluck the ears of corn.      1 Deut. xxiii. 25

24 And the Pharisees said unto him, Behold, why do they on the sabbath day that which is not lawful ?

---

23. "His disciples began, as they went, to pluck the ears of corn." Literally, "His disciples began to make a way, plucking the ears of corn." Vulg., *Cœperunt progredi, et vellere spicas.*

Sabbath observance than the religious leaders of that time permitted. The rules which the Pharisees had enforced seemed intended to make the Sabbath an intolerable burden, and the Lord having emancipated His disciples from any such yoke, proceeds to enunciate in a short and very decisive aphorism, preserved only by St. Mark, the true principle of the weekly day of rest and refreshment.

"He went through the corn fields on the sabbath day." Perhaps from one synagogue to another; but no doubt the incident was so ordered by God (Who had given Him commandment what He should say and what He should teach, John xii. 49) that it might afford Him opportunity to establish the greater freedom of the New Kingdom, the relation of the Sabbath to man as a great boon from God to those who live by hard labour, and His own power over the Sabbath as its Lord.

"To pluck the ears of corn." St. Matthew notices that the disciples were an hungred. The disciples in thus satisfying their hunger, did a thing which the law of Moses expressly permitted them to do; for we read, "When thou comest into the standing corn of thy neighbour, then thou mayest pluck the ears with thine hand; but thou shalt not move a sickle unto thy neighbour's standing corn" (Deut. xxiii. 25). Of course after they had done this, they must of necessity have rubbed the ears in their hands, or they could not have got at the kernels as they walked through the fields, and it would not have been lawful to take any quantity away. This we should have been sure of, even if St. Luke had not mentioned it. The Pharisees object, not to the plucking of the ears—that was clearly allowed—but to the action of rubbing them in their hands. And the Lord answered them by showing that it is according to the Father's will that all rules respecting outward things must give way to the needs of men. He cites as strong a case in point as can well

# 40   DAVID EATING THE SHEWBREAD.   [ST. MARK.

25 And he said unto them, Have ye never read ᵐ what
ᵐ 1 Sam. xxi. 6. David did, when he had need, and was an
hungred, he, and they that were with him?

26 How he went into the house of God in the days of
Abiathar the high priest, and did eat the shewbread, ⁿ which
ⁿ Ex. xxix. is not lawful to eat but for the priests, and gave
32, 33. Lev.
xxiv 9.    also to them which were with him?

---

26. "In the days of Abiathar the high priest;" or, "When Abiathar was high priest;"
*sub Abiathar principe sacerdotum*, Vulg.

be conceived. It was not lawful for any but the priests to eat the
shewbread, and yet David asked for this bread; and Ahimelech
(with whom was Abiathar, his son) gave it to him, and to those
that were with him, and very probably on the Sabbath day, for it
would appear from 1 Samuel xxi. 6, that it had been changed on
that very day.

A difficulty has been made respecting the name of the priest.
Ahimelech, the father of Abiathar, was the priest who gave the
bread to David, but Abiathar was certainly present, and would, no
doubt, concur in the act. This explanation is as old as the time of
Venerable Bede, who says, "There is, however, no discrepancy, for
both were there, when David came to ask for bread, and received
it: that is to say, Ahimelech, the high priest, and Abiathar, his
son; but Ahimelech having been slain by Saul (very shortly after),
Abiathar fled to David, and became the companion of all his exile
afterwards. When he came to the throne, Abiathar himself also
received the rank of high priest, and the son became of much greater
excellence than the father, and therefore was worthy to be mentioned as the high priest, even during his father's lifetime." Such
seems, in all respects, a fair and likely account of the substitution
of the son's name for that of the father. If, however, St. Mark
wrote Abiathar in mistake, it merely shows that the inspiration
vouchsafed to him, whilst enabling him to give the most graphic
account of the Lord's works of any of the four, was not intended
to raise him above the liability to make mistakes in matters of
chronology, or locality, or grammar, which could deceive no one,
and which any reader could correct for himself. (See particularly
my note on St. Matthew xxvii. 9.)

27 And he said unto them, The sabbath was made for man, and not man for the sabbath:

---

27. "And he said unto them . . . not man for the Sabbath." St. Mark omits the Lord's reference to the more laborious work of the priests in the temple on the Sabbath, and to Himself as one greater than the Sabbath, and the reference to the prophetical utterance, "I will have mercy and not sacrifice" (Matt. xii. 5, 6, 7), and proceeds to enunciate the principle on which such a day as the weekly festival can only be observed. The Sabbath was made for man, for his rest and refreshment, particularly if he has to labour to get his bread at the will of others, and so God says in the book of Deuteronomy: "Keep the Sabbath day to sanctify it . . . that thy manservant and thy maidservant may rest as well as thou" (v. 12, 14). But this gift of God to the sons of toil, whether the Sabbath of the Jew, or the Lord's Day of the Christian, is turned into an unbearable burden if it is to be kept after the manner of the Pharisees. It is then turned from its first intention of being a day of refreshment subordinate to man's needs, and so observed as if man was subordinate to it. It is surprising how many pious, God-fearing men have not seen this, and have refused, of set purpose, to set before themselves how every allusion to the Sabbath in the account of the Lord's ministry seems to tell against its too strict enforcement. Whole bodies of professing Christians seem to make the Pharisees rather than the Lord their exemplars in this matter. I read lately in the life of a pious Scotch minister of this generation how his home looked upon an open park in the suburbs of a crowded city, and how, when he saw his fellow-citizens taking a quiet walk for the sake of fresh air and innocent relaxation on the Sunday, he wondered how it was that the earth did not open her mouth and swallow them up as it did Korah and his company. But, on the other hand, man is robbed of this gift of God by laxity and self-indulgence on the part of employers. If men give sumptuous entertainments and use their costly equipages on this day, how can their man-servants and their maid-servants rest as well as they?

I am thankful to see that in this matter the great country of France seems returning to a better mind. The national church is everywhere encouraging societies and guilds whose work it is to form public opinion and so bring about a better observance of

* Matt. xii. 8.   28 Therefore °the Son of man is Lord also of the sabbath.

---

Sunday, and Services of Reparation are appointed by authority to deprecate God's anger for past violations of His holy day.

Quesnel expresses himself admirably upon this: "The usages and ordinances of religion ought to be regulated according to their end, which is the honour of God, and the advantage of men. It is the property of the religion of the true God, to contain nothing in it but what is beneficial to man. Hereby God plainly shows, that it is neither out of indigence nor interest that He requires men to worship and obey Him, but only out of goodness, and on purpose to make them happy. God prohibited work on the Sabbath day for fear lest servants should be oppressed by the hard-heartedness of their masters, and to the end that men might not be hindered from attending upon Him and their own salvation. Religion, therefore, salvation, and mercy, are the things which should employ us on that holy day."

28. "Therefore the Son of Man is Lord also of the Sabbath." Not, of course, Lord of the Sabbath as the Son of Man, for as Son of Man He is, as St. Paul says, "made under the law;" but the Son of Man is also the Son of God, and so being "God of the substance of His Father, begotten before the worlds," He is Lord of the Sabbath. Nothing can show the Divine Nature of our Lord more clearly than that He is above such a law of God, so that He should modify it, relax it, and change it at His pleasure. He exercised but a small part of this authority when He freed His disciples from the yoke of its burdensome Pharisaic observance. He exercised His lordship over the day far more royally when He by His Spirit made the day of His Resurrection the weekly religious festival of His Church. By this He gave it altogether a new character. Henceforth it is a day, not of mere rest, but of renewed life, the Life of His own Resurrection, and so its characteristic ordinance is not the slaying of beasts, but the life-giving celebration of the Sacrament of His risen Body.

## CHAP. III.

AND ᵃ he entered again into the synagogue; and there was a man there which had a withered hand.  ᵃ Matt. xii. 9. Luke vi. 6.

2 And they watched him, whether he would heal him on the sabbath day; that they might accuse him.

---

1. "Had a withered hand." Better, "Had his hand withered."

1. "And he entered again into [the] synagogue . . . withered hand." This narrative very fitly follows up the teaching of what has just preceded it; for, in the last verses of the former chapter, the Lord vindicates the lawfulness of works of necessity on the Sabbath—now He claims for Himself (and if for Himself, for His Church) the right of doing works of mercy on the same day. But He does more than this: He seems to teach us that works of healing and restoration are very appropriate to the holy festival; for it might have been supposed, even by those who were not Pharisees, that such a work as follows might have been postponed—that the man might have been bid to come to Christ on some other day; but the Lord does not put off the act of mercy on account of the day. He took into account that the healing of the man on the spot was saving him one day of discomfort and loss of means of livelihood, and so He delayed not a single hour.

"A man there which had a withered hand," or rather had his hand withered, intimating that the man was not born with the defect. The Gospel according to the Hebrews, or Nazarenes, quoted in Jerome, represented him as saying: "I was a mason seeking sustenance by my hands: I beseech thee, Jesus, that Thou restore me health that I may not shamefully beg for food." (From Nicholson's comment on St. Matthew xii. 10.)

2. "And they watched him, whether he would heal him on the Sabbath day," &c. What mingled impiety and malignity, that they should seek occasion against anyone for performing an act of benevolence, and not only of benevolence, but of Almighty power, for without such power the act could not have been performed at all!

3 And he saith unto the man which had the withered hand, † Stand forth.

4 And he saith unto them, Is it lawful to do

† Gr. *Arise, stand forth in the midst.*

---

3. " Stand forth." See margin, and old translation, quoted below.

I cannot help giving a very good reflection of Bishop Hall's (quoted by Ford) on this watching. "There is no public action which the world is not ready to scan; there is no action so private which the evil spirits are not witnesses of. I will endeavour so to live as knowing that I am ever in the eyes of mine enemies." ("Meditations and Vows," cent. iii. 78.)

St. Matthew does not mention that they watched Him, but that they first asked Him, " Is it lawful to heal on the Sabbath-day?" St. Augustine remarks: "We must understand that they first asked the Lord, if it was lawful to heal on the Sabbath day, then that understanding their thoughts, and that they were seeking an opportunity to accuse Him, He placed in the middle him whom He was about to cure, and put those questions which Mark and Luke relate. We must then suppose that when they were silent He propounded the parable of the sheep, and concluded that it was lawful to do good on the Sabbath day."

Canon Cook, in the "Speaker's Commentary," remarks that the word "watched" is scarcely strong enough, the original denotes jealous, perverse, uncandid observation, the watching of one already hostile. The word occurs but seldom, and only in passages where perverse intention is indicated. (Luke xiv. 1; Acts ix. 24; Gal. iv. 10.)

3. "And he said unto the man which had the withered hand, Stand forth." Our translation, "stand forth," scarcely gives the full meaning, which is, "Arise (and come forth) into the midst," as if He would have him come where all eyes might see him. Thus Wickliffe has: "And he seide to the man that hadde a drye honde, rise into the myddil." Tyndall has: "Arise, and stond in the middes." Perhaps, also, the Lord did this, that, by directing their looks to the sufferer, He might rouse the consciences of these men, or excite any better feeling which might be remaining in any of them.

4. "And he saith unto them, Is it lawful to do good . . . save life, or to kill?" &c. The instruction conveyed by this question is very remarkable. To "do good" is paralleled by to "save life;" to

CHAP. III.] THEY HELD THEIR PEACE. 45

good on the sabbath days, or to do evil? to save life, or to kill? But they held their peace.

5 And when he had looked round about on them with

---

"do evil" by "to kill." But "to kill," in the case before us, would be merely to defer relief, and that not of life, but of limb; but the Lord teaches us that the underlying principle is the same. It was a part of the same power of evil that a man's hand should be deadened by the withering of the nerve, as that his whole body should be dead by the extinction of the principle of life in all the nerves; and so it was a part of the same power of Good, that the life of the single limb should be "saved," as that the life of the whole body should be "saved." The benevolent power which would save the life of the limb would save that of the whole body; and, on the contrary, the malevolent wish which would, for base purposes, defer the healing of the limb, would not rest there, but would, if opportunity offered, destroy the whole life. This was, as we all know, proved to the letter when the enemies of Christ, in order that they might prevent men believing in Him, sought to put Lazarus to death. The Lord in a true sense saved this man's life when He saved to him the means of life. A modern expositor, Morison, has put this well: "All good-doing to men's bodies lies on the line of life; all withholding of good-doing lies on the line of killing, or of death. If it would be wrong, in the absence of higher claims, to withhold the good-doing that would save life, it must also be wrong, when the higher claims are still absent, to withhold the good-doing that may be needed to develop life into its fulness of vigour and beauty."

Lange also remarks well : "The Lord declares the work of compassionate love or doing good generally to be always urgent; and the thought is further involved, that sickness does not tarry at a stand, but that there is a continual sinking into deeper danger and need."

5. "And when he had looked round about on them with anger, being grieved," &c. Notice how he to whom St. Mark owed this whole account—no doubt, St. Peter—had had the look of mingled anger and grief indelibly impressed upon him. St. Mark could scarcely have derived such a fact, except from one who followed the Lord's eye, and observed every change in His Divine counte-

anger, being grieved for the ||hardness of their hearts, he ||Or, *blindness*. saith unto the man, Stretch forth thine hand. And he stretched *it* out: and his hand was restored whole as the other.

---

5. "Whole as the other" omitted by ℵ, A., B., C., D., K., Vulg., and Syriac; therefore most probably not a part of the original text, though inserted in L., later Uncials, and most Cursives.

nance. "He looked upon them with those eyes which, the Psalmist says, 'consider the poor,' and those eyelids which 'try the children of men.'" He looked upon them, says Chrysostom, that by His very eye He might win them over.

"With anger, being grieved." His anger was at their sin—*i.e.*, their hypocrisy and malice,—His grief at the state to which these sins had reduced their hearts. They were in the most pitiable condition, being hardened against compassion and goodness; and He Who knew what the future consequences of these sins would be was grieved. May we hope that this, His grief, was effectual to find, some day or other, a way for His mercy to reach them?

"Stretch forth thine hand." It is most probable that the withering of the hand had affected the whole arm. In such a case, the Lord here calls upon the man to perform an act of faith, to endeavour to do that which, a moment before, he had not power to do: and the Lord met this, his endeavour, by instantaneous restoration of health and strength.

"He stretched it forth, and his hand was restored," &c. We are to remember that this was a visible miracle—not merely a restoration of secret power to the internal nerves, but of fulness of flesh in the place of shrunken and withered muscle and sinew. All in the Synagogue witnessed this, and must have been, willingly or not, convinced of the exercise of Divine Power.

The whole miracle is suggestive to everyone who has the smallest spirituality of mind of the healing of the soul. "The man with a withered hand shows the human race, dried up as to its fruitfulness in good works, but now cured by the mercy of the Lord; the hand of man which, in our first parents, had been dried up, when he plucked the fruit of the forbidden tree, through the grace of the Redeemer, Who stretched His guiltless hands on the tree of the Cross, has been restored to health" (Bede, in "Catena Aurea").

6 ᵇAnd the Pharisees went forth, and straightway took counsel with ᶜthe Herodians against him, how they might destroy him.

ᵇ Matt. xii. 14.
ᶜ Matt. xxii. 16.

7 But Jesus withdrew himself with his disciples to the sea: and a great multitude from Galilee followed him, ᵈand from Judæa,

ᵈ Luke vi. 17.

---

6. "And the Pharisees went forth, and straightway took counsel with the Herodians." It is difficult to understand what common ground these two parties could have in seeking the life of the Lord. We can well understand the ground which the Pharisees, the upholders of formalism and spurious traditions, took against One Who laid bare their hypocrisy; but why the party of Herod, the secularists and worldlings, should trouble themselves with the matter, so as to unite with their theological adversaries (for it is generally understood that the adherents of Herod and the Roman power, if they professed any religion at all, would profess Sadduceeism) is more difficult to account for. Some (amongst them Theophylact) consider that the adherents of Herod claimed on his behalf certain Messianic pretensions, as the possessor of the throne of David. Others (amongst them Bede), that the adherents of Herod, on account of the hatred which their lord had for John, pursued also with treachery and hate the Saviour Whom John preached. But will not all anti-Christs sink their differences, and eventually unite against Christ? The claims of Christ, whether He was to be received or not, were at this juncture far more pressing than the decision as to whether formalists or secularists were nearest the truth. All questions, even between Pharisees and Sadducees, could and must wait. The question respecting whether Jesus was the Christ of God could not wait. Every miracle, every sermon forced them to a decision one way or another.

7. "But Jesus withdrew himself with his disciples to the sea." His hour was not yet come; so He went with His disciples to the borders of the lake of Galilee, where, if pursued, He could the more easily take ship, and escape to some other part, out of the reach of His persecutors.

"And a great multitude from Galilee followed him," &c. We should put a full stop after "followed him," and read the two verses thus: "And a great multitude from Galilee followed him.

8 And from Jerusalem, and from Idumæa, and *from* beyond Jordan; and they about Tyre and Sidon, a great multitude, when they had heard what great things he did, came unto him.

9 And he spake to his disciples, that a small ship should wait on him because of the multitude, lest they should throng him.

10 For he had healed many; insomuch that they || pressed upon him for to touch him, as many as had plagues.

|| Or, *rushed.*

---

And a great multitude from Judæa, and from Jerusalem, and from Idumæa, and from beyond Jordan, and about Tyre and Sidon, hearing what great things He did, came unto Him." The multitude from the neighbouring Galilee, in which He had been preaching and healing, *followed* Him; the multitude from Judæa, and Jerusalem, and from all the regions bordering on the Holy Land, attracted by the fame of His miracles, " came " to Him. Notice how, though He is rejected by the leaders both in Church and State, the people from all parts seem to accept Him. I say "seem," for the Evangelist is careful to inform us that they were attracted, not by His preaching, but by His miracles.

Let the reader notice how here, as before, this Evangelist loves to dwell upon the widespread popularity of the Lord.

9. " And he spake to the disciples, that a small ship should wait on him," &c. The word " wait " does not give the full meaning of the original, which is the same word as that used in the Apostolic precept, " continue instant in prayer," of Romans xii. 12. It means that the ship should be always at His beck and call, so that, by escaping the pressure of the multitude, He should not be unduly hindered in the exercise of His ministry.

10. " For he had healed many: insomuch that they pressed upon him," &c. " Pressed upon him " should rather be rendered "fell upon him," as if there was a rush towards Him of all who had plagues—plagues (literally " scourges ") describing the painfulness and distress of disease, as if it were a scourging inflicted on man as a punishment for his sin.

" To touch him." It was the Lord's will most frequently to heal

CHAP. III.]  THOU ART THE SON OF GOD.  49

11 ᵉ And unclean spirits, when they saw him, fell down before him, and cried, saying, ᶠ Thou art the Son of God.

12 And ᵍ he straitly charged them that they should not make him known.

13 ʰ And he goeth up into a mountain, and

ᵉ ch. i. 23, 24.
Luke iv. 41.
ᶠ Matt. xiv. 33.
ch. i. 1.
ᵍ Matt. xii. 16.
ch. i. 25, 34.
ʰ Matt. x. 1.
Luke vi. 12.
& ix. 1.

---

men by contact with His body. He makes communication with His Body the means by which virtue flows from Himself to those whom He wills to benefit. The reader will understand.

11. "And unclean spirits, when they saw him, fell down before him." The uniformity of action on the part of all evil spirits in the presence of the Lord, in that they should fall down and confess Him, is exceedingly remarkable (Matt. viii. 29; Mark i. 23, 24). These fallen beings seem to be under a law that they should thus acknowledge the Son of God. I cannot think that this is to be explained, as so many attempt to do, on the ground of diabolical cunning. It seems as if they were compelled to fall down, and confess their Maker, even though they had made it the one object of their existence to oppose and thwart Him.

12. "And he straitly charged them that they should not make him known." On this Bede remarks, "A sinner is forbidden to preach the Lord, lest any one listening to his preaching should follow him in his error, for the devil is an evil master, who always mingles false things with true, that the semblance of truth may cover the witness of fraud. But not only devils, but persons healed by Christ and even Apostles (Mark viii. 9) are ordered to be silent concerning Him before the Passion, lest by the preaching of the majesty of His Divinity, the economy of His Passion should be retarded."

13. "And he goeth up into a [the] mountain and calleth unto him whom he would," &c. St. Luke is more full upon this, inasmuch as he gives us the reason why He went up and how long He continued there: "He went out into a mountain to pray, and continued all night in prayer to God." St. Matthew makes this choosing of the twelve to follow upon the Lord beholding the multitudes, compassionating their condition as that of sheep without a shepherd, and calling upon His disciples, as distinguished from the Apostles, to pray the Lord of the harvest that He would send forth labourers

calleth *unto him* whom he would: and they came unto him.

into his harvest. The harmonists consider that this was said just before the Lord sent forth the Apostles to preach, but it seems very appropriately placed as preceding the designation of the twelve.

Respecting the doctrinal significance of the call of the apostles I have enlarged in my notes on St. Matthew x. 1, &c. Its importance, however, particularly at this time, is so great that I will reproduce in other words the substance of my former remarks.

There are two theories respecting the nature and origin of the Church of Christ. The first, that of the Catholic Church, that it was founded on the day of Pentecost through and by the Apostles, on whom the Lord had breathed the Holy Ghost for this purpose, so that from its very birth it was an organized body, and the means of its organization and consequent unity was the Apostolic company, the twelve. According to this view God has made the ministry essential to the Church, for in the Apostles the ministry was founded before the Church, and was the ordained means by which the Church was founded, so that the Church as it came from the hands of Christ cannot be conceived of apart from the ministry. This is perfectly compatible with the fact that the ministry is, in purpose, subordinate to the Church, that is, that it exists not for itself, but for the Church, *i.e.*, the whole mass of believers, for the "joints and bands" to which St. Paul compares the ministry (Coloss. ii. 19) are not the Church, but exist for it, that the whole body may receive in an orderly way grace from the Head, even Christ. According then to this view, the ministry in the Apostles derived its origin and commission, not from the Church, or from the people, but from Christ. It was in the power of Christ to have called all His people together, and bid them choose their future rulers from amongst themselves; but He did not so—they were chosen by Christ alone, Who Himself designated them, and afterwards breathed upon them when He ordained them with full Apostolic power. And when it pleased Christ to raise up another Apostle it was by the Holy Ghost, saying, "Separate me Barnabas and Saul for the work whereunto I have called them," and this Apostle expressly disclaims any commission from the people, for he calls himself "an Apostle, not of men, neither by man, but by Jesus Christ and God the Father, Who raised Him from the dead." (Gal. i. 1.)

14 And he ordained twelve, that they should be with him,

---

14. "He ordained." Literally, "He made twelve," or, "He constituted twelve." After "He ordained twelve" א, B., C., five or six Cursives, and some versions add, "Whom also He named Apostles."

The second theory is, that the Church is in the Divine mind an unorganized body to which God has given the Spirit, and that its ministry, *i.e.*, its organization, is an after-thought, as it were, not in the least degree of its essence, so that the model Church is like the Society of Friends or certain sects of the so-called "brethren" who are without an ordained or stated ministry: but, strange to say, this Church only exists in idea. It has had no existence in reality, for when the Church came into existence on the day of Pentecost it had a ministry already provided for it which instructed it, which held it together, and which claimed and received its obedience.

I do not know one single New Testament fact which can be appealed to in favour of this last theory, whilst every fact which bears upon the ministry upholds the former, *i.e.*, the Apostolic or Catholic view of the matter.

The first great fact is that this solemn choosing of the twelve Apostles took place after a night spent in prayer. It is recorded by each of the Synoptics, and is followed by a list of their names in each of the three, and there is another list at the outset of the history of the Church in the Acts of the Apostles (Acts i. 13), so that extraordinary emphasis is laid upon their names, and the number of these names as forming a definite company or college.

14. "And he ordained twelve, [whom also he named apostles] that they should be with him." No number had so many holy associations connected with it as this number of twelve: there were the twelve Patriarchs, the twelve wells in Elim, the twelve stones on the breastplate of the High Priest, the twelve loaves of the shewbread. It seems to have been because of the sacredness of this number that the Lord chose it to be the number of the Apostles, for we do not read that each Apostle had a particular tribe of Israel assigned to him.

"He ordained twelve." This was not their solemn ordination. It was rather designating them that they should be educated as it were, and trained, before they received their real ordination when He breathed on them, and said unto them, "Receive ye the Holy Ghost" (John xx. 21, 22).

## SIMON HE SURNAMED PETER. [St. Mark.

and that he might send them forth to preach,

15 And to have power to heal sicknesses, and to cast out devils:

*John i. 42.*    16 And Simon ¹ he surnamed Peter;

---

15. "Power to heal sicknesses, and." These words omitted by א, B., C., L., Coptic but retained by A., D., later Uncials, almost all Cursives, Old Latin, Vulg., &c.
16. The MSS. of the Neutral Text, א, B., C.*, repeat before this verse the words, "He ordained the twelve;" but A., D., L., most later Uncials, all Cursives, and most versions omit the words.

"That they should be with him." This was to be their real preparation for their high position in the Church, that they had been with Jesus so as to watch all His Holy Life, to see all His miracles, to hear all His words, to be carefully tended by Him, and reproved and exhorted, and so kept in the Name which He had given them (John xvii. 12). When one fell away another was chosen who, as near as may be, had enjoyed their privileges, for he was of the number of those men who had "companied with the Apostles all the time that the Lord Jesus went in and out among them" (Acts i. 21).

14, 15. "And that he might send them forth to preach, and to have power to heal sicknesses, and to cast out devils." He sent them to do the things which He did, or at least the most prominent. After this on His departure He enlarged their commission so that they should represent Him even in the remitting and retaining of sins.

16. "And Simon he surnamed Peter." The Neutral Text repeats before this mention of Simon the words, "and he appointed the twelve." If this be the true reading it still further emphasizes the call and designation of this definite number to be the fountain of the Christian ministry.

The name of Simon Peter is always mentioned as the first (Matthew x. 2). It was no doubt the intention of the Lord to assign to him a personal primacy, so that the Apostles should not choose their own leader, but one amongst them was designated to be their leader and spokesman by the Lord, Who saw in him, notwithstanding his faults, the courage and prompt decision which fitted him to take the first place. It was, no doubt, through this that the Church was kept together one and undivided in its infancy till it was established in faith and discipline. It is useless denying this primacy.

17 And James the *son* of Zebedee, and John the brother of James; and he surnamed them Boanerges, which is, The sons of thunder:

18 And Andrew, and Philip, and Bartholomew, and Mat-

---

It appears to me that they who do so for polemical purposes, pu' themselves in the wrong, and play into the hands of those who, also for polemical purposes, exaggerate Peter's position, and virtually ignore the Apostolic office, except as it existed personally in him.

17. "And James the son of Zebedee . . . . sons of thunder." Very much has been written upon this name. It is, however, interpreted for us by the Evangelist, and is no doubt the word Benaireges, pronounced broadly in the provincial accent of Galilee. In what sense it was applicable to the character or teaching of these two brethren is not certain, particularly in the case of St. John, the Apostle of Gentleness and Love. Perhaps, however, if we had heard him preach we should have discerned in a moment the fitness of the name. If he preached as he wrote in his Epistle there would be much to vindicate the title, for he wrote such terrible words as " Who is a liar but he that denieth that Jesus is the Christ ? " "He that committeth sin is of the devil." "Whosoever sinneth hath not seen him." "Whosoever hateth his brother is a murderer, and ye know that no murderer hath eternal life abiding in him." And respecting a certain troubler of the Church he writes, "If I come I will remember his deeds which he doeth." Much stronger and more scathing words than the platitudes usually uttered by those who in this day profess to follow him. And we must remember, too, that this Epistle was written in his old age, when years had toned down his decisiveness and vehemence. Respecting the preaching of the other brother we know nothing except this, that when Herod would gratify the Jewish hatred of the Gospel, he singled out James as his first victim, which he would hardly have done unless this Apostle also had been the foremost in aggressive energy of speech.

18. "And Andrew and Philip . . . went into an house." The length to which this note on the call of the Apostles has extended prevents me from speaking of what is known in Scripture and ecclesiastical history of the remainder of the Apostles. I must reserve this till (D.V.) I come to the parallel place in St. Luke. Suffice it to

**54**   HIS FRIENDS HEARD OF IT.   [St. Mark.

thew, and Thomas, and James the *son* of Alphæus, and Thaddæus, and Simon the Canaanite,

19 And Judas Iscariot, which also betrayed him : and they went ‖ into an house.

20 And the multitude cometh together again, so that they could not so much as eat bread.

21 And when his ‖ friends heard *of it*, they

‖ Or, *home.*

k ch. vi. 31.

‖ Or, *kinsmen.*

---

18. "The Canaanite." Spelt in Greek "Kananite;" derived not from "Canaan," but from "Kana," he was jealous. So "Zelotes" or "Zelot." But א, B., C., D., L., Vulg., and some versions read, "Cananean."

"And they went." Perhaps, "he comes;" but A., C., L., later Uncials, Cursives, Vulg., and Syriac as in Authorized.

say at present that the four lists (in the three Synoptics and Acts i.) resolve themselves into two—that in Matthew and that in Luke— the only discrepancy being in the name Lebbæus, or Thaddeus, in the first two lists, which answers to Judas the brother of James in the last two.

19. "And they went into an house." This is translated by many, they [or He came] came home, or into the house, where He usually lived, and from which He departed when He went out to spend the night in prayer. It is the beginning of a new paragraph describing the crowding of the multitude about Him, the unbelief of His friends, and the renewed and still more bitter opposition of the Scribes.

20. "And the multitude came together again . . . eat bread." Let the reader again notice how this Evangelist neglects no opportunity of showing how popular the Lord was with the multitude. It is also distinctly implied that the Lord neglected the supply of His own needs and of those attached to Him in order that He might minister to the people. " He teaches His ministers by His own example, to look upon themselves as the servants of those souls who are committed to their charge, to wait for and embrace every occasion that offers to promote their spiritual benefit, never to think any time inconvenient to themselves, when called to their service, and to forego even the necessary refreshments of life when the harvest is great, and an opportunity which may irrevocably be lost presents itself" (Quesnel).

21. "And when his friends heard of it, they went out to lay hold on him . . . beside himself." His friends, literally, they that were with Him, probably his kinsmen, including, it may be, His nearest

CHAP. III.]     HE IS BESIDE HIMSELF.     55

went out to lay hold on him: ¹for they said, He is beside
himself.

22 ¶ And the scribes which came down from
Jerusalem said, ᵐ He hath Beelzebub, and by the
prince of the devils casteth he out devils.

23 ⁿ And he called them *unto him*, and said

¹ John vii. 5.
& x. 20.

ᵐ Matt. ix. 34.
& x. 25. Luke
xi. 15. John
vii. 20. & viii.
48, 52. & x. 20.

ⁿ Matt. xii. 25.

---

relatives, who were alarmed for Him, when they heard how He was
neglecting His own bodily wants, and how He was stirring up still
more bitter enmity against Himself.

"They went out," literally, "they came out," perhaps out of the
home at Nazareth.

"He is beside himself," literally, "He stands out of himself."
This need not mean that he was insane, but that He was carried
away by His devotion and enthusiasm beyond all self-control. Thus
Lange: "It is designedly ambiguous, inasmuch as the word
[ἐξέστη] may mean, in a good sense, the being for a season wrapped
into ecstasy by religious enthusiasm (2 Cor. v. 13), as well as in a
bad sense, the being permanently insane. In His ecstasy, He is
no longer master of Himself."

22. "And the scribes which came down from Jerusalem said
. . . casteth he out devils." St. Mark here omits to mention the
particular miracle which gave occasion to this remark, which is
thus described in St. Matthew: "There was brought unto him one
possessed with a devil, blind, and dumb, and he healed him,
insomuch that the blind and dumb both spake and saw. And all
the people were amazed and said, Is not this the Son of David?"

Notice the fearful length to which the malignity of the Pharisees
proceeds. He is not only possessed of a devil, but by Satan himself. It is as if they said, "He is an incarnation of the Evil One,
and by Satan's own power He expels his subordinate spirits."

"The scribes which came down from Jerusalem." It would
seem from this that those in power in Jerusalem—the Sanhedrim—
were becoming thoroughly alarmed at the increasing popularity of
the Lord, and so they sent down scribes, chosen, no doubt, for
their ability as disputants and their unscrupulousness, to oppose
Him. From St. Matthew we learn that the Scribes were also
Pharisees.

23. "And he called them unto him, and said unto them in

unto them in parables, How can Satan cast out Satan?

24 And if a kingdom be divided against itself, that kingdom cannot stand.

25 And if a house be divided against itself, that house cannot stand.

---

parables, How can Satan cast out Satan?" Olshausen's remarks upon the mercy of the Saviour in thus endeavouring to bring to a better mind those who so malignantly opposed Him are very good: " This endeavour of the merciful Redeemer, Who knew what was in their hearts, is full of consolation. We are entitled to infer from it that He perceived in their hearts the germ also of something better, to the vivification of which He might direct His attention, in the course of His instruction. Had these unfortunate men, who called light darkness, and converted that which was holy into an unholy thing, not been blinded by passion, they would then have committed the sin against the Holy Ghost, and thus have been deprived of all hope of forgiveness. But in that case it would have been inconceivable that our Saviour should have addressed to those people who could not be redeemed words having a tendency to deliver them from their error.

24, 25. " And if a kingdom . . . that house cannot stand," &c. As if the Lord said, " What you allege against me is an impossible thing. I preach the law of God in all its spiritual fulness and significance. I uphold the honour of God and advance His kingdom over men's souls and spirits. All My teaching is on the side of goodness and righteousness. But to enforce this My teaching as coming from God I perform acts which it is within the power of God only to perform. In particular I cast out of their victims the spirits which belong to Satan's kingdom. Now, if I did this by Satan's power, or if he assisted me in doing this, he would work against himself; he would war against his own kingdom, and he would destroy it just as a kingdom weakened by civil war is ready to fall a prey to its enemies, and a house which has within it those who would open the door to its spoilers must be plundered and ruined."

As I remarked on the parallel place in St. Matthew, the Lord does not here allude to minor divisions on matters of policy in a senate or in a household, but divisions which touch the very existence of the kingdom

26 And if Satan rise up against himself, and be divided, he cannot stand, but hath an end.

27 °No man can enter into a strong man's house, and spoil his goods, except he will first ° Is. xlix. 24. Matt. xii. 29.

---

26. Revisers translate this, "And if Satan hath risen up against himself, and is divided, he cannot stand, but hath an end."

27. "But no one can enter into the house of the strong man, and spoil his goods, except he first bind the strong man, and then he will spoil his house."

26. "If Satan rise up against himself, and be divided, he cannot stand, but hath an end." This is as if the Lord said: "The power of Satan consists in this, that he is thoroughly and entirely evil. If he assisted Me in performing miracles which substantiate and enforce the truth of My doctrine, he could only do this because there is some good remaining in him, and this presence of good in him would immeasurably weaken his power for evil and eventually destroy it, for he would be then like weak, wavering mortals, whose nature, being a mixture of good and evil, is unable of itself to sustain a kingdom of evil, just as it is unable to sustain a kingdom of good."

27. "No man can enter into a strong man's house, and spoil ... he will spoil his house." In my comment on St. Matthew I explained the strong man's house as human nature in general, and the Lord as entering into it by His Holy Incarnation. But what is true of human nature is true of every unit which composes it. Satan is the strong man who, by nature, has hold of every human being. He is strong, so that nothing whatsoever can drive him out except that Second Man, Who is stronger than he. No power of education, for instance, apart from Christ, no change of circumstances, no example of goodness, none of these things will *of themselves*, dispossess Satan, though the Lord may use them in effecting His entrance into each soul whom He delivers.

But how is it that the Lord speaks here of *having* bound the strong man as if it was a thing past and completed, whereas we suppose that it was by His Death and Resurrection that He destroyed him that had the power of death. Probably He speaks by anticipation. God having brought about the Incarnation of His Son and sent Him into the world, all must follow in due course. What is fixed in God's will is as certain to be brought about as if it had already been brought about. Or the Lord may allude to some casting out

bind the strong man; and then he will spoil his house.

28 <sup>p</sup> Verily I say unto you, All sins shall be forgiven unto the sons of men, and blasphemies wherewith soever they shall blaspheme:

<small>p Matt. xii. 31.
Luke xii. 10.
1 John v. 16.</small>

---

28. The Revisers give the force of the definite article by translating, "All their sins shall be forgiven to the sons of men, and their blasphemies," &c.

---

of Satan which took place in the unseen world in accordance with His mysterious words: "I beheld Satan as lightning fall from heaven."

"Then he will spoil his house." He has spoiled his house and his goods. His goods are those men who are "delivered out of the power of darkness, and translated into the kingdom of God's dear Son" (Coloss. i. 13).

28, 29, 30. "I say unto you, All sins shall be forgiven . . . He hath an unclean spirit." We learn clearly from this place in what this fearful sin consists the only one of all the evils which the sons of men commit which will not be forgiven. Those with whom the Lord was now remonstrating were in danger of committing it, "*because* they said, He hath an unclean spirit." This was, in point of fact, almost equivalent to their calling the Lord an Incarnation of Satan. In order to see something of the wickedness of this sin we must realize that all our Lord's teaching was on the side of God and goodness, and all His miracles, especially that of the expulsion of evil spirits, were done to enforce such teaching, and to set forth the character of God—the God Who sent Him, as at once a holy and benevolent God, desirous to free men from the yoke of all moral and spiritual as well as of all physical evil. To call the Spirit of such an One as our Lord an evil spirit was the extremest form of that wickedness denounced by the prophet when he said: "Woe unto them that call evil good and good evil; that put darkness for light, and light for darkness" (Is. v. 20). For a man to have a mind which could deliberately ascribe such a spirit to the Saviour is, as far as man can, to cut himself off from redemption— to make the acceptance of redemption impossible to him. This will be more clearly seen if we remember certain words said on this occasion by the Lord, which are only given in St. Matthew, "Whosoever speaketh a word against the Son of Man it shall be forgiven him, but whosoever speaketh against the Holy Ghost it

## NO FORGIVENESS.

29 But he that shall blaspheme against the Holy Ghost hath never forgiveness, but is in danger of eternal damnation:

---

29. "Is." ℵ, D., L., Old Latin [a, c, e, f], Vulg. read shall be.
"In danger of eternal damnation." ℵ, B., L., D., two or three Cursives, Vulg., and some versions read, "Of an eternal sin;" A., C^r, later Uncials, and almost all Cursives read as in Rec. Text.

shall not be forgiven him." A man might, through prejudice, speak against the claims of Jesus to be the Messiah. He might not be the Messiah whom he expected. He might be led away by false hopes of an earthly temporal Messiah, to reject the true one. Such an one might continue in infidelity, but the door of repentance and faith would be open to him, because, as Saul of Tarsus, what he did in rejecting Christ he did ignorantly and in unbelief. But if such an one had an opportunity of observing the Spirit of Christ—the Spirit of goodness and love displayed in all His character and discourses, and enforced by His mighty deeds, all on the side of benevolence and holiness, and yet deliberately called such a Spirit the Spirit of Evil, then there was nothing left in him for Redemption to take hold of. He was reprobate in the deepest sense of the word. He had first given himself over, and then he was given over by God, to a reprobate mind—that is, to his own evil, absolutely evil, self. But if a person thus ascribed the works of Christ to the power of evil, would that not be blaspheming against the Son of Man—not against the Holy Spirit? No, we are told that both the teaching and the mighty works of Christ were done by the Spirit (Acts i. 2; Matt. xii. 28). Christ taught very emphatically that He did nothing of Himself. He must, consequently, act by some spiritual power not His Own. Was that power Divine or diabolical? Of God, or of God's enemy? If a man deliberately said it was from God's enemy he displayed an intensity of perverse and malicious wickedness almost incredible.

Some of the most acute observations on this difficult subject are to be found in Calvin's "Commentary on the Synoptics." "Shall any unbeliever curse God? It is as if a blind man were dashing against a wall. But no man curses the Spirit, who is not enlightened by Him, and conscious of ungodly rebellion against Him; for it is not a superfluous distinction, that all other blasphemies shall be forgiven, except that one blasphemy which is directed against the Spirit. If a man shall simply blaspheme against God, he is not

30 Because they said, He hath an unclean spirit.

31 ¶ ᵃ There came then his brethren and his mother, and, standing without, sent unto him, calling him.

ᵃ Matt. xii. 46.
Luke viii. 19.

---

declared to be beyond the hope of pardon, but of those who have offered outrage to the Spirit it is said that God will never forgive them. Why is this but because those only are *blasphemers* against the Spirit, who slander His gifts and power contrary to the conviction of their own mind?"

Two observations on all this may not be out of place.

1. It is clear that no one can have committed the sin against the Holy Ghost who desires the influence of the Holy Ghost to deliver him from sin, and to make him love God, for such an one must believe that the power exhibited in Christ was on the side of God and goodness. He must believe that Christ was actuated and impelled by a holy and good spirit, which must be from God.

2. Looked at in the light of this one exception to the forgiving power of God, how exceedingly broad and large is the promise implied in the 28th verse, "Verily, I say unto you, ALL sins shall be forgiven unto the sons of men." The one exception proves the universality of the rule. If any sinner has a mind to lay hold on the Divine mercy, no memory of past sin need deter him; and the state of mind which he has towards sin, and his desire of deliverance, forbids the idea that he has committed the one unpardonable sin. Quesnel concludes some good observations with this prayer: "Lord, it is Thou alone Who art my salvation; it is from Thy Spirit alone that I hope for the administration of those blessings and privileges which Thou hast purchased for me with Thy precious Blood. Absolve, justify, sanctify, and save me for Thy mercy's sake."

31. "There came then his brethren and his mother, and, standing without, sent," &c. From "the brethren" being here mentioned first, there can be little doubt but that they were the foremost in this well-meant, but mistaken, interference. They probably had regard either to the way in which He was wearing Himself out without due rest and sustenance (verses 20, 21), or they feared the ever-increasing malignity of His enemies the scribes. They brought His mother with them, that by her influence He might be induced to look more to Himself.

32 And the multitude sat about him, and they said unto him, Behold, thy mother and thy brethren without seek for thee.

33 And he answered them, saying, Who is my mother, or my brethren?

34 And he looked round about on them which sat about him, and said, Behold my mother and my brethren!

---

32. "And thy brethren." A., D., E., F., H., M., other later Uncials, above one hundred Cursives, Old Latin [a, b, e, f] add, "And thy sisters," but this is omitted by ℵ, B., C., G., K., L., Vulg., Coptic, Syriac.

32. "And the multitude sat about him, and they said unto him," &c. It is interesting to note the difference between the report of each of the Synoptics: St. Matthew, "one said unto him;" St. Luke, "it was told him;" St. Mark, "the multitude . . . said unto him." There is no discrepancy. It would be buzzed about in the crowded assembly that His mother desired to speak to Him, and one of them who sat near would be the spokesman.

33, 34. "And he answered them, saying, Who is my mother or my brethren? . . . The same is my brother, and sister, and mother." Notice how St. Matthew records that the Lord "stretched forth his hands;" but St. Mark describes the incident as it appeared to a close observer, one who watched His very looks: "He looked round about on them that sat about him" (see Mark iii. 5; x. 21, 23). Of course, St. Peter was the observer.

35. "For whosoever shall do the will of God, the same is my brother," &c. This is one of the household words of the kingdom of God. It teaches, with an emphasis which it seems impossible to exceed, that there are but two divisions of mankind—those who do the will of God, and those who disobey that will, and that not even the closest blood relationships, much less the possession of national, or Church, or religious privileges, can in the slightest degree affect the distinctness and permanence of the line between these divisions. Of all relationships, spiritual ones are the closest; and there is but one permanent relationship to God, and that is, conformity to His will.

In my note on St. Matthew, I drew attention to Chrysostom, as taking much too harsh a view of the conduct of the Virgin. The most lenient and charitable view seems that taken by one in whose

35 For whosoever shall do the will of God, the same is my brother, and my sister, and mother.

---

writings we should have least expected it—*i.e.*, John Calvin: "'His mother and brethren came to him.' The reason must have been either that they were anxious about Him, or that they were desirous of instruction; for it is not without some good reason that they endeavour to approach Him, and it is not probable that those who accompanied the Holy Mother were unbelievers. Ambrose and Chrysostom accuse Mary of ambition, but without any probability. What necessity is there for such a conjecture, when the testimony of the Spirit everywhere bestows commendation on her distinguished piety and modesty? The warmth of natural affection may have carried them beyond the bounds of propriety. This I do not deny; but I have no doubt that they were led by pious zeal to seek His society" (Calvin, in "Harmony").

And Augustine sums up the teaching thus: "Men are not blessed for this reason, that they are united by nearness of flesh unto just and holy men; but that, by obeying and following, they cleave unto their doctrine and conduct. Therefore, Mary is more blessed in receiving the faith of Christ (Luke i.) than in conceiving the flesh of Christ" (Augustine, "Tract. de Virginitate," quoted in Ford).

## CHAP. IV.

AND *he began again to teach by the sea side: and there was gathered unto him a great multitude, so that he entered into a ship, and sat in the sea; and the whole multitude was by the sea on the land.

* Matt. xiii. 1.
Luke viii. 4.

---

1. "And he began to teach by the sea side. . . . by the sea on the land." The place where He then taught was at the north end of the lake, "and probably near Bethsaida, where the beach rises rapidly, and there is deep water within a few yards of the shore, while at the same time a multitude of hearers could place them-

2 And he taught them many things by parables, ᵇ and said unto them in his doctrine, ᵇ ch. xii. 38.

3 Hearken; Behold, there went out a sower to sow:

4 And it came to pass, as he sowed, some fell by the way side, and the fowls of the air came and devoured it up.

5 And some fell on stony ground, where it had not much earth; and immediately it sprang up, because it had no depth of earth:

6 But when the sun was up, it was scorched; and because it had no root, it withered away.

---

4. "Fowls of the air." "Of the air" omitted by א, A., B., C., L., later Uncials, very many Cursives, Syriac, Vulg. [Cod. Amiat.], versions, &c.
5. "Stony." Properly, "rocky."

selves so as to see the Saviour in the boat" (McGregor's "Rob Roy on the Jordan").

2, 3. "And he began to teach them many things . . . a sower to sow." "The sower." The reader scarcely needs to be reminded how the Lord of all things, in striving to impress holy truths upon men, especially draws his illustrations from the works of husbandry: the sower and his seed; the reaper and his barns and fan; the shepherd and his sheep and goats; the gardener and owners of vineyards, and their figs, their vines, and winepresses. Men daily see these things; and the Lord would have those who see them daily reminded of the spiritual truths which He has so graphically drawn from them.

4. "And it came to pass, as he sowed, . . . devoured it up." Not, of course, the high road, but the narrow paths through the fields, trodden down hard by the feet of those continually passing; or, if it formed the division between two lots, not ploughed over.

5. "And some fell on stony ground." Not as ground in many of our fields, covered with stones on the surface, but a thin layer of earth spread over the hard rock, which here and there appears above it. The very shallowness of the ground would prevent its sinking to any depth, so that at first it would spring up, as if sown in a hotbed, but would the sooner wither, as the noontide heat would dry up all moisture.

The roots had no deep ground below them, where the scorching heat could not penetrate, into which they might strike down.

7 And some fell among thorns, and the thorns grew up, and choked it, and it yielded no fruit.

c John xv. 5.
Col. i. 6.

8 And other fell on good ground, <sup>c</sup> and did yield fruit that sprang up and increased; and brought forth, some thirty, and some sixty, and some an hundred.

---

4-8. The Revisers give the article before the words "sower," "stony ground," "thorns," "good ground;" but for reasons which I have given in my notes on the parable in St. Matthew, I do not think that our English idiom allows it.

7. "And some fell among thorns . . . yielded no fruit." Instead of being stubbed up by the roots, the thorns could be only burnt off the surface, and so would spring up together with the wheat, and, being the stronger plant, would deprive the wheat of all nourishment and air.

8. "And other fell on good ground . . . some an hundred." In Dean Stanley's " Sinai and Palestine," there is a remarkable passage which, though often quoted, we cannot omit: "Is there anything on the spot to suggest the images thus conveyed? So (if I speak for a moment of myself) I asked, as I rode along the track, under the hill-side, by which the plain of Gennesareth is approached. So I asked [myself], at the moment, seeing nothing but the steep sides of the hill, alternately of rock and grass. And when I thought of the parable of the sower, I answered, that here at least was nothing on which the Divine teaching could fasten: it must have been the distant cornfields of Samaria or Esdraelon on which His mind was dwelling. The thought had hardly occurred to me, when a slight recess in the hill-side, close upon the plain, disclosed at once, in detail, and with a conjunction which I remember nowhere else in Palestine, every feature of the great parable. There was the undulating cornfield, descending to the water's edge. There was the trodden pathway running through the midst of it, with no fence or hedge to prevent the seed from falling here and there on either side of it, or upon it; itself hard with the constant tramp of horse and mule, and human feet. There was the good rich soil, which distinguishes the whole of that plain, and its neighbourhood, from the bare hills elsewhere, descending into the lake, and which, where there is no interruption, produces one vast mass of corn. There was the rocky ground of the hill-side protruding here and there

CHAP. IV.]   WHEN HE WAS ALONE.   65

9 And he said unto them, He that hath ears to hear, let him hear.

10 ᵈ And when he was alone, they that were about him with the twelve asked of him the parable.

<small>ᵈ Matt. xiii. 10. Luke viii. 9, &c.</small>

---

through the cornfields, as elsewhere through the grassy slopes. There were the large bushes of thorn—the Nabk, that kind of which tradition says the Crown of Thorns was woven—springing up like the fruit trees of the more inland parts, in the very midst of the waving corn " (chap. xiii. p. 426).

9. "And he said unto them, He that hath ears to hear, let him hear." As often as this is inserted in the Gospel, or in the Apocalypse of St. John, that which is spoken is mystical, and is pointed out as healthful to be heard and learnt. For the ears by which they are heard belong to the heart; and the ears by which men obey, and do what is commanded, are those of an interior sense (Bede). And Quesnel well remarks: "Let all the world confess that it is God Who gives these ears of the heart, without which none can accomplish His Will, to the end that those who have received them may bless God for this free gift; and that those who have not may humble themselves, and have recourse to Him, in order to obtain them."

10. "And when he was alone, they that were about him with the twelve," &c. They that were about Him with the twelve. Who were these? The Lord having taught the multitudes out of the ship came ashore, no doubt, into some house, and then it was that, as St. Matthew says, the disciples came to Him. If He had continued out of doors, the people would have thronged about Him so that it could not be said that "He was alone." The persons, then, who were about Him may have been those in the house, for if the whole twelve were there, there could hardly have been other disciples—such as some of the Seventy. Still it is possible. How little of retirement or privacy was there in which the Lord could be at rest! For He had always twelve about Him, and often, it seems, more, and was ever answering their questions, resolving their doubts, dispelling their delusions, strengthening their wavering faith.

11, 12. "And he said unto them, Unto you it is given to know. . . . parables." Unto you is given the mystery of the kingdom of

F

11 And he said unto them, Unto you it is given to know the mystery of the kingdom of God: but unto ᵉ them that are without, all *these* things are done in parables:

ᵉ 1 Cor. v. 12.
Col. iv. 5.
1 Thess. iv. 12.
1 Tim. iii. 7.

11. "Unto you it is given to know the mystery of the kingdom of God." ℵ, A., B., C., K., L. read, "Unto you is given the mystery of the kingdom," &c.; Vulg. and Syriac, later Uncials, most Cursives, and Old Latin as in Rec. Text.

God. Why? Because, to use the figure of the next clause, they—the disciples—had come "within." They had accepted the call of God to come within, and abide within, the sphere, the teaching, the influence of the Lord; they were in His training, in His school, in His family, in His love. But those that were without, were without because they had refused to come within. They had heard His sayings, and had made no attempt to do them. Though He had invited them (Matt. xi. 28) they had not willed to come to Him that they might have life (John v. 40). And now He changed His mode of teaching. Before, in such sermons as that on the mount, and on the plain (Luke vi. 17, &c.) He had spoken plainly; now He began to speak enigmatically, mysteriously, in parables; the meaning of which did not force itself upon men's minds, but needed that men should have the seeing eye, and the hearing ear, and the understanding heart, so that they who cared to know would ponder and inquire, and come to Him to be taught, and they who cared not to know would say among themselves, "Why should we listen to such stories? What are they to us? We have no time for such inquiries. Let Him speak as before, and we will pay attention."

Such would be the disposition of mind of those "within" and those "without" respectively.

And now the Lord proceeds to give the reason for this change in His mode of teaching. As the words stand in St. Mark they are exceedingly difficult, for they seem to make the merciful Saviour utter parables, lest at any time those who heard him should be converted and forgiven. The words are:—

12. "That seeing they may see, and not perceive; and hearing they may hear, and not understand; lest at any time they should be converted, and their sins should be forgiven them." Now if the reader turn to the parallel place in Matthew xiii. 13, 14, 15, he will see that the Lord in the first place declares that He speaks to them

## SEE, AND NOT PERCEIVE.

12 'That seeing they may see, and not perceive; and hearing they may hear, and not understand; lest at any time they should be converted, and *their* sins should be forgiven them.

f Is. vi. 9.
Matt. xiii. 14.
Luke viii. 10.
John xii. 40.
Acts xxviii. 26.
Rom. xi. 8.

---

in parables, not to produce a certain state of heart in them, but because they had already, through their own fault, produced that reprobate state of heart in themselves which prevented them receiving the Word in love and obedience. "Therefore speak I unto them in parables, because they seeing see not," &c. And he proceeds to quote the prophecy of Isaiah, not according to the harsher reading of the Hebrew, but according to the milder reading of the Septuagint, which renders the prophet's Hebrew words, "Make the heart of this people gross, and make their ears heavy," &c., by the indicative, "This people's heart is waxed gross . . . and their eyes they have closed . . . lest at any time they should see with their eyes . . . and should be converted." In the quotation and application of the words of the prophet in St. Matthew, the Lord states that in them (*i.e.* those without) is fulfilled the words of the prophet, that "this people's heart is waxed gross and their eyes they have closed" through their hatred of good and love of evil before He began to speak to them in parables, and so His speaking to them in this dark enigmatical way was in mercy, as well as in judgment—it was that those amongst them who rejected His message, should not incur the greater guilt of rejecting plain words, the meaning of which forced itself, as it were, upon them, whilst those who accepted, or were inclined to accept His message, would be struck by the words and see in them mysteries of grace which they then would but faintly apprehend, but which would attract them to Him. The Lord's words as given in St. Matthew, being so much fuller, are evidently the words which He actually used; and this is in accordance with the characteristic difference between these Evangelists: St. Matthew giving more perfectly the Lord's words, whether in discourse or parable; St. Mark dwelling more circumstantially and graphically on His miracles and the incidents of His life.

To those then without faith in Him the Lord's parables veiled the mysteries of the kingdom, but to those who had faith and desired instruction, they unveiled and shed light on the same mysteries. "God gives sight and understanding to men who seek for

**13** And he said unto them, Know ye not this parable? and how then will ye know all parables?

g Matt. xiii. 19.

**14** ¶ g The sower soweth the word.

---

them, but the rest He blinds, lest it become a greater accusation against them, that though they understood they did not choose to do what they ought." (Theophylact.)

13. "And he said unto them, Know ye not this parable? ... all parables?" The Lord seems to imply that this parable was the easiest of all. And, indeed, to us it seems to bear its signification on the face of it. But we are living after Pentecost, and the Apostles were then living before the outpouring of the Spirit.

14. "The sower soweth the word." The sower was first of all the Lord Himself, and it may be a comfort to faithful preachers, who see so many utterly hard and unreceptive, so many falling away, so many bearing little or no fruit, that as it is with them so it was with the Lord and with His Apostles. To the hearers of Christ and the hearers of St. Paul the preacher was to some a savour of life unto life, to others of death unto death.

But Who is the sower now, and what is his sowing, and what is the seed he sows? The sower is the preacher, the sowing is preaching, the seed sown is the word preached. First of all the "word" is the word respecting repentance, for the Lord and His Apostles, first of all, in all cases preached repentance, or things that would lead to or bring about repentance, such as righteousness, temperance, and judgment to come. Then the word is the declaration of the truths of the Gospel, which would lead to living faith in the Saviour, that He is the Son of God, that by His Incarnation He became for us the Son of Man; that He lived a life which reveals to us the goodness and holiness of God Himself brought down to the level of our understandings and of our endeavours; that He died an atoning and reconciling Death; that through the Blood shed in His Death our sins can be blotted out; that He arose again to assure us of the truth of all His promises, and to impart to us of His new, His Resurrection Life; that He ascended to the right hand of God to intercede for us, and to order all things for the well-being of His Church; that He will come again to judge; that He has sent His Spirit Who now dwells in His Church, and by His entrance into each soul makes it a par-

## THEY BY THE WAY SIDE.

15 And these are they by the way side, where the word is sown; but when they have heard, Satan cometh immediately, and taketh away the word that was sown in their hearts.

---

15. "In their hearts." א, C., L. read, "In them;" B. and some Cursives read, "into them;" D., later Uncials, almost all Cursives, Old Latin, Syriac, and some versions as in Rec. Text; Vulg. [Cod. Amiat.], *In corda eorum*. A. alone reads, "From their hearts." The differences of reading are more important in this case than in many, as they raise the question, Could the word be said to have reached their hearts?

taker of the benefits of Christ's Incarnation, Death, and Resurrection; that in order that all may receive these inestimable blessings He gives them to our faith easily and as a free gift; that He has ordained such things as Sacraments, in one of which He grafts us into Himself, and makes us members of His Body, and branches of Himself the True Vine, and, in the other, He gives His Body and Blood to be our spiritual food and sustenance; that He has ordained a perpetual ministry to represent Himself, and that through the action of this ministry He instructs His people in His doctrines, makes them partakers of His Sacraments, and absolves them from sin. All these are parts of that word which the Apostles preached. They one and all set forth some aspect of God's grace and goodness. They are to be preached in their turn as men are able to hear and bear them; but they are all to be preached if the sower is to deliver his conscience in the matter of his sowing.

15. "And these are they by the way side, where the word is sown . . . taketh away the word that is sown in their hearts" [or in them]. Those by the way side may be divided into two classes, (1) the utterly indifferent, who shut their ears, and pay no attention whatsoever to the words of the preacher: and (2) those who hear and who, because they know what the word is about, that it demands of them that they turn from sin and turn to God, at once dismiss it from their minds. They dismiss it by forcibly turning their minds to other things: their business, their pleasures, their ambitions, their rivalries, their possessions, their fancies, are the things which make up their inner lives, and the thoughts of these are ever at hand, and at once rush in as birds swooping down on the grain on the hardened soil, and efface not only all impressions, but the very remembrance of the good things preached. Now the Lord teaches us that this indifference to the word by which it fails to convince and convert, is brought about, not through natural, but

16 And these are they likewise which are sown on stony ground; who, when they have heard the word, immediately receive it with gladness;

17 And have no root in themselves, and so endure but for a time: afterward, when affliction or persecution ariseth for the word's sake, immediately they are offended.

---

through supernatural agency. An enemy does this. In our present fallen state he is able to summon up thoughts which may distract the attention from the thoughts which the life giving Word suggests, and our evil wills fall in with the thoughts which he instils. These thoughts may not always be evil by any means, but they do his work, for they distract the attention, and being far more in accordance with the evil bent of the heart, the good thought is swallowed up, effaced, and forgotten. I think that there can be no minister who comes closely into contact with the souls of men but must be aware that there is not only an evil principle at work in the heart, but an evil personal agency which is able to suggest doubts and interpose difficulties, and assist the soul in barring out the word by placing all his cunning at the disposal of the evil will. Satan or his emissary, the evil spirit to whom he has committed the destruction of the man's soul, cometh immediately. See note on parallel passage in Matthew xiii.

16. "And these are they likewise which are sown on stony ground ["rocky places," Rev., 1881] ... with gladness." These differ from the first (those by the way side) in that they "receive" the word, which the first did not; and not only receive it, but do so "with gladness." As soon as ever they are converted, they seem to be able to rejoice in the Lord, and are in our day, on this account, pronounced "saved," whilst holier, humbler souls are held to be in darkness, because they have a deeper sense of sin, and a clearer view of the requirements of the Gospel. But it is only for a short time that this class of hearers make a profession even.

17. "And have no root in themselves ... immediately they are offended." Just as the rock underneath the thin soil prevents the roots from striking down, and becoming proportionate to the plant, so, in their souls, the hardness and unpreparedness of the will and all that forms the deep, abiding character, prevents the word from penetrating into the depths of the soul. If it does not do so, if it

## THOSE SOWN AMONG THORNS.

18 And these are they which are sown among thorns; such as hear the word,

18. "And these are they which are sown among thorns." So A., later Uncials, almost all Cursives, Syriac; but ℵ, B., C., D., L., Old Latin, Vulg., Coptic read, "And there are others which are sown among thorns; these are they which," &c.

does not penetrate deeply, there is no perseverance, no stability. "The hidden life must be nourished underground, or the outward will soon fail." And this agrees with the true theory of Divine grace: for it is from the secret depths of the soul that the Holy Spirit begins to act, not from the surface. He renews and sanctifies from within—from the very centre. Such hearers many of the Galatian Christians seem to have been of whom St. Paul writes: "Ye received me as an angel of God, even as Christ Jesus. Where is, then, the blessedness ye spake of? for I bear you record, that, if possible, ye would have plucked out your own eyes, and have given them to me" (iv. 14). The reader will also remember the example of Herod, who heard John gladly, and the Jews, who were willing, for a season, to rejoice in the Baptist's "burning and shining light."

But what makes these hearers to rejoice so soon? In my notes on St. Matthew, I said that it was that which was bright in Christianity—its promises of heaven, its security. I find that a similar explanation is given by Hammond (quoted in Ford): "These persons take Christ, but under a false person: either they take the promises only, and let Christ alone; or they take Christ the Saviour, but not Christ the Lord, are willing to be saved by Him, but never think of serving Him. They abstract the cheap and profitable attributes of Christ, His priestly office of satisfaction and propitiation; but never consider Him as a King."

18. "These are they [or there are others] which are sown among thorns . . . . cares of this world . . . . lusts of other things . . . , unfruitful." In this case, the seed springs and grows up; but, side by side with it, there springs up and grow noxious plants, stronger than itself; and these take away its nourishment, not perhaps at first, but when the ear begins to form, and shows signs of fruit, and before the ear can form any kernels worth speaking of. It may be profitable to consider how this takes place. In this way: the cultivation of Christian graces and habits of devotion and religious usefulness requires time, and thought, and watchfulness, and attention.

19 And the cares of this world, ʰ and the deceitfulness of riches, and the lusts of other things entering in, choke the word, and it becometh unfruitful.

ʰ 1 Tim. vi. 9, 17.

---

Now, if the Christian, neglecting the words of his Saviour respecting taking no anxious thought for the morrow, and not realizing the promise of God, that if he seeks the kingdom of God and His righteousness all needful things will be added, allows the anxieties of life always to be preying upon him, he cannot give the things of God and eternity the place in his soul which their importance requires. The fear that he shall lose what he has, or the desire of getting richer and richer, or some over-mastering longing to attain some higher worldly position, or to excel in such a pursuit or accomplishment: all these so fill the mind with other thoughts that there is no room for spiritual desires. The stated times of prayer, if kept to through habit, are yet curtailed and broken in upon by alien thoughts of all kinds, such thoughts are allowed unchecked to range through the mind, even in the house of God, perhaps even at the altar; and so, though there may be certain regular habits, and a respectable life, and abstention from gross vices, there is not those fruits of the Spirit which God looks for.

"The lusts of other things." St. Matthew only mentions "the cares of this world, and the deceitfulness of riches;" St. Luke mentions "pleasures of this life," as answering to "lusts of other things." Under this head, then, the Lord places the love of pleasure, of amusements, and sensual gratifications, and even the cultivation of refined tastes: all which have a tendency to engross the mind, and induce it quietly to take up with a world which yields it so much satisfaction.

"Entering in." This expression is only to be found in St. Mark's Gospel. And it is very suggestive: it teaches us that these cares of the world, and deceitfulness of riches, may not be present or sensibly felt when the word first springs up in the heart; but, when opportunity offers, they may make their appearance, and grow far faster and more vigorously than the true religious life, and ultimately destroy it.

"And it becometh unfruitful." The word " becometh " seems to imply that " fruit " had begun to be formed ; but these evil things " coming in," the growth of the grain is checked. Are we to

## SOWN ON GOOD GROUND.

20 And these are they which are sown on good ground; such as hear the word, and receive *it*, and bring forth fruit,

---

understand, then, that it is quite fruitless? The parallel expression in St. Luke—" bring no fruit to perfection "—seems to imply that there may be some scanty fruit of an inferior quality, but none answering to the goodness of the seed, or even of the soil, if it had not been robbed of its nourishing qualities by the thorns. So many a good heart may be spoilt as to its religion by unwatchfulness in prosperity.

20. "And these are they which are sown on good ground . . . . hundred fold." "Are sown" (lit., "have been sown," past participle). St. Mark uses a different form here, and in verses 16, 18. This seems to imply complete or effectual action (Canon Cook, in "Speaker's Commentary"); but St. Matthew uses the past participle in all four cases.

"Good ground." This is interpreted in St. Luke as "an honest [sincere] and good heart."

"Such as hear the word and receive it." It is interesting to compare the corresponding words in the two other Synoptics with these, as they mutually explain one another. St. Matthew has, "heareth the word, and understandeth it;" St. Mark, "hear the word, and receive it;" St. Luke, "having heard the word, keep it," or, rather, "keep hold of it." According to St. Mark, they hear the word, and receive it: doubtless, according to the highest meaning of the word "receive," *i.e.*, "receive in the love of it." These are they who, according to St. Matthew, "understand it"—not with the intellect only, but with the understanding heart; understand its application to themselves, and act on that understanding—as our Collect says, "inwardly digest it." And these are they who, according to St. Luke, "keep it"—*i.e.*, hold it fast, grasp it, embrace it.

"Some thirtyfold, some sixty, some an hundred." Everyone has observed the difference between those who may be called good Christians, in the matter of their good works—how some seem to produce twice or thrice the fruit that others do. Some are, compared with others, three times more attentive in prayer, three times more careful in all the trifling matters which make up so much of life; three times more self-denying, three times more liberal, three

some thirtyfold, some sixty, and some an hundred.

20. "Some thirty, some sixty," &c. Owing to the earliest MSS. being without accents, it is impossible to say whether this should be read "in [*b*] thirty, in sixty," &c., or, "some [*bv*] thirty, some sixty," &c., but there is not the slightest difference in meaning. The Vulgate has, *unum triginta*, as in Authorised; the Syriac, *tricenos et sexagenos*, &c.

times more humble, subdued, and thankful. Does not the Lord recognize this difference in the parable of the pounds—when the nobleman, in leaving, gives a pound to each of his servants ; and one servant makes it ten pounds, and another five; and he commends both, but gives to the more industrious worker twice the reward ? Look at the lives of John Wesley, Charles Lowder, Selwyn, Pattison, Fénelon, St. Theresa, Ridley, Latimer, Bernard, Anselm, Savanarola, Augustine, Ambrose, and see what sacrifices of time and labour and self-denial and prayer these have offered to God, not by fits and starts, but during their whole lives.

Such then is the parable of the sower. Its scope is admirably summed up by Bishop Beveridge: " We may observe in general, that of the three unprofitable hearers the first hear the word, but do not mind it ; the second minded it for a time, but did not keep it ; the third kept it, but did no good with it. But the fruitful hearers do all that these did and more; they hear so as to mind it, they mind so as to keep it: and they keep it so as to use and improve it to God's glory and their own good."

One word by way of caution. No one parable can possibly express every feature of the Divine life, or every circumstance bearing on it. In this parable the ground is represented as unchanged, and the fruit produced by the seed is according to the soil. But throughout all Scripture the soil, that is, the heart of man, is set forth as capable of being changed ; God, by the severest of all the prophets, says to His people, " I will take away the stony heart out of your flesh, and I will give you a heart of flesh " (Ezek. xxxvi. 26); and we are ourselves called upon to take our part in this : " Make you a new heart and a new spirit: for why will ye die, O house of Israel ? " (Ezek. xviii. 31).

Thus Chrysostom says : " And how can it be reasonable, saith one, to sow among the thorns, on the rock, on the way-side ? With regard to the seeds and the earth it cannot be reasonable, but in the case of men's souls and their instructions, it hath its praise, and that abundantly. For the husbandman indeed, would reasonably

## SET ON A CANDLESTICK.

21 ¶ ¹ And he said unto them, Is a candle brought to be put under a || bushel, or under a bed? and not to be set on a candlestick?

22 ᵏ For there is nothing hid, which shall not be manifested; neither was any thing kept secret, but that it should come abroad.

¹ Matt. v. 15. Luke viii. 16. & xi. 33.
|| *The word in the original signifieth a less measure, as* Matt. v. 15.
ᵏ Matt. x. 26. Luke xii. 2.

---

22. "Which shall not be manifested," rather "but that it should be manifested." ℵ, B., and some Cursives read, "Except that it may be manifested;" A., C., K., L., and many Cursives, "Except it be manifested;" Vulg., *Quod non manifestetur;* Syriac, *Quod non sit revelandum.*

be blamed for doing this, it being impossible for the rock to become earth, or the wayside not to be a wayside; but in the things that have reason it is not so. There is such a thing as the rock changing and becoming rich land; and the wayside being no longer trampled on, nor lying open to all that pass by, but it is possible that it may be a fertile field, and the thorns may be destroyed, and the seed enjoy full security. For had it been impossible, the Sower would not have sown. And if the change did not take place at all, that is no fault of the Sower, but of those who are unwilling to be changed" ("Homilies on St. Matthew," xiii. 19-21).

And Augustine: "Change the soil while you may. Break up your fallow-ground with the plough; from your field cast forth the stones, and pluck out the thorns. Be unwilling to have a hard heart, such as makes the word of God of none effect. Be unwilling to have a thin layer of soil, in which the root of Divine love can find no depth of entrance. Be unwilling to choke the good seed by the cares and lusts of this life, when by our labour it is scattered for your good. For God sows; while we are His workmen; but be the *good* ground." (Quoted in Ford from Serm. xiii. c. 3).

21. "And he said unto them, Is a [or the] candle brought to be put under," &c.

22. "For there is nothing hid which shall not be manifested" [or, save that it should be manifested].

These verses must be taken together, and their meaning seems to be something of this sort. The Lord had for certain wise, and, we believe, merciful reasons, adopted a new mode of teaching, in which He veiled His meaning from the multitude under parables, but this was not because He intended their meaning to be permanently hidden

> <sup>1</sup> Matt. xi. 15.
> ver. 9.

23 <sup>1</sup> If any man have ears to hear, let him hear.

---

from the world, but because He intended that it might be the better known to the world when the fitting time was come. To this end He made known the interpretation to His Apostles, not for themselves, but for the world. His truth—the truth of the Gospel—was the lamp; this lamp of truth He intended not for a corner of the world, or for a select few, but for all men of all nations, who would turn their faces towards it and receive it, and so He gave it now to the Apostles, who, after Pentecost, were to make it known to all nations for the obedience of faith.

God does not conceal any mystery, any religious truth, merely for the sake of concealing it. If He conceals any truth it is that He may ultimately make it the better known. This very parable is an illustration of this. If any truth ever shone forth upon the lamp-stand of the Church it is that which is taught us by this parable, that the word of the Gospel is efficacious or not, according to the state of heart of the recipients; so that men must in very deed "take heed" as to "how" they hear and "what" they hear. This meaning is still more clearly enforced by the true reading of the first clause of verse 22. There is nothing hidden, save that it should be manifested. So we have this parable given in full in three out of the four Gospels, and we may safely say that, with the exception of that of the returning prodigal, there is none which has been more expounded and enforced by preachers in all ages. The meaning, however, of verse 21, is much obscured by deficiency of translation. We lose much of the significance if we think of the modern candle and candlestick carried about in the hand. On the contrary, it is *the* lamp of the house put upon the lamp-stand, or candelabrum, which is so elevated that any lamp upon it can lighten up all the interior.

The reader will notice that the Lord uses this aphorism here with quite a different significance to that which He gives to it in Matt. x. 26.

23. "If any man have ears to hear," &c. If this was said not in the hearing of the multitude, but to the Apostles, or to those select ones to whom He had just expounded the parable, then it implies that there are still deeper mysteries of grace which require, for their apprehension, a more effectual opening of the soul's ear, and a deeper preparation of heart. Men have ears to hear certain funda-

## TAKE HEED WHAT YE HEAR. 77

24 And he said unto them, Take heed what ye hear: [m] with what measure ye mete, it shall be measured to you: and unto you that hear shall more be given.

[m] Matt. vii. 2.
Luke vi. 38.

25 [n] For he that hath, to him shall be given: and he that hath not, from him shall be taken even that which he hath.

[n] Matt. xiii. 12. & xxv. 29.
Luke viii. 18. & xix. 26.

---

24. "To you that hear shall more be given." "That hear" omitted by א, B., C., D., L. Vulg., and some other versions; but A., later Uncials, most Cursives, and Syriac read as in Rec. Text.

mental, or practical truths, who still have not as yet ears to hear certain deep mysteries.

24. "And He said unto them, Take heed what ye hear: with what measure ye mete," &c. This seems to mean, "Take heed that ye attend to and lose none of My present words. In proportion to your present profiting ye shall in due time receive more spiritual benediction and grace. This is also another instance in which the Lord uses a short aphoristic saying in another and totally different sense to that in which He had formerly applied it. In Matthew vii. 2 it is used with reference to retribution, and is in connection with "with what judgment ye judge ye shall be judged." Here it has to do with the dissemination of truth. The more industrious the Apostles should be in the preaching and expounding of the truth— the more would the treasures of Divine Truth be revealed to them. Or it may be more closely connected with "Take heed what ye hear," and may mean, "The more closely you apply yourselves to the understanding and preaching of revealed truth, the more you shall enter into its depths." So Theophylact: "That is, that none of those things which are said to you by Me should escape you. 'With what measure ye mete it shall be measured to you,' that is, 'whatsoever degree of application ye bring, in that degree ye will receive profit.'" But the former is preferable.

"And unto you [who thus measure] shall more be given," the words "that hear" being probably a later gloss. Nothing can be more apposite than the words of Venerable Bede on this: "Or else if ye diligently endeavour to do all the good which you can, and teach it to your neighbours, the mercy of God will come in to give you both in the present life a sense to take in higher things, and a will to do better things, and will add for the future an everlasting reward.

26 ¶ And he said, ° So is the kingdom of God, as if a man should cast seed into the ground;

° Matt. xiii. 24.

And therefore it is added, 'And to you shall more be given.'"

26. "And he said, so is the kingdom of heaven . . . . seed into the ground." The parable which follows—that of the seed growing secretly—is the only one peculiar to St. Mark. St. Mark, along with St. Matthew, gives the parable of the Sower, and of the Mustard Seed, but omits all the others which we have in Matthew xiii. It seems then to have been delivered at the same time as the rest of those given in St. Matthew, and as it is unlike any of them, I think we must take it as having a meaning peculiar to itself. We must not interpret it then by the parable of the leaven, as some have done, for that of the leaven has to do with the change of the body in which the leaven is deposited, whereas, in this parable, we have no such change. It is simply the history of the growth and development of the plant of grace. The teaching seems to be something of this sort. The greatest mystery in nature answers to the greatest mystery, or one of the greatest mysteries, of grace. The greatest mystery of nature—taking nature to mean the order of things in the world in which God has placed us—the greatest mystery of nature is Reproduction, the reproduction of new forms of the same living thing from seed, and the greatest mystery of grace is the reproduction of new forms of the New Man in the world, or in the Church, or, as we may say, in the soil of human nature, from the Divine Seed. If we hold fast to this as the one teaching of the parable, it will enable us in a very great degree to put aside such questions as "who is the sower of verse 26, or the reaper of verse 29?" The sower may be the Lord, or he may be the human minister; the reaper would appear, at first sight, to be the Lord only, at the last day by His ministers the angels reaping the world, but looking at such places as Matthew ix. 37, 38, John iv. 35-6, 38, it is clear that the Lord contemplates His ministers as being reapers as well as sowers, some as assisting at the beginning of any work of grace, some as gathering the fruits of it into comparative safety in the storehouse of the Church. Just as the sower of the earthly field sows the grain in the earth, and then must leave it so far as its germination and internal principle of growth is concerned, till its fruit is ready to be gathered, so in heavenly spiritual husbandry, the sower has to sow the seed, but when this is done he has done all

## HE KNOWETH NOT HOW.

27 And should sleep, and rise night and day, and the seed should spring and grow up, he knoweth not how.

---

that he can do to make it germinate. He has committed it to the earth, and there he must leave it. If it germinates it is owing to hidden processes of nature over which he has no control. If it appears above ground he cannot by any watching of it, or by anything he can do to the plant itself, make it grow faster or produce more grain. He can, it is true, dress the soil in which he sows it, or he can drain that soil of its superfluous moisture, and he can clear it of weeds, or gather the stones from the surface, but these operations are outside of the scope of this parable. It would be within the scope of this parable if the husbandman could go to each seed after it was sown, examine it, see if it was germinating, and if it was not, do something to it which would make it spring up, or if it was weakly, infuse by some process of his own, some new life into it, or restore it to life if it was dead. But the temporal husbandman can do none of these things. He must leave the grain to itself, so far as the vital principle of its springing up and its growth is concerned. And so with the spiritual husbandman in sowing the seed of the word. He sows it, but the reason why one seed germinates and another does not, is a thing known only to God, and one of the deepest of all mysteries. To say that this depends upon God's secret election is only putting the difficulty one step back, for God must have a reason for predestinating that the seed of the word should spring up in any particular soul. He must in such a matter act reasonably, and not as the Calvinists would have men believe, out of sheer wilfulness, indeed out of caprice. Now the secret cause of this springing up of the word we must leave to God, and with it the whole progress of spiritual growth and development. It is as completely out of the range of our faculties as the commencement and development of life in the world of nature.

In the production of spiritual fruit or corn, just as in the production of the natural, there are two agents—the seed, or rather the germ of life in the seed, on the one side, and the secret influence of the earth which receives it on the other. And the action and reaction of these upon one another is known only to Him Who knows what the mystery of life is, and what is the mystery of its nourishment. The first of these unknown agents, the life of the seed, we have in the words " the seed should spring up and grow,

28 For the earth bringeth forth fruit of herself; first the blade, then the ear, after that the full corn in the ear.

---

28. "For the earth." ℵ, A., B., C., L., omit "For;" later Uncials, almost all Cursives, some Old Latin, Vulg., Coptic, Syriac retain it.

he knoweth not how;" the second of these, the action of the ground or soil, we have in the words, "the earth bringeth forth fruit of itself." The gist of the parable is, that these are the only two agents in the development of life, and they postulate one another. The seed springs up only when sown in the ground, and the ground produces of itself only when it has received the seed. The part done by man, the sowing—the intermediate processes of dressing, weeding, and irrigating, and at last the reaping, are in no respect mysteries, but the beginning and continuance of the life is the deepest of mysteries.

And in what is the practical use of the lesson of the parable? Alford thinks that it warns us against undue interference with the seed when once sown. "No trouble of ours," he writes, "can accelerate the growth or shorten the stages through which each seed must pass. It is the mistake of modern Methodism, for instance, to be always working at the seed, taking it up to see whether it is growing, instead of leaving it to God's own good time, and meanwhile diligently doing God's work elsewhere." But many bodies and schools in the Catholic Church fall into this mistake quite as much as Methodists, and this simply by overdoing the "direction" of souls. This is not to be taken as disparaging the anxious and careful work of the pastor, for St. Paul bids the Ephesian Elders remember "that by the space of three years he ceased not to warn every one night and day with tears." Wesley has a most admirable pithy note on this parable: "Even he that sowed it cannot explain how it grows. For as the earth by a curious sort of mechanism which the greatest philosophers cannot comprehend, does as it were spontaneously bring forth first the blade, then the ear, then the full corn in the ear: so the soul in an inexplicable manner, brings forth first weak graces, then stronger, then full holiness: and all this, of itself, as a machine, whose spring of motion is within itself. Yet observe the amazing exactness of the comparison. The earth brings forth no corn (as the soul no holiness) without both the care and toil of man and the benign influence of heaven."

29 But when the fruit is ‖ brought forth, immediately ᵖ he putteth in the sickle, because the harvest is come.

| Or, *ripe*.
ᵖ Rev. xiv. 15.

29. "Brought forth." "Ripe," see margin. *Cum produxerit fructus*, Vulg.

Most commentators consider that the parable applies to the growth of the Church in the world, as well as to the growth of the plant of grace in the individual soul. "Again, the parable speaks of the whole Church. The Son of Man sows the seed, having prepared the ground and done His labour: and then He seems like a man gone into a far country—as He is described in another parable —as a husbandman who has done his work and leaves it. So it is now. He has prepared the ground, He has planted His Church; He may be even as one that sleeps while his enemy sows tares. He seems to have left it to itself, waiting for the end, and when He sees it is ripe, He will again visibly return. When the Day of Pentecost is fully come,—the time of the ingathering,—then that which is spoken of in the Revelation takes place. 'Upon the cloud sat one like unto the Son of Man, having on His head a golden crown, and in His hand a sharp sickle. And the voice is heard, saying, Thrust in thy sickle and reap, for the harvest of the earth is ripe." (I. Williams.)

In this latter case, of course, the full corn in the ear would not be good works only, but rather the perfect number of the elect.

And this leads to the further and far deeper question, "What is the seed?" It may be the Son of Man Himself, according to His words: "Except a corn of wheat fall into the ground and die, it abideth alone, but if it die, it bringeth forth much fruit." This is the true idea of Christian reproduction, the Son of Man, the New Man reproduced in the true members of His mystical Body.

But it may be asked, Why should the Lord set forth in a parable a mystery?" To which we answer that one chief part of the education of the soul for the eternal service of God, is the submission or bowing down of the soul and spirit before the revealed *mysteries* of God; the adoring acknowledgment of that which is not only difficult, but beyond the grasp of all our faculties; the confession that, as the mysteries of the natural life are unthinkable, so also are the mysteries of the Divine Life.

30 ¶ And he said, "Whereunto shall we liken the kingdom of God? or with what comparison shall we compare it?

*Matt. xiii. 31. Luke xiii. 18. Acts ii. 41. & iv. 4. & v. 14. & xix. 20.*

---

30. "Whereunto shall we liken?" So A., D., later Uncials, almost all Cursives, some Old Latin (c, f), Vulg., Syriac, Coptic; but ℵ, B., C., L., a few Cursives, Old Latin (b, e) read, "how."

"With what comparison shall we compare it?" "In what parable shall we set it forth?" (Revisers) is read by ℵ, B., C., L., Δ, a few Cursives, Old Latin (b, e); but A., D., later Uncials, most Cursives, Vulg., Syriac, as in Rec. Text.

30. "And he said, Whereunto shall we liken the kingdom of God? or with what," &c. No other parable is introduced in this way. It is as if the Lord had a multitude of illustrations before Him, and He was revolving in His human mind which to select. Or, perhaps, He prefaced it thus that the hearers might exercise their own minds as to what they thought the kingdom of God would be like, and so His own explanation would take firmer hold of them.

As the former parable—that of the seed growing secretly—sets forth the mysterious vitality of the seed of grace, so this teaches us its expansive power. It not only bears fruit for food, as in the parable of the "Sower," and the "seed growing secretly," but from a very small seed expands into a great tree which affords shelter to those which take refuge in it.

The Lord, as I explained in my notes on St. Matthew, made choice of the grain of mustard seed because of a common proverb among the Jews, "small as a grain of mustard seed," and we have the testimony of those who have seen it in warm climates, that it grows to such a size that it may be called the greatest of all herbs. Maldonatus speaks of it as in "very warm places rising above the height of a man. I have often seen, in Spain, large ovens heated by the mustard plant in place of wood. Birds are exceedingly fond of the seed, and when it is ripened settle on its branches, which are strong enough to bear them, however numerous they may be." There can be no doubt that this concluding part of the parable— where the plant which the Lord speaks of grows to such a size that it gives shelter to the fowls of heaven—is not thrown in by way of setting off the picture, but contains an important feature of the teaching, for the Lord, no doubt, had in His Mind one of the most remarkable prophecies in the Old Testament respecting the king-

31 *It is* like a grain of mustard seed, which, when it is sown in the earth, is less than all the seeds that be in the earth :

32 But when it is sown, it groweth up, and becometh greater than all herbs, and shooteth out great branches so that the fowls of the air may lodge under the shadow of

---

31. "Is less than all the seeds." Revisers (following Neutral Text, א, B., D., L., Δ, and one Cursive, 33), "though it be less than all the seeds," &c.; but A., C., later Uncials, Cursives, Vulg., and most versions read as in Rec. Text.

dom of the Messiah. It runs thus : " Thus saith the Lord God, I will also take of the highest branch of the high cedar, and will set it ; I will crop off from the top of his young twigs a tender one, and will plant it upon an high mountain and eminent. In the mountain of the height of Israel will I plant it; and it shall bring forth boughs, and bear fruit, and be a goodly cedar: and under it shall dwell all fowl of every wing ; in the shadow of the branches thereof shall they dwell" (Ezek. xvii. 22, 23). There can be no doubt that these parables of Ezekiel and of Christ relate to the same kingdom, and so the fact that the tree becomes a place of shelter and refuge for all the people of the world, is one principal purpose of it, if not the principal. Now this parable of our Lord's is, as much as that of Ezekiel's, a prophecy, and has been fulfilled to the letter. In the course of little more than one century after it was uttered there was not a city of any size in the Roman Empire which had not its bishop, with his priests and deacons, preaching the Word of God, baptizing, and so admitting men into the new kingdom, celebrating the Eucharist, and exercising discipline over the faithful. It was not the spread of a philosophy, or of a system of opinions, or even of a gospel only. It was the spread of an organization for purposes of rule and discipline, of exclusion of the unworthy, and of pastoral care over the worthy. And it went on progressing and prospering till it became a great power *in* the world, though not *of* it. For centuries, emperors, kings, and people had to take it into account in every department of government and civil policy. Its present weakness is a reaction against its former abuse of its power when it had become secular, and failed to fulfil some of the chief purposes of its institution.

But in all ages the Catholic Church has afforded to men what the

## 84 MANY SUCH PARABLES. [ST. MARK.

33 ʳ And with many such parables spake he the word unto them, as they were able to hear *it*.

ʳ Matt. xiii. 34.
John xvi. 12.

34 But without a parable spake he not unto them: and when they were alone, he expounded all things to his disciples.

35 ˢ And the same day, when the even was come, he saith unto them, Let us pass over unto the other side.

ˢ Matt. viii. 18, 23. Luke viii. 22.

---

34. "To his disciples." Revisers, "To his own disciples." So א, B., C., L., Δ, Vulg., and Syriac; but A., D., later Uncials, all Cursives, as in Rec. Text.

prophet and the Lord foretold, rest and shelter. No human philosophy has afforded any rest or refuge for the wandering spirit. Only the Church has done this, and the Church has been able to do this because the foundation of all her doctrine has been the Incarnation of her Lord. She teaches the soul to look for the foundation of her hope, not into herself, her frames and feelings, but to the historical facts of the Incarnation, Death, and consequent Resurrection and Ascension of the Eternal Son, together with the Church system and sacramental means which are the logical outcome of that Incarnation; and because of this, and this only, she is an abiding refuge.

33, 34. "And with many such parables spake he the word . . . . disciples." We have some of these "many such parables" in St. Matthew, viz., the wheat and tares, the leaven, the treasure hid in the field, the pearl of great price, and the net cast into the sea. All these are like the three which St. Mark has recorded, not only in their simplicity, but in their object, to set forth some aspect of the kingdom or Church of God.

"As they were able to hear." Even in the Lord's parables there was this difference, that some must be uttered by Him before others. They would not be able to apprehend or to hear as yet the parable of the ten virgins, or of the Vine and the branches.

"When they were alone, he expounded all things to his disciples." This was in accordance with what He had before said, "Unto you it is given to know the mysteries of the kingdom of God."

35. "And the same day, when the even was come, he saith unto them," &c. The account which follows of the miracle of the stilling

36 And when they had sent away the multitude, they took him even as he was in the ship. And there were also with him other little ships.

37 And there arose a great storm of wind, and the waves

---

36. "Little ships." "Little" omitted by ℵ, A., B., C., D., K., M., and some Cursives, Vulg.; retained in E., F., G., H., L., and most Cursives.

of the tempest, must have come from one who was in the ship, and kept all in a loving memory, as we shall notice as we go on.

"And the same day when the even was come." St. Mark alone gives this note of time, and the very words which the Lord used in bidding them pass over.

26. "And when they had sent away the multitude . . . even as he was." No doubt without any preparation for the journey, perhaps weary and needing repose, which he refused to take in the house on the land. "They made no special preparation. They did not land first to obtain provisions. It would have been inconvenient to go ashore in the midst of the crowd. They made at once, as He told them to do, for the other side." (Dean Bickersteth.)

"And there were with him also other [little] ships." No doubt, whilst He was preaching, others having boats on the lake, crowded around, each little ship, with its freight of eager listeners, and some of them would follow in the wake of His ship.

Archer Butler (quoted in Ford) has a suggestive remark: "When our Lord was in that ship in the tempest, which all ages have agreed in employing as a type of His Church, St. Mark alone of the Evangelists, as it were incidentally, observes, 'And there were also with him other little ships.' Yet they doubtless enjoyed a share in the blessing of calm obtained by the ship that bare Jesus. I have sometimes thought that they picture vividly the fortune of those societies, that, in these latter days, have moved in the wake of the ancient Apostolic Church, that, with it, are forced to endure the storms of a world impartially hostile to every form of religious effort, and that not without participating in the blessings of the Holy Presence, abiding in that Church as long as in sincerity of heart they endeavour to keep up with the Master in his course."

37. "And there arose a great storm of wind, and the waves beat into the ship," &c. We should have thought that there must have been indications in the heavens of the coming storm which would

## ASLEEP ON A PILLOW.  [ST. MARK.

beat into the ship, so that it was now full.

38 And he was in the hinder part of the ship, asleep on a pillow: and they awake him, and say unto him, Master, carest thou not that we perish?

---

38. "On a pillow." "On the pillow," probably a bench fixed on the ship.

have induced them to postpone their journey for a short time; but on inland lakes, as in Switzerland, as well as in Galilee, storms brew up with astonishing rapidity. Dr. Buchanan (quoted in Gray's "Museum") gives a strikingly graphic account of a storm springing up without the least perceptible warning. "While gazing upon the suggestive scene around us [on the sea of Galilee], our earnest conversation was suddenly disturbed by a movement among our Arab crew. All at once they pulled in their oars, shipped their mast, and began to hoist their long and very ragged lateen sail. What can the fellows mean to do with a sail in a dead calm? But they were right. There comes the breeze rippling and roughening the lately glassy surface of the lake. It reaches us before the sail is rightly set. A few minutes more and it is blowing hard. The bending and often spliced yard threatens to give way .... 'And where are we going now?' was our first inquiry, when things had been got a little into shape. 'Where the wind will take us,' was the reply of the old greybeard at the helm. And away we went, the lake all now tost into waves, and covered with foaming white heads, as if a demon had got into its lately tranquil bosom; an adventure that afforded us a fresh illustration of the reality of those events which the narratives of Scripture relate."

37. "The waves beat into the ship, so that it was now full." St. Luke says, that "they were filled with water, and were in jeopardy." This was, of course, permitted by the Lord, Who knew all that was coming, in order to test their faith.

38. "And he was in the hinder part of the ship, asleep on a [the] pillow." From the article before the Greek word, this was probably not a soft pillow, but a bench in the prow of the ship on which the captain rests his head, when, as is his custom, he sleeps on the quarter deck. (Speaker's Commentary).

How mysterious the sleep of the Lord! To recruit His wearied body He submitted to be unconscious, so far as His human faculties

CHAP. IV.]   PEACE, BE STILL.   87

39 And he arose, and rebuked the wind, and said unto the sea, Peace, be still. And the wind ceased, and there was a great calm.

39. "And he arose." Rather, "he awoke."

were concerned; and yet His Divine Personality could not sleep. Whilst He appeared to be sharing their danger He was watching over them.

"And they awake him, and say unto him, Master [Teacher], carest thou not," &c. These words are words of remonstrance, we may almost say, of presumption. Seeing that St. Peter was usually the spokesman of the Apostolic band, we can have little or no doubt that they were the exact words which he uttered in rousing the Lord. They savour of the same presumption as characterized his remonstrance with Christ when he said, "Be it far from Thee, Lord, this shall not happen unto Thee." They betray some unworthy doubt of the love of the Lord, but if taken as said, not in the hurry and fear of the moment, but in their full significance, they undoubtedly show some faith in His supernatural power; they seem to imply that though asleep, He was still in some degree conscious of the danger they were in.

39. "And he arose, and rebuked the wind, and said unto the sea, Peace, be still," &c. According to St. Matthew, He first rebuked the disciples; but according to St. Mark and St. Luke, He first rebuked the wind and sea. It is just possible that He rose from His slumbers with the words of St. Matthew, and after the stilling of the tempest again remonstrates with them for their unbelief. St. Mark, alone, notices the double rebuke which, doubtless, St. Peter had felt, and made special mention of in his preaching. And the double rebuke first of the wind, then of the sea, corresponds to the double miracle. For if the wind only had been suddenly arrested, the sea would have continued agitated, perhaps for hours, and in the then state of the ship, filled with water, the danger would seem prolonged; and unbelievers might have said that it was but a natural occurrence, the wind having sunk as suddenly as it arose. But the Lord, by separate words of power, restrained first, the fury of the wind, and then, as instantaneously, the natural effect of that fury in the surging of the waves, so that there could have been no doubt that He wielded that fulness of Almighty power with which

## THEY FEARED EXCEEDINGLY. [St. Mark.

40 And he said unto them, Why are ye so fearful? how is it that ye have no faith?

41 And they feared exceedingly, and said one to another,

---

40. "How is it that ye have no faith?" ℵ, B., D., L., Vulg., Old Latin, Coptic, &c., read "not yet;" but A., C., later Uncials, almost all Cursives, and Syriac, as in Rec. Text.

God rules the elements. Let me also be forgiven for repeating what I said in St. Matthew, that this was not only an instance of Divine omnipotence, but of Divine Majesty in its exercise. It forcibly reminds us of the words, "Thou rulest the raging of the sea, Thou stillest the storms thereof when they arise."

40. "And he said unto them, Why are ye [so] fearful? how is it that," &c. The MSS. of the Neutral Text, supported by the Vulgate, read the latter part of the rebuke more mildly. "Have ye not yet faith?" What was their unbelief? It was either that they supposed it possible that the ship should go down whilst He was in it, or that they could be in any real danger whilst he was in the ship. In the first case their faith in His Divine mission must have been very weak, if they imagined for a moment that it could be so cut short. In the second case, He had chosen them to be His Apostles and representatives; would He permit their work and witness to be so soon put an end to? In either case it was a sad eclipse of faith.

But in what was their unbelief shown? Was it in that they awoke Him? I think not. Knowing His power, and seeing that the ship was fast filling with water, they would naturally awake Him, and invoke His aid; but their unbelief was shown in their fear. They were afraid that they might perish whilst He was in the ship with them, and so in St. Matthew's account, he distinctly associates their fear with their unbelief. "Why are ye fearful, O ye of little faith?"

41. "And they feared exceedingly, and said one to another," &c. Mark how, when they seemed in danger of perishing, they feared; but when all danger was over, and their faith restored, it is said that they "feared exceedingly." The fear of incredulity lest they should perish in His presence, was changed into the fear of deep reverential awe at the nearness of the Divine and Supernatural. Was not this the very fear which God by His prophet demanded of His people? "Fear ye not me, saith the Lord? will ye not

What manner of man is this, that even the wind and the sea obey him?

tremble at my presence which have placed the sand for the bound of the sea by a perpetual decree that it cannot pass it: and though the waves thereof toss themselves, yet can they not prevail?" (Jeremiah v. 22.)

And does not all this instruct us as to our realization of the presence of Christ in His Church? If He be the ship of the Church, as He is, are not all fears respecting the safety of that Church guilty because unbelieving fears? And are not all compromises of God's truth to suit the taste of the unbelieving world, and to disarm its opposition, the offspring of this guilty fear? And, on the other hand, should not the assured presence of the Eternal Son in our midst fill us with deep reverential awe? Have we not reason to fall on our faces and say with Jacob, "God is in this place, and I knew it not"?

## CHAP. V.

AND <sup>a</sup> they came over unto the other side of    <sup>a</sup> Matt. viii. 28. Luke viii. 26.

1. "And they came over unto the other side of the sea," &c. The Lord having hushed the tempest of the natural elements, now exhibits His Divine Power in quelling a far more terrible storm. "In the former miracle we behold the visible creation obeying the Creator; in this the invisible; in the former things insensible; in this spiritual. The former teaches us to fly under the shadow of His wings from the evils of this world: this from the worse evils of the next. The storm at sea was not more awful than this tempest in the spiritual world. The nakedness, the chainless fury, the mountains and tombs, the crying night and day, the injuring others and himself; a sight indescribably fearful; as it were affording a glimpse into the unseen abyss of woe." (Williams.)

"They come over unto the other side of the sea." This implies that they merely crossed to some near point, not that they sailed to

the sea, into the country of the Gadarenes.

2 And when he was come out of the ship, immediately there met him out of the tombs a man with an unclean spirit,

---

1. "Gadarenes" read by A., C., later Uncials, most Cursives, Syriac; "Gerasenes" read by א, B., D., Old Latin, and Vulgate; but L., five or six Cursives, and some versions read, "Gergesenes." It is not impossible that either of the two readings, Gadara and Gerasa, may be right. If Gadara was the nearest city of importance, though at some distance, the whole district might be called the country of the Gadarenes, though Gerasa was the exact spot where the miracle took place.

the other end of the lake, which they would have had to do if the scene of what follows was at Gadara.

"Into the country of the Gadarenes." I mentioned in a critical note on St. Matthew viii. 18, 28, the differences of reading—Gadarenes, Gergesenes, or Gerasenes. Our opinion of the genuineness of the reading in the case of each Evangelist depends on the value assigned to certain manuscripts, and can (it seems to me) never be more than a matter of conjecture, but not so, happily, with the locality itself. There can be no doubt that Dr. Thomson has successfully identified the site with the ruins of Kerea or Gerea, near the part of the shore where Gergesha is marked on most maps. After showing conclusively that Gadara, or the district immediately about it, is impossible, he writes, "In this Gerea, or Chersa, we have a position which fulfils every requirement of the narrative, and with a name so near that in Matthew as to be in itself a strong corroboration of the truth of this identification. It is within a few rods of the shore, and an immense mountain rises directly above it, in which are ancient tombs, out of some of which the two men possessed of the devils may have issued to meet Jesus. The lake is so near the base of the mountain, that the swine rushing madly down it could not stop, but would be hurried on into the water.... The name, pronounced by Bedouin Arabs, is so similar to Gergesa, that, to all my inquiries for the place, they invariably said it was at Chersa; and they insisted that they were identical, and I agree with them in this opinion."

2. "And when he was come out of the ship ... a man with an unclean spirit." St. Matthew mentions two, St. Mark and St. Luke only one. All commentators seem agreed that the solution of this difficulty is that one was much more fierce and intractable than the other. St. Mark's narrative requires that one should have

3 Who had *his* dwelling among the tombs; and no man could bind him, no, not with chains:

4 Because that he had been often bound with fetters and chains, and the chains had been plucked asunder by him, and the fetters broken in pieces: neither could any *man* tame him.

---

3. "With chains." So ℵ, A., D., later Uncials, most Cursives, Old Latin (b, f), Vulg., &c.; "With a chain," B., C., L., Old Latin (c, e).
4. "Could any man." Properly, "Was any man strong enough."

been more prominent, as the Lord asks him his name, and receives as answer, "My name is Legion," as if one only made answer.

3. "Who had his dwelling among the tombs." The spirit or spirits which possessed him were unclean spirits. Literally, it is a man in an unclean spirit. No other demoniac whom our Lord dispossessed was like this. They came to the synagogues, or were brought to our Lord along with other diseased persons, but this man took refuge in the abodes of corruption, among bones and putrefying carcases. Archbishop Trench gives a strikingly illustrative passage out of Warburton's "Crescent and Cross." "On descending from these heights (those of Lebanon) I found myself in a cemetery whose sculptured turbans showed me that the neighbouring village was Moslem. The silence of the night was now broken by fierce yells and howlings, which I discovered proceeded from a naked maniac who was fighting with some wild dogs for a bone."

"No man could bind him, no, not with chains . . . cutting himself with stones." The description of his state in St. Mark is more fearful than those of the other Evangelists, far more so than that of St. Matthew, whose only words to this effect are, "exceeding fierce, so that no man might pass by that way." What a terrible parable this is of the possession of the soul by some master sin, at times, to all appearances, effectually restrained (bound with fetters and chains), but to no purpose; the evil habit may seem subdued, but it is only an outward restraint, the love of sin yet remains in possession of the soul, and till this is driven out by the power of Christ, and the soul becomes the dwelling-place of the Spirit of Christ, there is always a danger of relapse; the evil spirit returns with ten-fold violence, the chains of merely worldly fear and

5 And always, night and day, he was in the mountains, and in the tombs, crying, and cutting himself with stones.

6 But when he saw Jesus afar off, he ran and worshipped him,

---

shame, and the fetters of conventional restraint or respectability are snapped, and the wretched being is again an outcast from the true Church or kingdom of God.

"Crying, and cutting himself with stones." So that his cruel fierceness was not against his fellows only, but against himself. In this the possession by the external evil power was manifestly seen. The spirits within him were spirits of destruction. They compelled him to destroy and torment his own body. And this is a parable also. The sins of lust and drunkenness make a man the enemy, not only of his immortal spirit and eternal interests, but of his own body, his own flesh and blood. The sins of envy and malice lacerate and envenom, and fill sometimes with maddening anguish the man's soul, and at the same time make his whole frame to quiver.

The question arises, "How did he get into this state, why did God permit him to give entrance to such an enemy?" Almost all writers upon demoniacal possession (I mean, of course, those who look at it from a believing stand-point)—almost all such seem to agree that it was the man's own evil will which first opened the door. We are not, of course, for a moment to suppose that such were the most wicked of men. On the contrary, this man, in his worst state, was a happier being than Judas, into whom Satan was permitted to enter without injuring one of his natural faculties. All remains of good were expelled from such an one as Judas, and being wholly given up to the Evil One there was no conflict within. But in the demoniacs it was the struggle between the remaining good feeling and respect for virtue with the spirit of wickedness which gave rise to the internal war, and violently shook the soul from its resting-place of reason and sound sense. Whatever this man's sin had been, it might be truly said of him that for a brief time he was "given over to Satan for the destruction of the flesh, that the spirit might be saved in the day of the Lord Jesus." (1 Cor. v. 5.)

6. "But when he saw Jesus ... he ran and worshipped him." Who was it who came thus to Jesus? Was it the man who of his own

7 And cried with a loud voice, and said, What have I to do with thee, Jesus, *thou* Son of the most high God? I adjure thee by God, that thou torment me not.

8 For he said unto him, Come out of the man, *thou* unclean spirit.

---

accord, having perceived by some spiritual instinct that the Man Who had just landed was his deliverer, asserted his own freedom and ran to Him for salvation, or was it the indwelling evil spirit? It seems to have been the latter. For how could the mere human intelligence of the possessed man have addressed the Lord as the Son of the Most High God? How could such an one recognizing in some unknown way that the Lord was His deliverer, beseech Him to torment him not? The personality which thus recognizes and entreats the Lord is evidently that of the spirit, or the leader of the band of spirits. If it be asked, why should such an one run to the feet of Jesus? We answer, simply because the Lord compelled him. The Lord had come across the sea to restore this man, for He knew that he would be the only fruit of the toilsome and dangerous voyage. The man seems to have been, for the time, wholly overborne by the malignant spirit. The Lord, it is to be noticed, only addresses the spirit, "Come out of the man, thou unclean spirit," and these words of the Lord are given as the reason why the spirit deprecates His wrath in the words, "I adjure thee, by God, that thou torment me not."

But why should the spirit entreat the Lord not to torment him, when the Lord had simply said, "Come out of the man"? Some would gather from this that he would be in a state of torment if he could not disorganize or destroy. He must exercise his destructive powers upon something; and so we read elsewhere of the evil spirit who was cast out, wandering through dry places, seeking rest and finding none. These wicked beings having made evil their good, find their rest and an alleviation of the hell within them in the paroxysms and tortures of their victims. But may it not be simply the cry of fear? He knew that he was in the presence of the Supreme Judge, Whose will, ever since his fall, he had been thwarting, and Whose creatures he had been tempting, and deprecates His wrath, and asks for a respite, knowing that the hour of judgment was not yet fully come.

9 And he asked him What *is* thy name ? And he answered,

What follows in this account is exceedingly difficult, and contains glimpses of the spiritual world, which it seems unlawful to speculate upon, since we know nothing whatsoever about the conditions under which the world of evil spirits exist, and what is told us here enhances rather than dispels the thick darkness in which God has shrouded it.

9. "And he asked him, What is thy name? . . . Legion: for we are many." It has been conjectured that the Lord asked the man his name as a step towards his cure, to remind him of his personality, of what he once was before he allowed the first inroads into himself of these cursed spirits; but this is very unlikely, for, in the first place, the Lord never mixes up natural and supernatural modes of cure. It was His intention in all His miracles to exhibit the power of God, apart from, and independent of, all human means: and in the second place He was not likely to adopt a tentative method, which in His foreknowledge He must have seen would fail utterly, for the man was not reminded by the question of his human personality, but continued to answer solely as the Evil One within him dictated. "My name is Legion: for we are many," and as St. Luke explains, "because many devils were entered into him." I have no doubt that the Lord asked the question in order to elicit this answer. It was His will that the Apostles, and, through them, all after ages of the Church, should knew that this was not an ordinary case of possession, such as those with which they had, in time past, seen Him deal. It was unique amongst the multitudes of such cases as had come in His way, or been brought under His notice. He had crossed the sea in the fearful storm that they should be witnesses of this desperate subjugation of a fellow creature to many evil powers, and of His complete control over all such influences.

And now let us consider the import of this answer. It is generally taken to mean that the devils which had entered into this man were so many as to be comparable in number to a Roman Legion, a body of men, when complete, five or six thousand in number; but are we at all warranted in taking the words in this way? Is it not most probable that the man used the word with somewhat the same latitude as we use the term "host"? If a man were to tell us that he was overwhelmed with a "host" of troubles, we

## MY NAME IS LEGION.

saying, My name *is* Legion : for we are many.

10 And he besought him much that he would not send them away out of the country.

---

should not for a moment consider that he meant one thousand or one hundred, or even twenty. We should think him quite warranted in using the expression if five or six were worrying him. In writing this, the reader will, I trust, give me credit for making no concession whatsoever to Rationalism. It is just as contrary to the spirit of Rationalism that one evil spirit should so possess a man so as to inject thoughts into his heart, and speak words by his tongue, as that a thousand should; but it seems the most natural way of understanding the words, and goes far to remove somewhat of the grotesqueness which, in many minds, is associated with this miracle. It seems right to remark that, if we had only St. Matthew's account, we should certainly gather that there were only two, one in each demoniac. This in no way detracts from the truth of the fact that "many" had been permitted to take possession of the one, but it should make us hesitate in accounting the number so very large as some do.

From the answer of the evil spirit, "*My* name is Legion," we are led to conclude that there was one leading one who spoke for the rest, and held rule in the possessed man, and that the others were permitted by him to take part in exciting the turmoil. So in the moral world, one master lust given way to, opens the door to a multitude of others.

Drunkenness, for instance, opens the door to unbounded selfishness, and the use of profane and obscene language, and violent outbreaks of angry passion, and all sorts of fraudulent devices whereby the means for self-indulgence may be acquired.

With respect to the fact that a man may be possessed by more than one evil spirit, we are told by the Lord that the evil spirit when exorcised may return "with seven other more wicked than himself" (Matt. xii. 45). And out of Mary Magdalen He cast seven devils.

10. "And he besought him much that he would not send them away out of the country." This place also presents extraordinary difficulty, and I confess that I cannot explain the reason, nor have I seen any explanation which seems at all satisfactory, especially when we take into account that the parallel place in St. Luke is,

11 Now there was there nigh unto the mountains a great herd of swine feeding.

12 And all the devils besought him, saying, Send us into the swine, that we may enter into them.

---

12. "All the devils." So A., E., F., G., H., almost all Cursives, Old Latin (a); Vulg. and Syriac omit "all." א, B., C., L., and a few Cursives read, "they" besought Him.

"They besought him that he would not command them to go into the abyss," *i.e.*, the bottomless pit (Rev. ix. 2). I can only mention briefly the opinions of others. Canon Cook, in the Speaker's Commentary, says that they besought him not to send them out of the country, because it was a heathenish district. Olshausen, and after him Archbishop Trench: "These words are, doubtless, connected with the Jewish popular opinion, that certain spheres of operation were assigned to the bad angels as well as to the good (Daniel x. 13, 20, 21). The demon desires not to be removed out of his. If a removal out of one country into another was regarded as impossible, their being driven out of the country assigned would be precisely equivalent to being sent down into the abyss." Lange suggests: "The lawless nature of the country (where Jews lived mingled with Gentiles), which pleased the demons well."[1]

11. "Now there was there nigh unto the mountains . . . swine feeding." Dr. Thomson, in his "Land and Book," gives us a startling illustration of this also: "This Wady Semak (in which Gersa is situated) is everywhere ploughed up by wild hogs in search of the esculent roots upon which they live at this season of the year. . . . It is a fact, however, that these creatures still abound at this place, and in a state as wild and fierce as though they were still possessed."

As the whole region was partially Gentile, we are not to consider the possession of this herd as unlawful.

12. "And all the devils besought him saying . . . enter into them." Some think that this request proceeded from their being unclean and yet disembodied spirits: they could not be at rest, or the nearest state which they could enjoy approaching to rest was

---

[1] Cornelius à Lapide, Maldonatus, and Estius, none of whom seem to shirk difficulties, make no allusion to this in their notes on any of the Gospels.

## CHAP. V.] JESUS GAVE THEM LEAVE.

13 And forthwith Jesus gave them leave. And the unclean spirits went out, and entered into the swine: and the herd ran violently down a steep place into the sea, (they were about two thousand;) and were choked in the sea.

---

13. "A steep place." Properly, "the steep" (Revisers).

the possession of some living body, if not of a man yet of a brute; but the greater part of commentators seem to think that they requested this for the purpose of destroying the swine, in order that, through their loss, the people of the district might be turned against the Lord. I believe that this was the reason. If it be asked, Why should the Lord permit them thus to hinder His work? I answer, that His work was not hindered. He came over, as I said, simply for the restoration to a sound mind of the one or, rather, of the two men. When He had made them experience His almighty power in rescuing bodies and souls from Satan, He had done His work there. He left one monument of His power to be His witness and apostle in that region, and we know not how many were afterwards gathered into the Church through his testimony. Anyhow the men of the place were then wholly unfit to receive the preaching of the Lord.[1]

13. "And forthwith Jesus gave them leave . . . choked in the sea." There is no cliff or precipice near Chersa over which the swine could have thrown themselves into the lake, but there is a very steep descent down which animals rushing in a panic would infallibly be destroyed. "Take your stand," Dr. Thomson writes, "a little to the south of this Chersa. A great herd of swine, we will suppose, is feeding on the mountain that towers above it. They are seized with a sudden panic—rush madly down the almost perpendicular declivity—those behind tumbling over, and thrusting forward those before; and as there is neither time nor space to recover on this narrow shelf between the base and the lake, they are crowded headlong into the water and perish. All is perfectly natural just at this point; and here, I suppose, it did actually occur. Further south the plain becomes so broad that the herd might have recovered and recoiled from the lake, whose domain they would not willingly invade."

---

[1] See Excursus on Demoniacal Possession at the end of this volume.

14 And they that fed the swine fled, and told *it* in the city, and in the country. And they went out to see what it was that was done.

15 And they came to Jesus, and see him that was possessed with the devil, and had the legion, sitting, and clothed, and in his right mind: and they were afraid.

---

"They were about two thousand." We are not to suppose for a moment that by this is implied that there were so many evil spirits. All flocks of animals of every kind have leaders, and it would be quite sufficient to strike a panic into the whole herd, if they saw a very few rush down the steep.

14. "And they that fed the swine fled . . . what was done." They could give no rational account of matters. They would have noticed the demoniac of whom they were always in terror running and falling down at the feet of some one who had just disembarked. And a short time after this they would see the panic-stricken herd rush down into destruction. They would blindly connect these two things, and leave it to the inhabitants of the city to examine the matter as best they could. St. Matthew, whose account of the whole matter is very short, seems to give only the traditionary outline. St. Mark here is evidently more true to nature, as the swineherds are not likely to have been near enough to understand that a miracle had been wrought.

15. "And they come to Jesus . . . and they were afraid." Notice how instantaneous the cure had been. He who, not perhaps an hour before, had been rushing down from the tombs a raving, naked maniac, was now sitting quietly, clothed already by the kindness of some friendly hand, listening to the Lord. It is to be noticed that St. Mark never mentions that the man in his wild state was unclothed, whereas St. Luke alone tells us that he "wore no clothes." Another instance of undesigned coincidence.

St. Luke says, "sitting at the feet of Jesus;" both tell us that he was clothed, both that he was in his right mind. And is not this also a parable? Is not the man who is willingly under the dominion of sin, "naked," so that men see his shame, and "out of his mind," so that whilst confessing with his lips that he believes in God and in the life everlasting, he yet lives as if there were no God, no judgment, no heaven, no hell; and when the Lord restores him, does

## ALSO CONCERNING THE SWINE.

16 And they that saw *it* told them how it befell to him that was possessed with the devil, and *also* concerning the swine.

17 And [b] they began to pray him to depart out of their coasts.

[b] Matt. viii. 34. Acts xvi. 39.

18 And when he was come into the ship, [c] he that had been possessed with the devil prayed him that he might be with him.

[c] Luke viii. 38.

---

17. "Coasts." Rather, "borders" (Revisers).
18. "He was come." ℵ, A., B., C., D., K., L., M., Δ, some Cursives, Old Latin, Vulg., read, "When he was coming;" later Uncials and most Cursives read as in Rec. Text.

he not sit at His feet as a humble disciple, and is he not clothed with a better righteousness, and is not his mind now made "right" so that he sees all things—God, Christ, the Spirit, the Church, the world to come, judgment, and eternity—all in their true light?

16. "And they that saw it . . . concerning the swine." "They that saw it." These may have been the Apostles or the bystanders, who would naturally gather round any ship from which men were disembarking. Very probably they told it to the praise of the Lord; but there would be some who would be far more struck with the request to enter into the swine, and the permission so readily granted, and the consequent destruction of the unclean animals.

17. "And they began to pray him to depart out of their coasts." We are not to judge too harshly of these people, seeing that, in all probability, they were heathen, and so knowing little or nothing of the God of Israel, or of the promises of the Messiah, they could not but look upon the Lord with very mixed feelings; they would see the maniac restored to his senses evidently by an act of supernatural power, and they would see closely following upon this, and as an effect of it, the destruction of an immense herd of swine. So St. Luke says, "they were taken with great fear," as men always are in the presence of the supernatural, or the supposed supernatural. Of course, judged by Christian principles, they ought to have allowed the restoration of the maniac to his senses to outweigh the destruction of ten thousand swine, but they had never been taught Christian principles, and the Lord evidently did not hold them to be fit, at that time, to receive them. We are not warranted, I think, in ascribing their conduct so much to avarice as to fear.

18. "And when he was come into the ship . . . might be with

19 Howbeit Jesus suffered him not, but saith unto him, Go home to thy friends, and tell them how great things the Lord hath done for thee, and hath had compassion on thee.

20 And he departed, and began to publish in Decapolis how great things Jesus had done for him: and all *men* did marvel.

---

19. "Howbeit Jesus suffered." אּ, A., B., C., K., L., M., Δ, some Cursives, Vulg., and Syriac read, "And he suffered him not ; " but D., some later Uncials, most Cursives, and Old Latin read as in Rec. Text.

him." Some suppose that he imagined that he would be only thoroughly safe from a relapse and re-possession in the presence of his Deliverer; but may we not think that, out of gratitude and love, he desired to follow One to Whom he owed his very self?

19. "Howbeit Jesus suffered him not ... compassion on thee." How is it that the Lord commands this man to go home and tell his friends of the blessing he has received whilst he strictly charges others not to open their lips about it? No doubt the Lord had in each case regard to the natural disposition or temperament of the man healed. On the garrulous and self-asserting, on those who would be talking of themselves and directing attention to themselves He would enjoin silence, whilst others who would sink themselves in their Deliverer, as He saw this man would do, He commanded to spread abroad the fame of the mighty work among their friends.

Archbishop Trench has a valuable remark as to how the command had reference to the permanence of the cure: "Where there was a temperament over-inclined to melancholy, sunken and shut up in itself, and needing to be drawn out from self, and into healthy communion with its fellow-men, as was evidently the case with such a solitary, melancholic person as we have here, then the command was, that he should go and tell to others the great things which God had done for him, and in this telling preserve the healthy condition of his own soul."

20. "And he departed, and began to publish ... all men did marvel." So that he became the first missionary of the Lord to the heathen, for the region of Decapolis was mainly Gentile.

"All men did marvel." This is only noticed by St. Mark, and is another instance how he (or rather the great Apostle who was

CHAP. V.] JAIRUS. 101

21 ᵈ And when Jesus was passed over again by ship unto the other side, much people gathered unto him: and he was nigh unto the sea.

ᵈ Matt. ix. 1.
Luke viii. 40.

22 ᵉ And, behold, there cometh one of the rulers of the synagogue, Jairus by name; and when he saw him, he fell at his feet,

ᵉ Matt. ix. 18.
Luke viii. 41.

23 And besought him greatly, saying, My little daughter

---

22. "Behold" omitted by ℵ, B., D., L., Δ, Old Latin (a, b, e), Vulg., Coptic, Syriac; retained by A., C., later Uncials, and almost all Cursives.

the real author of this Gospel) takes every opportunity of noticing the stir which the Lord's mighty works made among the common people.

21. "And when Jesus was passed over . . . nigh unto the sea." From St. Mark we should infer that this gathering of the people to Him, as He was nigh unto the sea, took place immediately on His landing. St. Matthew, however, introduces here the healing of the man sick of the palsy, ix. 2-9; his (St. Matthew's) own call, ix. 9; the feast in his house, ix. 10-18. St. Mark reports these occurrences in ii. 2-23, evidently out of their proper order. The inspiration of not one of the three Synoptics reaches to their giving an exact chronological order of events.

22. "And [behold] there cometh one of the rulers of the synagogue . . . feet." As this took place in Capernaum, where the centurion of Matthew ix. had built a synagogue, it is not at all improbable that this man was one of those rulers, or elders, whom he sent to entreat the Lord on behalf of his servant. He is here called one of the rulers, there being several to each synagogue. "Jairus," the same as the Jair of Numbers xxxii. 41. Commentators notice that the word signifies "he shall enlighten" or "he shall gladden," and if God exercises any providence over the giving of names, doubtless He did so here. St. Mark writes as if the whole scene was before him. St. Matthew has, "he worshipped Him." St. Luke, "he fell down at Jesus's feet," but St. Mark, "having seen Him he fell down," as if the narrator had seen the man come near—seen him recognize the Lord and then fell down at once.

23. "And besought him greatly, saying, . . . she shall live." The Greek is more disjointed and broken than the authorized version. "My little daughter is at her last gasp—that thou wouldest come

lieth at the point of death: *I pray thee,* come and lay thy hands on her, that she may be healed; and she shall live.

24 And *Jesus* went with him; and much people followed him, and thronged him.

<sup>f</sup> Lev. xv. 25.
Matt. ix. 20.

25 And a certain woman, <sup>f</sup> which had an issue of blood twelve years,

---

23. "And she shall live." So **A.**, later Uncials, &c.; but ℵ, B., C., D., L., and some Cursives read, "And live;" Old Latin, Vulg., *Ut salva sit et vivat.*

and lay hands on her—that she may be healed [saved] and live." It seems from this as if the father's feelings had overcome him, and his utterance was choked through sorrow.

From St. Matthew, whose account is a mere outline compared to St. Mark's, we should at first sight gather that the man believed his daughter to be already dead. "My daughter is even now dead." In this case there would be a serious discrepancy between his account and St. Mark's, who represents the faith of this ruler to be much weaker and to require sustaining by the encouraging words of the Lord (verse 36), but St. Matthew's words must be taken as the words of earnest entreaty: "She is, maybe, even now dead, for I left her at the very point of death; delay not, or it will be all over." The words of those who came to meet him (verse 35) are more decisive as to death having actually taken place.

24. "And Jesus went with him; and much people followed him and thronged him." Notice how all things are ordered for the best. This man's faith was weaker than that of the centurion who asked our Lord to say but the word, but if the Lord had done this and not set out to the house of the ruler we should have lost the inestimable encouragement which we derive from the miracle which Jesus performed on the way.

"Much people thronged him." This is said as an introduction to what follows.

25. "And a certain woman, which had an issue of blood twelve years," &c. There are several legends respecting this woman: amongst them the following is preserved by Eusebius. "They say that the woman which had the issue of blood mentioned by the Evangelists, and who obtained deliverance from her affliction by our Saviour, was a native of this place (Panium), and that her house is shown in the city, and the wonderful monuments of our Saviour's

## SHE TOUCHED HIS GARMENT.

26 And had suffered many things of many physicians, and had spent all that she had, and was nothing bettered, but rather grew worse,

27 When she had heard of Jesus, came in the press behind, and touched his garment.

28 For she said, If I may touch but his clothes, I shall be whole.

---

benefit to her are still remaining. At the gates of her house, on an elevated stone, stands a brazen image of a woman on her bended knee, with her hands stretched out before her, like one entreating. Opposite to this there is another image of a man, erect, of the same materials, decently clad in a mantle, and stretching out his hand to the woman . . . This statue, they say, is a statue of Jesus Christ, and it has remained there even until our times; so that we ourselves saw it whilst tarrying in that place." (B. vii. c. 18).

26. "And had suffered many things . . . rather grew worse." Considering the remedies then tried, and of which we have accounts in Rabbinical writers, it is no wonder that she suffered much under such treatment and was the worse for it. This woman is a type of poor human nature which, by no skill of man, can bring about the remedy for its own loathsome and deep-seated disease, but must come to Him, Who by assuming our nature has endowed it with heavenly and supernatural virtue. Human nature must exercise faith in Him and strive to touch Him if it is to be healed and renewed.

27. "When she had heard of Jesus, came . . . his garment." Why did she not boldly come forward and beg a blessing? To which it may be replied, she was restrained through modesty from the nature of her disorder, or rather, as Chrysostom says, it might have been the sense of her ceremonial uncleanness which held her back.

28. "For she said, If I may touch but his clothes, I shall be whole." Chrysostom, unlike many modern commentators, instead of drawing attention to the want of faith exhibited in what she did, notices the strength of her faith. "For she did not doubt, nor say in herself, 'Shall I indeed be delivered from the disease? shall I indeed fail of deliverance?' But confident of her [sure restoration to] health, she so approached Him, for she said, 'If I may only touch his garment I shall be whole.' Yea, for she saw out of what

29 And straightway the fountain of her blood was dried up; and she felt in *her* body that she was healed of that plague.

30 And Jesus, immediately knowing in himself that ⁵ virtue had gone out of him, turned him about in the press, and said, Who touched my clothes?

⁵ Luke vi. 19.
& viii. 46.

---

30. "Knowing in himself that virtue had gone out of him." Revisers, "Perceiving in himself that the power proceeding from him had gone forth." So Vulg., *Cognoscens in semet ipso virtutem, quæ exierat de eo*.

manner of house He was come, that of the publican, and who they were that followed Him, sinners and publicans, and all these things made her to be of good hope."

But men blame her ignorance that she should think to steal healing virtue from the Lord by a mechanical act. As to her ignorance, she had to do with One Who "can have compassion on the ignorant," and He had compassion on her.

And in what consisted her ignorance? Not in her believing, as she did, that our Lord's Person overflowed with healing virtue, but in her imagining that this could be communicated to her without His knowledge, and apart from His Will.

Call it ignorance, or call it superstition, as we will, whatever was wrong in it the Lord pardoned, and then met, and rewarded her faith, for we read,

29. "And straightway the fountain of her blood was dried up .... that plague." The cure was instantaneous, and she was conscious of it. And so if the Lord will, the cure of any sin or evil habit may be instantaneous, and we may be conscious that the power of Christ has been manifested in us.

30. "And Jesus immediately knowing, &c., .... who touched my clothes?" This conduct of the Lord is exceedingly remarkable, for He speaks for the moment as if power had gone out of Him independent of His own will. In St. Luke it is still more emphatic: "I perceive that virtue is gone out of me." We should rather have expected Him to say: "Someone came behind Me to be healed, and touched Me, and I healed her, but I cannot suffer My act to be concealed." Now, the Lord speaks as if He desired to emphasize the fact that power or virtue was actually lodged (if one may use the expression) in His Body, and that that power or virtue would

31 And his disciples said unto him, Thou seest the multitude thronging thee, and sayest thou, Who touched me?

32 And he looked round about to see her that had done this thing.

33 But the woman fearing and trembling, knowing what

---

be given to the faith which discerned that this power or virtue was in His Body, or human person: in fact, the word must be spoken, He acted as if He would by this miracle adumbrate His Sacramental action in His Church, and prepare men to approach Him through the Sacramental Elements.

It was given to this woman to discern a stupendous truth, that the Lord's Human Person was full of healing power: but providentially it was not given to her to realize how the reception of this virtue depended on an act of the Lord's will—providentially, I say, for if she had realized this we should not, humanly speaking, have had this miracle and its wondrous teaching. If anyone hesitates about accepting this fulness of power in the Lord's Body, let him ponder over the words of the Spirit: "In him dwelleth all the fulness of the Godhead bodily" (Col. ii. 9).

31. "And his disciples . . . sayest thou, Who touched me?" The Lord instantly discerned the touch of faith. The touch of the crowd was that of mere external nearness, of indifference, perhaps of rudeness—aimless, purposeless, but the touch of the woman was for a purpose. The disciples (of whom Peter was the mouthpiece) have been blamed for their want of spiritual discernment, but how could they have divined that such an one was in the crowd with such secret thoughts respecting the Lord?

32. "And he looked round about to see her that had done this thing." It is very characteristic of St. Mark, and adds much to the vividness of this picture, that he on this and other occasions, notices the very look of the Lord (thus iii. 34 and x. 21). We can think we see Him scanning the crowd with a searching eye, and all wondering at the sudden pause—wondering at the Lord looking so earnestly into their faces—except one who had a sort of guilty consciousness of the meaning of it all, and would have hid herself, but found that that could not be.

33. "But the woman fearing and trembling . . . all the truth." Why did the Lord thus compel the woman to come forward, and

was done in her, came and fell down before him, and told him all the truth.

---

33. "In her." So A., most later Uncials, almost all Cursives, Vulg. [*in se*]; but אֵ, B., C., D., L., a few Cursives, some Old Latin (a has *ei*), Syriac, "to her."

declare before the crowd her uncleanness, and the virtue which she had received at the moment of the touch?

For three reasons especially. First, for the woman's own sake. Had she been allowed to carry away her blessing in secret, as she purposed, it would not have been at all the blessing to her and to her whole after spiritual life that it now was when she was obliged by this repeated question of the Lord to acknowledge that she had come to seek, and that she had found, help and healing.

Then, secondly, it was only by the confession which the Lord compelled her to make that the Church in all ages has seen in her so remarkable an example of faith of no common sort, a faith which realized not only the power of the Lord's Will, but the virtue and grace of the Second Adam in His human bodily Presence. Her faith which realized the virtue of His Body for the purpose of bodily healing, must be in us when we draw near to the Sacrament of His Body for the purposes of Spiritual healing. Her faith is that which animates our prayer of humble access. "Grant us, gracious Lord, so to eat the Flesh of Thy Son Jesus Christ and to drink His Blood, that our sinful bodies may be made clean by His Body and our souls washed through His most precious Blood;" and that of our prayer of Consecration, "Grant that we, receiving these Thy creatures of bread and wine, according to thy Son Jesus Christ's Holy Institution, in remembrance of His Death and Passion, may be partakers of His most Blessed Body and Blood."

And in the third place, the healing and the manner of it was made public in order to sustain the faith of Jairus. So Chrysostom: "Moreover the ruler of the synagogue, who was on the point of thorough unbelief, and so of utter ruin, He corrects by the example of the woman. Since both they that came said, 'Trouble not the master, for the damsel is dead,' and those in the house laughed him to scorn when He said 'She sleepeth,' it was likely that the father too should have experienced some such feeling."

34. "And he said unto her, Daughter, thy faith . . . . whole of thy plague." It was His power that had made her whole, but her

GO IN PEACE.

34 And he said unto her, Daughter, [h] thy faith hath made thee whole; go in peace, and be whole of thy plague.

[h] Matt. ix. 22. ch. x. 52. Acts xiv. 9.

35 [i] While he yet spake, there came from the ruler of the synagogue's *house certain* which said, Thy daughter is dead: why troublest thou the Master any further?

[i] Luke viii. 49.

36 As soon as Jesus heard the word that was spoken, he saith unto the ruler of the synagogue, Be not afraid, only believe.

---

34. "Thy faith hath made thee whole;" rather, "hath saved thee." The terms used to signify temporal or bodily healing marvellously run up into spiritual healing.

36. "As soon as." So A., C., later Uncials, most Cursives; but omitted by א, B., D., L., some Cursives, Old Latin, Syriac, and some versions.

"Jesus heard." So A., C., D., later Uncials, almost all Cursives, Old Latin, Vulg.; but א, B., L. read, "took no heed, neglected" [what was said].

faith had laid hold of His power, and won from Him the exercise of His healing Will. And this is a parable for us. We have not to come to Him to steal a blessing, but to receive one, which He, in the most open way, offers to our acceptance in His Church.

"Go in peace." "For thou hast in no way offended Me, but hast pleased Me in that thou hast set an example of faith to My people in all ages."

"Be whole of thy plague." But was not the woman already whole? Yes, but may not this be an assurance to her that her plague should never return again?

35. "While he yet spake, there came . . . . why troublest thou the Master any further?" Hitherto He had not shown His power over death, and so there may be an excuse for the message, but surely there might be some consolation in the words of such a Master! His presence need not be out of place in the house of mourning. There is a curtness and abruptness in this message which savours of unbelief.

36. "As soon as Jesus heard [or not heeding] the word . . . . Be not afraid, only believe." Jesus, perceiving the mischief which the message might work, at once put in a comforting and hope-inspiring word, "Be not afraid, only believe."

Belief is in one sense the only thing needful, because it is the one condition on which we can receive salvation and grace from the Lord. But what does the Lord here mean by "only believe?"

37 And he suffered no man to follow him, save Peter, and James, and John the brother of James,

38 And he cometh to the house of the ruler of the synagogue, and seeth the tumult, and them that wept and wailed greatly.

<small>38. "He cometh." So L., later Uncials, almost all Cursives, Old Latin (a, c, f), some versions; but ℵ, A., B., C., D., F., two Cursives (1, 33), Old Latin (b, e, g), Vulg., Coptic, Syriac read, "they come."</small>

Only believe what? Why, evidently, that "I have power after death, that My might reaches beyond death, beyond the grave." If the man believed that his daughter was dead, and the Lord bid him "fear not," it must mean "fear not, but that I will give her to you again." If He added to this "fear not" the words "only believe," it must mean, "Believe that I am life to the dead. You may not know how, but let not your faith in Me fail, and you shall see."

If it be said that this was too much to require of this ruler, we can only answer that the Lord thought otherwise. The man had known of the healing of the centurion's servant, and of the woman with the issue, most probably also of the casting out of the devils out of the Gergesenes; and we know not how many more mighty works performed in Capernaum, and around the borders of the lake, and now he was asked to go one step further in the same road, *i.e.*, to believe that death was not the termination of the Lord's power.

37. "And he suffered no man to follow him, save Peter, and James, and John," &c. The three who were to be witnesses of His Transfiguration, and of His Agony.

38. "And he cometh to the house .... wept and wailed greatly." From the parallel words in St. Matthew, "Saw the minstrels and the people making a noise," there is no doubt that these were hired mourners, such as are described in Jeremiah ix. 17, 18: "Consider ye, and call for the mourning women that they may come; and send for cunning women, that they may come, and let them make haste, and take up a wailing for us, that our eyes may run down with tears, and our eyelids gush out with waters."

Dr. Thomson, in "The Land and the Book," says: "Every particular here alluded to is observed on funeral occasions at the present day. There are in every city and community women exceedingly cunning in this business. These are always sent for and kept in readiness. When a fresh company of sympathizers comes in,

39 And when he was come in, he saith unto them, Why make ye this ado, and weep? the damsel is not dead, but <sup>k</sup> sleepeth.                                                                      <sup>k</sup> John xi. 11.

40 And they laughed him to scorn. <sup>l</sup> But when   <sup>l</sup> Acts ix. 40. he had put them all out, he taketh the father and the mother of the damsel, and them that were with him, and entereth in where the damsel was lying.

41 And he took the damsel by the hand, and said unto her, TALITHA CUMI; which is, being interpreted, Damsel, I say unto thee, arise.

42 And straightway the damsel arose, and walked; for she was *of the age* of twelve years. And they were astonished with a great astonishment.

---

41. "CUMI." Neutral Text reads, *cūm*, without final *i*, but manifestly wrong, as the final letter is the sign of the feminine imperative.

these women 'make haste' to take up a wailing, that the newly come may the more easily unite their tears with the mourners. They know the domestic history of every person, and immediately strike up an impromptu lamentation, in which they introduce the names of their relations who have recently died, touching some tender chord of every heart, and thus each weeps for his own dead."

39. "And when he was come in, he saith .... sleepeth." There can be little doubt but that the Saviour here employs the same way of speaking as when He says, "Our friend Lazarus sleepeth, but I go that I may awake him out of sleep;" and immediately afterwards He told them plainly, "Lazarus is dead." Some have said that the maiden had fallen into the death-like swoon which often precedes, and then passes into actual death; but those watching her must have been conscious that so far as the help of man was concerned, all was over, or they would not have sent the message to the ruler which they did.

40. "And they laughed him to scorn." This ridicule would be stimulated by their interests, for their wages as mourners depended on the death having actually taken place.

"Them that were with him." Only Peter, James, and John.

41, 42. "And he took the damsel by the hand .... Talitha cumi .... astonishment." The very Syriac or Aramaic words

43 And ᵐ he charged them straitly that no man should know it; and commanded that something should be given her to eat.

ᵐ Matt. viii. 4.
& ix. 30. & xii.
16. & xvii. 9.
ch. iii. 12.
Luke v. 14.

---

which the Lord used are here preserved by the Evangelist, doubtless from the recollection of St. Peter. The words properly translated are, "Girl, arise." Quesnel's remarks on this are well worth reproducing: "The sacred Humanity is, as it were, the hand and instrument of the Divinity, to which it is united in the person of the Word. It is from this Humanity that our life proceeds, because it was in this that Christ died and rose again, and completed His Sacrifice. He is man, since He takes the dead person by the hand; He is God since He commands her to live, and to arise, and is immediately obeyed."

43. "And he charged them straitly .... given her to eat." It is to be noticed that in the case of the Gergesene demoniac, after healing He bade him make known what God had done for Him, and He Himself compelled the woman, in the last miracle, to confess her healing before the crowd. How is it that here He forbids the parents to make it known? Very probably He foresees how in some cases the fame of some mighty deed might be an hindrance to, as in other cases it might forward His real work.

Or in each He might have had regard to the spiritual temperament of those whom He charged. Canon Farrar has a good remark: "If He added His customary warning, that they should not speak of what had happened, it was not evidently in the intention that the entire fact should remain unknown, for that would have been impossible, when all the circumstances had been witnessed by so many, but because those who had received from God's hand unbounded mercy are more likely to reverence that mercy with adoring gratitude, if it be kept like a hidden treasure in the inmost heart."

"And commanded that something should be given her to eat." There must be some reason why this is specifically mentioned. It may have been to show the completeness of the recovery, in that one, a short time before so utterly prostrated and weak, should be able to take ordinary nourishment. It may be mentioned for a mystical significance, that those to whom God has given spiritual life, require spiritual food for its continuance.

## CHAP. VI.

AND ªhe went out from thence, and came into his own country; and his disciples follow him. ª Matt. xiii. 54. Luke iv. 16.

2 And when the sabbath day was come, he began to teach in the synagogue: and many hearing *him* were astonished, saying, ᵇFrom whence ᵇ John vi. 42.

---

2. "And many." B., L., with four Cursives read, "The many," *i.e.* the most, the greatest part; but ℵ, A., C., D., later Uncials, and almost all Cursives as in Rec. Text.

1. "And he went out from thence, and came into his own country," &c. From thence, *i.e.* from Capernaum.

"Came into his own country." The things related in the following verses, as occurring immediately after the raising to life of the little maid, are related by St. Matthew as following close upon the setting forth of the parable in the 13th chapter. We have, I think, no certain key to the right order. A question of more interest is, Was this journey to Nazareth, and preaching there, the same as that related in Luke iv.? We can hardly think so, for though there are one or two points of resemblance, yet St. Matthew and St. Mark would certainly not have omitted all reference to the exhibition of angry feeling in the synagogue, when His enemies attempted His life, and He escaped by miracle. We must account this a second visit to Nazareth, in order to give His own city one more opportunity of receiving Him as the Messiah.

"And his disciples follow him." What means this passing remark? Did they not always follow Him, or does it mean that He went on this occasion some way in front? He may have wished to show to His townsmen that He was not now the despised, lonely Teacher which they had once known Him to be; but, like other rabbis, had a retinue of disciples who had given up all to follow Him.

2. "And when the sabbath was come, . . . wrought by his hands?" How besotted they were! Instead of receiving in faithful hearts what they acknowledged to be superhuman wisdom, and

hath this *man* these things? and what wisdom *is* this which is given unto him, that even such mighty works are wrought by his hands?

3 Is not this the carpenter, the son of Mary, <sup>c</sup> the brother of James, and Joses, and of Juda, and Simon? and are not his sisters here with us? And they <sup>d</sup> were offended at him.

<sup>c</sup> See Matt. xii. 46. Gal. i. 19.
<sup>d</sup> Matt. xi. 6.

2. "That even such mighty works are wrought." A., C². , E., F., G., H., M., S., and a large number of Cursives read, "And whence are such mighty works wrought?" The MSS., &c. are so conflicting upon the separate words that the true reading is very doubtful. The Revisers translate, "And what mean such mighty works wrought by his hands!"

availing themselves of His mighty power for the healing of their sick, they asked whence it all came from, insinuating apparently that it was from beneath, not from above.

3. "Is not this the carpenter, the son of Mary, &c.?" This seems to teach that the Lord Himself had worked in the shop of his foster-father. The reader has, no doubt, seen a passage quoted from one of the earliest of the Fathers, Justin Martyr, a native of Palestine, who writes thus:—"And when Jesus came to the Jordan, He was considered to be the son of Joseph the carpenter; and He appeared without comeliness, as the Scriptures declared; and He was deemed a carpenter (for He was in the habit of working as a carpenter when among men, making ploughs and yokes; by which He taught the symbols of righteousness and an active life)."

"The son of Mary." The omission of St. Joseph's name seems to show that that saint of God had long been called to his rest.

"The brother of James, and Joses (Joseph), and of Juda, and Simon?" Not His uterine brothers, but most probably His cousins; not the sons of Joseph by a former wife, for the two first, James and Joses, are called in this very Gospel (xv. 40) the children of another Mary, who stood at the foot of the cross. (See Excursus at the end of this volume.)

"And they were offended at him." They could not bear to think that one whom they had known so familiarly was now so immeasurably their superior. His reputation was not so sufficiently recognized by the world that they should be proud of Him; and the whole line of His teaching being so unworldly, forbids that they should look for advancement from Him.

CHAP. VI.]  HE MARVELLED.  113

4 But Jesus said unto them, ᵉ A prophet is not without honour, but in his own country, and among his own kin, and in his own house.   ᵉ Matt. xiii. 57. John iv. 44.

5 ᶠ And he could there do no mighty work, save that he laid his hands upon a few sick folk, and healed *them*.   ᶠ See Gen. xix. 22. & xxxii. 25. Matt. xiii. 58. ch. ix. 23.

6 And ᵍ he marvelled because of their unbelief. ʰ And he went round about the villages, teaching.   ᵍ Is. lix. 16. ʰ Matt. ix. 35. Luke xiii. 22.

---

4. "But Jesus." ℵ, B., C., D., L., two Cursives, most Old Latin, Vulg., Syriac, and Coptic read, "And Jesus;" but A., most later Uncials, almost all Cursives, and many versions read as in Authorized.

4. "But Jesus said unto them, A prophet is not without honour," &c. Jesus speaks of this as an universal truth, and, indeed, it is rooted in our nature to look down upon those with whom we are, or have been, familiar, and whom we have watched in the days of their infancy and weakness. But in an extended sense it applies to the people of the Jews. The Lord is now held in most dishonour by His own nation, whilst the Gentiles worship Him as a Person in the Godhead.

5. "And he could there do no mighty work," &c. It was His will to demand that those who came to Him for healing should believe that He was able to do the thing which they came to Him for. He would allow no tentative requests. Before He raised Lazarus, He set Himself forth to Martha as the Resurrection and the Life, and then put the direct question to her, "Believest thou this?" He *could* then do no miracles consistently with the rule He laid down, and which His Father had laid down for Him. It is necessary to draw attention to this, because some commentators, even believing ones, speak as if faith gave a man a sort of physical capacity for receiving benefits from Christ, just as faith in a physician is supposed to be a considerable step to the recovery of the patient.

6. "And he marvelled because of their unbelief." The reader cannot but contrast this marvelling at the unbelief of His townsmen with His wonder at the faith of the Gentile centurion. The Lord's true human nature, not crushed or obliterated by the indwelling of the Divine, was affected as our human nature is. It was astonished at that which is unlooked for, and in a way unnatural,

I

**HE CALLED THE TWELVE.** [St. Mark.

7 ¶ ¹And he called *unto him* the twelve, and began to
send them forth by two and two; and gave them
power over unclean spirits;

¹ Matt. x. 1.
ch. iii. 13, 14.
Luke ix. 1.

---

just as it was grieved at hardness of heart, and loved with a human as well as with a Divine love, and shrunk at the near approach of frightful suffering.

Lange has a very suggestive remark on the conduct of the Nazarenes. "The history of Nazareth has been repeated on a large scale in the history of Israel. Israel, as a whole, also made the nearness of Jesus, His external, 'not being afar off,' an occasion of unbelief, and fell. . . . This temptation . . . besets the dependents and fellow-citizens of chosen spirits, theologians in the daily study and service of the truths of revelation, ministers in their commerce with the ordinances of grace, and all the lesser officers of the house of God in their habitual contact with the externals of Divine things." This temptation is well expressed in the common saying, "familiarity breeds contempt."

7. "And he called unto him the twelve, and began . . . spirits." In St. Matthew's Gospel this mission of the twelve takes place after the Lord looked on the multitudes, and had compassion on them, and had bid those about Him to "pray the Lord of the harvest that he would send forth labourers into his harvest." This was some little time after the healing of Jairus's daughter, and the restoration of sight to two blind men. St. Mark, as is his wont, gives the words of the Lord with much less fulness than St. Matthew, who appends to the first short address as given in St. Mark some further instructions (x. 16-42).

St. Chrysostom remarks on the Lord not sending forth His Apostles till they had been well prepared and grounded in the true faith of His Messiahship: "Mark, I pray you, also, how well timed was the mission. For not at the beginning did He send them forth, but when they had enjoyed sufficiently the advantage of following Him, and had seen a dead person raised, and the sea rebuked, and devils expelled, and a paralytic new strung, and sins remitted, and a leper cleansed, and had received a sufficient proof of His power, both by deeds and words, then He sends them forth."

"And began." This was evidently their first mission.

"To send them forth by two and two." This is noticed only

CHAP. VI.]  NO SCRIP, NO BREAD, NO MONEY.  115

8 And commanded them that they should take nothing for *their* journey, save a staff only; no scrip, no bread, no ‖ money in *their* purse:

‖ The word signifieth a piece of brass money, in value somewhat less than a farthing, Matt. x. 9, but here it is taken in general for money, Luke ix. 3.

by St. Mark, who in his list of the names of the Apostles does not group them by pairs; whereas they are so grouped by St. Matthew and St. Luke, who say nothing of this sending by two and two. This is an undesigned coincidence worth remembering, as sustaining the naturalness, and so the truth, of the three-fold narrative.

He sent them "two and two that they might have the mutual help and comfort of one another's fellowship, in this resisting and rebellious world; because they were yet like us, poor weak men, not filled with the mighty rushing of the Holy Ghost, which after came on them, and enabled them to go (*sive binos, sive solos*, in pairs, or singly), as the Spirit should best direct them." From Ludolph's "Life of Christ," quoted in Ford.

"And gave them power over unclean spirits." It is remarkable that this casting out of evil spirits should be the first and foremost part of this their first commission to represent the Lord. It would impress upon them that, as Christ came to destroy the works of the devil, so the first work of His ministers is opposition to the Evil One. Their first crusade was not so much against the evils of humanity as against him who is himself the root of all evil.

8. "And commanded them . . . no money in their purse." In other words, they were to depend upon the providence of God, not only from day to day but from hour to hour—they were to make no provision for their next meal, no scrip in which to hold any provision, no money wherewith to purchase provision. They were to depend entirely upon God opening the hearts of those to whom they preached to give them their needful food and lodging. The reader will remember that the Lord subsequently appeals to the care which God took of them. "When I sent you without purse, and scrip, and shoes, lacked ye any thing? And they said, Nothing." (Luke xxii. 35.)

9 But ᵏ *be* shod with sandals; and not put on two coats.

ᵏ Acts xii. 8.
ˡ Matt. x. 11.
Luke ix. 4. &
x. 7, 8.

10 ¹ And he said unto them, In what place soever ye enter into an house, there abide till ye depart from that place.

ᵐ Matt. x. 14.
Luke x. 10.
ⁿ Acts xiii. 51.
& xviii. 6.

11 ᵐ And whosoever shall not receive you, nor hear you, when ye depart thence, ⁿ shake off the dust under your feet for a testimony against them. Verily I say unto you, It shall be more tolerable for Sodom † and Gomorrha in the day of judgment, than for that city.

† Gr. *or*.

---

11. "And whosoever shall not receive you." א, B., L., and a few Cursives read, "whatsoever place;" but A., C²., D., later Uncials, almost all Cursives, Old Latin, Vulg., and Syriac read as in Rec. Text.

"Verily I say unto you, it shall be more tolerable . . . than for that city." This clause omitted by א, B., C., D., L., two Cursives (17, 28), some Old Latin (b, c), Vulg., and some versions; but A., later Uncials, most Cursives, some Old Latin (a, f), Syriac, and some versions as in Rec. Text.

9. "But be shod with sandals; and not put on two coats." The coat was a tunic, or shirt; a second over-tunic was worn by persons of more consideration. Neither of these was, of course, the long robe or cloak (Matt. v. 40). They were to go about as poor men would do.

10. "And he said unto them, In what place soever ye enter into an house," &c. This means, of course, that having taken up their abode in any house they were not to leave it in the hope of getting better lodgings, or provision, or attendance at a richer man's house. In fact, that they were both to be, and to show themselves, indifferent to worldly comfort.

11. "And whosoever [whatsoever place] shall not receive you, nor hear you," &c. "It is a token," says Jerome, "that they would receive nothing from them." Perhaps it may be, as Origen explains it, a solemn act of adjuration and appeal to the Judgment. The expression, "for a testimony against them," seems to have this force. (Williams.)

The latter clause, "Verily I say unto you, It shall be more tolerable," &c., is probably supplied from St. Matthew's gospel.

12 And they went out, and preached that men should repent.

13 And they cast out many devils, °and anointed with oil many that were sick, and healed *them*.

° James v. 14.

---

12. "And they went out, and preached that men should repent." This was always the first message of the New Testament preacher. It was the first proclamation of the Baptist, of the Lord Himself, of St. Peter, of St. Paul. All preaching of the Gospel is unreal without it.

13. "And they cast out many devils, and anointed with oil many that were sick," &c. Some commentators gravely remind us that oil has medicinal virtues; but, as Calvin says, "Nothing is more unreasonable than to imagine that the Apostles employed ordinary and natural remedies, which would have the effect of obscuring the miracles of Christ. They were not instructed by our Lord in the art and science of healing, but, on the contrary, were enjoined to perform miracles which would arouse all Judea. I think, therefore, that this *anointing* was a visible token of spiritual grace, by which the healing that was administered by them was declared to proceed from the secret power of God; for, under the law, oil was employed to represent the grace of the Spirit."

The use of this anointing with oil in the case of the sick continued till the time of the writing of St. James's Epistle and was enjoined by him: " Is any sick among you? let him call for the elders of the Church, and let them pray over him, anointing him with oil in the name of the Lord: And the prayer of faith shall save the sick, and the Lord shall raise him up; and if he have committed sins, they shall be forgiven him" (v. 14, 15). Here the anointing mentioned by St. Mark is more directly connected with the grace of forgiveness (of course with prayer)—in other words, it is more sacramental; still, being used where there was hope of recovery, it does not appear to be the same as the later extreme unction. Of this, however, there can be no doubt, that the use of anointing with oil in a sacramental, or quasi-sacramental, sense, was universal in the Church from the earliest periods. It is distinctly mentioned by Tertullian as, in the second century, the means of miraculous healing. " Even Severus himself, the father of Antoninus, was mindful of the Christians. For he sought out also

14 ᵖ And king Herod heard *of him*; (for his name was spread abroad:) and he said, That John the Baptist was risen from the dead, and therefore mighty works do shew forth themselves in him.

ᵖ Matt. xiv. 1.
Luke ix. 7.

---

14. "And he said." B., D., two Uncials, some Old Latin (a, b) read, "They said;" but א, A., C., L., later Uncials, almost all Cursives, some Old Latin, Vulg., Coptic, Syriac, &c., read as in Rec. Text.

Proculus, a Christian, who was surnamed Torpacion, the steward of Euodia, who had once cured him by means of oil, and kept him in his own palace even to his death" ("Address to Scapula," iv). It is also mentioned by him as following upon Baptism: "After this, having come out from the bath, we are anointed thoroughly with a blessed unction, according to the ancient rule by which they were wont to be anointed for the priesthood with oil out of an horn. So in us also the anointing runneth over us bodily, but profiteth spiritually, as likewise in Baptism itself the act is carnal that we are dipped in the water, the effect spiritual that we are delivered from our sins."

14. "And king Herod heard of him . . . shew forth themselves in him." St. Matthew and St. Luke called Herod Tetrarch, which was, speaking strictly, his title as the ruler of the fourth part of the dominions of his father, but he might properly be called king, as ruling with royal power and state over the part which fell to his share.

"(For his name was spread abroad)." This parenthesis is an illustration of how St. Mark seems to lose no opportunity of noticing the impression which the works and teaching of Jesus made upon the people.

"And he said, That John the Baptist was risen from the dead." Herod's conscience smote him. He heard others speaking of the Lord as Elias—as the expected prophet—as one of the prophets, but remembering the virtues of him whom he had so wantonly murdered, he came to another conclusion; he exclaimed, "It is John the Baptist. He is risen from the dead, and therefore the powers of the unseen and eternal world energize in him."

Very probably Herod was an avowed Sadducee or Secularist, but this did not prevent his dread of a just retribution from conjuring up within him all sorts of uneasy fears, that he whom he had put, as he thought, out of the way, had, like others of the dead, returned to the earth to assert his innocence and terrify his persecutors.

CHAP. VI.] IT IS JOHN, WHOM I BEHEADED. 119

15 ᑫ Others said, That it is Elias. And others said, That it is a prophet, or as one of the prophets.   ᑫ Matt. xvi. 14. ch. viii. 28.

16 ʳ But when Herod heard *thereof*, he said, It is John, whom I beheaded: he is risen from the dead.   ʳ Matt. xiv. 2. Luke iii. 19.

17 For Herod himself had sent forth and laid hold upon

---

15. " Or as one." " Or " omitted by אּ, A., B., C., L., later Uncials, almost all Cursives, Vulg., Syriac, &c.; retained by D. It is most probably spurious.
16. " It is John, whom I beheaded." So A., C., later Uncials, most Cursives; but אּᶜ, B., D., L. read, " John whom I beheaded, he is risen." Vulg., *Quem ego decollavi Joannem hic a mortuis resurrexit*.
" From the dead." So A., later Uncials, almost all Cursives, Old Latin (b, c, d, f), and some versions; omitted by אּ, B., L., and two Cursives (33, 102).

Theological or dogmatic acknowledgment is one thing, practical belief is another. Olshausen well says, " A consistent carrying out of their sentiments on the part of such sensualists is not to be looked for; they deny the reality of what is Divine, yet amidst their very denial their heart quakes with the secret belief of it."

15. " Others said, That it is Elias. And others said, That it is a prophet [or] as," &c. According to the prophecy of Malachi a personal advent or resurrection of Elijah was expected before the coming of the Messiah.

There can be little doubt but that the " or " between the two last clauses of this verse is spurious, and being so, we should understand the sense to be, " It is a prophet, as one of the prophets," that is, that a prophet has appeared in all the mighty power of one of the former prophets, " of the old prophets," as St. Luke has it.

16. " But when Herod heard thereof, he said, It is John, whom I beheaded," &c. [the John whom I beheaded is risen]. The " others," *i.e.*, the holders of the various opinions respecting Jesus, surmised according to their religious belief or their imagination, Herod according to his guilty conscience.

17. " For Herod himself had sent forth and laid hold upon John," &c. It is to be remarked that the whole of what follows (to verse 30), respecting the martyrdom of John the Baptist, is given simply to account for the fact that Herod supposed Jesus to be no other than the Baptist returned again to this world. If it had not been for this, we should, most prabably, have had to rely upon the meagre account in Josephus for all that we could know respecting

John, and bound him in prison for Herodias' sake, his brother Philip's wife: for he had married her.

<sup>s</sup> Lev. xviii. 16. & xx. 21.
18 For John had said unto Herod, *It is not lawful for thee to have thy brother's wife.

¶ Or, *an inward grudge.*
19 Therefore Herodias had ‖ a quarrel against him, and would have killed him; but she could not:

<sup>t</sup> Matt. xiv. 5. & xxi. 26.
20 For Herod <sup>t</sup> feared John, knowing that he

---

18. "For John had said." Properly, "said," *i.e.* "continually said."
19. "Had a quarrel with him." Perhaps, "Set himself against him." Vulg., *Insidiabatur illi.*

the martyrdom of this great servant of God. So true is it that the Gospel was written for one purpose, to reveal what relates to the person and work of the Lord Jesus.

It is also to be noticed that the account in St. Mark, being much the most circumstantial, is more in favour of Herod, as it shows that not he, but Herodias, was the real cause of the persecution and murder of St. John.

"For Herodias' sake, his brother Philip's wife." This Herodias was the daughter of Aristobulus, his brother. She first married Philip, son of Herod the Great, and so her own uncle, thereby committing incest, and afterwards she deserted him for this Herod Antipas, thereby adding adultery to her incest.

18. "For John had said [or was continually saying] to Herod," &c. We learn from St. Luke that not only for this, but for *all* the evil which Herod had done, did St. John reprove him. Even if Philip had been dead, and there had been no relationship between them, yet according to Levit. xviii. 16 and xx. 21, it would have been unlawful for Herod to have married her.

19. "Therefore Herodias had a quarrel against him [or set herself against him—Revisers]," &c. No doubt she feared the preaching and reproofs of the holy man, lest they should work repentance in her paramour, and move him to discard her for his former wife whom he had divorced.

20. "For Herod feared John, knowing that he was a just man and an holy," &c. How was it that a king, having all power of life and death, feared a poor prisoner who was entirely at his mercy? Simply because evil has a divinely implanted instinct

## CHAP. VI.] HE DID MANY THINGS.

was a just man and an holy, and || observed him; and when he heard him, he did many things, and heard him gladly. ‖ Or, *kept him*, or, *saved him*.

21 And when a convenient day was come, that ᵘ Matt. xiv. 6.

---

20. "He did many things." So A., C., D., all later Uncials except L., all Cursives, Old Latin, Vulg., Syriac, &c.; but א, B., L., Coptic read, "he was perplexed."

within it that its power is but for a time, and that God must finally prevail against it, and judge it, and cast it out. There is nothing in all nature from which such a fear could arise. It could only come from God, the author of all good, and the hater and punisher of all evil.

"And observed him." Rather kept him in safe keeping, or custody, so that though he was a prisoner he was safe from the malice and wiles of Herodias.

"And when he heard him, he did many things, and heard him glady." "He did many things." Perhape this meane he was induced by the preaching or advice of the Baptist to do some acts of charity, or of common justice, or to initiate some reforms, but the one thing needful he did not do,—he did not repent and forsake sin, and put away the evil woman who was the curse of his life.

The reader will notice the extraordinary difference of reading in the MSS. of the (so called) Neutral Text: instead of "He did many things," they read, "He was much perplexed:" but this reading can only be accepted on the ground that it is a difficult, indeed an extremely unlikely one, as in direct opposition to the next words, "and heard him gladly." It is very likely that he should "do many things and hear St. John gladly." It is extremely unlikely that he should be perplexed and hear him gladly. (See Dean Burgon's "Revision Revised," p. 66.

"And heard him gladly." Here again is the God-implanted homage which vice pays to virtue. Men who have no desire to be holy, and good, and just, like to hear the claims of holiness, and goodness, and justice, warmly and eloquently asserted. Perhaps they secretly flatter themselves that loving to hear the praises of virtue shows that they have some good thing yet left in them—that they are not wholly abandoned to their own evil selves.

21. "And when a convenient day was come," &c. A convenient day, that is, an opportune or favourable day for carrying out the machinations against the life of the Baptist.

## 122   HEROD ON HIS BIRTHDAY.   [St. Mark.

Herod on his birthday made a supper to his lords, high
<sup>x</sup> Gen. xl. 20.   captains, and chief *estates* of Galilee;

22 And when the daughter of the said Herodias came in,
and danced, and pleased Herod and them that sat with him,
the king said unto the damsel, Ask of me whatsoever thou
wilt, and I will give *it* thee.

<sup>y</sup> Esth. v. 3, 6.   23 And he sware unto her, <sup>y</sup> Whatsoever thou
& vii. 2.   shalt ask of me, I will give *it* thee, unto the half
of my kingdom.

24 And she went forth, and said unto her mother, What
shall I ask? And she said, The head of John the Baptist.

25 And she came in straightway with haste unto the king,

---

22. "The daughter of the said Herodias." So A., C., later Uncials, almost all Cursives, Old Latin, Vulg., Syriac; but א, B., D., L., adopt the reading, "her daughter Herodias," contrary to the testimony of St. Matthew, who calls her "the daughter of Herodias," and of Josephus, who calls her "Salome."

"To his lords, high captains, and chief estates"—lit. his magnates, chiliarchs, and principal or first men. It is very probable, from the fact that Herod was afraid of the faces of these men, in the matter of the performance of his wicked oath, that they were heathen.

22. "The daughter of the said Herodias." Probably the daughter of Herodias herself. This daughter of a king demeaned herself to act the part of a lascivious dancing girl in order to accomplish the designs of her mother. Josephus tells us her name was Salome. Nicephorus, a late ecclesiastical historian, preserves to us a tradition that she perished miserably in a manner which cannot but recall the wicked act in which she took so prominent a part; for, walking over some ice, it gave way, and she fell under the ice, which closing round her neck, nearly severed her head from her body by its sharp edges.

23. "And he sware unto her, Whatsoever thou shalt ask of me," &c. Very probably at her mother's instigation she insisted on a solemn oath in addition to the promise.

24, 25. "And she went forth .... The head of John the Baptist." No doubt the bad woman insisted on the head being given to her on a charger, not only that she might glut her revenge by the sight,

and asked, saying, I will that thou give me by and by in a charger the head of John the Baptist.

26. ˣ And the king was exceeding sorry; yet for his oath's sake, and for their sakes which sat with him, he would not reject her.

<small>ˣ Matt. xiv. 9.</small>

27. And immediately the king sent ‖ an executioner, and commanded his head to be brought: and he went and beheaded him in the prison,

<small>‖ Or, *one of his guard.*</small>

28 And brought his head in a charger, and gave it to the damsel: and the damsel gave it to her mother.

---

<small>27. "Sent an executioner." "A soldier of his guard" (Revisers).</small>

but that she might be sure that no ignoble criminal had been sacrificed in the stead of her enemy.

26. "And the king was exceeding sorry; yet for his oath's sake," &c. There cannot be a moment's hesitation respecting the keeping of such an oath. Not only for his own sake, but for the sake of Herodias and Salome, that their guilt should not be increased by the consummation of their wicked intention, he was bound to break such an engagement. He ought to have said, "The Baptist is a great prophet, and his life belongs to God, not to me. In demanding such a thing you have asked me to commit a fearful crime, and it is my duty to God, as well as to yourselves and to all around me, to confess my folly in volunteering such an oath, and to disregard it utterly."

"For their sakes which sat with him." As I said, they were very probably heathen officers and soldiers, and had no respect whatsoever for human life; certainly none for the life of such a fanatic as they supposed John to have been.

27. "And immediately the king sent an executioner [or one of his guards] .... prison." Josephus tells us that St. John was imprisoned in the fortress of Machærus, within the walls of which Herod the Great had built a palace. It is probable, then, that Herod was keeping this feast within the same building in which St. John was immured.

"And brought his head in a charger .... to her mother." This murder seems to have deeply affected the Jews, or those of them, at least, who respected this great preacher of righteousness,

29 And when his disciples heard *of it*, they came and took up his corpse, and laid it in a tomb.

<sup>a</sup> Luke ix. 10.   30. <sup>a</sup> And the apostles gathered themselves together unto Jesus, and told him all things, both what they had done, and what they had taught.

<sup>b</sup> Matt. xiv. 13.   31. <sup>b</sup> And he said unto them, Come ye yourselves apart into a desert place, and rest a while:

<sup>c</sup> ch. iii. 20.   for <sup>c</sup> there were many coming and going, and they had no leisure so much as to eat.

---

for according to Josephus, they thought that the total destruction of Herod's army, which occurred afterwards, came from God, and that very justly, as a punishment for what he did against John that was called the Baptist." ("Antiquities," xviii. 5, 2.)

29. "And when his disciples heard of it . . . in a tomb." It is somewhat uncertain why this is mentioned. Some think that his body was cast out of the prison unburied, and so his disciples found it, and gave it decent burial; others, that Herod, out of respect for the remains of the man he had so foully murdered, sent for the disciples of John, and delivered to them the corpse, that their loving hands might commit it to the ground with all due solemnity. The wording of the verse, however, is decidedly in favour of the former view.

30. "And the apostles gathered themselves together unto Jesus, and told him," &c. At this time also the disciples of John, having buried the dead body of their Master, "went and told Jesus" (Matt. xiv. 12); and we should gather from what follows in that Evangelist that it was on account of this—*i.e.*, lest Herod, having slain the forerunner, should seek out Him Whose way the forerunner prepared—that the Lord departed privately by ship into a desert place. But this could scarcely have been the reason, for the place to which He retired was not sufficiently distant, nor was the Lord's retirement sufficiently long to enable Herod to forget his purpose. St. Mark then gives the true reason in the following verse.

31. "And he said unto them, Come ye yourselves apart into a desert place," &c. The Apostles were well-nigh overwhelmed with their labours, for work had made work: they were cumbered with much serving—not preaching the Gospel only, but healing and

32 And ᵈ they departed into a desert place by ship privately.

33. And the people saw them departing, and many knew him, and ran afoot thither out of all cities, and outwent them, and came together unto him.

34. ᵉ And Jesus, when he came out, saw much

ᵈ Matt. xiv. 13.

ᵉ Matt. ix. 36. & xiv. 14.

---

33. "And the people saw them departing, and many knew him." The most probable reading is that of א, A., B., D., L., later Uncials, most Cursives, Vulg., &c., "And many saw them departing, and knew them [or him]." *Et viderunt eos abeuntes, et cognoverunt multi*, Vulg.

exorcising; their meals and needful rest was broken in upon by importunate crowds; and so the Lord, to teach us that His ministers must have time for needful refreshment, does not recruit them by a miracle, but insists upon their using natural means. "Come ye yourselves into a desert place, and rest awhile." And is it not so now? Is not many an active and self-denying minister well-nigh broken down and worn out, because there is no time for thought and rest, and tranquil meditation, and a change of scene? Rich men, with many-roomed mansions, could not do a greater kindness to poor over-worked priests than by inviting them, from their crowded streets and alleys, to find a little rest and leisure in their multitudes of unused apartments.

32, 33. "And they departed . . . and came together unto him." It seems almost cruel that the little leisure which Christ won for His disciples should be so soon broken in upon; but it must have been specially ordered by God, for if it had not been for this pursuit of the Lord by the crowd into the desert place, far away from any town or village where they could buy food, we should not have had one of the most stupendous of the Lord's mighty works—that of the miraculous feeding of the multitudes.

We now enter upon the miracle of the feeding of the five thousand with the five loaves and two fishes. This is the only one of our Lord's miracles of which we have an account in each of the four Evangelists; and by this its teaching is emphasized as of the utmost importance for us to realize. I gave the principles of this teaching very fully in my notes on St. Matthew. I shall now consider the details of the miracle, and what instruction we can gather from them.

34. "And Jesus, when he came out, saw much people, and was moved with," &c. His first thought was of their ignorance and

people, and was moved with compassion toward them, because they were as sheep not having a shepherd: and *he began to teach them many things.

*f* Luke ix. 11.

35. *g* And when the day was now far spent, his disciples came unto him, and said, This is a desert place, and now the time *is* far passed:

*g* Matt. xiv. 15. Luke ix. 12.

36. Send them away, that they may go into the country round about, and into the villages, and buy themselves bread: for they have nothing to eat.

---

36. "And buy themselves bread, for they have nothing to eat." So A., later Uncials, most Cursives, &c.; but Neutral Text reads, " buy themselves somewhat to eat."

spiritual destitution—" they were as sheep not having a shepherd." Those who had assumed to teach them—the Scribes and Pharisees—had fouled the waters of life to which they professed to lead them (Ezek. xxxiv. 18).

"And he began to teach them many things." St. Luke has: "He received them, and spake unto them of the kingdom of God, and healed those that had need of healing."

Let it be particularly noted that, in doing this, the Lord kept them from returning home, or to the neighbouring villages for food, knowing how He was about to supply their wants.

35, 36. "And when the day was now far spent . . . nothing to eat." From St. John's narrative we gather that when He first discerned the vast crowd, He suggested to one of the Apostles, Philip, the difficulty of supplying such a multitude with food. "Whence shall we buy bread, that these may eat?" This He said to prove him— to try and see, that is, whether Philip, having witnessed such mighty exhibitions of supernatural power, had faith to suggest one more; but there was no response, only an answer of perplexity: "Two hundred pennyworth of bread is not sufficient for them, that every one of them may take a little."

It has been supposed, and with some show of reason, that two hundred pence (denarii) was the sum that they had then in the purse or chest, because, according to our Evangelist, they suggested, "Shall we go and buy two hundred pennyworth of bread?" They could scarcely have mentioned such a sum, much less volunteered to go and purchase bread with it, unless they had it by them.

37 He answered and said unto them, Give ye them to eat. And they say unto him, ʰ Shall we go and buy two hundred ‖ pennyworth of bread, and give them to eat?

ʰ Numb. xi. 13, 22. 2 Kings iv. 43.
‖ *The Roman penny is seven pence halfpenny; as* Matt. xviii. 28.

37. "He answered and said unto them, Give ye them to eat." Upon this, they mentioned the two hundred pence; and then the Lord inquired, "How many loaves have ye? go and see."
Then it was that Andrew said, "There is a lad here which hath five barley loaves and two small fishes." We gather from St. Mark and St. Luke that this was their stock of provision for the night, and that the boy was only carrying it. For they said, "We have no more, but five loaves." It is exceedingly important to note this, for apparently they at once and cheerfully made an offering of all the night's provision, still, however, doubting whether it could be of any use: "What are they among so many?" (John vi. 9). If any of them had been selfish or churlish, they would have asked, "What shall we do for the evening meal?"
Isaac Williams brings this out feelingly and well: "It must be noticed that they had just retired to this desert, because they had no leisure so much as to eat, which makes it likely that this was the very provision they had taken with them. This was, therefore, in St. Andrew, the eldest of that company, a giving-up of all they had for themselves; this adds a force to such his free oblation. It was, indeed, but little for their own number; but we must remember that, on one occasion, we find the disciples plucking for hunger the ears of corn; at another, that when at sea they had forgotten to take bread; here they have retired to the desert to eat, and yet have but five barley loaves. It is amid an overwhelming multitude, faint and weary; in the desert, and in hunger; and man's helplessness is God's opportunity. In the desert came the manna; in the desert was Elijah sustained; and Elisha multiplied barley loaves; therefore, in childlike, wondering, inquiring faith, looked up the disciple, bringing the child with five loaves; not shaping to himself a definite thought, but gazing up, not without hope; in perplexity, but not in despair." If this be so, and it seems true to nature, this stupendous miracle was consequent upon an act of self-denial and unselfishness on the part of the Apostles. And equally willingly did they offer to part with all that might be

38 He saith unto them, How many loaves have ye? go
¹ Matt. xiv. 17. and see. And when they knew, they say, ¹ Five,
Luke ix. 13.
John vi. 9. and two fishes.
See Matt. xv.
34. ch. viii. 5. 39. And he commanded them to make all sit down by companies upon the green grass.

40 And they sat down in ranks, by hundreds, and by fifties.

---

in the bag. "Shall we go and buy two hundred pennyworth of bread, that these may eat?"

39. "And he commanded them to make all sit down by companies." This is not mentioned by St. Matthew, nor by St. John, but it was evidently a necessity. Unless they were orderly arranged in groups, and all keeping their places, such a company could not have been fed before midnight. Such an arrangement is a foreshadowing of the parochial or territorial system of the Church, assigning definite districts with manageable numbers to individual priests, so that all may be within reach of instruction and worship, and none may be overlooked.

"Upon the green grass"—green, because it was then, being Passover time, the finest spring time. During a great part of the year there is no green to be seen on these hills by the Galilean lake, all is brown and scorched. This, too, must have been the reminiscence of an observant witness, who had himself assisted in seating the multitudes.

40. "And they sat down in ranks, by hundreds, and by fifties." "In ranks"—that is, in plots, like beds or plots of plants, with gangways or paths between, as in a garden. In order that the Apostles who had the office of distribution might get easily at each man, in order to give him his portion, it has been conjectured, with much show of reason, that they were groups of double rows, of one hundred each, fifty in front, and one behind each—*i.e.*, only two deep. There must have been some arrangement like this, because if there were but fifty persons in a square crowd, or knot, there would be difficulty and confusion in reaching those in the middle. Wesley has, " by hundreds and fifties—*i.e.*, fifty in a rank, and one hundred in file."

The exact spot where all this occurred seems to be ascertained by Dr. Thomson, in his "Land and Book," to be at a place called

41 And when he had taken the five loaves and the two fishes, he looked up to heaven, ᵏ and blessed, and  ᵏ 1 Sam. ix. 13. Matt. xxvi. 26.

---

Butaiha. "This bold headland marks the spot, according to my topography, where the five thousand were fed with five barley loaves and two small fishes. From the four narratives of this stupendous miracle we gather, 1st, that the place belonged to Bethsaida ; 2nd, that it was a desert place ; 3rd, that it was near the shore of the lake, for they came to it by boat ; 4th, that there was a mountain close at hand ; 5th, that it was a smooth grassy spot capable of seating many thousand people. Now all these requisites are found in this exact locality, and nowhere else, as far as I can discover. This Butaiha belonged to Bethsaida. At the extreme south-east corner of it the mountain shuts down upon the lake bleak and barren. It was, doubtless, desert then as now, for it is not capable of cultivation. In this little cove the ships (boats) were anchored. On this beautiful sward at the base of the rocky hill the people were seated to receive from the hands of the Lord the miraculous bread, emblematic of His Body, which is the true bread from heaven." I would beg the reader to remember that this closing observation respecting the typical and sacramental significance of the feeding is not mine but Dr. Thomson's, who is, I believe, a Presbyterian. It illustrates how true Christians, when not on their guard to defend the particular tenets of their sect, approach the doctrine, and fall into the language of the Catholic Church.

41. "And when he had taken the five loaves and the two fishes," &c. I pray the reader to notice the solemn, mysterious circumstantiality of what follows. The loaves were not suffered to lie about the ground at His feet ; neither did He say, "Take them yourselves, and begin to divide, for the time hastens away." Each Evangelist expressly notices the solemnity of His "taking" them ; then three—the Synoptics—make express mention of His looking up to heaven, then "He blessed them ; " He blessed not God only as the Giver, but the loaves, the gift of God. St. John says, also, "He gave thanks." He eucharistisized, then "He brake." The Jewish loaves were thin broad cakes, and must be broken, but the breaking is in each account mentioned, as if in this case it was not a thing of course, but a part of a great solemnity ; then He gave, or as St. John has it, He distributed to the disciples. He gave,

brake the loaves, and gave *them* to his disciples to set before them; and the two fishes divided he among them all.

42 And they did all eat, and were filled.

---

apparently, none with His own hands to the people, only through the hands of the Apostles, yet every morsel, over and above the first scanty basketful, was the immediate creation of His power.

Such was the action of the Lord in feeding the five thousand. It clearly adumbrates a far more mysterious "taking" of bread, and blessing it, and breaking it, and giving it to the very men who were the agents in carrying out this miracle. The Lord's action in this miracle, and in the institution of the Eucharist, are so reported to us that the one in thought leads on to the other. And, if so with us, what must it all have been to those who were present at both—at the miracle, and at the institution? In fact, the Lord's action at this miracle prepared the Apostles for the outward circumstances of the institution, just as His discourse in John vi., arising out of this very miracle, prepared for the doctrine of the Divine Gift vouchsafed under the outward signs. When they saw Him repeat the action of "taking," most probably looking up to heaven, "blessing," "breaking," "giving" to each, they would remember what He had done before, and they would naturally expect some great thing; they would see no outward creation of bread, but they would remember the discourse at Capernaum, how He set forth Himself as the Bread of Life, how His Flesh was to be that Bread, how they who received it would have eternal life, and their faith in Him as the Bread of Life would be strengthened.

42. "And they did all eat, and were filled." That is, they did not eat only a little, just sufficient to keep them from fainting, but each one had a full meal. As I showed in my notes on St. Matthew, the miracle must have taken place in the hands of the Apostles. If it took place in the hands of the Lord, much time would have been lost by the disciples having to go to and fro from the place where He was standing, and then distributing to the various groups which, from their numbers and orderly arrangement, must have covered a large area. Neither could it have taken place in the hands of the multitude, or in their bodies, by enabling them to be satisfied and strengthened by a few crumbs, for then no such amount of fragments would have been left; but it miraculously increased in the

43 And they took up twelve baskets full of the fragments, and of the fishes.

44 And they that did eat of the loaves were about five thousand men.

45 ¹And straightway he constrained his disciples to get into the ship, and to go to the other

¹ Matt. xiv. 22.
John vi. 17.

---

44. "Were about five thousand." A., B., D., L., later Uncials, most Cursives, many Old Latin, Vulg., Coptic, Syriac omit "about."

---

hands of each Apostle. It grew, as it were, in their hands, and as they brake off piece by piece to each man, woman, and child, a multitude of broken pieces would necessarily fall to the ground.

43. "And they took up twelve baskets full of the fragments." That is, more than twelve times as much as was originally blessed. Theophylact (quoted in Ford) remarks well: "It was a proof of overflowing power not only to feed so many men, but also to leave such a superabundance of fragments. Even though Moses gave manna, yet what was given to each was measured by his necessity, and what was over and above was overrun by worms. Elias also fed the woman, but gave her just what was enough for her; but Jesus being the Lord, makes His gifts with superabundant profusion."

This very plentiful miraculous supply bears upon the truth of a saying, now often repeated, that God employs the miraculous with great parsimony. If by this is meant that He performs miracles at few times in the world's history, and through the instrumentality of very few persons, it is undoubtedly true. If miracles were common they would lose all their evidential power. But it is absolutely contrary to the truth to say that this parsimony applies to the life and acts of our Lord. He performs His miracles royally. There is no stint of supernatural power. It is not doled out by measure, but bountifully, generously, unsparingly.

45. "And straightway he constrained his disciples," &c. Here we must notice the fact which St. Mark omits, but is mentioned by St. John, that the people exclaimed, "This is of a truth that prophet which should come into the world." Close upon this we read, also in St. John, that "Jesus perceived that they would come and take him by force to make him a king."

In my commentary on St. John, I quoted a remark of Godet's

132 WHEN EVEN WAS COME. [St. Mark.

|| Or, *over against Bethsaida.* side before || **unto** Bethsaida, while he sent away the people.

46 And when he had sent them away, he departed into a mountain to pray.

m Matt. xiv. 23. John vi. 16, 17. 47 ᵐ And when even was come, the ship was in the midst of the sea, and he alone on the land.

---

46. "A mountain." "The mountain."

on the use of this word "constrained." Why should the Lord use constraint with them? It is generally explained as if their affection for Him would make them anxious not to leave Him alone, but may it not be that the disciples were in danger of being infected with the desire of the multitude to make Him a temporal King, and so He wished to preserve them from the temptation to join in asserting claims which would have destroyed the whole value of His work hitherto?

"Unto Bethsaida." Bethsaida Julias was at, or near, the extreme north of the lake, and Capernaum a little further to the west, where the shores just begin to bend southward. He probably directed them to skirt by the shore, so as to take Him up at some point where the Jordan enters the lake near Bethsaida. They would set out then towards Bethsaida, but their ultimate point would be further in the same direction, *i.e.*, at Capernaum.

46. "And when he had sent them away, he departed .... to pray." St. John seems to tell us that this departure was in order that He might escape from the importunity of the multitude, but may it not have been for both reasons? This was a great crisis in His history, for the misdirected zeal of the multitude was hurrying matters on too rapidly, His disciples might be perverted by it, and lose faith when He disappointed them. And yet the zeal of the multitude must be kept up, or they would not pursue Him to the other side, to Capernaum, and their zeal in following Him thither would be the direct occasion for the delivery of the most important and deeply mysterious of His discourses. All this was before Him, for His Father had given Him a commandment respecting what He should do, and what He should teach. He might well then retire to unbosom Himself to His Father.

47. "And when even was come, the ship was in the midst," &c. What even was this? It is generally assumed to be the evening of

48 And he saw them toiling in rowing; for the wind was
contrary unto them: and about the fourth watch of the night

---

the same day on which He fed the multitude, and so was what the
Jews called the second evening. But is this possible? The day was
declining when His disciples asked Him to send away the multitude.
After this came the arrangement of the vast number in plots or
groups, then the feeding till they were all filled, and then the dismissal of the crowd. I cannot but think that it must have been
the evening of the next day.

"The ship was in the midst of the sea." The wind had driven
it far from its course. St. John alone mentions the very great
violence of the storm. St. Matthew and St. Mark merely tell us
that "the wind was contrary."

48. "And He saw them toiling in rowing; for the wind was contrary." "And such is our success, when Jesus is not with us: we
labour against the stream of our corruptions, even against the wind
of a thousand temptations. Save us, O Jesu, or else we perish!
Come thou into the ship, and immediately we arrive at the haven
of our wishes." [W. Austin, quoted in Ford.]

"He saw them . . . . and about the fourth watch of the night
he cometh," &c. Notice how He had His eye upon them, but He
suffered them to toil on, and be in jeopardy for many hours, because they had not learnt their lesson of faith in His Almighty
power.

And do we not learn a lesson from this, that no matter what the
tempest of trouble we are in, He sees us, He has His eye upon us,
and is trying us, and will help us at the fitting moment? So Theophylact: "Now the Lord permitted His disciples to be in danger,
that they might have patience; wherefore He did not immediately
come to their aid, but allowed them to remain in danger all night,
that He might teach them to wait patiently, and not to hope at
once for help in tribulations."

I must refer the reader to my notes on St. Matthew for an extract from Chrysostom, bringing out, with great force, another
teaching of this miracle as compared with the former one when
Christ was asleep in the vessel when the storm raged. "It was
His purpose in all the events of this night to discipline and lead
them up to higher things than hitherto they had learned." Again,
another writer: "In the first storm (Matt. viii. 24) He was present

he cometh unto them, walking upon the sea, and [n] would have passed by them.

[n] See Luke xxiv. 28.

49 But when they saw him walking upon the sea, they supposed it had been a spirit, and cried out:

50 For they all saw him, and were troubled. And imme-

---

49. "A spirit." The word rather signifies "apparition." See below.

in the ship with them, and thus they must have felt all along that, if it came to the worst, they might arouse Him; while the mere sense of His presence must have given them the feeling of a comparative security. But He will not have them to be clinging only to the sense of His bodily presence, not as ivy, needing always an outward support, but as hardy forest trees which can brave a blast; and this time He puts them forth into the danger alone, even as some loving mother-bird thrusts her fledglings from the nest, that they may find their own wings and learn to use them

"And about the fourth watch of the night he cometh unto them, walking upon the sea." This miracle was not a law of nature suspended. It was rather one of the forces of nature counteracted by a superior force, that is, a Divine force or power. It was the law of gravity counteracted by the innate force or power of the will of the God-Man (see note in St. Matthew). Let us remember that the Lord did not make a calm, but walked on the sea at its roughest, for the wind did not cease till He had got unto the ship (verse 51).

"Would have passed by them." Compare with this, Luke xxiv. 28, when "He made as though he would have gone further," for this very purpose that He might make them evince their love of the truth in which He was instructing them by constraining Him to abide with them. God cannot effectually discipline us, without at times seeming to take no notice, so that we may be the more importunate in prayer. See also the parable of the Unjust Judge and of the friend who was unwilling to be disturbed.

49, 50. "But when they saw him walking .... troubled." A spirit, rather an apparition, *i.e.*, of some inhabitant of the unseen world. The word employed (phantasma) is quite different from that indicating a spirit (pneuma).

"They all saw him." This is peculiar to St. Mark, and the fact would have made a deep impression on one who was present.

diately he talked with them, and saith unto them, Be of good cheer: it is I; be not afraid.

51 And he went up unto them into the ship; and the wind

---

If all saw Him, how is that not one recognized Him? It may have been because of the darkness, but probably their eyes were holden.

"And saith unto them, Be of good cheer: it is I; be not afraid." Would our Lord have after this fashion walked on the sea, and after this fashion reassured His disciples, unless He was fully conscious of the Divine within Him? For it was the especial glory of God thus to walk on the waters: "Thy way is on the sea, and thy paths in the great waters." Here we have, as I remarked on iv. 39, the Lord acting, not only with the power, but with the majesty of God. "How often does it happen that Christ comes to His people, and they do not know Him! He comes to them in some unexpected trouble or bereavement, or disappointment, or worldly loss, and they do not recognize Him. He comes to them in love and they are full of fear. But let it once be brought home to them that it is really He, and what peace and comfort does this assurance bring with it, 'It is I, be not afraid'" (P. Young). Quesnel has a remarkable application, which is very illustrative of the revival of Catholic teaching in our Church in our own day: "There is sometimes a kind of mutiny in the ship of the Church, and a great clamour is raised at the hearing of certain truths, as if they were errors; and even those who sit at the helm are alarmed at a phantom which they fancy they see. But as soon as Christ speaks, and they are capable of hearing Him, His truth manifestly appears, their apprehensions vanish, and all grows quiet."

At this point comes in the episode of the miracle of St. Peter walking on the water to meet Jesus. The only reason why it is omitted in St. Mark, who is much more full in his account of the miracles than St. Matthew, must be the desire of St. Peter that what in a measure distinguished him, should be omitted. Thus the words of the Lord to St. Peter, "Thou art Peter, and upon this rock I will build my Church," are not to be found in this (St. Peter's) Gospel, though Christ's rebuke, which followed upon it, is given in full.

51, 52. "And he went up unto them ... their heart was hardened." This, their unbounded astonishment, was a sign of their unbelief—

ceased: and they were sore amazed in themselves beyond measure, and wondered.

<sup>o</sup> ch. viii. 17, 18.
<sup>p</sup> ch. iii. 5. & xvi. 14.
<sup>q</sup> Matt. xiv. 34.

52 For °they considered not *the miracle* of the loaves: for their <sup>p</sup>heart was hardened.

53 <sup>q</sup>And when they had passed over, they came into the land of Gennesaret, and drew to the shore.

---

51. "Beyond measure." So A., later Uncials, almost all Cursives; omitted by ℵ, B., L., Syriac; Vulg., *Plus magis intra se stupebant*.

"And wondered." So A., D., later Uncials, almost all Cursives, Old Latin, and Syriac; omitted by ℵ, B., L., some Cursives, and Vulg.

52. "For they considered not the miracle of the loaves." More literally as Revisers, "They understood not concerning the loaves." *Non enim intellexerunt de panibus*.

"For." So A., D., later Uncials, most Cursives, most Old Latin, Vulg., Syriac—ℵ, B., L., one Cursive (33) read, "but" instead of "for."

53. "Into the land of Gennesaret." So A., D., later Uncials, almost all Cursives, Old Latin, Vulg., Syriac, and versions; but ℵ, B., L., two Cursives, "They came to the land unto Gennesaret."

---

but unbelief in what? Not surely in His Messiahship, but in His Divine Power. His Messiahship they must have believed in, or they would not have followed Him, but what they were slow to believe was that He was the Son of God in the true and natural sense of the word, so that He could wield the full power of God. If they had duly considered the miracle of the loaves,—how such a thing could have taken place—they must have seen that it could be only by a direct creative act, *i.e.*, an act of God.

But here we have to note an apparent discrepancy of a very marked character between St. Mark's narrative and that of St. Matthew. St. Mark finishes his narrative with a notice of the unbelief of the Apostles—St. Matthew of their belief, "They that were in the ship came and worshipped him, saying, Of a truth thou art the Son of God." But the reconciliation is plain to a believer. They were sore amazed—their heart was hardened—till He called Peter to come to Him—till He returned with Peter into the ship—till the wind ceased. Then their unbelief was dispelled—then they at once fell down and worshipped Him and acknowledged Him to be the Son of God.

53. And when they had passed over . . . drew to the shore." St. John alone notices that as soon as they had taken the Lord into the ship it was immediately at the land whither they went; but he says nothing of what follows that.

## CHAP. VII.] STRAIGHTWAY THEY KNEW HIM. 137

54 And when they were come out of the ship, straightway they knew him,

55 And ran through that whole region round about, and began to carry about in beds those that were sick, where they heard he was.

56 And whithersoever he entered, into villages, or cities, or country, they laid the sick in the streets, and besought him that ʳ they might touch if it were but the border of his garment: and as many as touched ‖ him were made whole.

ʳ Matt. ix. 20.
ch. v. 27, 28.
Acts xix. 12.
‖ Or, *it*.

---

54. "When they were come out of the ship, straightway they [the men of that place] (Matt.), knew him; . . . those that were sick, where they heard he was." All this took place the day on which He lands, and the day before He was found, by those who had pursued Him, in the synagogue of Capernaum. He probably landed some way beyond Capernaum, but His arrival was soon discovered. This seems implied in the words of St. Matthew: "When the men of that place had knowledge of him."

55. "Where they heard he was." This seems to imply that He did not go at once to Capernaum, but continued, perhaps a day, in the neighbourhood.

56. "And whithersoever He entered . . . were made whole." As this is the first time we read of the touching of His garment as a recognized means of receiving healing, it is probable that it took its rise from the report of the blessing which the woman had received who had endeavoured in this way to snatch a secret cure.

## CHAP. VII.

THEN ᵃ came together unto him the Phari-   ᵃ Matt. xv. 1.

---

1. "Then came together unto him the Pharisees . . . Jerusalem." From the Greek word used to express "came together," Lange supposes that this meeting was of the nature of an ecclesias-

sees, and certain of the scribes, which came from Jerusalem.

2 And when they saw some of his disciples eat bread with ¹ Or, *common*. || defiled, that is to say, with unwashen, hands, they found fault.

---

1, 2. "Which came from Jerusalem. And when they saw some of his disciples eat bread." The Revisers, following אּ, B., L., and one Cursive (33) read, "Which had come from Jerusalem, and had seen that some of his disciples ate their bread," &c. ; but A., D., later Uncials, and most Cursives as in Rec. Text.

"They found fault." So some later Uncials, most Cursives, and Syriac; but א, A., B., E., G., H., L., and many Cursives omit. Old Latin and Vulg., *Vituperaverunt.*

tical investigation—" an official interference of the Sanhedrim with our Lord." Olshausen and most others, however, see no such marked official action. The Pharisees, we must remember, were a religious sect, or school, rather than an authorized public legal corporation.

"And when they saw some of his disciples eat bread," &c. "Some of his disciples," apparently not all. Some out of a body of twelve would be less scrupulous about such matters than others.

"With defiled, that is to say, with unwashen hands." Defiled, *i.e.*, not ceremonially cleansed, literally "common." Thus St. Peter says (Acts x. 14) with reference to the eating of animals forbidden in the Levitical law, "Not so, Lord, for I have never eaten anything that is common or unclean."

It is to be noticed that the explanation of the word "common" or "unwashen" is thrown in for the benefit of the Roman Gentile Christians, at whose immediate instance St. Mark wrote this Gospel. The same applies to the fuller explanation of Jewish ceremonial ablutions in the following verses. These washings, it must be remembered, were not done for the sake of cleanliness, but as religious observances over and above what the Law had commanded.

"They found fault." These words are not in the great majority of the older Uncial MSS. If they are to be omitted the two verses should be read, "And there were gathered together unto him [the] Pharisees, and certain of the Scribes, which had come from Jerusalem, and had seen that some of His disciples ate bread with defiled, that is, unwashen hands. For the Pharisees," &c.; and then, after the parenthesis which sets forth the Jewish ceremonial washing in

## HOLDING THE TRADITION.

3 For the Pharisees, and all the Jews, except they wash *their* hands || oft, eat not, holding the tradition of the elders.

4 And *when they come* from the market, except

|| Or, *diligently*: in the original, *with the fist*: Theophylact, *up to the elbow.*

---

3. "Oft." See below and also margin.

verses 3 and 4, the thread is resumed at verse 5: "And the Pharisees and Scribes ask him," &c.

3. "For the Pharisees, and all the Jews, except they wash their hands oft," &c. "All the Jews" are mentioned to show that the Pharisees were the leaders in this ultra ceremonialism, and that the whole body of the Jews had been influenced by them to conform to it.

"Wash their hands oft," or, as the margin has it, "diligently," or, in the original, "with the fist." Immense difficulty has been made of this expression "with the fist." One commentary now before me has three large closely-printed pages upon it; but I confess I cannot see any, or at least very little difficulty, in the matter. The ceremonial rule was that they were not merely to dip their fingers into the water, but to dip in both hands, and first to rub one hand with the other hand doubled up, or clenched, and then the second with the first. That the Pharisees should have prescribed this particularity is only in accordance with all their system of making rules about trifles. Of course the first marginal reading "diligently," expresses the idea of the requirement.

The excess to which these regulations were carried is well illustrated by a tradition respecting one Rabbi Akaba, the abettor of Barchocab's rebellion, who, in his dungeon, being driven by a pittance of water to the alternative of neglecting ablution or dying with thirst, preferred death to failing in ceremonious observance. (From "Notes on the Gospels," by F. M.) The Vulgate, which our authorized translation on this point follows, has *crebro*, "frequently;" the Syriac, "carefully;" but the true reading is undoubtedly "with the fist."

"Holding the tradition of the elders." This tradition was asserted, most falsely, to have been handed down from the time of Moses, but its germs even could not well have been earlier than the time of the Captivity—as I have shown in notes on St. Matthew.

4. "And when they come from the market, except they wash," &c. "Except they wash." The word is, except they baptize them-

they wash, they eat not. And many other things there be, which they have received to hold, *as* the washing of cups, and || pots, brasen vessels, and of || tables.

| *Sextarius is about a pint and an half.*
|| Or, *beds.*
b Matt. xv. 2.

5 ᵇ Then the Pharisees and scribes asked him, Why walk not thy disciples according to the tradition of the elders, but eat bread with unwashen hands?

6 He answered and said unto them, Well hath Esaias

---

4. "Except they wash." Literally, "Unless they be baptized or bathe."
"Of tables." So A., D., later Uncials, almost all Cursives, Old Latin, Vulg., Syriac, &c.; but A., B., L., Δ omit.
5. "With unwashen hands." So A., L., later Uncials, almost all Cursives, Old Latin (b, e, f), Syriac; but ℵ*, B., D., and five Cursives (1, 28, 33, 118, 209), Old Latin (a, i, &c.), Vulg., and some versions read, "With common hands."

---

selves, or bathe themselves. It is difficult to believe that all such Jews as did business in market-places should have been obliged to take a complete bath afterwards. In fact, taking into consideration the rainless state of Palestine during much of the year, it seems impossible, and so this can only mean, unless they cleanse themselves more thoroughly.

The washing of cups, and pots, and brasen vessels." The cup (*poterion*) was a drinking vessel; the pot (*xestes*, corrupted from the Latin *sextuarius*), holding above a pint, was a vessel for holding or measuring fluids; the brazen vessel (*calcion*), probably a cauldron. It is to be remembered that this washing which is here noticed was over and above all washing of these objects for the sake of cleanliness or health: it was strictly ceremonial or quasi-religious.

"And of tables." If the word represented by this "tables" be a part of the original text, it must mean couches, or the furniture on which the guests reclined. It cannot mean such tables as we have.

5. "Then the Pharisees and scribes asked him . . . . unwashen hands." We know that, on a later occasion, a Pharisee marvelled that our Lord "had not first washed before dinner." So we cannot but gather from this that on the present occasion only some of the disciples had eaten without the customary ablutions. Otherwise His enemies would not have been slow to charge the Lord Himself.

6, 7. "He answered and said . . . teaching for doctrines the

prophesied of you hypocrites, as it is written, ᶜThis people honoureth me with *their* lips, but their heart is far from me.   ᶜ Is. xxix. 13. Matt. xv. 8.

7 Howbeit in vain do they worship me, teaching *for* doctrines the commandments of men.

8 For laying aside the commandment of God, ye hold the tradition of men, *as* the washing of pots and cups: and many other such like things ye do.

---

8. " As the washing of pots and cups: and many other," &c. So A., later Uncials, almost all Cursives, Vulg., Syriac, Old Latin, and versions; but omitted by ℵ, B., L., Δ, a few Cursives, and Coptic.

commandments of men." Our Lord here quotes, not the Hebrew, but the Septuagint: " Well, (that is, admirably,) hath Esaias prophesied of you hypocrites. As it is written, ' This people honoureth me,'" &c. It is the very essence of hypocrisy in religion to render to God an outward or lip service, while the heart is not His. And the quotation goes on: "In vain do they worship me"—that is, their worship, such as it is, is unaccepted by Me, because they teach doctrines which are not My commands, but the commands of men which overload, and obscure, and make void My commands.

It has been asked whether Isaiah had prophetically in his mind the Pharisees of our Lord's day, to which it may be answered, forms of sin and evil continually repeat themselves and reappear. The prophecy in Isaiah exactly describes the hypocritical or Pharisaic mind, substituting the merest and most meaningless external forms for internal purity and heart devotion, and so teaching the doctrines and commandments of men that there is no room for the pure word of God. Olshausen has a very suggestive remark: "The whole Old Testament history was prophetic of Christ, and of those around Him, in this respect, that everywhere, in the continually recurring contest between light and darkness, between truth and error, there were displayed the types of that which, in its highest energy, developed itself in and around Christ."

8, 9. " For laying aside the commandment of God . . . keep your own tradition." The extent to which the Pharisaic Jews went, in exalting their own traditions above the written words, seems incredible. One saying was, the Scriptures are like " water; "

9 And he said unto them, Full well ye ‖ reject the commandment of God, that ye may keep your own tradition.

‖ Or, *frustrate.*

10 For Moses said, ᵈ Honour thy father and thy mother; and, ᵉ Whoso curseth father or mother, let him die the death:

ᵈ Ex. xx. 12.
Deut. v. 16.
Matt. xv. 4.
ᵉ Ex. xxi. 17.
Lev. xx. 9.
Prov. xx. 20.

11 But ye say, If a man shall say to his father or mother, *It is* ᶠ Corban, that is to say, a gift, by whatsoever thou mightest be profited by me; *he shall be free.*

ᶠ Matt. xv. 5.
& xxiii. 18.

12 And ye suffer him no more to do ought for his father or his mother;

---

12. "And." So A., later Uncials, most Cursives, Vulg., Syriac; but omitted by ℵ, B., D., some Cursives, Old Latin, and Coptic.

the ⸤Mishna—*i.e.*, the text or body of the traditions, after they were committed to writing—is as "wine;" the Gemara—*i.e.*, the comment on the Mishna, embodying still more blasphemous absurdities—is as "spiced wine." Mr. Nicholson gives a passage out of Lightfoot, quoting from the Jerusalem Talmud, "out of infinite examples which we meet in their writings," the following: "The words of the scribes are lovely, above the words of the Law: for the words of the Law (of Moses) are weighty and light, but the words of the scribes are all weighty." And, again: "The words of the elders are weightier than the words of the prophets." It is, however, improbable that they went to such depths of blasphemy in our Lord's time. It was after their rejection of Him that they were wholly given over to such a reprobate mind. In their case, the latter part of this prophetic utterance of Isaiah, as read in the Septuagint, seems to have been most literally fulfilled, both in their temporal and spiritual punishment: "Therefore, behold, I will proceed to remove this people, and I will remove them. And I will destroy the wisdom of the wise, and will hide the understanding of the prudent."

10, 11, 12. "For Moses said, Honour thy father and thy mother . . . his father or his mother." This place is somewhat obscured by the insertion of the words, in italics, "he shall be free," with the copula, "and," in verses 11 and 12. The meaning is plainer,

13 Making the word of God of none effect through your tradition, which ye have delivered: and many such like things do ye.

---

if we read and expound it thus: If a man shall say to his father or mother, "Whatsoever thou mightest be profited by me, whatever income or allowance I ought to make for thy support, or whatever gift I ought, as a son, to give thee, is corban—*i. e.*, dedicated to the temple service, and to be put into the treasury;" then, no matter how hastily or rashly he has said this, the vow is registered against him: "Ye suffer him no more to do ought for his father or his mother." The moment it rises up in his mind to give anything to his father, the vow intervenes, and stays his hand. He need not actually pay the money into the temple treasury, he may keep it in his own possession, or spend it on himself; but the only person to whom he is not to give it, is his father.

The reader will not fail to notice how the Lord here lays His finger on the fifth commandment, and upholds its authority. He was subject to His earthly parent and her husband (Luke ii. 51), and it was His meat and drink to do the will of His Heavenly Father, and to finish His work (John iv. 34).

13. "Making the word of God of none effect by your traditions ... do ye." "Many such like things do ye." Through their traditions, they made the Sabbath a burden; through their traditions, they inverted the relative obligation of oaths (Matt. xxiii. 16-22); through their traditions, they allowed frequent divorces, and so destroyed the sanctity of marriage (Matt. xix. 3).

It may be well, now, to restate shortly, in other words, some of the leading points of my note in St. Matthew on Christian tradition, or what is so called, as distinguished from Jewish.

The traditions of the Jews—*i.e.*, the traditions of the elders or rabbis, were all, without exception, the product of the later ages of the Jewish dispensation in the time of its decay and fall, when it was at its worst; whereas the opinions and practices, which are invidiously called traditions in these days, *i.e.*, the opinions and practices of the earliest Fathers of the Christian Church, are the products of the earliest ages of the Christian Religion, when it was at its best, and was least contaminated with the influence of the world from without, and kept most pure by godly discipline from within. The opinions of the Fathers on the interpretation of

14 ¶ ᵍ And when he had called all the people *unto him,* he said unto them, Hearken unto me every one *of you,* and understand:

15 There is nothing from without a man that entering into him can defile him: but the things which come out of him, those are they that defile the man.

ʰ Matt. xi. 15.    16 ʰ If any man have ears to hear, let him hear.

ᵍ Matt. xv. 10.

---

14. "All the people." So A., later Uncials, most Cursives, Syriac (Schaff); but ℵ, B., D., L., Δ, Old Latin, Vulg., Coptic read, The people again ("called the people again").

16. "If any man," &c. So A., D., later Uncials, most Cursives, Old Latin, Vulg., and versions; but ℵ, B., L., and Coptic omit the verse.

Scripture, when they can be ascertained, are far more likely to be in accord with the real meaning of the words of the Apostles than any opinions or practices of later ages, whether so-called Catholic or so-called Protestant. It is on these principles that the Reformation of the Church of England was brought about, retaining what was early and primitive, and rejecting what was merely mediæval, no matter how far-spread, as the denial of the cup to the laity.

14. "And when he had called all the people . . . understand." Compared with the parallel passage of St. Matthew (xv. 10), these words evince far more earnestness on the Lord's part that all the people should hear and receive this His saying, for by it He once and for ever distinguishes between ceremonial and personal religion. And so in a matter of such moment He summons all the people, and says to them, "Hearken unto Me every one of you (for it concerns you all), and understand."

15. "There is nothing from without a man . . . the man." This saying of the Lord's contains a principle or rule of the widest application. "It is," as Quesnel writes, "a rule of great importance and full of instruction and comfort to souls which seek God, that no sin or spiritual defilement can arise from anything but the will, as nothing sanctifies our food but the word of God, and prayer from the heart renewed by grace. Whatever proceeds from the desire of an impure heart is evil, and whatever does not, cannot but be good. It is not that which enters into the mouth which defiles even him who sins in eating and drinking to excess, but the

17 ¹And when he was entered into the house from the people, his disciples asked him concerning the parable. ¹ Matt. xv. 15.

18 And he saith unto them, Are ye so without understanding also? Do ye not perceive, that whatsoever thing from without entereth into the man, *it* cannot defile him;

19 Because it entereth not into his heart, but into the belly, and goeth out into the draught, purging all meats?

---

19. "Purging." Properly, "cleansing." This participle is in the masculine gender in ℵ, A., B., E., F., G., H., L., some Cursives, and a quotation from Origen in Tischendorf; K., M., and most Cursives, as in Rec. Text.

will and disposition of the heart, which inclines him to transgress the Divine Law."

17, 18, "And when he was entered . . . it cannot defile him." This is one of the many places which show us the enormous difference made in men's knowledge of spiritual things by the coming of the Saviour and the descent of the Spirit. It seems incredible that the Apostles should consider the words of the Saviour in which He speaks of nothing from without defiling a man, as a parable—that is, a dark saying, which required explanation. Even if they had in their minds the Levitical law of meats, they should have seen—if they had any spiritual perception—that if a man transgressed this law unwittingly, that is, if by mistake or accident he ate of some unclean animal, he could not be morally defiled, and that if a man transgressed the law of meats willingly to gratify his appetite, it was his evil will, which had its rise in his heart, which really defiled him. To take the strongest conceivable case, it was not any physical property of the forbidden fruit which defiled Adam and his descendants, but it was the evil will, which, contrary to God's will, made him desire to be as a god, and plunged him and all his descendants into sin.

19. "Because it entereth not into his heart . . . purging all meats." No food, of course, can enter into the heart, and our Lord is upon the subject of the defilement occasioned by meats; but temptations to sin from Satan or from our fellows come from without, and by assenting to them or harbouring them, they may defile us, but even in this case the real defilement is in our own evil assent—in other words, in our will. The outer defiling word or sug-

20 And he said, That which cometh out of the man, that defileth the man.

<sup>k</sup> Gen. vi. 5. & viii. 21. Matt. xv. 19.

21 <sup>k</sup> For from within, out of the heart of men, proceed evil thoughts, adulteries, fornications, murders,

---

gestion is like a seed which finds corrupt ground in the soul in which it can germinate.

"Purging all meats." The translation "purging" is exceedingly misleading. It really signifies "cleansing." It is commonly taken as alluding to the process by which the meat which enters into the body by the mouth is, by the process of digestion, which takes place within the body, separated, or purged from all useless particles, which are received into the sewer or drain, and those only which can be converted into blood are retained. In this case the participle "cleansing," is in the neuter. But the best manuscripts read it in the masculine gender, in which case it refers to the Lord Himself, and the words which He was then uttering. These words uttered by Him as the supreme Lawgiver abrogated all distinctions between meats as clean and unclean, and made from that moment all equally clean.

Chrysostom takes it in this sense. In his comment on the parallel place in St. Matthew, he refers to these words of St. Mark, "Mark saith, He spake this cleansing the meats." So that this was the cleansing alluded to by the voice from heaven in Acts x. 15, "What God hath cleansed, that call not thou common."

21. "For from within, out of the heart proceed evil thoughts," &c. Notice how evil thoughts are by the Saviour said to be the first of the evil things which, coming out of the heart, defile. *We* should not, I think, have put evil thoughts amongst the things which come *out* of the heart, because we suppose them to be *in* the heart. But is not what the Saviour says true of that which He alone knows—the very nature and substance of the soul? In its very centre, or close to its centre, the evil has its root or fountain. The evil suggestion arises, and then the will or affection takes notice of it. If the will is right with God, it immediately puts out the evil thing as if it were a loathsome reptile, but if the will be not right with God, it harbours the first suggestion of evil, it cogitates it, thinks it over and over, dwells upon it in imagination, chews the food of the evil fancy, desires to

CHAP. VII.] THESE EVIL THINGS DEFILE. 147

22 Thefts, †covetousness, wickedness, deceit, lasciviousness, an evil eye, blasphemy, pride, foolishness:  † Gr. *covetousnesses, wickednesses.*
23 All these evil things come from within, and defile the man.
24 ¶ ¹ And from thence he arose, and went into   ¹ Matt. xv. 21.

do the evil deed, resolves to do it, and so has already done it in the heart. So that out of the heart, out of the unseen and unthinkable depths within, proceed the evil thoughts which become evil acts within before they are incarnated, as it were, in some evil deed without.

The word employed by the Saviour certainly implies more than sudden or chance thoughts. It even means reasonings put into words, whereby we unsettle the faith of one another (thus Luke ix. 46, Rom. xiv. 1).

Of all evils, we account evil thoughts the least. "What! thoughts defile a man? What, so light a matter as thoughts? Can they make any impression? Yes, and defile a man too, leaving such a spot behind as nothing but the hot blood of Christ can wash away." (Archbp. Usher, quoted in Ford.)

It is to be particularly noted that, according to St. Mark, the Saviour specifies many additional evil things defiling the man, which are not mentioned in St. Matthew's account, viz., covetousness, wickedness, deceit, lasciviousness, an evil eye, blasphemy, pride, foolishness. How few think that covetousness, or deceit, or an evil eye, *i.e.*, envy, defile! Christian people who pronounce these things wrong would hesitate to say that they *defile;* and how few, how very few, would allow that pride defiles! and yet the Saviour enumerates covetousness and pride among such defiling things as fornication and lasciviousness. Well may the wise man say, " Keep thy heart with all diligence, for out of it are the issues of life " (Prov. iv. 23). Well may we say to God in daily worship, " O God, make clean our hearts within us, and take not Thy Holy Spirit from us." Surely it was a man after God's own heart who said, " Try me, O God, and seek the ground of my heart, prove me and examine my thoughts. Look well if there be any way of wickedness in me, and lead me in the way everlasting" (Ps. cxxxix. 23, 24).

24. " And from thence he arose.... He could not be hid." Not to Tyre and Sidon themselves, but into the coasts or borders, the

the borders of Tyre and Sidon, and entered into an house, and would have no man know *it*: but he could not be hid.

25 For a *certain* woman, whose young daughter had an unclean spirit, heard of him, and came and fell at his feet:

---

24. "And Sidon." So אּ, A., B., N., all later Uncials, almost all Cursives, Old Latin (c, f), Vulg., Coptic, Syriac, and some versions; only D., L., Cursive 28, and some Old Latin (a, b, ff) omit. Notwithstanding the apparently enormous preponderance in favour of the reading, Tischendorf omits it, and Westcott and Hort mark it as doubtful by putting it in brackets.

parts adjacent. From this verse we learn that He did not go into these parts to preach, and to do miracles, for He endeavoured to keep Himself in retirement, otherwise it would not have been said, "He could not be hid."

For what purpose then did He take this journey? It could only have been for one. He saw that there was one living in these parts whom He could set forth to all after ages as an extraordinary example of persevering faith. To call forth such faith, and to show it to His disciples, so that they should have it deeply impressed upon them, and should afterwards embody it in the tradition which was the groundwork of the written Gospels, in two of which it should in due time be embodied, and be read now as an example for all ages, to show them what difficulties true faith can conquer— this was worth the journey in the sight of the Son of God.

25. "For a certain woman . . . cast forth the devil out of her daughter." From St. Matthew's account we should gather that she accosted first Himself, and then the body of the disciples as they passed on the road. From St. Mark, that she came and fell at His feet when He was seeking retirement in a house. St. Mark says nothing about the request of the Apostles to the Lord to grant her prayer, "Send her away, for she crieth after us." It is just possible that St. Peter was for some reason not in the company of the Apostles when they preferred this request.

"She was a Greek, a Syrophenician by nation." That is, she was not only a Gentile, and so out of the pale of God's covenanted mercies, but of a race accursed beyond all others, a descendant of one of those nations whom God commanded His people to exterminate.

"Whose daughter had an unclean spirit." From her words as recorded in St. Matthew, "My daughter is grievously vexed with a

26 The woman was a || Greek, a Syrophenician by nation; and she besought him that he would cast forth || Or, *Gentile.* the devil out of her daughter.

27 But Jesus said unto her, Let the children first be filled: for it is not meet to take the children's bread, and to cast *it* unto the dogs.

---

devil," we should gather that this possession was attended with violent paroxysms.

"And she besought him that he would cast forth." From St. Matthew we learn that she appealed to Him as Son of David. From this we should infer that she was not altogether ignorant of the Messianic hopes of the Jews, and that they looked for some mighty deliverer who should be a Son of David.

27. "But Jesus said unto her, "Let the children first be filled," &c. This was her third repulse. First, when she accosted Him, even as Son of David, He answered her not a word (Matth. xv. 23). Then when the disciples besought Him, He said, "I am not sent but to the lost sheep of the house of Israel," and now He answers still more strangely, "Let the children first be filled: for it is not meet to take the children's bread, and to cast it unto the dogs." This was indeed the severest trial of her faith, but as the Lord foresaw, it came forth as the "silver purified seven times in the fire." The one great lesson we learn from this is, that the truest faith is the humblest. Would not any of us, if we had heard such words, have started and shrunk away, or in wrath returned bitter words? It would have been human nature so to do; but this woman must have been a humble believer in the one true God. She must have realized that it was in wisdom and justice, and perhaps too, even in far-seeing mercy, that the God of Israel had, till then, made Himself known to one race only, and had so shut out others from the knowledge of Himself, that, compared with those who knew or could know Him, they were as a lower order of creatures. This is akin to what the Psalmist says in describing the exaltation of those to whom the Word of God came, "I have said, ye are Gods, and ye are all the children of the Most Highest" (Ps. lxxxii. 6, John x. 34, 35). The Lord Himself in His pre-existent state, as the Giver of the Mosaic Law, had constituted this difference between His people and all other nations; and within a very short time from this He was about to "break down

28 And she answered and said unto him, Yes, Lord: yet the dogs under the table eat of the children's crumbs.

---

**28.** "*Yes, Lord: yet the dogs,*" &c. See below for translations of Revisers. So Vulg., *Utique, domine! nam et catelli.*

the wall of partition," and to reconcile all to His Father in One Body on His Cross, but till this took place He respected the requirements of the system of which He Himself had been the Author. He went not into the way of the Gentiles to teach and to heal; when He crossed the sea, to land for a short time on heathen soil, it was to heal but one possessed man. All this state of things was shortly to cease, but it had not yet ceased, and so here, for the last time, He asserted the ancient exclusion; and yet, all through, He was secretly upholding the faith of this poor creature, so that she should knock the more importunately at the seemingly closed door, and cause that it should be opened to her, and receive as her reward not only the salvation of her daughter, but that everywhere where the Gospel is preached what she had done should be spoken of as a memorial of her. But even this is not all. As Keble reminds us in his wonderful sermon on this woman's faith, "We adopt her language in the deepest prayer of our Eucharistic Service. There we are taught by the Church to confess that we are not worthy so much as to gather up the crumbs under God's Table; and yet, at the same time we ask for the highest blessing He can give—that our sinful bodies may be made clean by His Body, and our souls washed through His most precious blood, and that we may ever more dwell in Him, and He in us." ("Sermons for the Christian Year," vol. iv. Sermon xiv. I desire very earnestly to commend this sermon to the reader, so that he should make some endeavour to become acquainted with its contents.)

28. "And she answered and said unto him, Yes, Lord .... children's crumbs." The translation of this in the Revised version, brings out more fully the real meaning. "Yea, Lord, even the dogs under the table eat of the children's crumbs." Upon this Archbishop Trench remarks: "She accepts the Lord's declaration, not immediately to make exception against the conclusion which He draws from it, but to show how, in that very declaration, is involved the granting of her petition. 'Saidest Thou dogs? It is well: I accept the title and the place: for the dogs have a portion of the

29 And he said unto her, For this saying go thy way; the devil is gone out of thy daughter.

---

meal, not the first, not the children's, but a portion still, the crumbs which fall from the master's table. In this very statement of the case thou bringest us heathen, thou bringest me within the circle of the blessings which God the great Householder is ever dispensing to His family. We also belong to His household, though we occupy but the lowest place in it. According to Thine own showing I am not wholly an alien, and, therefore, I will abide by this name, and will claim from Thee all which is included in it.'"

29. "And he said unto her, For this saying go thy way," &c. The full words of the Lord (as reported in the two Evangelists) were, "Oh, woman, great is thy faith; be it unto thee even as thou wilt. For this saying go thy way: the devil is gone out of thy daughter." Truly it may be said of her, "With the heart she believed, and with the mouth she made confession unto salvation." Quesnel remarks, "How great comfort is it to a Christian mother, when God is pleased at last to grant to her prayers the salvation of a daughter possessed with the spirit of the world!"[1]

---

[1] Keble also, in the sermon to which I have just alluded, makes a still closer application. "The woman's daughter was 'vexed with an unclean spirit.' Poor creature! she was like thousands more who grow up and go on in uncleanness till they are quite possessed with it as with a bad and fallen angel. They feel as if they could not help themselves, so entirely subject have they become to evil lust, 'The law in their members warring against the law of their mind.' 'Having eyes full of adultery, and that cannot cease from sin.' God help them, poor creatures, against the great enemy! May God touch and turn their hearts, for vain is the help of man. But then, the less you can do for them, the more you should pray for them. The woman of Canaan could, of herself, do nothing for her child, but this one thing she could do, she could find out Jesus, and pray to Him, and this she did with all her might. She prayed and prayed, and by-and-by came the answer. Will you do the same for any friend or kinsman of yours whom you believe or fear to be living in uncleanness? Try! it will be the least you can do, but it will prove a great thing if you try in earnest."

30 And when she was come to her house, she found the
devil gone out, and her daughter laid upon the bed.

---

As in all probability extremely few of those who read these
notes will possess the Biblical Commentary of Olshausen on the
Gospels, I will conclude my remarks on this miracle with a
passage from him of remarkable power, which sums up its teaching:
"This little narrative lays open the magic that lies in a humbly
believing heart more directly and deeply than all explanations or
descriptions would do. Faith and humility are so intimately at
one, that neither can exist without the other, both act as by a
magic spell on the unseen world of the spirit, they draw the
heavenly essence itself down into the earthly. In this case faith is
again obviously seen, not as knowledge, not as the upholding of
certain doctrines for true, but an internal state of the mind—the
tenderest susceptibility for what is heavenly—the most entire
womanhood of the soul." And respecting our Lord's seeming
severity he remarks : " It would seem as if He Who knew what was
in man (John ii. 25) must have been constrained at once to help
*this* woman, as her faith could not have been concealed from Him,
and even though, for wise reasons, He was led to confine His
ministry to the Jews, yet as in other instances He made exceptions
(comp. on Matt. viii. 10), so might He have done in her case at
once, without laying on her the burden of His severity . . . . It
is Christian experience alone which opens our way to the right
understanding of this. As God Himself is compared by our Lord
to an unjust judge who often turns away the well-grounded supplication (Luke xviii. 32), as the Lord wrestles with Jacob at Jacob's
ford, and thus exalts him to be Israel (Gen. xxxii. 24), as He seeks
to kill Moses, who was destined to deliver his people (Exod. iv. 21),
so faith often in its experience finds that 'the heaven is of brass,'
and seems to despise its prayers. A similar mode of dealing is here
exhibited by the Saviour. The restraining of His grace, the manifestation of a treatment wholly different from what the woman
may at first have expected, acted as a check usually does on power,
when it really exists: the whole inherent energy of her living faith
broke forth, and the Saviour suffered Himself to be overcome by
her as He had when wrestling with Jacob. In this mode then of
Christ's giving an answer to prayer we are to trace only another

## CHAP. VII.]   ONE THAT WAS DEAF.   153

31 ¶ ᵐ And again, departing from the coasts of Tyre and Sidon, he came unto the sea of Galilee, through the midst of the coasts of Decapolis.   ᵐ Matt. xv. 29.

32 And ⁿ they bring unto him one that was deaf, and had an impediment in his speech; and they beseech him to put his hand upon him.   ⁿ Matt. ix. 32. Luke xi. 14.

---

31. "Departing from the coasts of Tyre and Sidon, he came unto the sea of Galilee," &c. So A., later Uncials, almost all Cursives, Syriac, and some versions; but ℵ, B., D., L., Δ, Cursive 33, Old Latin, Vulg., Coptic, Æthiopic read, "From the coasts of Tyre he came through Sidon unto," &c.

form of His love. Where faith is weak, He anticipates and comes to meet it; where faith is strong, He holds Himself far off in order that it may in itself be carried to perfection."

31. "And again, departing from the coasts . . . coasts of Decapolis." The following miracle is peculiar to St. Mark. Not being related in either SS. Matthew or Luke, it seems to have not been embodied in the original tradition of the Lord's life. May not this be accounted for if we suppose that when the Lord took the man aside, only Peter, and James, and John were witnesses of the miracle, and not the whole body of the Apostles?

"Departing from the coasts . . . Decapolis." Whether we read with the Authorized or with the Vulgate (departing from the borders of Tyre, he came through Sidon to the Sea of Galilee through the midst of the coasts of Decapolis), the Lord, in either case, made a considerable circuit through a heathen region to get back to the Galilean Sea. Of the incidents of this journey we are told nothing, so that it is not at all likely that in making it He either preached to the people or healed those that were sick.

32. "And they bring unto him one that was deaf." "Had an impediment in his speech." Not one absolutely dumb, as some would have it, but one who spoke with difficulty.

"They beseech him to put his hand upon him." It has been suggested by some (among them I. Williams) that this request arose from imperfect belief. The object of their petition, that He would lay His hand on him, though a sacred and priestly custom, yet implied less of an inherent Divine power than any other mode of healing, just as on another occasion it is said that He did not many miracles there because of their unbelief. "Except," adds St. Mark,

**33** And he took him aside from the multitude, and put his fingers into his ears, and ᵒ he spit, and touched his tongue;

* ch. viii. 23.
John ix. 6.

---

"that He laid His hands on a few sick folk"—a customary action, too, among the prophets, which Naaman the Syrian expected of Elisha.

**33.** "And he took him aside from the multitude, and put . . . and he spit, and touched his tongue." "There must be a deep meaning in all the variations which mark the healings of different sick and afflicted ones, a wisdom of God ordering all the circumstances of each particular cure. Were we acquainted as accurately as He Who 'knew what was in man' with the spiritual condition of each one who was brought within the circle of His grace, we should then perfectly understand why one was healed in the crowd, another led out of the city ere the work of restoration was commenced; why for one a word effected a cure, for another a touch, while a third was sent to wash in the pool of Siloam 'ere he came seeing;' why for some the process of restoration was instantaneous, while another 'saw men as trees walking.' Our ignorance prevents us from at once seeing the manifold wisdom which ordered each of His proceedings, and how it was conducted so as best to make the bodily healing a passage to the spiritual which the Lord had ever in His eye" (Trench).

Many reasons have been given for the Lord's thus taking the man aside; as that He wished to avoid unnecessary display, or that the presence of the multitude was distracting to His own prayers, and hindered the devotion with which He desired to inspire the deaf man. A more ingenious reason is that being in a heathen country He wished to avoid giving the slightest encouragement to superstitious practices, which they might have learnt if they had seen Him touch the man's tongue with his finger moist with saliva; but is it not probable that this "taking aside" is most consonant with that privacy in which He desired to be all through this journey? At the beginning it is said that He could not be hid, though He evidently desired it, and of this journey no public acts are recorded.

Why did the Lord put His fingers into the ears of the deaf man, and spit and touch His tongue? On two other occasions He made use of spittle in healing—in the case of a blind man at Bethsaida, whom He also led out of the town (Mark viii. 23), and when He

CHAP. VII.]            HE SIGHED.                155

34 And ᵖ looking up to heaven, ᑫ he sighed, and

ᵖ ch. vi. 41.
John xi. 41. &
xvii. 1.
ᑫ John xi. 33, 38.

healed the man born blind (John ix. 6), and there may have been many others unrecorded. There must be some significance in so strange an act. I have not the least doubt that it was to emphasize the truth that the healing of our whole nature proceeds from His own Person. It is not an act of His power only, but an emanation from His Person through its lower part, His Body. Let the reader remember how He said, "Somebody hath touched me, for I perceive that virtue is gone out of me." (Luke viii. 46.) Remember also how it is said, "The whole multitude sought to touch him: for there went virtue out of him and healed them all." (Luke vi. 19.)

Of course there was not the least natural virtue in saliva, or in any bodily contact, but the Lord had it in His Mind that we are to receive healing virtue not merely from the teaching of His higher or intellectual and spiritual Nature, but also from partaking of His lower—His Body. The Lord's action must have been either natural in the way of medical application, or mystical; the former is absolutely inadmissible, and without curiously searching, much less defining, we must see the significance of such actions of His in the latter. "It is not for its medicinal virtue that use is made of this, but as the suitable symbol of a power residing in and going forth from His Body." (Trench.)

34. "And looking up to heaven, he sighed." Looking up to heaven, *i. e.*, putting Himself into direct and open communion with His Father, without Whom He did nothing (John v. 19, 30). Remember Mark vi. 41, when He looked up before He brake the loaves, and John xi. 41, before He raised Lazarus.

"He sighed," or "groaned." The reader will remember how just before the raising of Lazarus, when He knew that He was about to restore him to life He "groaned in the spirit." How was it that He exhibited sorrow when He was on the point of imparting such joy? It may be that these instances of relief vouchsafed to His fellows, so very few in comparison with what He could have performed for them if they had only believed in Him, brought before His soul more feelingly the mass of misery which they represented, but which, owing to men's perverseness and rejection of

saith unto him, EPHPHATHA, that is, Be opened.

35 ʳAnd straightway his ears were opened, and the string of his tongue was loosed, and he spake plain.

36 And ˢhe charged them that they should tell no man: but the more he charged them, so much the more a great deal they published *it*;

37 And were beyond measure astonished, saying, He hath

---

Himself, He was not able to alleviate. Did not our great Christian poet strike the true chord when he wrote,—

> "O'erwhelming thoughts of pain and grief
>   Over His sinking spirit sweep:
> What boots it gathering one lost leaf
>   Out of yon sere and withered heap,
> Where souls and bodies, hopes and joys,
> All that earth owns or sin destroys,
> Under the spurning hoof are cast
>   Or tossing in the autumnal blast?
>
> The deaf may hear the Saviour's voice,
>   The fettered tongue its chain may break,
> But the deaf heart, the dumb by choice,
>   The laggard soul, that will not wake,
> The guilt that scorns to be forgiven,
> These baffle e'en the spells of heaven.
> In thought of these, His brows benign
>   Not e'en in healing cloudless shine."

"Ephphatha." How wondrously large the spiritual application of these words! They may be said to closed eyes (Psalm cxix. 18), to closed ears (Isaiah l. 4, 5), to closed lips (Psalm li. 15), to closed hearts (Acts xvi. 14). Quesnel founds on them a very simple, but all-embracing prayer: "O Jesus, pronounce over mine, over the hearts of sinners, and of all those who ought to hear Thee, and to speak in Thy stead, these words, Be opened, and Thou shalt be forthwith obeyed."

36, 37. "And he charged them that . . . . deaf to hear, and the

done all things well: he maketh both the deaf to hear, and the dumb to speak.

---

dumb to speak." Why He gave such a charge on this occasion, knowing that it would not be obeyed, we cannot tell. It may have been because in certain cases, and this one of them, His spiritual ministry of teaching and preaching was seriously hindered by the crowds of those who came with no other thought than either to be cured of bodily infirmities, or to gaze idly upon the performance of His mighty works. We shall know one day that, whether He forbid men to proclaim His mighty deeds of grace, or whether He encouraged them so to do, "He hath done all things well."

## CHAP. VIII.

IN those days ᵃ the multitude being very great, and having nothing to eat, Jesus called his disciples *unto*  ᵃ Matt. xv. 32. *him*, and saith unto them,

---

1. "The multitude being very great." So A., E., F., H., K., other later Uncials, most Cursives, and Syriac; but ℵ, B., D., G., L., M., N., fourteen or fifteen Cursives, Old Latin, Vulg., Coptic, and other versions read, "There being again a great multitude."

1. "In those days the multitude being very great," &c. We now come to what is called "the Second Miracle of the loaves." From the fact that we have two miracles performed almost under the same circumstances, and in the same manner, and the accompanying details very much resembling one another in both cases, we cannot but gather that we have here a peculiar phase of Christ's love and power presented to us, and by its repetition commended very urgently to our notice, so that we should be very anxious to realize all that is taught us in these two accounts. It would seem at first sight impossible to do more than repeat what has been before remarked on the two miracles, as related in St. Matthew, and on the first one which has already been fully described in St. Mark, but it is not so. We have yet many fragments to gather

2 I have compassion on the multitude, because they have now been with me three days, and have nothing to eat:

3 And if I send them away fasting to their own houses, they will faint by the way: for divers of them came from far.

4 And his disciples answered him, From whence can a man satisfy these *men* with bread here in the wilderness?

---

up if nothing is to be lost. In the first place, then, the Lord here takes the initiative.

2. "I have compassion on the multitude, because they have now been with me three days," &c. In the former miracle He felt equal compassion for the multitude, but did not express it. The disciples urge upon Him to send them away, and then He, as it were, invites them to suggest some exercise of the mighty power which they had so repeatedly seen put forth by Him. But they can suggest nothing except what is natural, that they should be dismissed to take care of themselves. Now the Lord Himself begins: " I have compassion on the multitude, they have been with me three days. If I send them to their own houses, they will faint by the way," &c. Here was the hint given that they should ask Him to do as He had done just before, but apparently not a thought of the former mighty work presented itself. They seem to have altogether forgotten it.

4. "And his disciples answered him, From whence," &c. We marvel at (must not the word be said?) this stupidity, but is it not natural? This surprise arises out of our ignorance of man's heart, of our own hearts, and of the deep root of unbelief therein. " It is ever more thus in times of difficulty and distress. All former deliverances are in danger of being forgotten, the mighty interpositions of God's hand in former passages of men's lives fall out of their memories. Each new difficulty appears insurmountable, as one from which there is no extrication; at each recurring necessity it seems as though the wonders of God's grace are exhausted, and have come to an end. God may have diverted the Red Sea for Israel, yet no sooner are they on the other side than, because there are no waters to drink, they murmur against Moses, and count that they must perish through thirst (Exod. xvii. 1-7), crying ' Is the Lord amongst us or not?' Or, to adduce a still nearer parallel, once already the Lord had covered the camp with quails (Exod. xvi. 13),

5 ᵇ And he asked them, How many loaves have ye? And they said, Seven.   ᵇ Matt. xv. 34. See ch. vi. 38.

---

yet for all this, even Moses himself cannot believe that He will provide flesh for all that multitude." (Abp. Trench.)

But the backwardness of the Apostles to believe in Christ's readiness to feed the multitudes miraculously, is in strong contrast with their readiness to believe in His powers of healing. They had but a short time before urged the Lord to grant the request of the Syrophenician woman, when He seemed unwilling. May it not, in part, have arisen from the infrequency of this sort of miracle? As Theophylact says, "He did not always work miracles for the feeding of the multitude, lest they should follow Him for the sake of food."

And may there not be also something typical, something prophetical, about it? Do not many true disciples of the Lord in these days, who thankfully acknowledge the Lord's power to cleanse and heal, seem to have their eyes closed to the supernatural or eucharistic feeding, of which this miracle is so remarkable an adumbration?

Again, do we not learn from this miracle how Christ will exercise acts of special providence to help and succour those who are following Him? Is there any life of a poor humble Christian which does not contain some account of interpositions almost supernatural in favour of those who have given up all to follow Him? Dean Hook, in a lecture on this very miracle, gives a striking one: "There was an individual who gave up a profitable employment, acting under advice, and not from the mere caprice of his own judgment, because he thought, taking his temptations into account, he could not follow it without peril to his soul. And after many reverses he was reduced to such a state of distress, that the last morsel in the house had been consumed, and he had not bread to give his children. His faith did not, however, forsake him; and when his distress was at the height, he received a visit from one who called to pay him a debt he had never hoped to recover, but the payment of which enabled him to support his family until he again obtained employment." And he adds, "Many a similar tale can our poorer brethren tell."

5. "And he asked them, How many loaves have ye?" &c. This question was not for information. He knew well how many

6 And he commanded the people to sit down on the ground: and he took the seven loaves, and gave thanks, and brake, and gave to his disciples to set before *them;* and they did set *them* before the people.

<sup>a</sup> Matt. xiv. 19. ch. vi. 41.

7 And they had a few small fishes: and <sup>a</sup> he blessed, and commanded to set them also before *them.*

---

they had, but he asked it that there should be no mistake about the miraculous nature of the feeding. There were two more loaves and a somewhat smaller multitude than on the former occasion, but this does not, in the smallest degree, affect the character of the mighty work.

6. "And he commanded the people to sit down on the ground," &c. From the fact that it is expressly mentioned in the account of the former miracle, that there was much grass in the place, and that they sat by companies on the green grass, it has been argued with much probability that this second miracle took place at a much later time in the year, when the grass had been dried up by the scorching rays of the sun.

"And gave thanks." We have before noticed the symbolical character of this "giving thanks" as foreshadowing the Eucharistic Benediction; but we learn also from it a more homely lesson, how that for all food, whenever received, thanks should be rendered, and we also learn how we ought to be thankful for all means and opportunities of doing good. The thanks of the Lord would be tendered to His Father not only in anticipation of the actual food soon to be so marvellously provided, but for the opportunity of showing forth the Divine glory and power, and also of relieving the wants of so many who were following Him for a good purpose.

"And gave thanks, and brake, and gave to his disciples," &c. From the circumstantiality with which these details are given in each of the four accounts, it is clear that there is some particular lesson which the Lord and His Spirit would have us draw from this. That lesson seems to be that the true feeding in the Church of Christ is not that each man should take for himself, but that all that can be called food is to be given through ministerial intervention.

7, 8. "And they had a few small fishes . . . . seven baskets

## CHAP. VIII.] SEEKING A SIGN FROM HEAVEN. 161

8 So they did eat, and were filled: and they took up of the broken *meat* that was left seven baskets.

9 And they that had eaten were about four thousand: and he sent them away.

10 ¶ And ᵈ straightway he entered into a ship with his disciples, and came into the parts of Dalmanutha.

ᵈ Matt. xv. 39.

11 ᵉ And the Pharisees came forth, and began to question with him, seeking of him a sign from heaven, tempting him.

ᵉ Matt. xii. 38. & xvi. 1. John vi. 30.

---

9. "And they that had eaten." So A., C., D., later Uncials, almost all Cursives, Old Latin, Vulg., Syriac, &c.; but א, B., D., L., Cursive 33, and a few others, and Coptic, omit "they that had eaten."

..... sent them away." From the mention of a few small fishes, it seems evident that the disciples gave all their provisions of every kind for the sustentation of the multitude; but notwithstanding this they were not in want, for a much larger quantity of fragments or broken pieces was taken up than in the case of the miracle of the feeding of the five thousand: the word here used signifying hampers or panniers, rather than baskets. The same word is used to denote the basket in which St. Paul was let down from the walls of Damascus (2 Cor. xi. 33).

10. "And straightway he entered into a ship .... parts of Dalmanutha." Dr. Thomson, in "The Land and the Book," thinks that he can identify this place with a certain Dalhamia, about halfway down on the western side of the Lake. It is about two miles south of El Medjet, which has been supposed to be the site of the ancient Magdala [or Magadan] Matt. xv. 39).

11. "And the Pharisees came forth, and began to question with him," &c. How diffused and ramified throughout the whole of the country this sect must have been, if even at these insignificant places they were ready to meet and oppose the Lord as soon as He landed.

"Seeking of him a sign from heaven." They made an absurd difference between a miracle wrought upon the surface of the earth, and one which seemed to have its sphere of action above this world. They considered that, if the Lord had caused the food for the five

M

12 And he sighed deeply in his spirit, and saith, Why doth this generation seek after a sign ? verily I say unto you, There shall no sign be given unto this generation.

13 And he left them, and entering into the ship again departed to the other side.

f Matt. xvi. 5.   14 ¶ ᶠ Now *the disciples* had forgotten to take bread, neither had they in the ship with them more than one loaf.

g Matt. xvi. 6. Luke xii. 1.   15 ᵍ And he charged them, saying, Take heed,

---

thousand and the four thousand to descend from the sky, it would have been a greater proof of His Messiahship than the creation of new food in the hands of His Apostles.

12. "And he sighed deeply in his spirit, . . . . no sign be given to this generation." He sighed deeply, because He read their hearts, and saw that their implacability was the real cause of their unbelief. If the signs already vouchsafed on the shore of this very lake had not already convinced them, nothing would. They asked for a sign from heaven, believing that He would not perform it. Their demand was not prompted by the spirit of inquiry, and the desire to ascertain the truth, but because they had already forejudged Him. They would not be persuaded though one rose from the dead.

14. "Now the disciples had forgotten to take bread." Bede says: "Scripture relates that they had forgotten to take bread with them, which is a proof how little care they had for the flesh in other things, since in their eagerness to follow the Lord, even the necessity of refreshing their bodies had escaped from their mind."

How plain and coarse must have been the fare of these princes of the kingdom of God ! Five barley loaves and two fishes; again, seven loaves and a few fishes—only the barest necessaries !

15. "And he charged them, saying, Take heed, beware of the leaven of the Pharisees . . . . leaven of Herod." In Luke xii. 1, our Lord explains this "leaven of the Pharisees" as being "hypocrisy"—the show of religion without the substance. In St. Matthew, on the contrary, it is explained as the doctrine or teaching of the Pharisees. But these things agree together. For the doctrine of the Pharisees against which our Lord inveighed was

beware of the leaven of the Pharisees, and *of* the leaven of Herod.

that part of their teaching by which through their traditions they made void the law of God. It was the attention to ceremonial minutiæ (much of it mere human invention) whilst they neglected judgment, mercy, and faith. Such teaching, by its very nature, engendered and fostered hypocrisy, for it enabled men to make a show of religion without any corresponding internal substance. The substance of religion is that which requires faith and prayer and pains, and the doctrine of the Cross in all its forms is the cleansing of the heart, the rectifying of the conscience, the right direction of the will, the crucifying the flesh with its affections and lusts. Now the putting of what is external in the place of these, so as to make a fair show externally, is in very deed, wherever and whenever it occurs, the leaven of the Pharisees.

The question must now be met, is Sacramentalism (commonly so called) the leaven of the Pharisees? for it is continually insinuated that it is. Now what is Sacramentalism? By the very name is implied a high view of the Sacraments as being not mere forms or external rites, but outward visible signs of inward spiritual grace. The Sacramentalist, as such, believes that the Son of God would not have ordained mere external forms, mere ceremonies, mere types teaching only the need of grace, mere shadows of good things to be received at almost any time rather than the time when men receive the outward sign; on the contrary, he believes that the Son of God ordained these Sacraments to make us partakers of His own Adorable Human Nature as the Second Adam, and this for the highest moral and evangelical purposes, "that our sinful bodies may be made clean by His Body, and our souls washed through His most precious Blood," and "that we may evermore dwell in Him, and He in us." The Sacramentalist [so called] believes all this simply on the words of the Lord. He cannot see that these words mean anything else except the conveyance of a very great Gift indeed, in and through and by the Sacraments. He is exceedingly afraid to lower, or explain away, or in the very least detract from, the mysterious meaning of these words, lest at the last he be found to have done this through the leaven of the Sadducees, which is, in its root, the denial of the Supernatural and so is the leaven of Infidelity. So far from Sacramentalism being opposed

16 And they reasoned among themselves, saying, *It is* ʰ because we have no bread.

ʰ Matt. xvi. 7.

16. "They reasoned among themselves, saying, *It is* because," &c. So A., C., L., N., later Uncials, almost all Cursives, Vulg., Syriac, Coptic, &c. B. and D., omit "saying," and read, "[Because] they had no bread."

to Spirituality, the most Spiritual Christians have been Sacramentalists in the sense of holding the highest views of the grace of Sacraments, witness Augustine, Bernard, Anselm, Thomas à Kempis, Quesnel, Keble.

"And of the leaven of Herod." In the parallel passage of St. Matthew we read (the leaven) of the Sadducees, and it is supposed from this, with much reason, that the party of Herod were mostly Sadducees, if they professed any religion at all. The leaven of Herod would be the *secular* leaven, which not only the Apostles, but all generations of Christians, need to beware of. It is at the bottom the leaven of unbelief. Amongst the Jews it appeared in the denial, as far as was possible, of everything divine in their religion—in the denial of the existence of angels, of spirits in a separate state, of the resurrection, and of judgment to come. In fact, it was a religion of sight, a creed whose dogma was the non-existence of the unseen and spiritual world. And constantly has this leaven reappeared in the Church of Christ, under the form of Arianism, Socinianism, Rationalism, but wherever it has worked it has destroyed all true faith, witness the state of Protestantism in France, Holland, Switzerland, and to a very great extent, in Germany. It is in direct opposition to the very intent and purpose of the revelation of the Son of God, which is given for the express purpose of evidencing to us things not seen. Let us remember also that the words of Christ bid us beware not merely of an openly professed doctrine, but of a *leaven*, *i.e.*, a secret working, an infection, a spirit rather than a definite form of evil.

16. "And they reasoned among themselves, saying, . . . . It is because we have no bread." Commentators ask what is the immediate link between the Lord's mention of leaven, and their being conscious that they had forgotten to take bread? Some suppose it to be, that in bidding them beware of the leaven of the Pharisees, they thought He had denounced even their bread as polluted, but need we seek any such reason? When a person has committed a fault, any chance word dropped by a second party will suggest

17 And when Jesus knew *it,* he saith unto them, Why reason ye, because ye have no bread? ¹ perceive ye not yet, neither understand? have ye your heart yet hardened?

18 Having eyes, see ye not? and having ears, hear ye not? and do ye not remember?

19 ᵏ When I brake the five loaves among five thousand, how many baskets full of fragments took ye up? They say unto him, Twelve.

20 And ˡ when the seven among four thousand, how many baskets full of fragments took ye up? And they said, Seven.

21 And he said unto them, How is it that ᵐ ye do not understand?

¹ ch. vi. 52.

ᵏ Matt. xiv. 20. ch. vi. 43. Luke ix. 17. John vi. 13.

ˡ Matt. xv. 37. ver. 8.

ᵐ ch. vi. 52. ver. 17.

---

**21.** "That ye do **not understand?**" A., Vulg., Syriac, and most other MSS. (except B.) add "yet."

blame, though the connection is of the remotest. Surely here is a touch of nature which is beyond the reach of the cleverest invention.

17, 21. "And when Jesus knew it.... How is it that you do not understand?" As if He said, Did I ever blame you for forgetfulness about the goods of this world? Are not My reproofs always addressed to you because you know not yet, after all My teaching, the good things of that heavenly and eternal kingdom which I am come to reveal? Whilst I am in your company, how can you perish with hunger? I have but very lately twice multiplied a very small amount of bread, so that in the one case you gathered of fragments twelve smaller baskets after feeding five thousand, and in the other seven panniers full after feeding four thousand. Are you not yet in many things in much the same spiritual condition as the multitude to whom I spake in parables, because seeing they see not, and hearing they hear not, neither do they understand? After all My miracles, and all My teaching, and all My explanation of My teaching, do *ye* not yet understand?

Must we not learn from this how the all-sympathizing Lord can enter into the feelings of teachers of the Scriptures in this day, whose scholars, whilst they are capable of understanding all else,

## 166 THEY BRING A BLIND MAN TO HIM. [St. Mark.

22 ¶ And he cometh to Bethsaida ; and they bring a blind man unto him, and besought him to touch him.

23 And he took the blind man by the hand, and led him

---

22. "He cometh." So ℵ, A., N., later Uncials, most Cursives, and Syriac; but B., C., D., L., some Cursives, Old Latin, Vulg., Coptic, &c., "they come."

seem unable to take in, sometimes even to remember, the plainest Gospel truths ?

And, on the other hand, may not the same teachers take heart when they remember how these dull and ignorant fishermen, unable to associate leaven with anything but barley loaves, became, shortly after this, the overthrowers of idolatry and false philosophy, and the instructors of the world in the knowledge of God?

22. "And he cometh to Bethsaida." It is doubtful whether this is the city of Bethsaida Julias, or a small unimportant fishing village on the coast, very near Capernaum.

"And they bring a blind man unto him, and besought him to touch him." This miracle strangely resembles the miracle of the restoration to his hearing and speech of the deaf and stammering man narrated in the last chapter. It may be worth while drawing attention to the resemblances. In both cases the men were brought by friends. In the first case the friends besought the Lord to lay His hands upon the man ; in the second, to touch him. In both cases the Lord leads the person to be healed away—in the first case, from the crowd, in the second, out of the town. In both He touched the affected part with His spittle, and also put His hands upon the blind man, answering to putting His fingers in the ears of the deaf man. But the difference is, that in the first case the man was at once restored to hearing and distinct utterance, whilst in the second there were two stages in the progress of the cure.

23. "And he took the blind man by the hand, and led him out of the town." Here we have mystically the Lord foretold by the prophet "leading the blind by a way that they knew not" (Isaiah xlii. 16).

It has been supposed that the Lord led the man out of the city in order that the inhabitants of that city (Bethsaida) who had rejected His teaching might not incur greater guilt, by still further making nought of the witness of this exceedingly great miracle; but may it not have been that the presence of a crowd, many of

CHAP. VIII.]   I SEE MEN AS TREES, WALKING.   167

out of the town ; and when [n] he had spit on his eyes, and put his hands upon him, he asked him if he saw ought.  [n ch. vii. 33.]

24 And he looked up, and said, I see men as trees, walking.

---

24. "I see men as trees, walking."  A., ℵ, B., C., L., M., N., later Uncials, almost all Cursives read, " I see men, for I behold [them] as trees walking."  So Revisers ; but D., Old Latin, Vulg., Coptic, Syriac, as in Rec. Text.

whom, perhaps, would jeer and flout, was inimical to the spiritual effect which the Lord desired each of His miracles to have ?

Is not this leading the blind man typical ? Are not many who are spiritually blind led, even in their blindness, by the compassionate Lord, till the fit time and opportunity comes for their restoration to spiritual sight ?

" And when he had spit on his eyes, and put his hands upon him, he asked," &c.  For the significance of this spitting see my note on corresponding part of the former miracle (Mark vii. 33).

" He asked him if he saw ought."  He asked this, of course, for the sake of the spectators, among whom, probably, were St. Peter and other Apostles, that they might notice how in this case He chose to heal gradually.

24. " And he looked up, and said, I see men as trees, walking."  That is, he saw certain forms moving about him, but without the power of discerning their shape and magnitude—" trees he should have accounted them from their height, but men from their motion."

Theophylact supposes that the imperfection of his vision was owing to his want of faith. "The reason why he did not see at once perfectly, but in part, was that he had not perfect faith ; for healing is bestowed in proportion to faith " (quoted in Ford, "Cat. Aurea "). Also I. Williams : " It was probably thus to lead him on by degrees to the full faith required. Although it is the only instance in which the attempt is thus repeated, as if the first were not altogether successful ; yet it is in this respect similar to that gradual drawing on to the fulness of belief which is found in other miracles : as in our Lord's conduct to Jairus, and to Martha on raising her brother Lazarus, and others ; it is like supporting Peter on the water by the hand, when his own faith was too imperfect to sustain him ; it is like the carrying in His arms, or gently leading, the weak ones of His flock."

25 After that he put *his* hands again upon his eyes, and made him look up: and he was restored, and saw every man clearly.

26 And he sent him away to his house, saying, Neither go

---

25. "And made him look up." So A., N., later Uncials, almost all Cursives, some Old Latin (a, f, g): but ℵ, B., C., L., Δ, and four or five Cursives read, "And he looked steadfastly." So Revisers. D., some Old Latin, and Vulg., "he began to see."

But must we not remember that this man was brought by the faith of others, who certainly believed that our Lord's touch would cure him?

25. "After that he put his hands again upon his eyes," &c. May not the Lord's conduct in healing this blind man gradually be best explained by taking into account the typical import of the miracle? This miracle sets forth the restoration, to the spiritually blind, of their sight of God and eternal things. And are not men's eyes gradually opened, at least for the most part? Bishop Hall, than whom a better judge in spiritual matters could hardly be found, seems to think that the cure of spiritual blindness is always gradual. He writes: "I find but one example, in all Scripture, of any bodily cure, which our Saviour wrought by degrees: only the blind man, whose weak faith craved help by others, not by himself, *saw* men first, *like trees;* then in their true shape; all other miraculous cures of Christ were done at once, and perfect at first. Contrarily, I find but one example of a soul fully healed, that is, sanctified and glorified, both in a day; all others by degrees and leisure. The steps of grace are soft and short. Those external miracles He wrought immediately by Himself; and therefore no marvel if they were absolute [at once perfect] like their Author. The miraculous work of our regeneration He works together with us; He giveth it efficacy: we give it imperfection." ("Holy Observations," quoted in Ford.)

Even in men who are suddenly converted, *i.e.*, turned from sin, the opening of the eyes to see some of the greatest wonders of the kingdom of God is very gradual. It requires a man to be fully enlightened indeed to see in their due proportions all the great truths of the Catholic faith.

26. "And he sent him away to his house, saying, Neither go into the town," &c. May not the Lord, in giving this strict injunction, have

CHAP. VIII.] WHOM DO MEN SAY THAT I AM? 169

into the town, ° nor tell *it* to any in the town.   ° Matt. viii. 4. ch. v. 43.
27 ¶ ᵖ And Jesus went out, and his disciples, ᵖ Matt. xvi. 13. Luke ix. 18.
into the towns of Cæsarea Philippi: and by the
way he asked his disciples, saying unto them,
Whom do men say that I am?

---

26. "Nor tell it to any in the town." So A., C., N., later Uncials, most Cursives, Syriac, &c.; or..itted by א, B., L. Vulg., *Et si in vicum introieris nemini dixeris*.

foreseen that many in the town, Pharisees and Scribes, would strive to destroy the weak faith of this man, as they did in the case of the man healed at the pool of Siloam? Perhaps the Lord, Who knew this man's heart, foresaw that he would not be able to give to his questioners the noble answer, "One thing I know, that, whereas I was blind, now I see" (John ix. 25).

27. "And Jesus went out, and his disciples, into the towns of Cæsarea Philippi." Called Cæsarea Philippi to distinguish it from the Cæsarea on the coast of Palestine where Cornelius lived. There is a very interesting account of it in "The Land and the Book," to which I refer the reader. The question arises, why did the Lord take the Apostles thus northward, almost out of the Holy Land, Cæsarea itself being a heathen city? It is not, however, said that He took them as far as Cæsarea, but to its coasts or borders. I think it must have been for retirement, and that they might have leisure and quiet to think upon the meaning of the marvellous acts which for a long time past they had seen Him performing, and in many of which they had themselves taken part. What was the significance of the Lord's wonder-working power? They had called Him—nay, they had even worshipped Him as—the Son of God; but now He desired a more deliberate and distinct confession—deliberate, as not being the product of the temporary excitement produced by some mighty act, and distinct, as distinguished from, and in contrast to, the vague and inadequate opinions of the multitude.

St. Mark then tells us that "by the way," *i.e.*, whilst they were on the journey, not in a house or village, He asked them the all-important question, and St. Luke tells us that it was after prayer: "It came to pass, as he was alone praying, his disciples were with him." Perhaps He had withdrawn Himself to a very short distance, and then beckoned them to Him. First of all He prepared

28 And they answered, ⁹ John the Baptist: but some *say*, Elias; and others, One of the prophets.

29 And he saith unto them, But whom say ye that I am? and Peter answereth and saith unto him, ʳ Thou art the Christ.

⁹ Matt. xiv. 2.
ʳ Matt. xvi. 16. John vi. 69. & xi. 27.

---

them for the home question respecting their own faith, by asking them what others said of Him; and from the answers we gather that the people thought him to be a messenger of God, John the Baptist, or Elijah, or one of the old prophets returned to earth; but none believed Him to be the Very Christ, the long looked for Messiah. And then the Lord put the solemn question to them, "Whom say ye that I am? Ye whom I have chosen and separated from all other men to be with Me, to see all my life, to hear all My words, to be witnesses to all My works. Whom say ye that I am?" The question was to all, "Whom say YE," and so the answer was in the name of all. There was no division, no hesitation, "Thou art the Christ." St. Matthew appends to this answer the words, "the Son of the Living God." St. Luke, " of God," "the Christ of God." Now how is it that St. Mark omits the most important, if not all important words, " the Son of the Living God ?" Simply for this reason, that the confession that Jesus was the Christ necessarily carried with it the confession of the truth of all that Jesus claimed to be. Was Jesus the Christ, the Messiah? then He was the Messenger, or Apostle, or Representative of God in a sense in which none else could be. He was the promised Seed of Abraham, the "anointed king on God's holy hill" of David; the "Wonderful Counsellor" of Isaiah; "the Lord our Righteousness" of Jeremiah; the Lord and "Angel of the covenant" of Malachi. Without, however, insisting that the Apostles grasped the significance of all these Divine titles, one thing is abundantly plain, that the true Messiah must be whatsoever He claimed to be, and that the development of His claims, and functions, and offices, and prerogatives was only a matter of time; and another thing, also, was as perfectly plain, (as we shall soon see,) that the danger of the Apostles was not on the side of unbelief in the glories of Christ's Person, but on the side of unbelief in the humiliation, and shame, and death, which were equally associated with the Lord's redeeming work. In fact, so far as the supernatural—the (humanly speaking) incredible was

CHAP. VIII.] THE SON OF MAN MUST SUFFER. **171**

30 ˢAnd he charged them that they should tell no man of him.   ˢ Matt. xvi. 20.

31 And ᵗhe began to teach them, that the Son of man must suffer many things, and be rejected of the elders, and *of* the chief priests, and scribes,   ᵗ Matt. xvi. 21. & xvii. 22. Luke ix. 22.

---

concerned—these very Apostles had passed unscathed through an ordeal which could hardly be equalled. They had but very lately heard the Lord give utterance in the synagogue of Capernaum to words which had sifted and winnowed the disciples of inferior faith, so that many had left Him, and they had stood firm and accepted all these words, no matter how incomprehensible, in simple faith. "Lord, to whom shall we go? thou hast the words of eternal life, and we believe and are sure that thou art the Christ, the Son of the Living God [the Holy One of God]." No, their stumbling-block was not the glories of the throne, or, much less, the enunciation of the mysteries—it was THE CROSS.

30. "And he charged them that they should tell no man," &c. Why? Simply because the Jews to a man mistook the nature of the office and kingdom of the Messiah. They looked for a Messiah who should conquer through armies : the true Messiah was to conquer by the Cross. To proclaim, then, that He was the Christ would utterly mislead all who heard them. They must first learn what sort of a deliverer the true Messiah was to be : and the next verses show that the Apostles themselves were unable to teach them that, because to a great extent they shared in the mistake of their countrymen.

31. "And he began to teach them," &c. This was the first distinct teaching on the part of the Lord of His coming Sufferings and Death. Before this time they could not have borne it, and, indeed, now they could not bear it. But they must now be told all, for otherwise, when the terrible events come to pass, they would make utter shipwreck of faith and hope.

So "he began to teach them, that the Son of man must suffer many things, and be rejected of the elders," *i.e.*, of the governing body in the Jewish Church ; " of the chief priests," *i.e.*, of the God-ordained ministers of the Jewish sacrificial system ; "and of the scribes," *i.e.*, of the authorized expounders of the law.

"And be killed." Mark that the Lord does not, as yet, distinctly

**172   PETER BEGAN TO REBUKE HIM.   [St. Mark.**

and be killed, and after three days rise again.

32 And he spake that saying openly. And Peter took him, and began to rebuke him.

33 But when he had turned about and looked on his dis-

---

foretell the cruel and degrading form of death that awaited Him. That He reserved till He set out on His last journey to Jerusalem (Matth. xx. 19). It required the sight of His Transfigured Body to enable them to bear such an announcement.

"And after three days rise again." The significance of this we know was especially "hidden from them." They seem never to have dreamt of taking comfort under the thought of the coming Death, by setting against it this most distinct enunciation of the Resurrection.

32. "And he spake that saying openly," &c. This seems to mean that He spake it in such a way as to show that He did not desire it to be concealed, in contrast to what He had said respecting His being the Christ, which was not to be openly made known. Perhaps others might have just before joined the company. With this, perhaps, agrees the fact that Peter "took him"—that is, aside.

"And began to rebuke him." If St. Matthew gives the words which St. Peter actually used ["Mercy on thee, Lord, this shall not be unto thee"], then our word "rebuke" is too strong. It should be "remonstrated" with Him, or some similar expression. The original is capable of expressing somewhat milder meanings, which our word "rebuke" cannot.

33. "But when he had turned about and looked on his disciples," &c. He "looked on His disciples," such was His manner when He would, at once, solemnly, and yet lovingly, impress them with some truth. "He looked round about to see her that had touched the hem of His garment" (Mark v. 32). "He looked on" the rich young man, and "loved him" (x. 21). He "looked round about" when he warned his disciples of the danger of riches (x. 23). He "looked round about on the Pharisees, being grieved for the hardness of their hearts" (iii. 5.) "He looked round about on them that sat about Him," when he spake of them as those who were spiritually nearest to Him (iii. 34). Most of these, if not all, we owe to St. Mark, who, himself, owed them to the observant eye of St. Peter.

ciples, he rebuked Peter, saying, Get thee behind me, Satan: for thou savourest not the things that be of God, but the things that be of men.

34. ¶ And when he had called the people *unto him* with

---

33. "Thou savourest not." Revisers, 'Thou mindest not."

---

"Get thee behind me, Satan.' Does the Lord here rebuke Peter under the name of Satan? If so, we must, undoubtedly, take the word Satan in its original meaning as adversary. Our Lord's way to His throne was through His Sufferings and Cross. He that would stand in the way of His suffering, and beseech Him to spare Himself, in reality, though he knew it not, stood in the way of Christ's greatest glory—the overcoming of evil through humiliation and self-denial. Quesnel well remarks, "How dangerous a counsellor is natural tenderness in the affairs of salvation!"

"Thou savourest not the things that be of God, but the things that be of men." The "thing of God" which the Lord had then before Him, was obedience to His Father's will in submission to death. "I have power to lay down my life, and I have power to take it again. This commandment have I received of my Father" (John x. 18). The things that be of men are that men should look to their own interests, and spare themselves, and exalt themselves, and above all things, avoid a cruel and shameful death.

34. "And when he had called the people unto him with his disciples," &c. St. Matthew reports merely that "Jesus said unto his disciples." St. Luke that "He said unto them all," but St. Mark is much more full: "When he had called the people unto him with his disciples also." The significance of this is well brought out by Quesnel: "Self-denial concerns everybody, and consists in renouncing, not only some external things, but the old man entirely, namely, whatever is corrupt in the understanding, judgment, memory, will, and affection, and whatever is therein opposite to the Spirit of Christ and His Gospel. There is no privilege, nor any difference of exemption from the Cross, betwixt the pastors and the flock, with respect to evangelical self-denial: it is for this reason that Christ joins the people with His disciples."

his disciples also, he said unto them, ᵘ "Whosoever will come after me, let him deny himself, and take up his cross, and follow me.

35 For ˣ whosoever will save his life shall lose

ᵘ Matt. x. 38.
& xvi. 24.
Luke ix. 23.
& xiv. 27.
ˣ John xii. 25.

---

35. "Will save his life," *i.e.* desires or wills.

"Whosoever will come after me," rather, whosoever desires; "whosoever has a mind to come after me." It may be that attracted by His words and struck by the power of His marvellous work, some were saying, "Lord, I will follow thee whithersoever thou goest." But as the way to His glory was through the Cross, so must theirs be. They must mortify their ambitious self-seeking, so as to accept Him as a spiritual and suffering Messiah. They must mortify their love of this world's goods, as the Apostles had done, by giving up all, and as the Pentecostal Christians did, by selling their possessions and goods, and parting them to all men. They must mortify themselves in the matter of favour with the great, and of self-esteem, and self-righteousness, as Saul of Tarsus did, when " those things which were his worldly gain, he counted loss for Christ." Such was the lot of those who followed Christ then, to be the first missionaries and heralds of His truth. The question is, Is this true now of us, in these quiet calm days ? Unquestionably it is, according to the words of the Apostles: "They that are Christ's, have crucified the flesh with its affections and lusts." No words illustrating this can be given better than those of Bishop Wilson : " Every day deny yourself some satisfaction. Deny the eye all objects of mere curiosity ; the tongue everything that may feed vanity, or vent enmity; the palate what it most delights in (but this not to be seen by others) ; the ear by rejecting all flattery, all conversation that may corrupt the heart ; the body all delicateness, ease, and luxury, by bearing all inconveniences of life for the love of God, cold, hunger, restless nights, ill-health, the negligence of servants and friends, contempt, calumnies, our own failings, melancholy, and the pain we feel in overcoming the corruptions of nature." (" Maxims of Piety," quoted by Ford.)

35. " For whosoever will save his life shall lose it." There is a remarkable saying of one of the fathers : " If you keep your seed you lose it : if you sow it, you will find it again." It is first spoken

it; but whosoever shall lose his life for my sake and the gospel's, the same shall save it.

36 For what shall it profit a man, if he shall gain the whole world, and lose his own soul?

37 Or what shall a man give in exchange for his soul?

---

36. "What shall it profit?" So A., C., D., Δ, later Uncials, almost all Cursives, Old Latin mostly, Vulg.; but ℵ, B., L., Old Latin (a), Syriac (Schaaf) read, "What doth it profit?"

---

of martyrdom, and of him who shall sacrifice this temporal life for the sake of God; but from thence the principle extends to all sacrifices of bodily health, worldly advantage, and reputation with men.

"For my sake and the gospel's." The words "and the gospel's" are peculiar to St. Mark, and they are written for those who in this day cannot follow Christ personally, as the Apostles did. They teach us that those who now forsake the comforts of home and intellectual society, and the prospects of preferment in a wealthy Church, to preach the Gospel amongst uncivilized or savage tribes, in so doing lose their lives, or all that worldly men esteem life worth living for, not only for the Gospel, or for the Church's sake, but for Christ Himself.

The term "save his life" has a very wide application. It means not only "save his life from death," but save his life, *i.e.*, save himself from the bearing of the cross, from labour for Christ, or for the people of Christ. He shall lose it in eternity.

36. "For what shall it profit a man, . . . lose his own soul [or life"]. The word "soul" is the same as that which is translated "life" in the previous verse. It is true both of the higher and the lower sense of $\psi\nu\chi\eta$ or "life." What use would it be to a man if on one day he had all the riches and honours that this world could bestow upon him, if he knew that he must die the next day; or what profit would it be to a man, if he should have all the wealth and enjoyments and sumptuous fare of Dives, if in hell he must lift up his eyes being in torments, and see afar off the blessed ones from whose society he is excluded?

37. "Or what shall a man give in exchange for his soul?" Chrysostom asks: "When a man at the cost of his soul, that is, his life, gains the whole world, what has he besides, now that his

38 ʸ Whosoever therefore ᶻ shall be ashamed of me and of my words in this adulterous and sinful generation; of him also shall the Son of man be ashamed, when he cometh in the glory of his Father with the holy angels.

ʸ Matt. x. 33.
Luke ix. 26. &
xii. 9.
ᶻ See Rom. i.
16. 2 Tim. i.
8. & ii. 12.

---

soul is perishing? Has he another soul to give for his soul? For a man can give the price of his house in exchange for the house, but in losing his soul he has not another soul to give. And it is with a purpose that He says, "Or what shall a man give in exchange for his soul?" for God, in exchange for our salvation, has given the precious Blood of Jesus Christ."

38. "Whosoever therefore shall be ashamed of me and of my words, &c. . . . holy angels." St. Matthew does not give these words, but only "The Son of man shall come in the glory of his Father with his angels, and then he shall reward every man according to his works." No doubt the Lord said the latter words respecting the judgment according to works immediately after the words in St. Mark. They teach us that our great "work for Christ" is to confess Him. But this confession of Christ's—this not being ashamed of Him and His words—is different in different generations and in different societies. In the earliest age of all the offence was the offence of the Cross,—that men should be ashamed to confess that they believed that He Who was crucified was the Son of God, and that they hoped to be saved by His very Cross. Since then this offence has ceased in outward form, but in reality it has reappeared under different forms of religious cowardice. In licentious ages and societies men have been ashamed of the self-denying words and example of the Lord; in superstitious ages of upholding the purity of His religion; in heretical ages of manfully contending for the faith of His true Godhead; in later periods of our history men seem to have been ashamed of confessing that we are saved through Christ alone, and in this age and in learned and scientific societies are not men ashamed of confessing those words of Christ and of His servants which assert the supernatural in our Holy Religion, especially as it appears in the mysteries of the Divine life and of the Sacraments? At the same time, the thoughtful reader will remember that these pearls of Divine truth are the very last which are to be cast before swine.

## CHAP. IX.

AND he said unto them, <sup>a</sup> Verily I say unto you, That there be some of them that stand here,   <sup>a</sup> Matt. xvi. 28. Luke ix. 27.

1. "And he said unto them, Verily I say unto you, . . . come with power." Upon this exceedingly difficult place I can only repeat what I said in my notes on St. Matthew, that I have not met with any exposition of it at all satisfactory. There seems to me now, however, a certain connection with the last five verses of the last chapter which may be worth stating.

The words of the Lord were, "Whosoever will come after me, let him take up his cross;" "Whosoever will save his life shall lose it;" "What shall a man give in exchange for his soul (or life)?" "Whosoever shall be ashamed of me in this adulterous generation, of him shall the Son of man be ashamed when he cometh," &c.

Now what would be the effect of these words on the minds of the Apostles? Evidently a very discouraging one. They would think that, if they were true followers of their Master, they would have soon, perhaps very soon, to be called upon to suffer death ; and if they confessed His words, the reward which they would look for in the sight of His triumph (coming in the glory of His Father) would be very remote. Now in these words, Christ promised that the three leading ones (there be *some*, *i.e.*, a very few, standing here) should see a glimpse of His heavenly glory long before they were called upon to choose death with Him, rather than life with the world.

But why, then, does the Lord express Himself obscurely, which He undoubtedly does? Evidently because He had reasons—known only to Himself in their fulness—why the Transfiguration should be kept secret from the body of His disciples. If He strictly enjoined them, after it had taken place, to tell the vision to no man, then, if He found it needful to give some promise of it beforehand, that promise must be expressed obscurely—it could not be given plainly, or it would undo the purpose which He had in commanding it to be kept secret.

The Transfiguration was as near an approach as could then be

which shall not taste of death, till they have seen ᵇ the kingdom of God come with power.

2 ¶ ᶜ And after six days Jesus taketh *with him* Peter, and James, and John, and leadeth them up

ᵇ Matt. xxiv. 30. & xxv. 31. Luke xxii. 18.
ᶜ Matt. xvii. 1. Luke ix. 28.

given to men in flesh and blood, of "the Son of man coming in His kingdom," or of "the kingdom of God coming in power." The Lord's Person was ineffably glorious, His face shining as the sun, His raiment white as the light; He came not alone or unattended, but with two of the greatest saints of the old covenant as the earnest of His coming with ten thousand of His saints. The sight was vouchsafed to the leaders, to those on whose faith the faith of the weaker Apostles very much rested. It had a very deep and lasting effect upon the two who have left us any writings. Both St. John and St. Peter speak of it as if of all the visible manifestations of Christ it struck them most; St. John in part at least where he writes, "We beheld his glory, the glory as of the Only Begotten of the Father" (John i. 14); and St. Peter, where he writes, "We have not followed cunningly devised fables when we made known unto you the power and coming of our Lord Jesus Christ, but were eye witnesses of His majesty. For He received from God the Father honour and glory, when there came such a voice to him from the excellent glory, This is my beloved Son, in whom I am well pleased. And this voice which came from heaven we heard when we were with him in the Holy Mount" (2 Pet. i. 17, 18).

So that, remembering the influence of these men in the earliest Pentecostal Church, we can scarcely overestimate the power of the Transfiguration in confirming and exalting the faith of the Saints. These considerations may abate some of the difficulty in interpreting this saying of the Lord, of that event to which it appears so immediately to refer, but I do not put them forward as a solution by any means.

2. "And after six days." St. Luke says, "about an eight days after," adopting a frequent mode of reckoning among the Jews, in including parts of days as wholes. No doubt it was six full days, and a small part of the day before the first, and of the day after the sixth, reckoned as whole days. This bears on the notices of the Resurrection, that He was three days in the tomb, the parts of Friday and Sunday being counted as "days."

"Leadeth them up into a high mountain apart by themselves,"

CHAP. IX.] THE TRANSFIGURATION. 179

into an high mountain apart by themselves: and he was transfigured before them.

It is very difficult to set aside the tradition of the Palestinian Christians that this was Mount Tabor. Cyril, Bishop of Jerusalem, early in the fourth century, speaks of it as a thing commonly known and recognized. "There, Moses and Elias were present with Him in Mount Tabor when He was Transfigured." Commentators continually assert that the tradition dates from this time, as if Cyril himself invented it, but this is impossible. It must have been held for years before he wrote; and yet it could hardly have been Tabor, for Tabor was in Galilee, and putting together all the notices of our Lord's movements at this time, He could not now have been either travelling about or sojourning in Galilee. Dr. Thomson, in "The Land and the Book," gives the preference to Panium: "If all that is recorded," he writes, "in the 16th and 17th of St. Matthew, in immediate connection with the visit of our Saviour, actually occurred in this neighbourhood (Cæsarea Philippi, now Banias), it has been the scene of some remarkable transactions, and among them the Transfiguration. I have supposed, ever since my first visit to Tabor, that that could scarcely have been the place, for the whole summit was covered by a vast castle, which we know was occupied, if not then, yet shortly after, by soldiers. It is true that Josephus says he built the castle, the only foundation for which assertion being that he repaired one that had been there for ages. Moreover, that locality does not suit the accounts given of events immediately connected with the Transfiguration, as recorded by the Evangelists: though it must be confessed that these are not definite or very decisive. I would not, therefore, contend with those who prefer the old tradition in favour of Tabor, and yet I think it probable that it was somewhere in this direction, and see no good reason why it may not have been on this lofty and lonely Panium, or rather Hermon, of which it forms the southern termination." St. Luke alone mentions that He went up to pray, and that the transfiguration took place while He prayed. "And he was transfigured before them."

8. "And his raiment became shining, exceeding white as snow." This, as I have shown in my notes on St. Matthew, was the glory of His Godhead which was suffered for a very brief season to shine through the veil of His humanity. So Cyril of Jerusalem: "Where-

3 And his raiment became shining, exceeding <sup>d</sup> white as snow; so as no fuller on earth can white them.

<sup>d</sup> Dan. xii. 9. Matt xxviii. 3.

4 And there appeared unto them Elias with Moses; and they were talking with Jesus,

---

3. "As snow." So A., D., N., later Uncials, almost all Cursives, Old Latin, Vulg.. Syriac; omitted by א, B., C., L., d. (Latin of D.), and some versions.

fore, since no man living could see the face of the Godhead, He took on Him the face of human nature, that we, though seeing it, might live. Yet when He wished to show even that with a little majesty, when *His face did shine as the sun*, the disciples fell to the ground affrighted: if, then, His Bodily countenance, shining not in the fulness of Him Who wrought, but in the measure of those who followed Him, yet terrified them, and was too much for them, how could any man gaze on the majesty of the [unveiled] Godhead?" (x. 7.)

"Exceeding white as snow; so as no fuller on earth can white them." Archbishop Trench well remarks on this: "All words seem weak to the Evangelists, all images to fail them here. St. Mark, whose words I have quoted, borrows one image from the world of nature (snow), another, homely but effective, from that of man's art and device (that of the fuller): struggling by aid of these to set forth and reproduce for his readers the transcendent brightness of that light which now clothed from head to foot the person of the Lord, breaking forth from within, and overflowing the very garments which He wore: until in their eyes who beheld, He seemed to array Himself with light, which is ever the proper and peculiar investiture of Deity (Ps. civ. 2), 'as with a garment.'"

4. "And there appeared unto them Elias with Moses: and they were talking," &c. Tertullian, in his Treatise against Marcion, has a very remarkable chapter on the Transfiguration, dwelling particularly on this appearance of Moses and Elias in glory with Jesus, and conversing with them, as setting forth in the most sensible way how Christ came, not to destroy the Law and the Prophets, but to fulfil them. "What could so befit the Creator's Christ as to manifest Him in the company of His own fore-announcers? to let Him be seen with those to whom He had appeared in revelations? to let Him be speaking to those who had spoken of Him?—to share His glory with those by whom He used to be called the Lord of

## CHAP. IX.] A VOICE OUT OF THE CLOUD.

5 And Peter answered and said to Jesus, Master, it is good for us to be here: and let us make three tabernacles; one for thee, and one for Moses, and one for Elias.

6 For he wist not what to say; for they were sore afraid.

7 And there was a cloud that overshadowed them: and a voice came out of the cloud, saying, This is my beloved Son: hear him.

---

5. " Three tabernacles." Better, " booths " (Revisers).
6. "What to say." So A., D., N., later Uncials, most Cursives, Old Latin, Vulg., Syriac &c.; but א, B., C., L., and two or three Cursives read, " What to answer."

Glory, even with those chief servants of His, one of whom was once the moulder of His people, the other afterwards the reformer thereof?" (Bk. iv. ch. xxii.)

5-6. "And Peter answered and said to Jesus, Master," &c. Many commentators reflect with somewhat of scorn on the suggestion of Peter, but it was said as "not knowing what he said;" and well might he be so overwhelmed with awe and astonishment as to be at a loss for words, for no eye of man had seen what these simple Galileans were then seeing. But what he said was to his honour, he wished to detain Jesus and the two heavenly visitants, so that from their converse they might learn more of heavenly and eternal truth.

It is surprising that some should have asked such a question as "how came the Apostles to know that the two were Moses and Elias?" Surely the same Power Who brought them out of the unseen world, and made them visible to the eyes of the Apostles, would take care that the whole significance of their appearance should not be lost through ignorance of their names. Tertullian says that it was through Peter and the Apostles being in the Spirit. " Now it is no difficult matter to prove the rapture of Peter. For how could he have known Moses and Elias except by being in the Spirit ? People could not have had their statues, or images, or likenesses: for that the law forbade. How, if it were not that he had seen them in the Spirit ? "

7. "And there was a cloud that overshadowed them." St. Matthew calls it a bright cloud. In 2 Pet. i. 17, it is called the excellent glory, but the word "excellent" is much too feeble. It is rather the very magnificent glory. It was, no doubt, that Shekinah, respecting which God said, "I will appear in the cloud above the mercy seat."

8 And suddenly, when they had looked round about, they saw no man any more, save Jesus only with themselves.

* Matt. xvii. 9.   9 * And as they came down from the mountain, he charged them that they should tell no man what things they had seen, till the Son of man were risen from the dead.

---

From this cloud of glory, as from God Himself, proceeded the Voice, "This is my beloved Son [in whom I am well pleased], hear Him." This witness of the Father to the Divine Sonship of the Lord was to the Apostles what the same Voice at the Lord's Baptism had been to the Baptist. It was the most direct witness from God the Father which was ever vouchsafed to them. The Resurrection, and the Descent of the Spirit, and the miracles they performed in His Name, were sure and certain witnesses, but inferential so far as the Eternal Father was concerned. Here was His very Voice out of the outward visible sign of His presence, and so the Apostle who heard it looks back upon it as the Eternal Father personally acknowledging and so glorifying His Son. "He received from God the Father honour and glory, when there came such a voice to Him from the excellent glory. This is my beloved Son in whom I am well pleased" (2 Pet. i. 17).

8. "And suddenly, when they had looked round about," &c. To understand this we must refer to St. Matthew's account. From him we learn that when they heard the Voice of the Father, they were a second time overwhelmed with fear. "When the disciples heard it, they fell on their face and were sore afraid, and Jesus came and touched them, and said, Arise, and be not afraid." And when thus aroused suddenly by the touch and voice of the Lord, they looked round and saw none but the Lord with them. So suddenly did the glorious sight come to an end.

9. "And as they came down from the mount, he charged them . . . risen from the dead." Probably this was principally for their own benefit. If they had been permitted to make known the revelation vouchsafed to them, they would have spoken of it in a boastful spirit; for two of the three very shortly afterwards asked for the highest places in His kingdom. Such glimpses of heaven were to humble and to abase, not to exalt. Thus St. Paul, under great constraint and unwillingly, and not till it was forced upon him, spake of the visions and revelations of the Lord,—of being "caught

## ELIAS MUST FIRST COME. 183

10 And they kept that saying with themselves, questioning one with another what the rising from the dead should mean.

11 ¶ And they asked him, saying, Why say the scribes ᶠ that Elias must first come?

<small>ᶠ Mal. iv. 5.
Matt. xvii. 10.</small>

12 And he answered and told them, Elias verily

---

up unto the third heaven"—of seeing Paradise, and hearing unspeakable words, but adds that, "lest he should be exalted above measure" by the revelations, there was given him "a thorn in the flesh," the messenger of Satan to keep him low and humble.

10. "And they kept that saying with themselves," &c. Probably the saying that they were not to speak of the vision which they had seen. They religiously observed the injunction respecting silence, but withal wondering at the nature of that Resurrection from the dead, after which they were no longer to keep silence respecting the glory just revealed. As Jews they must have believed in the Resurrection from the dead. There were many prophecies of it in the Scriptures, but these were of a general Resurrection. Would the Lord rise again before this? Must He die in order to rise again? The Resurrection of the Lord, as I have more than once noticed, seems to have been providentially hidden from the Apostles, so that none can say with the least shadow of truth that they expected it, and so imagined it, and so pictured it to themselves till they thought they saw their risen Master. (See observations on the Resurrection of our Lord in my notes on St. Matthew, pages 468 and 470.)

11. "And they asked him, saying, Why say the scribes that Elias," &c.? This, which may be either a question, or an assertion put in order to elicit an explanation, was probably suggested by the appearance of Elias with the Lord. "Surely this appearance of Elias in glory with you, speaking of your shortly approaching Exodus, is not the appearance which the Scribes bid us look for. If you are the Messiah, you must be preceded by Elias."

12. "And he answered and told them, Elias verily cometh first, and restoreth," &c. Two very different meanings have been assigned to this restoration of all things by Elias. First, that Elias shall restore all things by reconciling the fathers with their children, in bringing them to the faith of the Apostles. "Reconciling the unbelieving fathers the Jews, to the Apostles, their children," says Chrysostom: but Augustine, "reconciling their fathers the Prophets

cometh first, and restoreth all things; and <sup>g</sup> how it is written of the Son of man, that he must suffer many things, and <sup>h</sup> be set at nought.

13 But I say unto you, That <sup>i</sup> Elias is indeed come, and they have done unto him whatsoever they listed, as it is written of him.

14 ¶ <sup>k</sup> And when he came to *his* disciples, he

g Ps. xxii. 6.
Is. liii. 2, &c.
Dan. ix. 26.
h Luke xxiii. 11. Phil. ii. 7.
i Matt. xi. 14. & xvii. 12.
Luke i. 17.
k Matt. xvii. 14. Luke ix. 37.

---

13. "How it is written." Revisers, "How is it written?" &c.
14. "When he came . . . he saw." So A., C., D., I., N., later Uncials, almost all Cursives, all Old Latin (except k), Vulg., Coptic, Syriac, Gothic, Æthiopic; but ℵ, B., L., Δ, and Old Latin (k) read, "When they came . . . they saw."

with their unbelieving children the Jews." But must not the true meaning be of this sort? The Baptist restored and rectified the natural conscience of the people in the matter of domestic virtue and the plain rules of righteousness. The former he did when he turned the hearts of the fathers to their children, and conversely the hearts of the children to their fathers, making goodness [as they say of charity] to begin at home. The latter he did when he bid the soldiers do no violence, the publicans exact no more than their due, and the body of the people lay aside their covetousness and be charitable to one another (Luke iii. 10-14). The importance of all this had been utterly obscured by their Pharisaic traditions, and the Baptist, by awakening the slumbering conscience, restored all the fitness for the coming of the Messiah.

"And how it is written of the Son of man that he must suffer many things." This place is at first sight somewhat obscure, however translated, but a glance at the parallel places in St. Matthew seems to clear up its meaning. St. Matthew adds to the saying of the Lord, "They have done unto him whatsoever they listed," the words, "likewise shall also the Son of man suffer of them." The Saviour seems to say that His case would be parallel to the Baptist's: as they knew not the forerunner and destroyed him, so they would not know Him Whose way he prepared, but would do unto Him also whatsoever they listed: they would make Him suffer many things, and set Him at naught, and this according as it is written of Him. As it is written of the Christ that He should have a forerunner, so also the prophets foretold that He must suffer and be set at naught.

14. "And when he came to his disciples, he saw a great multi-

saw a great multitude about them, and the scribes questioning with them.

15 And straightway all the people, when they beheld him, were greatly amazed, and running to *him* saluted him.

---

tude," &c. This is one of the almost innumerable indications in this Gospel that its real author was an eye-witness of all that he describes. St. Peter having seen, with his two fellow Apostles, the Transfiguration, descended with the Lord, and watching, as he ever did, his Master's countenance, observed how the Lord took particular notice of what was going on among the rest—how a great multitude were crowding about the disciples, and how, above all, His enemies were at their old work of instilling unbelief.

15. "And straightway all the people, . . . were greatly amazed," &c. St. Mark alone notices this also. St. Matthew says, "when they came to the multitude." St. Luke, "much people met him." How was it that the people, when they beheld Him, were "greatly amazed?" The word is a remarkable one, and is used to describe the commencement of our Lord's Agony. "He began to be sore amazed." It denotes very great awe and prostration of spirit. How, then, were the multitude thus affected? It has been supposed that the Lord retained on His countenance some remnant of the brightness of His Transfiguration. Thus Archbishop Trench: "Suddenly He, concerning Whom the strife was, appeared, returning from the Holy Mount, His face and person yet glistering, as there is reason to believe, with traces of the glory which had clothed Him there." The strong objection to this is, as Williams remarks, that not a word is said about it in the narrative, and the words of the Evangelist, v. 8, seem to imply that all trace of the Transfiguration had disappeared when the three were aroused by the Lord from their stupor. May not their astonishment have been occasioned by the strange suddenness of the appearance of the Lord, and its opportuneness, just when the bewildered disciples were overwhelmed with the questionings of the scribes?

It is to be remembered that we are not at all called upon to believe that the Lord led the Apostles to the very top of the mountain. If the mountain be a spur of Hermon, He would have led them almost into the region of perpetual snow. May He not have led them to a point sufficiently high to be above the world, as it were,

16 And he asked the scribes, What question ye ‖ with them?

<sup>|</sup> Or, *among yourselves?*

17 And ¹ one of the multitude answered and said, Master, I have brought unto thee my son, which hath a dumb spirit;

¹ Matt. xvii. 14. Luke ix. 38.

---

16. "The Scribes." So A., C., N., later Uncials, almost all Cursives, Old Latin (a), Syriac; but א, B., D., L., Δ, three Cursives (1, 28, 209), most Old Latin, Vulg., and Coptic read, "them"—["He asked them"].

and yet not so far above but that He might suddenly reappear to aid His own in their strife and perplexity? I confess that all my ideas of the Transfiguration are taken from Raphael's picture—for no effort of man's imagination can well be worthier of the reality; but one of the most striking features of that grand conception is the proximity of the scene of glory and peace above to the scene of hellish confusion and strife below. The Lord seems just hovering over the war of passionate words and frantic gestures, so that He might descend and reappear as a visitant from above would do. Of course this is imagination, but may it not point to the reality? The words of our Evangelist certainly seem to postulate an almost miraculous suddenness in the Lord's appearance. But beyond all doubt, that picture of pictures is a grand parable, teaching us how near the glory of heaven and the confusion and hate of hell may be to one another.

16. "And he asked the scribes [or them], What question ye?" If the words "the scribes" be genuine, then the Lord first addressed His enemies; but for very shame and awe they could not answer, and the man most concerned, the father of the maniac boy, came forward.

17. "And one of the multitude answered and said, Master, I have brought," &c. This was a case of possession, akin to that of the Gergesene demoniac, as violent and as destructive, not only racking his victim with spasms ["teareth him"], and afflicting him with fits akin to epilepsy ["he foameth and gnasheth with his teeth"], but urging him to destroy himself ["ofttimes it hath cast him into the fire, and into the waters, to destroy him"]. Archbishop Trench quotes a remarkable passage out of Lucian, the scoffer at Christianity, in which he seems to make special allusion to this case of demoniacal possession: "All know the Syrian of Palestine, the clever man in matters of this kind, how many lunatics (persons

CHAP. IX.]  HE TEARETH HIM.  187

18 And wheresoever he taketh him, he || teareth him: and he foameth, and gnasheth with his teeth, and pineth away: and I spake to thy disciples that they should cast him out; and they could not.  *|| Or, dasheth him.*

19 He answereth him, and saith, O faithless generation, how long shall I be with you? how long shall I suffer you? bring him unto me.

---

19. "Answereth him." So later Uncials, most Cursives, some Syriac; but א, A., B., D., L., several Cursives, most Old Latin, Vulg., Coptic, and some Syriac read "them."

falling down before the moon), and distorted in eye, and full of foam in mouth, at the same time he raises up and sends them away whole for a great fee, having delivered them from their terrible sufferings."

"And I spake to thy disciples that they should cast him out," &c. Very probably the faith of the nine was very sensibly lessened by the absence of the Lord, and of the three leading ones. Williams notices aptly the example of the people when Moses was withdrawn from them: "It was, perhaps, in this respect, as well as in others, strangely corresponding with the descent of Moses from the Mount. For then, at the instigation and gainsaying of the people, Aaron made the molten calf; as now, the disciples seem to give way under the urgency of the Scribes, and that faithless generation."

19. "He answereth him, and saith, O faithless generation, how long," &c. This exclamation is levelled against all around—the disciples, who had, but a short time before, been sent on a mission to cast out evil spirits, "and who had returned with joy, saying, Lord, even the devils are subject to us in thy name" (iii. 15; Luke x. 17); the multitude, who would not have come together unless they expected to see some mighty work similar to those they had seen or heard of very frequently, for the Lord's fame had spread over all the districts round about the Holy Land; and the Scribes, who, maliciously ignoring all former exorcisms, insisted on this single failure as destructive of the claims of Jesus.

"How long shall I be with you? how long shall I suffer you?" &c. From this we learn that it is lawful for the ambassadors of God to groan under the unbelief and opposition of a world at enmity with God, and to long for peace and rest. So the Lord's

HE WALLOWED FOAMING. [ST. MARK.

20 And they brought him unto him: and ᵐ when he saw
ᵐ ch. i. 26.    him, straightway the spirit tare him ; and he fell
Luke ix. 42.
on the ground, and wallowed foaming.

21 And he asked his his father, How long is it ago since this came unto him? And he said, Of a child.

22 And ofttimes it hath cast him into the fire, and into

---

great forefather: " The enemy crieth so, and the ungodly cometh on so fast . . . . and I said, O that I had wings like a dove, for then would I flee away and be at rest."

20. "And they brought him unto him: and when he saw him, straightway," &c. The evil spirits seem always compelled to recognize the presence of the Lord. The reader will remember how the unclean spirit of chapter i. 24, cried out, "What have we to do with thee ? " and how in chapter iii. 11, all seem forced to fall down before Him, and so also, "he that had the Legion ran forward to fall down before Him." Here, however, a spirit more inveterate in malice acknowledges the Divine presence by defiance, as 'it were, and more violent attempts on the life of his victim. Peter Chrysologus, a father of the fifth century, Bishop of Ravenna, remarks: "The youth fell on the ground : but it was the devil who was racked with pain : the possessed had trouble ; but the usurping spirit was convicted before the awful Judge : the captive was detained, but the captor was punished : through the suffering of the human body, the punishment of the devil was made manifest." (Quoted in Ford.)

21. "And he asked his father, How long is it ago since this came unto him ? " &c. This He asked, not for His own information, but for the benefit of the bystanders, that they might know how inveterate this case was, and above all, that the providence of God had so guarded the youth that the evil spirit was restrained from destroying him. Again : " In this, as in some other remarkable instances, our Lord seems long to linger and to ask questions, before He works the miracle, as if thus by degrees, and by the aid of His voice and presence, to call every latent germ of faith into operation : by His words as the dew of heaven ; by His countenance as the genial sun, eliciting and giving strength."

22. " If thou canst do anything, have compassion on us, and help us." Here was seen the mischief which the questioning of the

the waters, to destroy him : but if thou canst do any thing, have compassion on us, and help us.

23 Jesus said unto him, [n] If thou canst believe, all things *are* possible to him that believeth.

24 And straightway the father of the child cried out, and said with tears, Lord, I believe; help thou mine unbelief.

[n] Matt. xvii. 20. ch. xi. 23. Luke xvii. 6. John xi. 40.

---

23. "Believe" omitted by א, B., C.*, L., Δ, four Cursives (1, 118, 209, 244), Coptic, Armenian, Æthiopic; but retained by A., D., N., later Uncials, almost all Cursives, Old Latin, Vulg., and Syriac.

24. "With tears." So A. (very early correction), D., N., later Uncials, almost all Cursives, Old Latin (a, b, e, i, l), Vulg., Syriac; omitted by א, B., C., L., three or four Cursives, Coptic, Armenian, Æthiopic. (In Cowper's edition of the Codex Alexandrinus there is a note, "παιδιου μετα δακρυων.—παιδιου μετα addita in marg., *et δακρυων prius omissum scriptum super rasura ; 1 m. [primâ manu] ut videtur.*")

Scribes had done. It had well-nigh deprived the man of the blessing he desired. How different from the words of the Centurion, "Speak the word only," or of the Leper, "If thou wilt, thou canst make me clean," or of the woman with the issue, to herself, "If I may but touch his clothes, I shall be whole!"

23. "If thou canst believe, all things are possible to him that believeth." A large number of authorities omit the word "believe" from the clause, "If thou canst believe," supposing the word to be spurious. Thus the Lord's words may be paraphrased. As to this, "If thou canst" what meanest thou by it? Then, after a short, emphatic pause, "All things are possible to him that believeth."

If we retain the word "believe," the meaning may be, "Thou saidst to me, If thou canst do anything. I say, If thou canst believe, all things are possible," &c.

24. "And straightway the father of the child . . . . help thou mine unbelief." These words of the afflicted father are priceless, as revealing to us, more clearly than, perhaps, any other in Scripture, the first effect of grace on the soul, how by its entrance it shows to the soul its want, and deficiency, and weakness. The first spark of true faith reveals to the man the extent of the darkness of his unbelief, and draws from him a prayer of mingled faith and humility. Thus Quesnel excellently says, " The humble man is himself distrustful of his faith, and prays without ceasing for an increase of it. It is

25 When Jesus saw that the people came running together, he rebuked the foul spirit, saying unto him, *Thou* dumb and deaf spirit, I charge thee, come out of him, and enter no more into him.

26 And *the spirit* cried, and rent him sore, and came out of him : and he was as one dead; insomuch that many said, He is dead.

27 But Jesus took him by the hand, and lifted him up; and he arose.

---

often so weak that it scarce deserves the name. Who amongst us has, after the example of this man, made use of prayers and tears to obtain it? An humble acknowledgment of the imperfection of our faith, and of our other defects, is capable of making up anything which is wanting to us; or rather, nothing is wanting to him who has humility." Thus, also, Wesley: "Although my faith is so small, that it might rather be termed unbelief, yet help me." Leighton also: "The direct and proper act of faith is of perpetual use and necessity, and then most where there is least of assurance; and it is no other than a remembrance or reliance, a rolling over of the soul upon free mercy." (Ford.) These words may be applied to every Christian grace or feeling. "Lord, I repent; help Thou mine impenitency." "Lord, I love; help Thou my coldness." "Lord, I resolve; help Thou the weakness of my will."

25. "When Jesus saw that the people came running together," &c. The Lord had most probably taken the man and his son aside. The crowd running up to them from mere curiosity, and crowding about, would tend to destroy all the spiritual effect of the mighty work which the Lord intended, and so He at once, with words of irresistible power, cast forth the evil spirit. "Thou deaf and dumb spirit, I command thee, come out of him, and enter no more into him."

26, 27. "And the spirit cried, and rent him sore . . . . and he arose," &c. It has been remarked that this cry of the boy was the first sign of restoration; before, he had been dumb and foamed at the mouth only; now the sharp cry is the prelude to restoration, to speech and reason. Here the Lord permits the violence and power of the spirit to be seen in this last paroxysm, so that when He took him by the hand and lifted him up, it was all but a restoration to

28 ° And when he was come into the house, his disciples asked him privately, Why could not we cast him out? ° Matt. xvii. 19.

29 And he said unto them, This kind can come forth by nothing, but by prayer and fasting.

---

29. "And fasting." So A., C., D., L., N., later Uncials, almost all Cursives, all Old Latin except k, Vulg., Syriac, Coptic, Gothic, &c.; but ℵ, B., and one Old Latin only omit. This is one out of many cases in which certain critics (Tischendorf and Westcott and Hort) make two MSS., noted for scandalous omissions, nullify all other evidence.

life, and so the most violent commotion of the spirit, at times, precedes restoration to spiritual life.

28, 29. "And when he was come into the house . . . . prayer and fasting." St. Matthew adds, "because of your unbelief, for verily I say unto you, If ye have faith as a grain of mustard seed . . . . nothing shall be impossible unto you."

But the answers, as given by the two Evangelists, supplement each other, for true faith will be shown in the earnest and continual use of the means of grace, such as prayer and fasting, not in their neglect. No human being ever had such confidence in God as Christ had, and yet in the view of His great conflict with Satan, He fasted forty days and forty nights. If His great servants the Apostles Peter and Paul were men of faith, they were equally men of fasting. (Acts x. 30; xiii. 2, 3; xiv. 23; 2 Cor. vi. 5; xi. 27.) The more a man has true faith in God, the more likely he is to use extra means of humbling himself before God. Wesley remarks on the parallel text in Matt. xvii. 21: "What a testimony is here of the efficacy of fasting, when added to fervent prayer!" And Calvin's words are also worth reproducing: "The meaning, therefore, is, that it is not every kind of faith that will suffice, when we have to enter into a serious conflict with Satan, but that vigorous efforts are indispensably necessary. For the weakness of faith, He prescribes prayer as a remedy, to which He adds fasting by way of an auxiliary: 'You are effeminate exorcists,' said He, 'and seem as if you were engaged in a mock battle got up for amusement; but you have to deal with a powerful adversary, who will not yield till the battle has been fought out. Your faith must, therefore, be excited by prayer, and as you are slow and languid in prayer, you must resort to fasting as an assistance.'"

30 ¶ And they departed thence, and passed through Galilee ; and he would not that any man should know *it*.

<sup>p Matt. xvii. 22. Luke ix. 44.</sup> 31 <sup>p</sup> For he taught his disciples, and said unto them, The Son of man is delivered into the hands of men, and they shall kill him ; and after that he is killed, he shall rise the third day.

---

31. " He shall rise the third day." So A., N., later Uncials, almost all Cursives, some Old Latin, Vulg., Syriac (Schaaf); but ℵ, B., C., D., L., Δ, most Old Latin and Coptic read, " after three days."

Certain MSS. noted for their monstrous omissions, leave out the words " and fasting," but the reader will see that the overwhelming mass of authorities are in favour of retaining the words. And the sense is on the side of so doing. All attempts at expelling evil spirits must be preceded by prayer, *i.e.*, by invoking the Name and power of God, but in the case of certain more stubborn forms of evil something must be added to prayer. Our Lord Himself adds fasting to prayer as a means of grace, in His Sermon on the Mount (Matt. vi.). He added intense and long-continued fasting to prayer in view of His own conflict with the most powerful of evil spirits, and so the sense here requires that something more than mere prayer is wanted to expel an evil spirit of more than ordinary power and malignity.

30, 31. " And they departed thence, and passed through Galilee .... he shall rise [again] the third day." " Thence " indicates the place where the Transfiguration occurred, probably much to the north of Galilee, near Cæsarea Phillippi. If the previous events had occurred near Mount Tabor, it could hardly have been said that He departed thence and " passed through Galilee," and afterwards that He " came to Capernaum." Lange supposes that this secret abode of Christ's in Galilee coincides with the Lord's refusal, on occasion of His brethren's challenge to Him to go up with them to the feast of Tabernacles in Jerusalem (John viii. 1), and that took place before the penultimate, and certainly concealed journey of Jesus to Jerusalem.

Why should He wish now to be in retirement (" He would not that any man should know it ") ? Evidently because the matter upon which He was now instructing His disciples, His fast approaching Passion and Resurrection, could not be spoken of in public. We

## WHO SHOULD BE THE GREATEST.

32 But they understood not that saying, and were afraid to ask him.

33 ¶ ᑫ And he came to Capernaum: and being in the house he asked them, What was it that ye disputed among yourselves by the way? <sup>ᑫ Matt. xviii. 1. Luke ix. 46. & xxii. 24.</sup>

34 But they held their peace: for by the way they had disputed among themselves, who *should be* the greatest.

---

33. "He came." So A., C., L., N., later Uncials, almost all Cursives, Coptic, Gothic; but א, B., (D.), three Cursives (1, 118, 209), most Old Latin (a, b, c, g, i, k, l), Vulg., Syriac (Schaaf) read, "they came."

must remember that what he is represented in verse 31 as teaching, was not said once for all, but was the continuous theme of His discourses. He had now done with teaching and healing the multitudes. He had borne His witness, and now He laid Himself out to prepare His followers for His Death and Resurrection.

32. "But they understood not that saying, and were afraid to ask him." The truth, respecting the atoning Sacrifice of Himself, which He was about to offer, seems preternaturally hidden from them. Not in such a sense as that they were without blame in not receiving it. But their intense personal love to Him, their admiration of Him, their hopes of His future glory closed their ears to the truth of His sayings. Their secret thought ever was, "Be it far from thee, Lord: this shall not be unto Thee." And so putting away the idea of His Death, they could not receive what He said of His Resurrection: wherefore, for His own purposes, God permitted the veil which they had woven for themselves out of blind love and misplaced hope to abide on their hearts.

33, 34. "And he came to Capernaum . . . . by the way . . . . who should be the greatest." This is the only instance on record, in which the Lord questions them respecting their conduct. With their low and imperfect views of the Kingdom of God, it was only natural for them to dispute who should be the greatest in it, but being natural, *i.e.*, the outcome of the natural and only partially renewed heart, it must be corrected. And according to the Lord's words as recorded in St. Matthew, it could only be corrected by their "conversion." Wonderful fact this, that the men who had given up all to follow Christ needed to be converted. But

35 And he sat down, and called the twelve, and saith unto them, ʳIf any man desire to be first, *the same shall be last of all, and servant of all.*

36 And ˢhe took a child, and set him in the midst of them: and when he had taken him in his arms, he said unto them,

ʳ Matt. xx. 26, 27. ch. x. 43.
ˢ Matt. xviii. 2. ch. x. 16.

---

from what, and to what did they need to be converted? They needed to be converted as to their whole views of the relative importance of things, so that they should desire to be the last of all, and the servants of all—so that they should esteem it the greatest honour and privilege to receive not a king, or a governor, or a philosopher, or a statesman, but a little child in the Name of Christ. How little do those who go about amongst us preaching conversion, preach such a conversion as this!

"But they held their peace." That is, they were thoroughly ashamed. This shame was the beginning of the particular conversion which the Lord declared to be needful.

35. "And he sat down." Not for rest's sake, but to assume the attitude of the teacher.

"And called the twelve." He summoned together the whole body, or college, for the lesson was one which touched the spiritual life of each and every one of them.

"And saith unto them .... last of all, and servant of all." This may be understood in one of two senses; either, "if any desire to be the first in Christ's kingdom hereafter, he must be on earth the lowliest of all, and minister as a servant to others;" or it may be, "if any one be ambitious of pre-eminence above his brethren here on earth, he shall be the last in that eternal kingdom." I incline to the last; for I do not see how any one could set before himself the definite desire to be first either here or hereafter, without forfeiting all claim to be first or indeed great in any way, even though he would attain the object of his desire by self-abnegation, and self-humiliation. Such humiliation for a set purpose could not be true humility.

36. "And he took a child, and set him in the midst . . . said unto them." Some great writer—I am not certain who it is—has noticed the extreme originality, as well as appositeness, of this illustration. It has also been noticed that only a little child would not

37 Whosoever shall receive one of such children in my

---

be injured in heart by so extraordinary a distinction being put upon him. "These children," says St. Hilary, "follow their father, love their mother; wish no ill to their neighbour; have no care for wealth; vaunt not; hate not; nor deceive; believe what is told; hold as true what they hear. And these affections, received into the heart and the will, lay open to us the way to heaven."

Let us put together the things which we learn from each Evangelist of this lovely scene. St. Matthew tells us that He called the child to Him, and St. Matthew and St. Mark that He put him "in the midst" of the disciples, after which St. Mark alone tells us that He "took him up in His arms," and St. Luke, that He set him by Him.

37. "Whosoever [therefore] shall receive one of such children in my name," &c. What is the meaning of "receiving" such a child? Chrysostom thinks it means so as to educate it and bring it up; but probably the meaning is to do to it any sort of kindness whatsoever.

"One of such *children*." Almost all expositors consider that such a term includes all who are in any way like such children, as, for instance, all who are helpless, as children are; all who are simple-minded, or even weak in mind, or, particularly all who are young in the faith, who, like children, require the "milk" of the Word, and not its "strong meat" (Heb. v. 12-14).

"In my name," *i.e.*, for My sake; not only because they are baptized or belong to Christian parents, though these are good reasons indeed, but because they partake of the nature which Christ took upon Him, because they belong to the race which Christ redeemed—because like Him they are poor, and have no settled homes, or because He may be honoured in their after life.

Such children are received in Christ's Name, not only in orphanages or in Sunday schools, but by many of the Christ-loving poor, who have children of their own, and yet take into their homes some poor waif or stray, and cherish it as their own flesh and blood for no reward except the Lord's approval.

"Receiveth me." The grace of this promise seems almost incredible. What an honour would any Christian have esteemed it, if he had been permitted to receive Christ under his roof for a single hour, and yet that receiving might have been external and transi-

name, receiveth me: and ᵗwhosoever shall receive me, receiveth not me, but him that sent me.

38 ¶ ᵘAnd John answered him, saying, Master,

ᵗ Matt. x. 40.
Luke ix. 48.
ᵘ Num. xi. 28.
Luke ix. 49.

tory, but the Lord here, undoubtedly, promises that to receive a little one in His Name, is to receive Him effectually. But this is not an isolated promise. There are several such. "He that receiveth you, receiveth Me." "Verily, I say unto you, inasmuch as ye did it unto one of the least of these, My brethren, ye did it unto Me."

"Whosoever shall receive me, receiveth not me, but him that sent me." This sentiment is Johannine in its character and expression. It belongs to that numerous class of passages, mostly in the fourth Gospel, which set forth the oneness of nature, character, attributes, will, action between the Father and the Son. Just as "he who hath seen Me, hath seen the Father," "he that believeth on Me, believeth on Him that sent Me;" "he that hateth Me, hateth My Father also;" so here, "he that receiveth Me, receiveth Him that sent Me."

38. "And John answered him, saying, Master, we saw one casting out devils," &c. It is very remarkable that this question is the only one word of St. John which he himself addressed singly to our Lord, which has come down to us. Along with his brother James, he moved his mother to ask for the first places in Christ's kingdom, and along with his brother he asks whether they should call down fire from heaven upon the Samaritan village; but in this case only does he address the Lord by himself. It is interesting to consider what it was which moved him. Most probably his conscience; he had just heard the Lord say, "Whoso shall receive one such little child in My Name." Then it struck him that lately he, in common with the rest, or some of them, had forbidden someone to do a good thing in the Name of Christ, and had forbidden him because he did not belong to, or follow, the Apostolic company. The man in question must have been a believer in Christ, and must have been in heart attached to Him. The Lord in His answer claimed him as "for Him," *i.e.*, on His side (Luke ix. 50). Owing to the attention with which the Lord's preaching was listened to, and the effect of His miracles, there must have been many who, without attaching themselves to Him as the Apostles

we saw one casting out devils in thy name, and he followeth not us: and we forbad him, because he followeth not us.

**38.** "And he followeth not us." This first "followeth not us" omitted by ℵ, B., C., L., Δ, three Cursives, Coptic, Syriac, and some versions; but retained by A., D., N., later Uncials, almost all Cursives, Old Latin, Vulg., some Syriac, Gothic, &c.

did, yet believed in Him as the Christ. We know that there were more than two such among the rulers themselves (John xii. 42). The Lord had not as yet laid it upon these that they should openly join themselves to the Church; indeed they could not, for there was, as yet, no organized body to receive them, as there would be after the Day of Pentecost. So that the Lord naturally said, "Forbid him not." If he was sincere we may be sure that the providence of God would, in due time, bring him into the Apostles' fellowship and add him to the Church (Acts ii. 42, 47).

This account is exceedingly important as bearing upon the present state of religion amongst ourselves. There are great numbers of persons amongst us who are preaching Christ after their fashion, who have had not only no commission from the Church, but no training even in the Scriptures from any professedly religious body whatsoever. Are we of the Church to forbid them, *i. e.*, to denounce them as necessarily schismatic and anti-Christian? I think that this place, together with such words as those of the Holy Spirit by St. Paul, in Phil. i. 18, settles the matter that we are not. But then we are bound to do that which will entail upon ourselves far more trouble and far more odium. We are bound to witness to such preachers and their followers, that Christ desires the absolute Unity of His Church, and exhibited His desire by very earnestly praying for it (John xvii. 20, 21), so that if they preach such things as conversion and present acceptance of Christ without regard to the truth that there is not only "one Spirit" but "one body," they may destroy with one hand what they think they build up with the other. Christ by no means laid it upon all those who had received the most signal benefits from Him, that they should so much as tell to others what they had received (Matt. viii. 4; ix. 30; xii. 16; Mark v. 43), and such would show their truest gratitude by obedience to what must have been to their grateful hearts a very hard command. Again, we are bound to do another thing, which will entail still more trouble and odium. We must bring before such irregular preachers, and those influenced by them, as opportunity offers, that in all

39 But Jesus said, Forbid him not: ˣ for there is no man which shall do a miracle in my name, that can lightly speak evil of me.

ˣ 1 Cor. xii. 3.

40 For ʸ he that is not against us is on our part.

ʸ See Matt. xii. 30.

40. "Against us is on our part" [or, "for us"]. So ℵ, B., C., Δ, many Cursives, and the Elzevir edition of Stephens; but A., D., N., later Uncials, seventy Cursives, Old Latin, Vulg., Syriac, Gothic, &c., "Against you is on your part."

probability they hold an imperfect, indeed, a very mutilated Christianity; for all such persons are, by the necessity of their position as external to the Catholic Church, unable to comprehend the truths which relate to the Mystical Body, and, in consequence, they ignore the leading truths of the Apostolic writings, especially those of the Apostle Paul (Rom. vi. xii. 1-4; 1 Cor. vi. 18-20; x. 16-18; xii. 12-30; Ephes. i. 22, 23; iii. 6; iv. 4-6); they, in consequence, disparage altogether the grace of Sacraments, holding them, at the highest, to be mere badges of fellowship; they have, to a man, the most imperfect views of the holiness of the Christian's body, and of set purpose absolve their followers from all need of preparation for the judgment of Christ.

The loss of these truths we should bring before them very prayerfully and very humbly, knowing that the Church herself has in time past, through her ministers, imperfectly taught them; but still we should set them before them very decidedly, for they are not our truths, but the Lord's, and in so doing we shall not be without success. I have now before my mind one whose conscience was awakened by one of the most fanatical and wrong-headed of such irregular preachers, but who through instruction was brought to see the Catholic truth in its full proportions, and is now a priest second to none in usefulness and zeal. The Catholic Church alone is capable of setting forth the whole truth, the whole historical, doctrinal, evangelical, moral, sacramental truth of God.

"Lightly speak evil of me. "Rather, "quickly speak evil of me." Most likely meaning, he may gradually fall away from Me, but whilst he performs miracles in My Name, he must be a true believer in Me.

40. "He that is not against us is on our part." This is not for a

## A CUP OF WATER IN MY NAME.

41 ᵃ For whosoever shall give you a cup of water to drink in my name, because ye belong to Christ, verily I say unto you, he shall not lose his reward.

ᵃ Matt. x. 42.

---

41. "In my name." So א*, C³., D., later Uncials, almost all Cursives, Old Latin, Vulg., &c. ; but אc, A., B., C., K., L., some Cursives, and Syriac omit.

moment to be taken as if a man indifferent to religion or to the Church or the Gospel were not against Christ, for the Lord had said, "He that is not with Me is against Me, and he that gathereth not with Me scattereth" (see my note on this place—Matt. xii. 3). The man whose conduct gave rise to this saying was not indifferent and careless of the honour of Christ. On the contrary, he was a believer above the common run of believers, for he invoked the Name of Christ over those possessed, and on account of the sincerity of his faith, was successful, and so was decidedly on the side of Christ in His contest with the powers of darkness, but if after the Lord had on Pentecost established the fellowship of the Apostles, and began to add to the Church those who were being saved, he had continued in his isolation, then his conduct would have been mischievous and schismatical. He would have attempted to divide that for whose unity Christ had earnestly prayed. And this is the case with many irregular and unauthorized preachers now—they begin through religious fervour to preach Christ, but are afterwards, through vanity, or the evil influence of others, persuaded to act in opposition to Catholic truth.

41. "For whosoever shall give you a cup of water only . . . his reward." This verse seems to follow close upon verse 37, and to be a continuation of a short discourse which seems to have been interrupted somewhat abruptly by the question of St. John, and the Lord's answer in verses 38, 39, 40.

Both Theophylact and Augustine, however, as quoted in Catena Aurea, connect the sense with what immediately precedes. Thus Augustine:—"By which He shows that he of whom John had spoken, was not so far separated from the fellowship of the disciples as to reject it as a heretic, but (in the same way) as men are wont to hang back from receiving the sacraments of Christ, and yet favour the Christian name, so as even to succour Christians, and do them service only because they are Christians. Of these he

42 ᵃ And whosoever shall offend one of *these* little ones that believe in me, it is better for him that a millstone were hanged about his neck, and he were cast into the sea.

43 ᵇ And if thy hand ‖ offend thee, cut it off: it is better for thee to enter into life maimed, than

ᵃ Matt. xviii. 6. Luke xvii. 1.

ᵇ Deut. xiii. 6. Matt. v. 29. & xviii. 8.

‖ Or, *cause thee to offend;* and so ver. 45, 47.

---

42. "In me." So A., B., C.³, L., N., later Uncials, all Cursives, many Old Latin (e, f, g, l, q), Vulg., Syriac; "in me" omitted by ℵ, Δ, and a few Old Latin.

says, 'They shall not lose their reward;' not that they ought already to think themselves secure on account of this goodwill which they have towards Christians without being washed in His Baptism, and incorporated in His Unity, but that they are already so guided by the mercy of God, as also to attain to these, and thus to go away from this life in security."

42. "Whosoever shall offend one of these little ones that believe," &c. This applies equally to little children whose souls are ruined by the bad example of those to whom they look up, or to weak believers, who are perverted from the truth into heresy, or some form of false religion, by the persuasion of those who seem to speak with more confidence.

"Shall offend"—*i.e.*, "shall cause to fall," "shall trip them up in their Christian walk." "It is better for him that a millstone," &c. A millstone here is probably one of such size and weight that it could not be turned by the human hand, but required an ass to move it. [See my note on St. Matthew respecting the allusion to that which was considered so terrible in those days, the loss of religious burial—for the weight of the stone would prevent the body being raised up from the depths of the sea to receive burial.]

"Better for him," &c. What a fearful passage this is against those who have seduced female innocence, or instilled the seeds of infidelity into the minds of those once religious, or initiated any of their brethren into evil practices. If this meets the eye of any such, let them, as they value their eternity, repent, and seek out those whom they have wronged, and strive to undo the effects of their wicked seduction. and pray God without ceasing for the souls once

Chap. IX.]     THE FIRE IS NOT QUENCHED.      **201**

having two hands to go into hell, into the fire that never shall be quenched:

44 ᶜ Where their worm dieth not, and the fire is    • Is. lxvi. 24.
not quenched.

44. "Where their worm dieth not, and the fire is not quenched." This verse with verse 46 omitted by ℵ, B., C., L., Δ, four or five Cursives; but retained both here and in verse 46 by A., D., N., later Uncials, most Cursives, Old Latin, Vulg., Syriac, Gothic, Æthiopic.

wronged by them, or assuredly they will find that the Lord will keep His word, and His word is very terrible.

43-48. "And if thy hand offend thee, cut it off.... where their worm dieth not, and the fire is not quenched." We earnestly wish that it was allowable for us not to comment upon this passage, but to leave it as it is, in its unutterable power, grandeur, and awfulness. As Williams says: "With regard to what is here represented as the parts of the body to be cut off, all comments on the passage are remarkable as showing how human explanations limit, weaken, and darken what is in itself so great; there is an all-seeing eye in God's Word which meets every case, as being Omniscient, Infinite, and Omnipotent. It is rightly understood by a child or illiterate person; it is sufficient to carry those who would pass thereon to the heavenly Canaan, but contains depths which no one can fathom." This is very true, but still the hands, the feet, the eyes, are set forth in God's Word as the instruments of the soul in compassing the gratification of certain distinct evil lusts: the hand is the instrument of covetous grasping and of violence; the feet are the means of evil companionship, and running into the ways of temptation and sin; through the eyes the soul covets what is not her own, and lusts after what is forbidden and polluting; through the eyes also the soul envies and hates, and the Lord classes "an evil eye" amongst the things that defile. But it may be asked, seeing that the members are but the instruments of the evil will, why does not the Lord denounce that, and that only? He does so, we answer, when occasion serves, as we have lately seen where He speaks of what defiles coming out of the heart: but now He sets forth the all important truth that the evil will is mortified and slain not by arguing with it, but by starving it; i.e., by forbidding the members to yield themselves to its gratification. When the Lord bids a soul for the sake of eternity mortify its members, its outward

45 And if thy foot offend thee, cut it off: it is better for thee to enter halt into life, than having two feet to be cast into hell, into the fire that never shall be quenched:

46 Where their worm dieth no, and the fire is not quenched.

‖ Or, *cause thee to offend.*

47 And if thine eye ‖ offend thee, pluck it out: it is better for thee to enter into the kingdom of God with one eye, than having two eyes to be cast into hell fire.

---

45. "Into the fire that never shall be quenched" omitted by א, B., C., L., Δ, a few Cursives, Old Latin (b, k), Coptic, Syriac; but retained by A., D., N., later Uncials, almost all Cursives, Vulg., many Old Latin, &c.

members, He necessarily speaks to one who has two wills, an evil will belonging to the old man, and a better and holier belonging to the new. The evil will would gratify its lusts through its members, but the better will can forbid the members to lend themselves to the evil within, and can call to its aid the Sprit of God by prayer, and can mortify the flesh, and use in faith the means of grace.

44, 46, 48. "Where their worm dieth not, and the fire is not quenched." " The awful and solemn emphasis which the distinction of the clauses and the repetition of words gives this passage, renders it, for the form of expression, the most remarkable in the Bible; the three-fold enunciation having, in Divine sayings, a peculiar force, as the Three Persons of the Godhead setting thereon their seal. The triple declaration of the latter part is, doubtless, on account of the unwillingness of the human heart to accept the doctrine of Eternal Punishment. The worm that preys on the dead body yet is no worm, for it dies not, and a fire that consumes the dead corpse yet is no fire, for it never goes out; a never-dying death, a never-living life; a punishment of the body when the body has been no more (?), the instruments of sin, the hand, the foot, the eye, taken into a state of suffering; these all are replete with mystery; clouds that envelop the King of Terrors." So Williams, and Quesnel writes: " These words, repeated three times, are so many admonitions to avoid the last, great, general and eternal excommunication, which will separate the sinner from all happiness, and overwhelm him with all internal and external miseries, denoted here

48 Where their worm dieth not, and the fire *is* not quenched.

48. This verse in all MSS. Tischendorf appends, *hunc versum nemo omittit*.

by the worm and the fire. Let us hearken to this wholesome advice of our Blessed Saviour, while, as yet, the worm may be crushed by faith in Him."

That He Who is at once the manifestation of the eternal Truth, and the eternal Son of God, should utter, with such emphasis, such words as these must impress upon us all two things :—

1st. That the condition of those who have finally rejected the redeeming grace of God will be unutterably fearful; so that the wrath to come is indeed a thing to be fled from, the Being Whose wisdom sees it necessary for the sake of the intelligent universe to inflict such a punishment, is in very deed a Being to be feared, the means by which this wrath is to be escaped must in very deed be known and be grasped with all the strength of our wills, the soul which is capable of suffering such a doom, must unceasingly commend itself to the safe keeping of Him Who has redeemed it.

2. And secondly, no soul which consistently with the interests of the intelligent universe He can save from this doom will perish in it. He Who, as Mediator, now carries on the perpetual application of His redeeming work, and Who will hereafter pronounce the sentence upon each and every soul, is the Lamb of God Who takes away the sins of the world, the Shepherd Who goes after the lost sheep till He find it, the Receiver of the fulness of the Spirit in order that He may bestow it, the Drawer to Himself of all men who will not resist His drawing. May I here quote words of surprising beauty, cited with manifest approbation by Dr. Pusey, in his answer to Canon Farrar: "I have no profession of faith to make about them (those without) except that God is infinitely merciful to every soul; that no one has been, or ever can be lost by surprise, or trapped in his ignorance; and as to those who may be lost, I confidently believe that our Heavenly Father threw His arms round each created spirit, and looked it full in the face with bright eyes of love, in the darkness of its mortal life, and that of its own deliberate will it would not have Him." (From Faber, "The Creator and the Creature," cited in Pusey's "What is of Faith as to Everlasting Punishment?" p. 17.)

# 204    EVERY ONE SALTED WITH FIRE.    [St. Mark.

<sup>d</sup> Lev. ii. 13.
Ezek. xliii. 24.

49 For every one shall be salted with fire, <sup>d</sup> and every sacrifice shall be salted with salt.

<sup>e</sup> Matt. v. 13.
Luke xiv. 34.

50 <sup>e</sup> Salt *is* good: but if the salt have lost his

---

49. " Every sacrifice shall be salted with salt." So A., C., D., N., later Uncials, almost all Cursives, Old Latin, Vulg., Syriac, Coptic, Gothic, and other versions; omitted by א, B., L., Δ, several Cursives, and some Coptics.

49, 50. "For every one shall be salted with fire . . . . peace one with another." According to the unanimous confession of all commentators, these are as difficult verses as any in the New Testament; but wherein consists the difficulty? Evidently in making out their connection with what precedes, and with one another. For in the two verses there are four distinct propositions, each of which has a good meaning in itself, but it is next to impossible to ascertain the sequence of thought. I believe the explanation of this to be that we have not the whole of the discourse, and by comparing the parallel places in St. Matthew and St. Mark, it is perfectly clear that we have not. For in this Gospel, immediately after the words "have peace one with another," which is the conclusion of the discourse which arises out of the dispute of the disciples in the way respecting precedence, the Lord arises and goes unto the coasts of Judæa; whereas in St. Matthew the discourse occupies twenty-five more verses, including the parable of the lost sheep, the instructions respecting the treatment of the brother who trespasses, Peter's question respecting forgiveness, and the parable of the unmerciful servant arising out of it. The only thing in St. Mark answering to all this matter peculiar to St. Matthew, being the words, "Have peace one with another." It seems quite clear then that verses 49 and 50 are fragments. Indeed they cannot be otherwise than fragments to us in our present state of knowledge, for we are obliged to supply long sentences and whole trains of thought between each to connect them together. Let us now take each clause separately.

"For every one shall be salted with fire." This admits of two meanings—one a very terrible one, fearful to contemplate. It is that the words " every one " refer to those lost ones just mentioned "whose worm dieth not," and it means that the fire of Gehenna will act like salt, it will preserve them from perishing as salt does those things which are salted by it, whilst it is the instrument of their punishment. But it is hard to believe that such is the meaning. Has God provided us in His word with any passage which will sug-

saltness, wherewith will ye season it? *Have salt* <sup>f</sup> Eph. iv. 29. Col. iv. 6.

gest a better? I think He has, and in a place which, like this, asserts the universal application of fire. This is 1 Corinth. iii. 11-15, where we are told that at the day of judgment the fire [whatever it be] will try every man's work; and this work, be it remembered, must be primarily the work of each man in building up his own soul on the One Foundation. Now the action of that fire will be like that of salt in this respect, by consuming that which is corrupt in the soul it will preserve what is left which is incorrupt, and so indestructible. It is that which is sinful and corrupt which destroys the soul in which it dwells. If that corruption be purged out, there is nothing left which can destroy the soul or spirit. By thus understanding the verse we give a meaning to the words of Christ which in itself is true, that is, if 1 Cor. iii. 11-15 gives us a true view of the judgment; and we preserve the universal application of the verse "*every one* shall be salted with fire." What the fire actually is, we must leave to God, only it acts as salt and it acts on all.

"And every sacrifice shall be salted with salt." Here the Lord seems to pass somewhat abruptly to a different kind of salting; but, perhaps, if we had the whole discourse verbatim we should find that the transition was by no means so abrupt. Fire has two uses. It has a purifying one, and a sacrificial one. The Lord passes from the purifying to the sacrificial. The sacrifices which God ordained were "offered by fire" (Exod. xxix. 18, 25, 41, "An offering made by fire unto the Lord," and so a vast number of other places); but there was a preliminary absolutely necessary, they must all be salted (Levit. ii. 13). Now all Christians, as far as I can see, are agreed upon the typical meaning of these sacrifices being never without salt. It is that the living sacrifices of themselves which men offer to the Lord (Rom. xii. 1, 2), must be salted with Divine Grace, *i.e.*, the Holy Spirit incorruptible in Himself, and destroying the corruption of those who are sprinkled with Him, or salted by Him. And now comes the real crux of the passage, the transition from the salting of the sacrifice to "the salt which may lose its saltness," but we have, from the Lord Himself, a sufficient guide as to the meaning of this in Matthew v. 13, where the Lord speaks, as here, of salt losing its saltness. The significance is plainly this: Divine grace is not only salt (and so good in itself), but it makes those to whom it is given to be in their turn "salt." The Apostles were, as the Lord

in yourselves, and ᵍ have peace one with another.

<small>ᵍ Rom. xii. 18. & xiv. 19.
2 Cor. xiii. 11.
Heb. xii. 14.</small>

says, "The salt of the earth," and this not from anything in themselves, but because they were the recipients of the salt of Divine grace to a greater extent than any other men. But there was this difference between the Divine Incorruptible Salt of Grace, and those which were made the salt of the world by receiving it, that the latter had to retain the grace and to increase in it. And so the Lord says, "Have salt in yourselves," *i.e.*, retain, hold fast, increase, and grow in, Divine grace, and this you cannot do unless you continue in the Divine fellowship in which you are, by being at peace one with another.

## CHAP. X.

AND ᵃ he arose from thence, and cometh into the coasts of Judæa by the farther side of Jordan: and the people resort unto him again; and, as he was wont, he taught them again.

<small>ᵃ Matt. xix. 1.
John x. 40. &
xi. 7.</small>

1. "By the farther side of Jordan." So A., N., later Uncials, almost all Cursives; but ℵ, B., C., L., Coptic read, "And beyond Jordan." C.², D., G., Δ, some Cursives, Old Latin, Vulg., Syriac, and some versions omit "and."

1. "And he arose from thence, and cometh into the coasts of Judæa by the farther," &c. It will be necessary to say a word or two respecting the sequence of events. Gresswell, with whose "Harmony" most commentators substantially agree, having inserted as the continuation of this discourse, as given in Matt. xviii. 10-35, the dealing with an offending brother, and St. Peter's question respecting how often he ought to forgive, and the parable of the Unmerciful Servant, then puts down the events from Jesus's going up to Jerusalem at the Feast of Tabernacles in John vii. 2, to the departure of the Lord, after His discourse respecting the Good Shepherd, to Bethany, beyond Jordan, where John first baptised (John x. 40). Either during this stay at Jerusalem, or at its conclusion, the Lord enters into a certain village, no doubt Bethany, near Jerusalem, where

2 ¶ ᵇ And the Pharisees came to him, and asked him, Is it lawful for a man to put away *his* wife? tempting   ᵇ Matt. xix. 3. him.

---

He is entertained by the sisters Martha and Mary (Luke x. 88). After this when in Bethany, beyond Jordan, he hears of the sickness of Lazarus, and returns to Jerusalem and raises him from the dead, then He again retires, but now into the "city called Ephraim" (John xi. 54). Between this retirement and the final entry into Jerusalem occur most of the events recorded between Luke x. 1 and Luke xviii. 14, and at the account of the Lord's taking up and blessing the little children the three Synoptics again coincide (Matt. xix. 13; Mark x. 13; Luke xviii. 15) and substantially continue to do so to the end.

We cannot then understand the word "thence" as referring to the place where the Lord had been speaking of the salt losing its savour, and was urging the Apostles to "have salt in themselves." It is quite necessary to understand it, so far as we are concerned, indeterminedly as referring to some place in Galilee not mentioned.

"Cometh into the coast of Judæa by the farther side of Jordan," *i.e.*, by Peræa. This was the second residence in Peræa, and so the Evangelist intimates, by twice making use of the word "again."

"And the people resort unto him *again*; and as he was wont he taught them *again*."

2. "And the Pharisees came to him, and asked him ... tempting him." In what consisted the tempting? Most probably in this. The whole of that generation, Jewish and heathen, was, as the Lord declares, adulterous to the last degree; not only "adulterous" in the spiritual sense of forsaking God, but adulterous in the sense of utterly disregarding the sanctity of marriage. The Lord's questioners hoped—nay, they were sure, that the Lord would express Himself on the side of strictness in respect of the marriage contract. He had done so before in the most public manner in His Sermon on the Mount (Matt. v. 32): and so, as divorces were then shamefully frequent, He would render Himself unpopular with the adulterous generation. It has been supposed, however, that they wished to entangle Him with Herod, who had put away his own lawful wife and taken his brother's: for being in Peræa, He was in the dominions of Herod. Or, it may be, that they simply wished to try to which school of opinion on the subject

3 And he answered and said unto them, What did Moses command you?

<sup>c</sup> Deut. xxiv. 1. Matt. v. 31. & xix. 7.

4 And they said, <sup>c</sup> Moses suffered to write a bill of divorcement, and to put *her* away.

---

of divorce He belonged—the school of Schammai, or that of Hillel. In Notes on the Four Gospels by F. M., which I have several times quoted, there is a comprehensive but terse note which gives all that need be given for the understanding of this abominable subject: "The School of Hillel, who affirmed that a man might divorce his wife for the most trivial matter, such as over-salting or over-roasting her husband's food (nay, R. Akiba taught, it sufficeth if a man see a woman handsomer than his own wife, for it is written: ' If she find not favour in his eyes,' Deut. xxiv. 1): and the school of Schammai, who from the succeeding words ('because he hath found some uncleanness in her') allowed it only in cases of adultery. Josephus, a respectable Pharisee, put away his second wife, by whom he had three children, because he did not fancy her (Life, 76)."

3, 4. "And he answered and said unto them, What did Moses . . . put her away?" In St. Matthew's account the question comes later on, and is asked of the Lord by the Pharisees. The command of Moses was intended to be a restraint upon divorce. It would serve to prevent the Jew doing anything in the heat of passion. St. Augustine remarks well on this: "Moses, however, was against a man's dismissing his wife, for he interposed this delay, that a person whose mind was bent on separation might be deterred by the writing of the bill, and desist; particularly since, as is related, among the Hebrews no one was allowed to write Hebrew characters but the Scribes. The law, therefore, wished to send him, whom it ordered to give a bill of divorcement, before he dismissed his wife, to those who ought to be wise interpreters of the law and just opponents of quarrel. For a bill could only be written for him by men who, by their good advice, might overrule him, since his circumstances and necessity had put him into their hands, and so by treating between him and his wife, they might persuade them to love and concord."

5. "And Jesus answered and said unto them, For the hardness of your heart," &c. This precept means that a man, if he divorced

5 And Jesus answered and said unto them, For the hardness of your heart he wrote you this precept.

6 But from the beginning of the creation <sup>d</sup> God made them male and female.   <sup>d</sup> Gen. i. 27. & v. 2.

7 <sup>e</sup> For this cause shall a man leave his father and mother, and cleave to his wife;   <sup>e</sup> Gen. ii. 24. 1 Cor. vi. 16. Eph. v. 31.

8 And they twain shall be one flesh: so then they are no more twain, but one flesh.

9 What therefore God hath joined together, let not man put asunder.

---

6. "God made them." So A., D., N., later Uncials, almost all Cursives, most Old Latin, Vulg., Gothic, Syriac; but ℵ, B., C., L., Δ, Old Latin (c), Coptic omit "God."

7. "And cleave to his wife." So A., C., L., N., later Uncials, almost all Cursives; omitted by ℵ, B., Gothic.

his wife, must give her a bill of divorcement. The precept involved the permission, and it was the permission that was given "because of their hardness of heart," as appears from what immediately succeeds.

6. "But from the beginning of the creation God made them male and female." St. Matthew inserts before this, "but from the beginning it was not so," *i.e.*, not so ordered by God that a man could put away his wife; because, at the beginning, God made one man and one woman, by this intimating His will that each man should have one wife and one only.

7. "For this cause shall a man leave . . . cleave to his wife . . . one flesh." The bearing of this on the indissolubleness of marriage is well brought out by Chrysostom: "If, however, He had wished one wife to be put away, and another to be brought in, He would have created several women. Nor did God only join one woman to one man, but He also bade a man quit his parents, and cleave to his wife." Wherefore it goes on: "And He said [that is, God said by Adam], For this cause, shall a man leave his father and mother, and cleave to his wife. From the very mode of speech, showing the impossibility of severing marriage, because He said, 'He shall *cleave*.'"

9. "What therefore God hath joined together, let not man put asunder." A somewhat deep and difficult question arises out of the foregoing argument. The law of God, from the creation itself,

P

10 And in the house his disciples asked him again of the same *matter*.

11 And he saith unto them, ᶠ Whosoever shall put away his wife, and marry another, committeth adultery against her.

ᶠ Matt. v. 32.
& xix. 9. Luke
xvi. 18. Rom.
vii. 3. 1 Cor.
vii. 10, 11.

12 And if a woman shall put away her husband, and be married to another, she committeth adultery.

---

was that marriage should be indissoluble. One female was created for one male, and when they were given to one another in marriage they became one flesh, so that it was like dividing asunder one person to sever the marriage tie. But Moses evidently gave the man a power, under certain restrictions, to put away his wife. Was this from God, or from Moses—from the Divine or from the human lawgiver? Evidently from the human; but with permission (and if it be lawful we should say with reluctant permission) from the Divine. For the Divine law of indissolubility was based on the original law or act of creation, as well as on the fact of marriage making man and wife, in God's sight, one flesh; so that the Mosaic indulgence was temporary, and like many other things in that dispensation, only till "the time of Reformation," and that time of Reformation was the coming of the Son of God, Who brought into the world a new Nature and a far more abundant Gift of the Spirit, and a new and far stricter and holier example. This case of Moses giving permission is in some sort parallel to that of St. Paul, who at times spoke not by the full authority of the Holy Spirit, but "by permission," as in 1 Corinth. vii. 6.

10. "And in the house his disciples asked him again," &c. St. Matthew seems to recognize this more private word to the disciples when He makes the Lord say, "I say unto you." Why was it said to the disciples when in the house? Because the disciples, or apostles, represented the Church, and there was to be in the Church a return to the original strictness of the Paradisaical state.

I must refer the reader to what I have said in my notes on St. Matthew on marriage contracted by divorced persons. I cannot add anything to what I have there said. Quesnel's remark on these verses is worthy of consideration: "The union of marriage resembles that of Christ with His Church, which He will never forsake to take another, as the faithful members thereof will never

CHAP. X.]  JESUS MUCH DISPLEASED.  211

13 ¶ ᵍ And they brought young children to him, that he should touch them: and *his* disciples rebuked those that brought *them*.   ᵍ Matt. xix. 13. Luke xviii. 15.

14 But when Jesus saw *it*, he was much displeased, and said unto them, Suffer the little children to come unto me,

---

forsake Him. God suffered divorce in the synagogue, to signify the future rejection of the people which that assembly represented; He re-established the indissolubility of marriage in the Church, to show that she is the inseparable spouse of Jesus Christ. It is upon this account that the adulterer does, by his lewdness and injustice, particularly dishonour Christ and His Church, Whose mysterious figure he so shamefully violates and abuses."

13. "And they brought young children to him, that he should touch them," &c. St. Luke calls these children "infants," thereby assuring us of their very tender years—that they were not of an age to understand what was implied by being blessed by the Lord.

"And his disciples rebuked those that brought them." By this we are certified that they were not brought to be healed of any infirmity or sickness, for the disciples were accustomed almost hourly to see such brought to our Lord. They could only be brought to Him as the great Prophet, that He should impart such unseen and spiritual blessing to them as they in their then tender years were capable of receiving.

14. "But when Jesus saw it, he was much displeased." The translation "much displeased" is not at all too strong. It is the same word as is similarly rendered in verse 41 of this chapter, and in every place where it is used signifies not only to be angry, but to be very angry.

"Suffer the little children to come unto me." It is particularly to be observed here that our Lord imputes to the children's benefit the faith of those who brought them. He accounts the parents or friends "bringing" to be the child's "coming." What an economy is this, not of superstition, as some most vainly talk, but of love! (Ford).

"And forbid them not." The reader will be grateful to me for giving him a comment on this passage, not in my own words, but in those of that great saint and ornament of our Church of England, John Keble. "That displeasure of His was one token of His special

and forbid them not: for ᵇ of such is the kingdom of God.

<sup>ʰ</sup> 1 Cor. xiv. 20. 1 Pet. ii. 2.

---

love for young children. Another was His express command, 'Suffer them to come to Me,' as if He should say, 'There is something in them which will cause them, if let alone, to come to Me: do not you hinder them. They cannot do without Me, and I, in a manner, cannot do without them. They want Me for a Saviour, and I want them for members. Who dare take on him to hinder us from coming together?' Then our Lord's saying, 'Suffer them to come' is a second and most clear token of His love. A third is His adding, 'Forbid them not.' For when a master not only commands his servant to do a thing, but adds, 'Take care you leave it not undone,' the servant understands that his master's heart is more than usually set upon that thing. But again our Master gives the reason why He is so earnest upon having all the little ones brought to Him; and this is another and an unspeakable token of His love. For what is the reason? 'Of such is the kingdom of God,' *i.e.*, the blessed condition which I came into the world to provide for men belongs, as it were, by right to them, and to such as they are. Instead of being unfit they are the very measure and standard of fitness for it, so that by comparison of them shall be known who are true children of the kingdom." Again, in the page before, he writes: "The Church, which is Christ's Body, pertains to such as they are; they were made for it, and it for them: and what right they have to the Church, just the same, of course, they have to the way into the Church, *i.e.*, to Holy Baptism. For if God calls them into His house, of course He calls them to go through the door. If the kingdom is theirs, so is the entrance into it. And so, as the Jews knew for certain that all their boys were to be circumcized, so Christians know for certain that all their children are to be baptized: not only that they *may* be, but that our Lord is very earnest, very desirous to have them all so brought to Him." (From "Village Sermons on the Baptismal Office," pp. 109-111.)

The reader will see that the spirit of faith which pervades this passage is but an echo of that of the Church. It is the reproduction and expansion of the words of the Church, "Ye perceive how by His outward gesture and deed He declared His goodwill towards them . . . Doubt ye not, therefore, but earnestly believe, that He

15 Verily I say unto you, ¹Whosoever shall not receive the kingdom of God as a little child, he shall not enter therein.   ¹ Matt. xviii. 3.

will likewise favourably receive this present infant, that He will embrace him with the arms of His mercy."

But we must remember that this bringing of little ones to Christ is not done and over when we have brought them to Him in baptism. This first bringing must be followed up by a continual, in fact, by a daily bringing. The more we believe in the reality of Christ's reception of little ones in Baptism the more we shall pray that they may continue and grow in the grace of it—the more carefully we shall shield them from evil influence, the earlier we shall sow in their minds the seed of God's Holy Word.

15. "Verily I say unto you, Whosoever shall not receive . . . not enter therein." In the first ages of the Church this was literally true. We can now scarcely realize of what a world of pride and prejudice a man then had to divest himself, to submit to receive baptism; for instance, an educated Gentile had to account Plato, Socrates, Aristotle, as at the best but very partially enlightened teachers, and to submit to receive the salvation of his soul and the resurrection of his body by believing that a Crucified Jew was the only Son of God. At the same time the Rabbinical Jew had to cast aside the traditions of his elders, over which he had spent the best years of his life, as mischievous nonsense, and to receive at the hands of a fisherman initiation into a system which was to supersede his own. The nearest thing to it in this our day is the baptism of a high caste Brahmin, so that he may receive salvation on the same terms as a Sudra (*i.e.*, one of the lowest caste), and kneel by the side of the same Sudra to receive the pledges of it.[1]

---

[1] The following is related in one of our missionary journals. A high caste Brahmin came to receive Holy Baptism. He approached the font wearing the sacred thread which, amongst his Hindoo co-religionists was the badge of his being amongst the "twice born," and entitled him to little short of religious worship from those of a lower caste. But at the moment when he answered, "I renounce them all," he stripped off the sign of idolatrous pre-eminence and trampled it under his feet.

16 And he took them up in his arms, put *his* hands upon them, and blessed them.

17 ¶ ᵏ And when he was gone forth into the way, there came one running, and kneeled to him, and asked him, Good Master, what shall I do that I may inherit eternal life?

18 And Jesus said unto him, Why callest thou me good?

<small>ᵏ Matt. xix. 16. Luke xviii. 18.</small>

---

16. "And he took them up in his arms, put his hands," &c. Notice not one, but three signs of goodwill. He took them up in His arms as a sign of fatherly affection, He laid His hands upon them in token of blessing proceeding from Himself, and He blessed them, and so by word of mouth assured all of His heavenly Father's benediction, for they had asked Him " to lay His hands upon them *and pray*."

17. "And when he was gone forth . . . there came one running . . . eternal life." St. Mark's narrative, as usual, bears every sign of having been learned from an eye-witness, for whereas St. Matthew merely notices that one came to Him, and St. Luke that a certain ruler asked Him, St. Mark mentions that it occurred when the Lord was going forth, no doubt out of the house, and that this young man, evidently one of rank and consideration, came running, that is, in haste and eagerness, and kneeled to Him, that is, in lowly deference, and asked—

"Good Master, what shall I do that I may inherit eternal life?" The question was evidently asked in all sincerity, by one who had listened to the words of the Lord, and been convinced by His mighty works that He was a teacher sent from God. We cannot help remarking that his coming to our Lord thus in public when He was in the way, and confessing His greatness by kneeling to Him, is in honourable contrast to the coming of another ruler secretly, by night.

18. "And Jesus said unto him, Why callest thou me good? . . . God." Why did the Lord so abruptly meet his inquiry with this question? In my notes on St. Matthew I said that it was as if the Lord asked, "Dost thou call me good out of mere courtesy, as thou wouldst call any scribe or Rabbi good?" And so He did this in order to rectify the man's views of what was good. He had come asking "what good shall I do?" and the Lord directs him at once

*there* is none good but one, *that is*, God.

---

to the only true standard of goodness, God Himself, and to His Law, which sets forth the goodness which God, the only Good, desired to see in His creatures.

Was, then, this young man wrong in thus addressing the Lord (he being, of course, ignorant of our Lord's claim as the Eternal Son of God, to partake of the essential goodness of His Father)? No, for Christ Himself had continually applied the term "good" to the imperfect human being, as when He said, "a good man out of the good treasure of his heart bringeth forth that which is good," and He speaks of "an honest and good heart." He was not wrong, but ignorant—ignorant of the infinite depth and meaning of the word he used, and the thing respecting which he came to inquire. "What shall I do?" St. Matthew alone represents him as asking "What good shall I do?" St. Mark and St. Luke merely, "What shall I do?" Very many of the best commentators believe that by what the Lord asked, He intended to lead the young man to the knowledge and confession of His Godhead. Thus Lange: "Jesus teaches him to apprehend good in its absoluteness, and to that end he must understand the being good, which he ascribes to Christ as being founded in God. Thus the answer is not to be explained Deistically, but Christologically; 'If thou wouldest call Me good, thou must apprehend My unity with God, and My Divine Nature.' Now without for a moment denying, but rather affirming, that any true, honest, searching investigation of the character, claims, mighty works and superhuman words of Christ, would infallibly lead to the belief of His absolute union with God, I do not think that the Lord means this by His question. I think He means to lead the man to a simpler issue, more on his level as not yet a disciple, and so not instructed in the mysteries of the kingdom, of which our Lord's essential Godhead is the highest. I think the Lord's drift will be best ascertained by considering what answer the young man must necessarily have given if the Lord had compelled him (and He may have done so) to say why he called Him good. He could only say, " I call you good because you seem to me, and to all who observe you, to do the will of God. You seem to keep all God's commandments, and to keep them in the highest and most spiritual way that men can. If the Scriptures give us the true character of God as good and merciful, and yet severe, then you set

## 216  THOU KNOWEST THE COMMANDMENTS. [St. Mark.

19 Thou knowest the commandments, [1] Do not commit adultery, Do not kill, Do not steal, Do not bear false witness, Defraud not, Honour thy father and mother.

[1] Exod. xx.
Rom. xiii. 9.

---

forth the character of God, for you go about doing works of mercy and goodness; you set forth forgiveness to the penitent, and yet you give no indulgence whatsoever to any sin." Such must necessarily have been the substance of the young man's answer if the Lord had compelled him to give one to His question, "Why callest thou Me good?" And with respect to the Lord's further remark, "There is none good but One, that is God," we can well suppose him to say, "There is, it is true, but One Who is really good, but then He is the Author of all good, He does not keep His goodness to Himself, He diffuses it. The Scriptures teach us that He is able and willing to make men good after the pattern of His own goodness; and He has made You thus good, and we know this because You so faithfully keep His commandments and do His will."

We must assume that the young ruler, from his position, must have been educated in the Scriptures, and, if so, he must have known all this. He must have known, for instance, that God promised to circumcise the hearts of His people, and he must have known that the Psalms, which he constantly used in his synagogue, supplied him with prayers in which to ask God to do this in each man's case, such as "Create in me a clean heart, O God, and renew a right spirit within me." "Make me to go in the path of Thy commandments."

So then the Lord evidently intended to remind him of what he knew, and bid him realize it, and follow up his knowledge to its issues, and above all not speak words or ask questions hastily and thoughtlessly, but consider and weigh his words well, for he had to do with One Who was able to hold him to what he might say, and would so do.

And now the Lord, having reminded him of the one standard and source of goodness, proceeds: "Thou askest the way of Eternal Life: Do the will of Him Who is Life, and thou shalt enter into His Life. If thou wilt enter into life, keep the commandments, for they were given to lead men to life." "Which?" was his reply. To which the Lord rejoins, "Thou knowest the commandments,

## ALL THESE HAVE I OBSERVED.

20 And he answered and said unto him, Master, all these have I observed from my youth.

---

Do not kill; do not commit adultery; do not steal; do not bear false witness; defraud not; thou shalt love thy neighbour as thyself." Now the reader will notice that the Lord here does not bring forward some test commandment, such as "Thou shalt love the Lord thy God with all thy heart," which would at once, and without any further trouble, have convicted the man as a transgressor, but He brings forward commandments which anyone respectably religious might have kept, and when the young man answered, "All these have I kept from my youth up," the Lord's conduct is in the most marked contrast to what, according to all principles of so-called Evangelical Religion, we should have expected. Instead of saying to him, "You miserably deceive yourself, for you have never really obeyed any one of these commandments in the spirit. Every single act you have performed is tainted with sin. Your supposed righteousness is a delusion. You are utterly alienated from God, for you are a prey to the worst of all evils—self-righteousness." Instead of this, it is said by our Evangelist that "the Lord looked upon him, and loved him." This action of the Lord's is unique. The look of the Son of God must have searched him through and through, and yet notwithstanding the imperfection He saw within him, He loved him. This would not have been if He had seen in him insincerity, or hypocrisy, or pride, or selfishness. If the righteous Lord loveth righteousness, He must have seen something very lovable and good in this man, so as to call forth His love, after that, by His look, the Lord had searched his heart.

But the young man asked, "What lack I yet?" and the Lord answered, "One thing thou lackest: if thou wilt be perfect, sell that thou hast, and give to the poor: [so that thou altogether partest with it and canst not ask it back again, or receive any further benefit from it in this world], and come, take up the cross, and follow me."

Now it is of the utmost importance to the understanding of the whole transaction, that we do not mistake the purport of this answer. If we understand that this answer was designed to convict this man openly of secret covetousness, and so to dismiss him to the fate of Balaam or Judas, or any other covetous reprobate, we

## ONE THING THOU LACKEST. [St. Mark.

21 Then Jesus beholding him loved him, and said unto him, One thing thou lackest: go thy way, sell whatsoever

---

lose the whole lesson which the Lord intended to teach us. We have only to contrast the Lord's conduct in respect of this rich young man with that to another rich man, viz., Zacchæus, to see this. It is said of Zacchæus that he was the chief of the publicans, and that he was rich; and it is also said that he stood and said unto the Lord, " Behold, Lord, the half of my goods I give unto the poor," and the Lord, instead of requiring of him the remaining half, approved of the partial surrender, which no doubt would have left him a comparatively wealthy man, and said, " This day is salvation come to this house, for as much as he also is a son of Abraham." Now why was this difference made? Why did the Lord approve of the surrender by Zacchæus of half of his goods, and require the surrender of *all* this young ruler's? It could not have been because it was necessary to salvation, or the Lord would have required the same of Zacchæus, and of every other man whom He willed to save. Why was it then required in this case? Simply because the man had asked the way of perfection. He had asked, " What lack I yet?" and the Lord sets before him the way of perfection, *i.e.*, the Apostolic life. " Sell that thou hast, and come, take up the cross, and follow me. Do what these My twelve companions have done, they have forsaken all and followed Me, in the way of enduring hardship; follow their example."

This incident is of the utmost importance, as showing that Christ distinctly recognizes two ways of religious life, the ordinary religious life, and the life of perfection. The ordinary religious life, so far as the retention of worldly possessions is concerned, is set forth in the injunctions of St. Paul to Timothy: " Charge them who are rich in this world . . . (not that they surrender at once all that they have, but) that they be not high minded, nor trust in uncertain riches, but in the living God . . . that they do good, that they be rich in good works." The life of perfection was set forth in the life of St. Paul himself. The Lord, then, did not require this young man to embrace the Apostolic life in order that he might enter into life—the way to that the Lord *had* set before him at the first; but because his self-esteem had prompted him to inquire after the way of perfection. [What lack I yet? If thou wilt be perfect.]

All professing Christians are called to the ordinary religious life,

thou hast, and give to the poor, and thou shalt have ᵐ treasure in heaven: and come, take up the cross, and follow me.

22 And he was sad at that saying, and went away grieved: for he had great possessions.

ᵐ Matt. vi. 19. 20. & xix. 21. Luke xii. 33. & xvi. 9.

---

*i.e.*, to a godly, righteous, and sober life, springing (in this dispensation) out of faith in the Person and Work of the Redeemer, guided by His Spirit, accepted through His Merits and Intercession, and nourished by His Body and Blood; but so far as we can see, all are not called to the Apostolic Life; though how many may be secretly called by God to a higher life, even a life of Apostolic perfection, which call of God they resist as this young ruler did, is known only to the Searcher of hearts.

Anyhow, the place teaches us the danger of using unreal words. How much, in this day, we hear of self-surrender which means only a surrender of self-righteousness, so that we should lean, not on ourselves, but on Christ, and submit to be saved, as the expression is, not in our own way, but in His; whereas, the self-surrender which the Lord required of this young ruler was a very different thing indeed, for it was a surrender of all that ministered to self. It was a surrender, not only of worldly company, that of course was included, but of worldly possessions. It was that he should enter upon a life of " simple " faith, which simple faith was to be shown not in words and phrases of reliance on Another's merits, but in the surrender of all settled income, so that he should rely for his daily sustenance on the Lord's opening the hearts of the brethren to minister to his necessities. The writer of these lines has not lived this life himself, nor anything like it; but as he is called upon in due course to expound this remarkable incident, he feels that he must do it honestly, and not deprave Scripture by ignoring the existence of this higher and more perfect way of serving God.

22. "And he was sad at that saying, and went away grieved," &c. It is a sad ending of the interview, but we may be sure that, since the Lord loved Him, it could not have been the ending of his day of grace. The author of the " Christian Year," asks, "Who can say that his heart did not turn afterwards, that He was not among those whom the Holy Ghost at His first coming moved to

28 ¶ ᵃ And Jesus looked round about, and saith unto his disciples, How hardly shall they that have riches enter into the kingdom of God!

ᵃ Matt. xix. 23. Luke xviii. 24.

---

lay all at the Apostles' feet?" (Keble's "Sermon on Prov. xxii. 2," quoted in Ford.)

28. "And Jesus looked round about, and saith unto his disciples," &c. Notice how the real author of this Gospel observed, not only the actions, but the very looks and gestures of the Lord. This "looking round about" implied a solemn pause, and a call to thought and serious reflection, for He was about to enunciate a truth very difficult for the world to receive when He exclaimed "How hardly shall they that have riches enter into the kingdom of God!"

The kingdom of God here does not mean the eternal state of future blessedness in the immediate presence of God, but that visible state of things upon earth—that Church, the body of Christ, which God designed to be the state of preparation for it. It was a fact that for years, we might almost say for centuries, the saying of the Apostle was literally true, "not many wise men after the flesh, not many mighty, not many noble were called." It was the reproach of the philosophers and the higher classes against the Church that it chiefly consisted of low-born persons and slaves. This I have noticed in my note on verse 15.

Now riches gave men consideration in this world. The wealth of this world made its possessors looked up to, and they were loth to enter into a society which was then looked down upon as low, and vulgar, and joyless. Some author has remarked that if a rich man was converted and baptized, he might find his former slave his bishop to exercise discipline over him, or his priest to administer to him elements which, on no account, could he consecrate or administer to himself. And that which would be an hindrance to a man in those days entering into the visible kingdom of God upon earth, would also be then and will be now an hindrance to him in attaining that heavenly state of final glory for which the Church upon earth is intended to be the state of preparation. For a man may be in the Church outwardly and visibly, and yet not of it—not of it in spirit, for the wealth of this world is certainly not conducive to poverty of spirit, and the Lord's first blessing is, "Blessed are the poor in spirit, for theirs is the kingdom of heaven."

24 And the disciples were astonished at his words. But

---

There can be no doubt of the fact, that all Christians, especially all teachers of religion, must face it, that the Lord of salvation lays down with very great seriousness and very great earnestness the hindrances which all worldly advantages are to attaining spiritual and eternal benefits. This is, in many ways, contrary to our worldly reasonings. We are tempted to think that the superior education which naturally accompanies wealth—that the broader and wider views of things which a higher worldly position assists men in taking—that the desire to maintain respectability of demeanour in a sphere above that of the many—that these things must be on the side of religion, but our Lord, Whose heavenly wisdom must have taken into account all such considerations, makes nothing of them, literally nothing, and lays down in the broadest and most absolute way, that wealth and the things which wealth procures are not only detrimental, but dangerous to the soul. Now it seems to me that those who teach the religion of Christ are bound to set this forth, though it may be urged against them. "See," it may be flung in our teeth, "see what comparative affluence you possess, what a position even in the eyes of the world you occupy, what society you are able to enjoy!" Well, if we are faithful we must submit to this taunt, and we must reproduce the words of our Master and Judge. We can, of course, take off much of the edge of such reproaches by self-denial—by simplicity of manners and living, and by liberality. No matter what the difficulty, either on our part or on the part of those we teach, the words of the Lord must be set forth, "How hardly shall they that have riches enter into the kingdom of God."

24. "And the disciples were astonished at his words." But had He not said the same thing in effect before, as in the Sermon on the Mount, and when He sent them forth on their first mission? Yes, but He had never before enunciated it so broadly, so unreservedly, so like an universal axiom as now. Might they not also be astonished at the differences between the new and the old state of things in this respect? Under the Old Covenant the man who obeyed God was to be blessed in his basket and in his store. David sang of him, "Blessed is the man that feareth the Lord," for "Riches and plenteousness shall be in his house," Ps. cxi. But now all is reversed.

Jesus answereth again, and saith unto them, Children, how hard is it for them ᵒ that trust in riches to enter into the kingdom of God!

<sup>o</sup> Job xxxi. 24. Ps. lii. 7 & lxii. 10. 1 Tim. vi. 17.

24. "*For them that trust in riches.*" So A., C., D., N., later Uncials, all Cursives, all Old Latin except one (k), Vulg., Syriac, Coptic, Gothic, Armenian; omitted by א, B., Δ, Old Latin, &c.

"But Jesus answereth again . . . Children, how hard is it for them that trust." Before we comment on this, we must ascertain what the true reading is. The Vatican and Sinaitic MSS. in company with two other authorities only, which I have given in the critical notes above, omit the words, "for them that trust in riches," and read "how hard it is" (*i.e.*, for anyone rich or otherwise) "to enter into the kingdom of God." Now, these MSS. are noted for their omissions, so that if our copies of the New Testament were based on them, we should have what all true Christians would consider a very mutilated Word of God. But the sense and consistency of the whole argument requires that these words should be genuine, for in the twenty-third verse we have the Lord speaking of the danger of riches, and in the twenty-fifth verse reiterating in a parabolic expression what He had said before respecting this particular danger. So that if in this intervening verse our Lord speaks generally, that salvation is a very difficult matter to all alike, the whole point of His argument is destroyed. It is hard for rich men to be saved, only because it is hard for any man to be saved. Thus the most solemn warnings of the Son of God upon a point in which His principles are irreconcilably at variance with the principles of the world are neutralized. The two MSS. which omit these words are derived from one which must have been the production of some scribe who did not do his work conscientiously.

We must treat then these words as part of the words of the Lord.

They teach us, taken in connection with His preceding words, that the danger of riches is, that they almost compel us to trust in them. We naturally look to them rather than to any superior power "for defence, or happiness or deliverance, from the thousand dangers that life is continually exposed to." See what they do—they procure us friends, deference, influence, honourable office: if carefully used and invested they relieve us from all anxiety about the future, and at very little sacrifice indeed they win for us a reputation for generosity and kindness. So that, as I said, they

25 It is easier for a camel to go through the eye of a needle, than for a rich man to enter into the kingdom of God.

26 And they were astonished out of measure, saying among themselves, Who then can be saved?

27 And Jesus looking upon them saith, With men *it is* impossible, but not with God: for ᵖ with God all things are possible.

p Jer. xxxii. 17. Matt. xix. 26. Luke i. 37

---

compel us to trust in them as being our fast friends. At times they fail us, but very seldom, if we exercise prudence and foresight, so that, as Wesley turns it, "It is easier for a camel to go through a needle's eye than for a man to have riches and not trust in them."

25. "It is easier for a camel to go through the eye of a needle than," &c. Of course this betokens an impossibility, and was intended to do so. An impossibility on man's side, left to himself with only a common measure of grace, and so it is said:

26. "They were astonished out of measure, saying among themselves, Who, then, can be saved?" As Jews they thought of the promises of the Old Testament of prosperity and safety to those who kept the law. It may be, also, that they considered among themselves that riches raise men above certain temptations, and put it in their power to relieve the poor, and to do much good.

27. "And Jesus looking upon them." They had said among themselves, not apparently to Him, or so that He should hear, "Who, then, can be saved?" and by His look He at once riveted their attention and, as Chrysostom explains, dispelled any unnecessary fear. "With a mild and meek look having soothed their shuddering mind, and having put an end to their distress [for this the Evangelist signified by saying, 'He beheld them'] then by His words also he relieves them, bringing before them God's power."

27. "With men it is impossible, but not with God: for with God all things are possible." With men (*i.e.*, with men without God's Spirit and Grace), it is impossible, but what is impossible? Not merely to save themselves, but to deliver themselves from the power of things temporal. Just as God only can deliver men from the love of sin, so God only can deliver men from reliance on riches.

"With God all things are possible." Thus God saved Zacchæus,

28 ¶ ᵃ Then Peter began to say unto him, Lo, we have left all, and have followed thee.

ᵃ Matt. xix. 27. Luke xviii. 28.

---

and in this our day some rich and noble men seem to abound in every Christian grace; but though it be possible with God, we may be sure that the Lord did not intend by these words to cancel the warnings He had just uttered. Does the Lord here mean that all things are equally easy to God? By no means. All things may be equally easy to Him as looked at from the side of mere power— mere physical force; but God does not deal with intelligent creatures in the way of overwhelming power. So far as their will is concerned He deals with them, then, after such sort that they should co-operate with Him, and yield willingly to Him: and the Lord if He teaches us anything by the whole matter teaches us this, that it requires more spiritual effort on God's part to deliver a man from the love of the world, when the man's wealth enables him to enjoy all that the world has to offer.

28. "Then Peter began to say unto him." Why is it particularly stated that Peter *began* to say? It seems as if he began and did not finish. Lange seems to have hit upon the right explanation when he says, "It is evident that the beginning signifies a venturesome interruption, or taking up the word [compare chap. viii. 31, 32] followed by embarrassment. According to Mark, Peter himself seems here to have broken off in inward confusion, or at the suggestion of modesty."

"Lo, we have left all, and have followed thee." St. Matthew adds, "What shall we have, therefore?" This is omitted by both St. Mark and St. Luke. May we suggest, that it was meant, and must necessarily be supplied to complete the sense, but that it was not expressed in words?

After this the Lord, as reported by St. Matthew, proceeds to give the promise of the twelve thrones on which the Apostles were to sit and judge the twelve tribes of Israel. Of this St. Mark says nothing, and it has been suggested that, as he was writing for Gentiles, such a promise would not be well understood by them; but in the vast majority of cases no account can be given why one Evangelist omits a matter, and another inserts it. The Spirit, in inspiring them to relate the Lord's words or actions, "Divided to every man severally as He willed" (1 Cor. xii. 11).

29 And Jesus answered and said, Verily I say unto you, There is no man that hath left house, or brethren, or sisters, or father, or mother, or wife, or children, or lands, for my sake, and the gospel's,

---

29. "Or wife" omitted by ℵ, B., D., Δ, Cursives 1, 66, 209, most Old Latin (a, b, c, &c.), Vulg., Coptic, Armenian; retained by A., C., N., later Uncials, almost all Cursives, Old Latin (f), Syriac, Gothic, Æthiopic.

29, 30. And Jesus answered and said, Verily I say unto you, there is no man that hath left house or brethren . . . world to come eternal life." In my notes on St. Matthew I remarked on the difficulty of this saying of the Lord as we have it in his gospel, but that the words as given by St. Mark being more circumstantial are still more difficult. It is only right to state and face this difficulty, though we can only indicate the direction in which we believe the true solution is to be found. St. Matthew's words, "shall receive an hundredfold, and shall inherit eternal life," *may* be explained of a reward in the future state: but the words "now in this time," which are added by St. Mark and virtually by St. Luke, altogether forbid this explanation, and show that the reward is to be expected here. Much more do the words, "with persecution," peculiar to St. Mark, forbid us to look for the fulfilment in heaven only.

Neither do I think it is possible to explain the words of the Lord merely in a spiritual way—as that we receive Christ, and in Him we receive all things: as the Apostle says, "All things are yours . . . and ye are Christ's, and Christ is God's." This is a most blessed truth, but the words of the Saviour are very express as to the man who surrenders certain worldly blessings for the sake of Christ receiving *at this present time* these blessings back again increased a hundredfold. The history of the New Testament forbids us to take the words literally, and yet the very circumstantial terms of the promise compel us to seek for as literal an interpretation as we can.

First let us take the relationships mentioned here. Suppose that a man, one out of a family of many brothers and sisters, was converted and felt it his duty (being clearly called by God to preach the Gospel) to leave his home and their society; or suppose, which must have been much more common, that a man belonging to such a family was converted to see the wickedness of idolatry, and the

30 ʳ But he shall receive an hundredfold now in this time, houses, and brethren, and sisters, and mothers,

ʳ 2 Chron. xxv. 9. Luke xviii. 30.

profane and immoral character of the whole heathen family life, so that, consistently with his duty to God, he could no longer live in a house where all sorts of pollutions were daily taking place—by so doing did he cut himself off from all fellowship, all society? So far from it, instead of one brother or sister in the flesh, with whom from their abominable idolatries and degrading habits he could no more hold pleasant converse, he was welcomed into the society of a multitude, all like himself enlightened and purified, all the children of the same Heavenly Father, and the brethren of the same Saviour, with whom, as his brethren, he could hold perpetual intercourse on the greatest things which can possibly engage the heart or mind of a human being. We thus see in a moment how, in the matter of human converse and fellowship, he would literally receive an hundredfold in return for what he surrendered for Christ's sake. He would not receive a hundred natural brothers or sisters, but he would receive a hundred brethren who would be far more to him than his own natural brethren as long as they continued what they were.

Then take the case of wife and children: it is not to be supposed for a moment that he would have to desert these. What the Lord says must be taken on the principles of common sense, that, for the sake of the Gospel, the man would remain unmarried, and so give up the innocent pleasures of home and family. Such an one would find in the souls won by him to the Church of Christ, a joy and satisfaction which Christ would take care should be a far greater recompense to him than children of his own.

And this helps us to meet the more difficult question of what we are to understand by "houses" and "lands"—how they who give up such purely material things for Christ, shall receive an hundredfold more *of such things* in this life. This is not to be understood, as some seem to take it, in the sense that he who, like Barnabas, surrendered his property would become a member of a society which, having all things in common, would see that none should want anything, and so would relieve each Christian of all worldly anxiety. This seems an unworthy meaning; to arrive at the true one we must consider what is wealth in houses or lands valuable for? Simply and solely for the satisfaction or gratification it affords. It can

and children, and lands, with persecutions; and in the world to come eternal life.

31 *But many *that are* first shall be last; and the last first.

<sup>*</sup> Matt. xix. 30; & xx. 16. Luke xiii. 30.

only be prized for the happiness or feeling of security, which it gives, or is supposed to give. Now, what our Lord promised to those who should surrender any good things of this world for His sake was, that even in this present time, so far from losing they should be gainers by it. They should be very much happier indeed for the surrender. His words are to be understood, not of spiritual joys only, but of happiness in its plainer and more common sense; of happiness as it is derived from things out of ourselves, from our worldly condition, and the treatment which we meet with from those around us. Just as they who lost the love of their natural friends and relations would have the place thus left empty in their hearts filled with more and dearer friends than nature had given them, so they that parted with house and lands for Christ's sake, would have their loss more than made up to them in such things as contentment, absolute freedom from the trouble and worry which almost always accompany worldly possessions, in peace of mind, not merely religious peace, but tranquillity in respect of all the changes and chances of this mortal life: above all, in the fact that their happiness does not depend upon what the world can deprive them of, for they have it very deeply engraven in their hearts that "the world passeth away and the lusts thereof, but he that doeth the will of God abideth for ever."

But the Lord adds that this manifold recompense *in* this world will not be *of* the world, for it will be attended with persecutions. "In the world ye shall have tribulation." "If they have persecuted Me they will also persecute you." But these persecutions will have two good effects. They will drive the soul more and more from the world to take refuge in God, and they will make the Christian long for *His* return, Who, when He comes, will destroy every enemy, and turn this present very imperfect state of happiness into a perfect one; but a perfect one in which this rule will hold good, that they who have laboured most, surrendered most, denied their wills most, will receive the greatest recompense of reward.

31. "But many that are first shall be last, and the last first." These words, as they are read in St. Matthew's Gospel, seem to

32 ¶ ᵗ And they were in the way going up to Jerusalem;
and Jesus went before them: and they were
amazed; and as they followed, they were afraid.
ᵘ And he took again the twelve, and began to tell
them what things should happen unto him,

ᵗ Matt. xx. 17.
Luke xviii. 31.
ᵘ ch. viii. 31.
& ix. 31. Luke
ix. 22. & xviii.
31.

33 *Saying*, Behold, we go up to Jerusalem; and the Son of man shall be delivered unto the chief priests, and unto the scribes; and they shall condemn him to death, and shall deliver him to the Gentiles:

---

32. "And as they followed, they were afraid." So A., N., later Uncials, almost all Cursives, some Old Latin, Vulg., Gothic, Syriac; but א, B., C., L., Δ, one or two Cursives, Coptic, Armenian, "They that followed were afraid."

introduce the parable of the "labourers in the vineyard," of which St. Mark says nothing. They have, however, a meaning, or indirect meaning, independent of the significance of that parable. One of the original twelve then present was cast away, and one not yet called [called, as he says, "out of due time"] laboured more abundantly than they all. "It also," as Williams says, "seems to refer to the last in time; that although the Apostles were first to give up all, yet even to the end the same renunciation of the world for Christ's sake, were it to exist, would raise to an equal dignity with them."

32. "And they were in the way going up to Jerusalem . . . were amazed . . . were afraid . . . should happen unto him." They were amazed at the alacrity with which He went up to the place where they knew His most bitter enemies were plotting His destruction [Let the reader remember how they said, "Master, the Jews of late sought to stone thee, and goest thou thither again?"]. They knew He was rushing into danger, but they did not know the form which the persecution would take. Naturally, as they followed they were afraid.

And the Lord now took them aside and told them the worst more distinctly than He had done before.

33, 34. "Saying, Behold, we go up . . . the third day he shall rise again." Notice the two deliverings up, first by Judas to the chief priests, then by them to the Gentiles. They were both betrayals of Him Whom the betrayers knew to be innocent. Notice also how the indignities and insults are dwelt upon as well as the death. "They shall mock Him, and scourge Him, and shall spit upon Him" (see note on Matt. xxvii. 26, 27, 28). Theophylact writes

34 And they shall mock him, and shall scourge him, and shall spit upon him, and shall kill him : and the third day he shall rise again.

35 ¶ ˣ And James and John, the sons of Zebedee, come unto him, saying, Master, we would that thou shouldest do for us whatsoever we shall desire.

ˣ Matt. xx. 20.

---

on all this, "He did this to confirm the hearts of the disciples, that, from hearing these things beforehand, they might the better bear them afterwards, and might not be alarmed at their suddenness, and also in order to show them that He suffered voluntarily : for he who foreknows a danger and flies not, though flight is in his power, evidently of his own will gives himself up to suffering."

"The third day he shall rise again." This is the third plain declaration of His Resurrection which the Lord had given to them. When we add to these the intimations in His last discourse, such as, "I go away and come again to you;" "Ye now therefore have sorrow, but I will see you again," &c., their want of expectation of His Resurrection seems almost miraculous. It is one of the grossest of all falsehoods to assert that He first rose again in their loving imaginations, and then they turned the creation of their fancies into reality.

35. "And James and John, the sons of Zebedee, come unto him," &c. In St. Matthew we read that it was their mother who came and spoke for them, of which St. Mark says nothing : so there is at first sight a discrepancy, but there is underlying the account a real and manifestly undesigned coincidence, for the Lord, having heard the mother's petition, turns to the two disciples, and treats it as if it was theirs, not hers, implying that the mother was merely prompted by the two. St. Mark, well informed by St. Peter of the nature of the matter, ignores the mother, and treats it as the petition of the disciples, which it was.

"Master, we would that thou shouldest do for us," &c. This seems a very unworthy way of preferring their petition. It seems as if, through His known affection and regard for them, they would entrap our Lord to promise something which they were afraid would be denied, if it was boldly mentioned at first.

36. "And he said unto them, What would ye," &c. The Lord knew well what they wanted to ask; but for the sake of the all-

36 And he said unto them, What would ye that I should do for you?

37 They said unto him, Grant unto us that we may sit, one on thy right hand, and the other on thy left hand, in thy glory.

38 But Jesus said unto them, Ye know not what ye ask:

---

important lesson which he foresaw that he should be able to draw from it, and from the indignation which it excited in the ten against the two ambitious brethren, He made them repeat it themselves, probably in the hearing of the rest.

37. "They said unto him, Grant unto us that we may sit, one on thy right hand," &c. But had He not said to all, "Ye shall sit upon twelve thrones, judging the twelve tribes of Israel?" Bishop Bull suggests that " as in the ancient kingdom of Israel the two first places belonged to the Princes of the Tribes of Judah and Joseph; these two places, therefore, she asks for her two sons in the kingdom of Christ." A more important question is, what prompted them to prefer the request at this time? For the Lord had just been speaking of the deep suffering and humiliation He was shortly about to undergo. Very probably, from all that the Lord had been saying, they knew that the crisis was at hand. What the events of that crisis were they most probably refused to steadily contemplate, but they were certain of its issue in the speedy establishment of the Messianic kingdom: and so they thought that they would be beforehand, and secure the first places of honour.

This was the first ecclesiastical intrigue for high places in the Church. The Lord exposed it and did not allow it to be kept secret, though the two were His most loving friends and followers. And is not this an earnest that in the great day all attempts at attaining high places in so holy a Society by favour, will be made known to the shame of those who have engaged in them?

38. "But Jesus said unto them, Ye know not what ye ask," &c. Ye vainly imagine that I shall give the places on my right hand or on my left, as Cæsar or any earthly king does—that I shall give them to those whom I favour, and that I bestow my favour as men do, through caprice, or through partiality, or because they are importuned, or to those who have made themselves useful to them: but I tell you that it is not so. For men to share with Me in my

CHAP. X.]     CAN YE DRINK OF MY CUP?     231

can ye drink of the cup that I drink of? and be baptized with the baptism that I am baptized with?

39 And they said unto him, We can. And Jesus said unto them, Ye shall indeed drink of the cup that I drink of; and with the baptism that I am baptized withal shall ye be baptized:

---

glory they must share with Me in My labours and sufferings. To sit on the right hand of God is not given even to Me of mere favour. "Because I drink of the brook in the way, God will lift up My head." "Because I make Myself of no reputation, and being found in fashion as a man I humble Myself, and become obedient unto death, even the death of the cross,—because of this, God will highly exalt me." This is My Cup—this is My Baptism.

"Can ye drink of the cup that I drink of, and be baptized with the baptism?" &c. Can ye cast in your lot with Me, and face the sufferings and contumely and cruel death which I have told you that I must undergo? "There are inward mortifications, which pierce the heart, expressed here by the cup, which is to be drunk of; and there are outward, denoted by the Baptism." So Quesnel, and Bengel remarks: "The mention of both [Cup and Baptism] is suitably introduced, for they who receive the Sacraments, share in the Baptism, and in the Cup of the Lord. The Baptism of Christ and our Baptism, and the Holy Supper, are closely allied with the Death and Passion, both of Christ and of ourselves."

39. "And they said unto him, We can," &c. There is a strange mixture of faith and of presumption in this answer. Of presumption, arising from their want of self-knowledge. They had been astonished that the Lord so boldly stepped forward to go to the place where His enemies were plotting His Life, and they were afraid. How, then, could they say that they were able to drink of His Cup? They could and they did say it, and apparently in faith and sincerity; for the Lord, instead of blaming them for their presumption, or prophesying of their approaching cowardice and desertion, accepted their words. Is it too much to suppose that they said it relying on His help and grace? And so with all Christ's followers. They are not able, and they are able. They are "not able of themselves to do anything as of themselves," but they are able through the strength of Christ to do and to endure what Christ allots to them.

40 But to sit on my right hand and on my left hand is not mine to give; but *it shall be given to them* for whom it is prepared.

And Jesus said unto them, " Ye shall indeed drink of the cup that I drink of," &c. Jerome writes: " It is made a question, how the sons of Zebedee, James and John, did drink the cup of Martyrdom, seeing that Scripture relates that James only was beheaded by Herod, while John ended his life by a peaceful death. But when we read in Ecclesiastical History that John himself was thrown into a cauldron of boiling oil with intent to martyr him, and he was banished to the isle of Patmos, we shall see that he lacked not the will of martyrdom, and that John had drunk the cup of confession, the which also the three children in the fiery furnace did drink of, albeit the persecutor did not shed their blood."

40. " But to sit on my right hand, and on my left is not mine to give, but for whom it is prepared of my Father." The words inserted in italics, both in the Authorized and in the Revised of 1881 (which professes to be an improvement upon the older versions) give a wrong meaning. A plain man would understand, that not Christ but someone else will assign these rewards, when he reads, " Is not Mine to give, but it shall be given," &c., as if He did not, as the Judge of all, assign all and every place in His Eternal Kingdom. But it is remarkable that He Himself, in His message to the Church of Laodicea, claims to give the highest conceivable glory : " To him that overcometh will I grant to sit with me on My throne, even as I also overcame and am set down with My Father on His Throne." (Rev. iii. 21.) And St. Paul asserts that he will receive his reward from the hands of Christ Himself, when he says, "Henceforth there is laid up for me a crown of righteousness which the Lord, the righteous judge, shall give me that day, and . . . to all that love His [Christ's] appearing." So that whatever places in His Kingdom are given, will be given by Christ Himself, but not according to a rule of favour, but to a rule of right and justice, which rule is laid down by the Holy Ghost in the words, " Every one shall receive his own reward according to his own labour." (1 Cor. iii. 8.) Bede remarks, " The kingdom of heaven is not so much of Him that giveth, as of him that receiveth." For " there is no respect of persons with God." My Father hath prepared it for those who conquer and triumph. If such be your character you will

CHAP. X.] WHEN THE TEN HEARD IT. 233

41 ʸ And when the ten heard *it*, they began to be much displeased with James and John. ʸ Matt. xx. 24.

42 But Jesus called them *to him*, and saith unto them,

---

obtain it. It belongs not to Me to give it to the proud. Do you wish to receive it? be dissatisfied with your present state. It is prepared for others: be no longer like yourselves [be other than you are in self-seeking], and it is prepared for you."

41. "And when the ten heard it, they began to be much displeased," &c. Thus one evil begets another. The self-seeking of the two brothers very naturally called out bitter feelings in those over whom they sought pre-eminence; feelings which, though provoked, sprang naturally from the same evil root as the ambitious request of James and John.

42. "But Jesus called them to him, and saith unto them, Ye know that they which are accounted . . . . your minister . . . . servant of all." In these words the Lord lays down, not the principle, but the spirit of all Ecclesiastical Rule. It is to be the rule not of servants only, for servants may be proud, tyrannical, and overbearing; but of servants who feel that their service, their holy, unselfish service, is their exaltation. A few remarks in addition to those I have written on the corresponding passage in St. Matthew's gospel will be necessary.

First of all, notice that the Lord does not meet the spirit of ambition and self-seeking which, as long as men are what they are, must exist in every large society like the Church, by laying down the principle of equality. On the contrary, he presupposes that some will be great, and that some will be chief in the Church; but this greatness and pre-eminence is to be attained by becoming ministers and servants—not by self-exaltation, but by self-abasement. Now a very little thought will make it clear that though a position of honour and rule may be accorded to self-abasement, yet it never can be sought by self-abasement, because in such a case self-abasement would be consciously used as the instrument of self-aggrandizement.

If, then, there are to be, as there must be, first and second places in the Church, and the first places are not to be attained by interest, canvassing, pushing ourselves forward, constituting ourselves leaders, and certainly not by an hypocritical show of humiliation,

ᵃ Ye know that they which || are accounted to rule over the Gentiles exercise lordship over them; and their great ones exercise authority upon them. 43 ᵃ But so shall it not be among you: but who-

ᵉ Luke xxii. 25.
|| Or, *think good*.
ᵃ Matt. xx. 26, 28. ch. ix. 35. Luke ix. 48.

42. "They which are accounted." See margin. Vulg., *Qui videntur principari Gentibus*; Syriac, *ii qui reputantur principes Gentium*.
43. "So shall it not be." So A., N., later Uncials, almost all Cursives, some Old Latin, Coptic, Syriac, Armenian, Gothic; but ℵ, B., C., D., L., Δ, most Old Latin, Vulg. read, "is" (" so it is not ").

then it follows that these places of honour and power are not to be sought by any members of the Church for themselves; and that is precisely what the Lord indicates in these words of His to the disciples. The whole history of Christendom shows that there can be no equality properly so called, in any organized body of professing Christians. There must be either the pre-eminence of bishops, or of party leaders. Now the pre-eminence of the latter is doubly wrong, because it not only engenders the use of all sorts of arts for gaining influence, but is founded upon that which is in itself contrary to the mind of Christ, viz., Church parties.

We will now make some remarks on the separate verses.

42. " Ye know that they which are accounted to rule," &c. There seems to be but one meaning which can be attached to this, viz., that all rule in the Church is to be very different from that exercised by the Cæsars, and those who govern under them. For Church rule is not to be arbitrary, autocratic, tyrannical, but paternal; resting on love and reverence, not on force. The rule of the Gentile powers is described by a word which expresses not only lording over, but lording it down upon those beneath. Dr. Morison has "exercise authority upon them." But not so much " up " on them as " down " on them. The preposition (κατά) in the Greek is well expressed by the homely and somewhat vulgar but graphic phrase, " coming down upon one."

" But so shall it not be [or so it is not] among you, but whosoever will be great," &c. Olshausen writes: "The idea of a special exaltation and glory in the kingdom of God is not the least condemned, but is acknowledged as correct." For the comparison of the rulers (ἄρχοντες) and great ones (μεγάλοι has positively no meaning, if it was intended that there should be no " first " or " great ones " in the kingdom of God.

CHAP. X.] WHOSOEVER WILL BE GREAT. 235

soever will be great among you, shall be your minister:

44 And whosoever of you will be the chiefest, shall be servant of all.

45 For even <sup>b</sup> the Son of man came not to be ministered unto, but to minister, and <sup>c</sup> to give his life a ransom for many.

<sup>b</sup> John xiii. 14.
Phil. ii. 7.
<sup>c</sup> Matt. xx. 28.
1 Tim. ii. 6.
Titus ii. 14.

---

43, 44. "Will be." "Desires to be." *Quicunque voluerit,* Vulg.

43. " Whosoever will be great among you, shall be your minister .... servant." Not only all Church rule, but all Church functions which reflect any degree of honour or pre-eminence in the administrator are to be administered in the spirit of service. As the Apostle writes, " ourselves your servants for Jesus' sake." All ministers, bishops, priests, deacons, are in the first place the servants of Christ, and in the second His servants towards the flock. So that self is to be completely sunk, and all exaltation on account of the service to be avoided. The spirit of this is admirably expressed by Quesnel : " The greatest minister of the Church is he who is most conformable to the example of Christ by humility, love, and continual attendance on his flock, and also looks upon himself as a servant to the children of God. We do not know what an exceeding honour it is to serve one single soul for the sake of God, in the spirit of the Holy Servitude of Christ."

45. " For even the Son of man came not to be ministered unto, but to minister," &c. The word used by the Lord for "minister" is usually derived from διά, a preposition signifying through, and κόνις, dust, one who works in the dust and runs through the dust, by this signifying low and hard labour : and His life was a life of hard labour, and unceasing spending of Himself for His fellow men. He was perpetually labouring as through the dust for the good of the bodies and souls of His fellow men, unceasingly healing, and preaching ; having, as I remarked on St. Matthew, so far as we can learn, no hired servant, having a following of poorly-clad men, not to wait upon Him, but to learn of Him.

" And to give his life a ransom for many." These many, we know, from various assertions in Holy Writ, are all mankind : " Who gave himself a ransom for all " (1. Tim. ii. 6). " He is the propitiation for our sins, and not for ours only, but also for the sins of the

46 ¶ ᵈ And they came to Jericho: and as he went out of Jericho with his disciples and a great number of people, blind Bartimæus, the son of Timæus, sat by the highway side begging.

ᵈ Matt. xx. 29.
Luke xviii. 35.

46. "Blind Bartimæus, the son of Timæus, sat by the highway side begging." So A., and the MSS. usually following it; but ℵ, B., L., Δ read (with Revisers), "The son of Timæus, Bartimæus, a blind beggar, sat by the wayside." Many small insignificant differences amongst MSS. and versions.

whole world" (1 John ii. 2). The assertion, in all probability, is not spoken doctrinally or dogmatically, but in sequence to the former clause. He came to minister, and He ministered not only in His Life, but, above all, in His Death. He ministered to very many in His Life, but to far, far more in His Death: inasmuch as by His Death He ransomed them from the worst of evils, the dominion of sin, death, and Satan. [For comparative infrequency of the mention of the atonement in our Lord's discourses, see my note on St. Matt. xx. 28.]

56. "And they came to Jericho: and as he went out of Jericho," &c. They came to Jericho, probably from Ephraim, to which place the Lord had retired after the raising of Lazarus (John xi. 54), but upon the sequence of events the Harmonists are divided.

There seems to be an irreconcileable discrepancy between the three Synoptics on the circumstances of this miracle. St. Matthew mentions two blind men—St. Mark only one, giving us his name. St. Luke mentions only one, as "a certain" blind man. Again, St. Matthew and St. Mark tell us that He restored the blind man to sight "as he went out of Jericho" ["as they departed from Jericho," Matt.], but St. Luke says, "as he was come nigh to Jericho." May I be permitted to repeat the substance of what I wrote on St. Matthew (xxvi. 69-75)? For the more confirmation of our faith in the power of His Son, God has given to us a threefold account of some of the principal miracles and incidents; and these accounts, in order that we may the more rely upon their truth, are evidently independent accounts; but how is their independence to be manifested? I answer, by those small discrepancies which would exist in any threefold account whatsoever, if we had an account of it from three independent persons. It is not in human nature that any three men, however truthful, should give exactly the same account of any transaction

47 And when he heard that it was Jesus of Nazareth, he began to cry out, and say, Jesus, *thou* son of David, have mercy on me.

48 And many charged him that he should hold his peace:

---

which was made up of a number of details more or less minute. If there was exact accord in all the lesser circumstances it would show either that the three accounts were copied from one original, and so were in fact only one, or that the three witnesses, or narrators, had met together to consult about the elimination of discrepancies—in fact, to use the vulgar expression, had cooked their account. The discrepancy has been met and explained in this way. As the Lord enters Jericho from the north, Bartimæus prays the Lord that he may receive his sight; his prayer is not answered then, but the Lord passes on and spends the night at the house of Zacchæus. And on the morrow as He left the city, Bartimæus and another who had joined him, called to the Lord, Who now takes notice of them, and they receive their sight; but is it not far better to suppose that the inspiration of the Evangelists did not extend to minutiæ of this sort, and that there is a mistake in the narrative, and that either St. Luke on the one side, or St. Matthew and St. Mark on the other, were misinformed?

"Bartimæus, the son of Timæus." On account of the mention of his name it is supposed that he was afterwards well known in the early Church.

47. "And when he heard that it was Jesus of Nazareth," &c. The name was first given by way of reproach, but in the later period of the Lord's ministry it seems to have been the most popular appellation. When men asked, as he entered into Jerusalem, Who is this? they were answered, "This is Jesus, the prophet of Nazareth of Galilee."

"Jesus, thou son of David." Thus addressing Him as the Messiah. If the Syrophenician woman thus called on Him (Matt. xv. 22), much more would one of His own nation who had heard the fame of His mighty works.

48. "And many charged him that he should hold his peace," &c. It has been supposed that the Lord was teaching as He went on His way; and certainly a very little after this, whilst on the journey, He set forth the parable of the Pounds (Luke xix. 11); but was it

but he cried the more a great deal, *Thou* son of David, have mercy on me.

49 And Jesus stood still, and commanded him to be called. And they call the blind man, saying unto him, Be of good comfort, rise: he calleth thee.

---

not most probably out of mere officiousness? The Lord had set forth on His last journey full of holy resolve to finish at Jerusalem His great work, and many had caught some of His enthusiasm, and were accompanying Him. They knew not distinctly for what He went up, and were annoyed that the progress should be interrupted.

But the blind man, sustained, no doubt, in his importunity by the secret grace of God, " cried the more a great deal, Thou Son of David, have mercy upon me." This showed his true faith in the power of Christ, and also in His compassionate loving character. It is as if he had heard and realized the words, " Him that cometh to me I will in no wise cast out."

49. " And Jesus stood still, and commanded . . . . Be of good comfort, rise: he calleth thee." Very probably the very persons in the crowd who had, but a little before, officiously bidden him to hold his peace, now turned and encouraged him. So thought Augustine when he wrote: " When a Christian first enters into a religious life, and begins to be zealous in good works, and to despise the world, he finds at this early stage of his amendment of life many lukewarm Christians who are ready to blame, and to oppose him; but should he persevere, and overcome them by continuance in well doing, these same persons will take his part. As long as they entertain the least hope of gaining their point, they molest and find fault; but when they are outdone by resolute determination, they change sides and exclaim, ' This is really a great man, a blessed man, to receive such grace from God.' "

" Be of good comfort, rise: he calleth thee." There can be no greater encouragement to the sinner than to know that the Saviour calls him, not only calls him by the general call which all share in the preaching of the Word, and the witness of the Church and Sacraments; but with that particular call which moves him personally to come to the Lord—that Divine call heard within, with the ear of the soul, which assures the sinner that amidst the distracting crowd the Saviour recognizes *him*, and desires that *he* should come

50 And he, casting away his garment, rose, and came to Jesus.

51 And Jesus answered and said unto him, What wilt thou that I should do unto thee? The blind man said unto him, Lord, that I might receive my sight.

---

50. "R«se." So A., C., later Uncials, almost all Cursives, Syriac, Armenian, Æthiopic; but אּ, B., D., L., Old Latin, Vulg., Coptic read, "leapt up" or "sprang up."

and partake of His restoring, and enlightning, and sanctifying grace.

50. "And he, casting away his garment, rose, and came to Jesus." Is not this a parable teaching us that we must show our earnestness and our sincerity, by casting aside every impediment which hinders us in coming to the Lord? This does not mean that we are to wait till we are cured before we come to Him. The blind man did not wait till he partially saw before He came, but we are to lay aside all in our surroundings which hinders us, such as evil companions, evil books, evil gains, evil practices in business or in daily life.

"And came to Jesus." Quesnel remarks well: "The blind man stands before Jesus without seeing Him, yet he believes and hopes in Him, which gives us a representation of this life, wherein our cure is wrought under the obscurity of faith. We shall see this adorable Truth which is at present veiled from our sight, when our cure shall be perfected and our eyes opened, and the darkness of faith (1 Cor. xiii. 12) changed into the light of glory."

51. "And Jesus answered and said unto him, What wilt thou?" &c. He had before cried out, "Thou son of David, have mercy upon me." Now the Lord requires that he should openly and distinctly state the particular mercy he needed. And this, also, is a parable for us. In our prayers we must not only ask in general terms, but we must particularize the mercy we need. We must come to Him Who saves His people from their sins, not merely asking to be saved from our sinfulness, or sinful nature, but from this or that particular sin, in which our sinful nature makes itself known. We must look into ourselves so as to understand what are the wounds and ailments of our souls, and come to Him mentioning each one thing of which we have reason to be ashamed.

52 And Jesus said unto him, Go thy way; ᵉthy faith hath made thee whole. And immediately he received his sight, and followed Jesus in the way.

* Matt. ix. 29.
ch. v. 34.
∥ Or, *saved thee*.

52. "And Jesus said unto him, Go thy way; thy faith," &c. Faith is believing. What did this man believe? In the first place, he believed that the Lord was the Messiah, or he would not have called on Him as the Son of David. In the next place, he believed that as the Messiah He could open the eyes of the blind, *i.e.*, that He could heal the disease, or restore the substance of the most delicate and tender and withal perishable organ of the body. In the next place, he believed that the Lord was so benevolent and merciful that He would do this, no matter what else He was engaged in doing; for he had heard how the Lord had suffered His teaching to be interrupted in order that He might heal a paralytic (Mark ii. 2-12), and so he thought that the same Lord would stay His journey for a few minutes in order to heal him. This was his belief, and it made him persevere in asking for mercy, when those who seemed to surround the Lord bid him be silent, and so, though nothing in itself, it won the blessing from the Lord.

"And immediately he received his sight, and followed Jesus in the way." No doubt that he might be to others a proof of the power and goodness of the Lord. And those too who have received spiritual sight from the Lord will follow Him in the way of life.

The Lord now having done this great work proceeds on His journey to Jerusalem. As He drew nigh He utters the parable of the Pounds (Luke xix. 11, 28). Then He lodges at Bethany, and there in the house of Simon the Leper they make a supper for Him, at which Mary anoints His feet with the ointment (Mark xiv. 37) and excites the anger of Judas (John xii. 4-8), who then determines to betray the Lord. Then many of the Jews from Jerusalem, when they knew He was in Bethany, came that they might see Him and Lazarus (John xii. 9-11), and then began to occur the events recorded in the next chapter. So that the matters narrated in Mark xiv. 1-10, occur earlier in the history, and are only mentioned there because of their connection with the Passover and the Betrayal.

## CHAP. XI.

AND <sup>a</sup> when they came nigh to Jerusalem, unto   <sup>a</sup> Matt. xxi. 1.
Luke xix. 29.
John xii. 14.

1. "And when they came nigh to Jerusalem, unto Bethphage and Bethany," &c. Almost all commentators believe that this triumphal procession of the Son of God into His own city, "The city of the Great King," took place on the first day of the week in which the great events of Redemption took place, *i.e.*, on Palm Sunday. The Lord had spent the Sabbath (Saturday) in Bethany; on the evening of that Sabbath He partook of the feast in Simon's house, and the next morning, perhaps after He had set out for a short way on foot, He sent the two disciples to find the colt on which He was to ride and fulfil the prophecy.

"When they came nigh to Jerusalem," &c. This verse, if the events of it were fully related so as to include the incidents mentioned only in St. John, would run: "They went on their way from Jericho to Jerusalem, and, as they drew nigh to Jerusalem, they halted at Bethany, where the Lord spent the Sabbath, and on the morning of the first day, leaving Bethany, He set out on His way to Jerusalem, through Bethphage, over the south side of the Mount of Olives."

"He sendeth forth two of his disciples," &c. The two Synoptics Matthew and Mark being led to omit, at the exact time, the account of the Supper at Bethany and the anointing which there took place in order to connect it more intimately with the betrayal, speak as if the Lord made no halt on His journey; and also since Jerusalem was the termination, mention it first, and Bethphage and Bethany in the order of their nearness to it.

This entry of the Lord into the city of David is described by each of the four Evangelists, so that we must consider well its meaning. Its significance is twofold. It is the great King coming, as was prophesied of Him, to receive the homage of the people of His own city—to be acknowledged by them, if but for a brief season, as the Son of David, in fact to receive praise and adoration as if He was a Divine Being—and it is the Priest Victim of Humanity coming at the time appointed to offer Himself to be slain, so that

R

Bethphage and Bethany, at the mount of Olives, he sendeth forth two of his disciples,

---

1. "**Unto** Bethphage and Bethany." So ℵ, A., B., C., L., later Uncials, almost all Cursives and versions; but D., Old Latin, and Vulg., omit "Bethphage."

He might fulfil all that was written of Him; and become in His own Person that all-reconciling Sacrifice, of which the sacrifices of the temple which He entered and cleansed were but forecasts and shadows.

Hitherto He had steadily avoided all public recognition of His claims to be the Messiah. He had even refused to say publicly, and before friends and foes alike, Who He was. Now He Himself made preparation to be received as the King of Sion; coming, it is true, in lowly guise, but coming as it had been foretold that the long expected Son of David should come. He bowed the hearts of the vast crowd to go before Him, and to follow Him with shouts of welcome which seemed in the eyes of His enemies to be nothing short of the adoration due to God only, and He went to the temple of God, and acted in it with the authority of a Son over His own house.

And yet this Melchizedec, King of Salem, entered into His city as the Priest Victim. His hour was come, and He came as a lamb to the slaughter. He came to be lifted up not on a throne, but on a cross. Hitherto as He had withdrawn Himself from public recognition, so He had withdrawn Himself from threatened danger, but now, unarmed and undefended, He put Himself into the hands of His enemies, that they should do to Him "whatsoever they listed," and what they "listed" to do for the gratification of their malice was no other than that "which was written in the Law and in the Prophets, and in the Psalms concerning Him."

The entry in triumph as King, and the succeeding Crucifixion as the Priest Victim, were as cause and effect. If He had not thus entered as a King and been hailed as a King, they could not possibly have acted on Pilate's fears as they did. All their accusations respecting His being "the King of the Jews," would have been meaningless unless there had been some show of public recognition. And all the city must have heard of the entry, and of the shouting "Hosanna to the Son of David," "Blessed be the King that cometh in the name of the Lord." And Pilate, we may be sure, was not the last to hear of it. Amongst such a vast and excited concourse there were sure to have been some of his soldiers watching what was going on. And when

CHAP. XI.] THE MOUNT OF OLIVES. 243

2 And saith unto them, Go your way into the village over against you: and as soon as ye be entered into it, ye

---

he inquired about it, they would assure him that there was no need for the smallest alarm, for it was all beneath contempt, very like a stupid joke—they were in the very midst of the throng, and they saw nothing but a fanatical crowd shouting and waving palms round a poor humble man whom they had seated on a colt because these besotted Jews believed that he had raised a dead man to life.

Such was the triumphal entry. It was the necessary prelude to the Crucifixion. His own city must acknowledge Him, and glorify Him before it rejected Him and cried " Crucify Him." There must have been some public act recognizing His Royalty known to Pilate, or they could hardly have approached the Governor with such accusations as " He stirred up the people," and "made Himself a King." There must have been some extraordinary disappointment of Messianic hopes, or the multitude could not so speedily have turned against Him with the cry, " Crucify Him," or have left Him to His fate. There must have been some pregnant crisis which compelled the chief priests to delay no longer, but at all risks to take that bold and decisive action to put Him to death at once, which resulted in the true Paschal Lamb being sacrificed at the moment of the Paschal solemnity.

We must now examine the narrative in detail.

"He sendeth forth two of his disciples." No doubt Peter was one of them, as the succeeding narrative bears strong marks of being derived from an eye-witness.

2. "And saith unto them, Go your way into the village over against you," &c. Most probably Bethphage. This village has perished, but there are old tanks and discernible foundations of houses on the spot which is its most probable site.

"As soon as ye be entered into it, ye shall find a colt tied," &c. St. Matthew alone makes mention of the ass, the mother which was with it; and this, no doubt, because writing especially for the chosen people, he was led to cite the prophecy mentioning together both the ass and the colt, the foal of the ass. St. Mark, writing in Rome for Gentiles, would only mention the creature on which the Lord actually rode.

"Whereon never man sat." The Lord, in giving this direction, acted as if He were Divine, for God required that the creatures

shall find a colt tied, whereon never man sat; loose him, and bring *him*.

3 And if any man say unto you, Why do ye this? say ye that the Lord hath need of him; and straightway he will send him hither.

---

3. "And straightway he will send him hither." So A., C.³, later Uncials, almost all Cursives, Old Latin, Vulg., Sah., Copt., Syriac, Goth., Arm., Æth.; but א, B., C.*, D., L., Δ, a few Cursives, and Origen add "again," "And straightway he [the Lord] will send them hither *again*," *i.e.* he will return them. The latter seems most unlikely. Dean Burgon has discussed this reading at page 58 of his "Revision Revised."

offered, or dedicated to Him, should be unused; thus Numbers xix. 2 ["Speak unto the children of Israel, that they bring thee a red heifer without spot, wherein is no blemish, and upon which never came yoke." So also Deut. xxi. 3, and 1 Sam. vi. 7]. The Lord under such a dispensation as the Jewish never could have made such a requirement if He had been a mere man.

3. "And if any man say unto you, Why do ye this? say ye that the Lord hath need," &c. Several questions present themselves here: first, were the words which our Saviour commanded the disciples to say ordinary words, which the owners of the colt would understand as a message from One Whom they knew well, having often seen Him pass between Jerusalem and Bethany, and Whom they would connect with the raising of Lazarus; and so, looking upon Him as a great Prophet, they would readily send the colt; or were they words which were to be addressed to strangers, and which, when they were uttered, the Lord would accompany with a secret putting forth of His power, so that they at once compelled the obedience of the owners? It appears to me that the owners must have been strangers, as the disciples were not sent to the house of a particular person, but into a village in the open street of which they were to find the colt tied. When they found all as Jesus had said unto them, they are distinctly reported to have said the very words which the Lord commanded, and it is noticed by the Evangelists that they had the immediate effect which the Lord intended and foretold.

All this circumstantiality seems exceedingly unlike an ordinary case of borrowing, and could not be well expressed differently, if the words which Jesus commanded them to use were to be words of compelling power. Besides, the two disciples were not to wait to

CHAP. XI.] WHAT DO YE LOOSING THE COLT ? 245

4 And they went their way, and found the colt tied by the door without in a place where two ways met; and they loose him.

5 And certain of them that stood there said unto them, What do ye loosing the colt?

6 And they said unto them even as Jesus had commanded: and they let them go.

---

see the owner, and ask his leave; but to act as if the Owner of all things were simply exercising His right in demanding the use of the animal.

4. "And they went their way, and found the colt tied by the door in a place," &c. This must have come from one of the two who were sent. They found a colt tied by a door, in a place where two ways met, *i.e.*, in a crossing. All this is very different from St. Luke's "they found even as He had said unto them." The one mentions what he had heard, the other describes circumstances which made an impression upon him.

5. "And certain of them that stood there said unto them . . . let them go." Notice that they entered into no explanations such as seem to have been required, but simply repeated the words, "The Lord hath need of them." They must have known and felt that their conduct was unusual. It was not taking the colt by stealth, but in the highway, in the sight of the owners. Their words implied that the animal belonged to the Lord more than to the owners, as in fact all which we call our own does. This was a foreshadowing of that absolute demand which Jesus Christ makes on all we possess,—property, intellect, time, even life.

7. "And they brought the colt to Jesus, and cast their garments on him, and he sat upon him." The Lord thus prepares to make His triumphal entry into the city of God riding on a colt, the foal of an ass. Now, the significance of this to the bystanders would altogether depend upon their knowledge of Scripture, together with the views which they took of the claims of Jesus to be the Messiah. If they considered the time, that it was the period when the prophecies were rapidly receiving fulfilment, and already the impending coming of the Messiah had been announced by John whom all men looked upon as a prophet; if they remembered that the Messiah was to be a king, such as the Holy City had never

7 And they brought the colt to Jesus, and cast their garments on him; and he sat upon him.

---

before seen, and if they remembered that the most distinct prophecy of His personal appearance when He came to take possession of His city was, that He should come riding " on the foal of an ass;"—if they realized all this, they would, beyond all doubt, consider that no Messianic claims which Jesus had ever made came near to this, that He should come after this fashion into the city of David. If He had entered on a richly caparisoned steed at the head of a mounted troop, with all the insignia of a military triumph, the observant Jew, who knew the words of the prophets, would say, " This is very grand, very imposing, but it is not what Zechariah has led me to expect." But if the same man was cognizant of the claims of the Lord, and rejected them, he would exclaim, " What amazing presumption thus to ride into Jerusalem! Does He pretend to be the King who rides upon the colt, and is to cut off the chariot from Ephraim, and the horse from Jerusalem . . . and speak peace to the heathen, and reign from sea to sea? And does He hear what the crowds are shouting, 'Hosannah to the Son of David, Hosannah in the highest?' What presumption! What arrogance! What blasphemy!" So it would be to the unbelieving Jew who knew the prophecies. And yet the ass's colt was without all doubt the symbol of meekness and patience, just as the horse would have been the symbol of pride and bloodshed. The King coming to His Kingdom was actually to triumph through humiliation and patience under blows and insults; He was to "have salvation," and to "speak peace to the heathen" by an ignominious death. In the prophecy of Zechariah there is a contrast between the ass and the horse. He Who is lowly, riding upon the ass, is to cut off the horse, the war-horse from Jerusalem. Williams remarks well: " The more noble animal, the horse, as ministering to human pride, does not appear to be praised in Scripture, nor selected for Divine purposes, but the contrary. It is connected with Pharaoh and Sennacherib, 'The horse and his rider hath He thrown into the sea' (Exod. xv. 1), and 'at thy rebuke both the chariot and the horse are fallen' (Ps. lxxvi. 6), and 'woe to them that go down to Egypt and stay on horses' (Is. xxxi. 1). The celebrated description of the horse in Job (xxxix. 18), is all of war: 'his neck is clothed with thunder,' and "he rejoices in the sound of the trumpet.' " The very contrast

CHAP. XI.]                HOSANNA.                     247

8 ᵇ And many spread their garments in the way: and others cut down branches off the trees, and strewed *them*  ᵇ Matt. xxi. 8. in the way.

9 And they that went before, and they that followed, cried, saying, ᶜ Hosanna; Blessed *is* he  ᶜ Ps. cxviii. 26. that cometh in the name of the Lord:

---

8. "*Others* cut down branches off the trees." The alteration made by the Revisers in this place is remarkable. In the margin for "branches" they read, "layers of leaves," appending the letters Gr., implying that it is the literal translation of the Greek; but Dean Burgon, in his "Revision Revised," remarks that the word which they have translated thus (*stibas*) never signified "layers of leaves," but rather, "a rough bed, pallet, or mattress." The word in A., C., and in most Cursives is *stoibas*, which may signify "small branches," "foliage," and so agrees better with the "branches" of St. Matthew. By far the greater part of Uncials, however (ℵ, B., D., E., G., H., K., L., M.), and many Cursives read *stibidas*, acc. of *stibas*. Liddell and Scott in their last edition make no distinction between the words.

"Off the trees." Some MSS., ℵ, D., L. read, "from the fields."

"Strawed them in the way." So A., D., later Uncials, Cursives, Old Latin, Vulg., Syriac, &c.; omitted by ℵ, B., C., L., &c.

---

to all this is this meek animal; and therefore it is said to Jerusalem, "Fear not." "Fear not, but feel confidence," says St. Chrysostom, "it is not as the unjust and warlike kings of the world, but One meek and gentle, which He shows by the ass, for He cometh not with an army, but with the ass alone."

8. "And many spread their garments in the way," &c. The welcome on the part of the multitude was unpremeditated, and so they honoured Him with what came first to their hands, some with their garments which they were wont to spread in the paths of kings (2 Kings ix. 13), others with the waving of palm branches, others with twigs of trees cut from the neighbouring fields and copses.

9. These shouts and songs of praise are mostly part of a Psalm of God, the one hundred and eighteenth; the Hosannah is the "Save now, I beseech thee," of the 25th verse, and is compounded of two words, "Hoshia," "save," and "na," "I pray." "Blessed be he that cometh in the name of the Lord," is taken verbatim from the 26th verse. That the anthem of praise, or parts of it, should be taken from this Psalm, is exceeding significant, for just before it we have, "The stone which the builders rejected is become the head stone of the corner," and just after, "God is the

10 Blessed *be* the kingdom of our father David, that
<sup>d</sup> Ps. cxlviii. 1. cometh in the name of the Lord: <sup>d</sup> Hosanna in
the highest.
<sup>e</sup> Matt. xxi. 12.   11 <sup>e</sup> And Jesus entered into Jerusalem, and into
the temple: and when he had looked round about upon all
things, and now the eventide was come, he went out into
Bethany with the twelve.
<sup>f</sup> Matt. xxi. 18.   12 ¶ <sup>f</sup> And on the morrow, when they were
come from Bethany, he was hungry :

---

10. " In the name of the Lord." So A., N., later Uncials, most Cursives, Syriac, Gothic,
Æthiopic; omitted by א, B., C., D., L., eight or ten Cursives, Old Latin, Vulg., Coptic,
Syriac (Schaaf).

Lord, who hath showed us light; bind the sacrifice with cords, yea
even unto the horns of the altar." The King in triumph was to be
Himself, the sacrificial Victim, as He was Himself, "the light of
the world."

Here St. Luke tells us that the Pharisees desired the Lord to
rebuke His disciples, and that the Lord wept when the view of
Jerusalem in all its grandeur rose before Him, as He descended the
Mount of Olives.

11. "And Jesus entered into Jerusalem, and into the temple
. . . Bethany with the twelve," &c. St. Matthew here tells us
what a stir the triumphant procession had made in the city, how
all asked, "Who is this?" how He healed the blind and the lame
in the temple, how the chief priests would have Him restrain the
children who shouted "Hosanna," and how He claimed in their
behalf and for Himself the words of the Psalmist, "Out of the
mouths of babes and sucklings Thou hast perfected praise."

He did nothing that evening in the way of cleansing the temple, as
probably the buyers and sellers had left the scene of their unholy
traffic for the night, but "looked round about upon all things."
The reader will remember how repeatedly this Evangelist speaks
of the Lord looking around Him, surveying the crowd, His disciples,
or His enemies.

12. "And on the morrow, when they were come from Bethany, he
was hungry." Chrysostom (who believes that our Lord was not really
hungry, but that from His going up to the fig tree to see if there
were fruit on it, His disciples thought Him to be so) asks, "What

13 *And seeing a fig tree afar off having leaves,*    *Matt. xxi. 19.*

prevented the Lord from eating before He left Bethany?" Some suppose that He did not lodge that night in His accustomed home, the home of Lazarus and the two sisters, but that He and the disciples slept all night in the open field, wrapped up, as Jews were often wont to be, in their large outer garments. And there is this to be said in favour of such a supposition that, according to St. John's account, at this time He "departed, and did hide Himself from them," so that probably He would not sleep in a house to which His enemies knew that He resorted. It was also the common custom of those from a distance who came up to Jerusalem for the Passover to camp out in the fields.

13. "And seeing a fig tree afar off having leaves . . . for the time of figs was not yet." In entering upon the examination of this most remarkable and unique miracle, we are to remember that *that* is more especially applicable to it which is said of all the Lord's miracles, that it is an acted parable. The true meaning of every part of it is to be brought out and vindicated on this principle only. The Lord then sees a fig tree afar off covered with leaves. Now, inasmuch as in the fig tree the fruit appears and gets to some size before the leaves are well out, there was some prospect of finding a few figs on such a tree, and so the Lord came up to it if haply He might find any thereon. Now, the question has been repeatedly asked, Did not the Lord, Who knew all things, know that there were no figs on the tree? To this some believing expositors have replied, that as man He did not know it, or He chose not to know it. It was hidden from His human cognizance, just as many other things must have been, if it could be said of Him that He "increased in wisdom" (Luke ii. 52). But is it not the case that He often asked for information in order that those about Him might learn something from the answer? And is it not also the fact that God Himself is represented in Scripture as coming down to see what men were doing? Thus it is said (Gen. xi. 5) that "The Lord came down to see the city, and the tower which the children of men builded." And as soon as He did so He executed judgment upon them, and confounded their language. Again (Genesis xviii. 20), "The Lord said, Because the cry of Sodom and Gomorrha is great, and because their sin is very grievous, I will go down now, and see whether they have done altogether according to

he came, if haply he might find any thing thereon: and when

---

the cry of it which is come unto Me, and if not I will know." Now just as God knew every sin of Sodom, and had all written in His books for judgment, so His Son knew that there were no figs on this tree. Why, then, do God and the Son of God feign ignorance? In order to impress upon us that He has "times of visitation." He judges and condemns, or acquits at all times; but there are times when He comes *near* to judgment. At such times He does what a human judge does. A criminal's guilt is perfectly plain; not only the judge, but every person in the court knows it, and yet the judge acts as if he were ignorant, and looks into the matter as if it required to be proved, when really it does not. Now, this tree was emblematical or typical, 1st, Of the people of the Jews who professed the religion of the true God, and the hope of the Messiah; and, 2nd, Of every kingdom, society, church, or individual similarly circumstanced, *i.e.*, called by God to the profession of His truth. In addition to the constant, never-ceasing observation with which the unseen Judge watches them, there is a time, or there are times, in which God or Christ come near [perhaps in the sight of angels, and of the powers of the unseen world] and conduct a sort of formal examination, though perfectly knowing what the result will be. It is one great part of the duty of a nation, or church, or soul to be prepared for such a visitation. Now, taking this miracle, as I said, as an acted parable, which it unquestionably is, the hunger of the Saviour, the seeing the leafy fig tree when all others of its kind were leafless, afar off, the coming, the searching, the disappointment, the condemnation, the withering, all are significant, and all are indispensable, if the lesson is to be impressed upon us. I look upon it, then, that the Saviour acts here as God the Observer, the Visitor, and the Judge, all which He is. Besides this, the Saviour sets forth two other matters, viz., God, as ever earnestly desiring the fruits of righteousness in His people, so that He hungers for them; and God seeing ostentatious or conspicuous profession afar off, and being attracted to it, to see whether the fair profession is accompanied by fruits answering to its attractiveness. So that in this case we cannot tell how far the human soul of the Saviour was ignorant, or kept itself ignorant. If the actions have any typical meaning, then the Lords acts here as the Supreme Judge, *i.e.*, as a Divine Being, a Person in the Trinity.

## NOTHING BUT LEAVES.

he came to it, he found nothing but leaves; for the time of figs was not *yet*.

---

13. "The time of figs was not yet," or, as Revisers, "It was not the season of figs," after Neutral Text.

"And when he came to it, he found nothing but leaves; for the time of figs was not yet." It is very surprising that so many difficulties should have been raised upon the statement "the time of figs was not yet," for this sentence is the key of the whole parable. All know that the fig tree shows its fruit before its leaves. If then our Lord had seen a fig tree at some distance without leaves, He would have known that in the course of nature no figs sufficiently ripe for eating were, at that time of the year, to be looked for on it; but if it was covered with leaves He might naturally expect to gather some of the first ripe figs from it. The only remaining point to be ascertained is, can instances be found of fig trees so forward as to be covered with leaves so early as the middle of April, which would then be about the Passover time?[1] Now we have a distinct and satisfactory answer to this question in Dr. Thomson's "The Land and the Book." He proposes the question, Have you met with anything in this country (Palestine) which can clear away the apparent injustice of seeking figs before the proper time for them? And he answers: "There is a kind of tree which bears a large green-coloured fig that ripens very early. I have plucked them in May, from trees on Lebanon, a hundred and fifty miles north of Jerusalem, and where the trees are nearly a month later than in the south of Palestine; it does not, therefore, seem impossible but that the same kind might have ripe figs at Easter, in the warm sheltered ravines of Olivet. The meaning of the phrase, 'the time of figs was not yet,' may be, that the ordinary season for them had not yet arrived, which would be true enough, at any rate. The reason why He might, legitimately, so to speak, seek fruit from this particular tree at that early day, was the ostentatious show of leaves. The fig often comes with, or even before the leaves, and especially on the early kind. If there was no fruit on this leafy tree, it might justly be condemned as barren, and hence

---

[1] See Smith's "Dictionary of the Bible," article "Month," page 417.

14 And Jesus answered and said unto it, No man eat fruit of thee hereafter for ever. And his disciples heard it.

the propriety of the lesson it was made to teach—that those who put forth in profusion only the leaves of empty profession are nigh unto cursing." This seems as complete and satisfactory an answer as can well be given.

Another objection is, that this "tree did not belong to the Saviour, but must have been the property of some other person; so that He had no right to take its fruit." This is also answered perfectly by the same author. "Referring to the Mosaic law in such cases, Josephus thus expounds it: "You are not to prohibit those that pass by where your fruit is ripe to touch them, but to give them leave to fill themselves full with what you have." And the custom of plucking ripe figs as you pass by the orchards, is still universal in this country, especially from trees by the road side, and from all that are not enclosed."

But did the Lord do right in destroying the property of another man? Now the very great probability is, that it was not the property of any one in particular, but by the side of a road, or on an unenclosed space, and its very barrenness goes far to prove this, for the same author tells us: "There are many such trees now; and if the ground is not properly cultivated, especially when the trees are young . . . . they do not bear at all; and even when full grown they quickly fail and wither away if neglected. Those who expect to gather good crops of well-flavoured figs are particularly attentive to their culture; not only do they plough and dig about them frequently, and manure them plentifully, but they carefully gather out the stones from the orchards, contrary to their general slovenly habits."

One objection more. Did not the Lord by withering the fig tree prevent future wayfarers from being refreshed by the fruit? No; from what has been just quoted this tree had no owner, was never likely to have any pains taken with it, and so the Lord saved future wayfarers from disappointment.

14. "And Jesus answered and said unto it, No man eat fruit of thee hereafter for ever." In St. Matthew we read, "And presently the fig tree withered away," as if the word of the Lord at once took effect. It is not impossible that such should have been the case, for the disciples were on their way, and would not turn or look back;

CHAP. XL.] JESUS IN THE TEMPLE. 253

15 ¶ ʰ And they come to Jerusalem: and Jesus went into the temple, and began to cast out them

ʰ Matt. xxi.
12. Luke xix.
45. John ii. 14.

---

but St. Mark notices that "the disciples heard it," but not till the next day did they see what had taken place.

[20. "And in the morning, as they passed by, they saw the fig tree dried up by the roots."] This is the one miracle which sets forth Christ as the Judge and the Executor of the wrath of God. In all His other miracles He appears as the Saviour from sin and all forms of spiritual evil, spiritual blindness, spiritual dumbness, spiritual hunger, spiritual death. In this alone we have Him "retaining sin." "Our most merciful Lord, Who expressed His everlasting bounties towards us by numberless miracles, with one miracle only (and that not in the case of a man, but of an insensible tree) denoting the severity of His judgment against unprofitable men; that we might be certain of this fact, that barrenness in good works is punished by the witholding of that grace which causes to fructify." So Grotius, and he seems to have taken the idea from St. Hilary: "Herein we find proof of the Lord's goodness. When He was minded to show forth an instance of the *salvation* procured by His means, He exerted the power of His might upon the persons of *men*, by healing their sicknesses, encouraging them to hope for the future, and to look for the healing of the soul; but now, when He would exhibit a type of His *judgments* on the obstinately rebellious, He represents the picture by the destruction of a *tree*." So that this miracle, so unlike any other in its severity, was done in great mercy. It sets before us the severe side of His character, that He is the Judge and the Executor of God's wrath, and that God will punish not only the wicked, as we call gross and open sinners, but the fruitless. What is the reality of the "withering?" Is it not that which the Lord sets forth in the parable of the vine: "If a man abide not in Me, He is cast forth as a branch and is withered"?

15. "And they come to Jerusalem: and Jesus went into the temple, and began to cast out," &c. It seems, at first sight, almost incredible that men who professed such reverence for the temple, and were so scrupulous about the slightest ceremonial defilement (John xviii. 28), should actually let out, as they did, a portion of the sacred precincts, the court of the Gentiles, or a part of it, to dealers in cattle and sheep and doves, and to money-changers, but

that sold and bought in the temple, and overthrew the

unscrupulous men will do anything for the sake of gain. It would be a great convenience to a Jew from a distance to buy his Passover Lamb close to the spot where it had to be killed ; and the Sadducean priests, taking advantage of this, were themselves the real desecrators of the most sacred building of which they were the guardians, by encouraging the unholy traffic. But the Lord, Who ever regarded the temple as His Father's house, and looked upon the very building as imparting its sanctity to all in it, resented this as He had done on a former occasion, alone and unaided, for this occurred on the day after His arrival, and the enthusiastic crowds were dispersed. He drove out all the traffickers, overthrew the tables of the moneychangers, and the seats of those who sold doves to those who were too poor to bring a more costly offering, and, according to our Evangelist, even went further, by forbidding the temple to be made a thoroughfare, so that vessels should be carried through it.

Now we must ask first, " Was this an ordinary exercise of power? " and then, " What was its significance ? "

It would have been a natural, though, of course, a remarkable exercise of power if it had been, as is asserted, through the personal greatness and intensity of will that showed itself in our Lord's look and word and tone. But if this personal greatness means a very commanding presence, so that all enemies should be at once overawed, why did not this save Him from the insults and outrages which were heaped upon Him during this very week ? We have no reason to believe from anything in the gospel that the Lord had a presence which greatly overawed men, and He must have had a very commanding personal presence indeed, to disperse without apparently the faintest opposition a crowd of cattle-dealers and money-changers. It seems to me that the faculty of transfiguring Himself at will, so as on one day to put on an appearance which overawed the roughest of men, and on the next day so to disguise His majesty as that the very slaves should spit on Him and strike Him, is as much a supernatural endowment as the power of healing the sick or casting out devils.

Why do men treat the exercise of the Lord's Divine power as if it were something immoral, something to be ashamed of, something that we must get rid of even at the expense of common sense, unless we are compelled to acknowledge it ? It may interest the reader to

tables of the moneychangers, and the seats of them that sold doves;

---

contrast with the modern view, that of a Father of the Church, St. Jerome: "To me it appears that amid all the signs of our Lord, this was the most wonderful; that one single man, at a time too when He was an object of scorn, and accounted so vile as soon after to have been crucified, while the Scribes and Pharisees [chief priests?] moreover were furiously raging against Him, on account of the loss through Him of their worldly gain, should nevertheless have succeeded with a whip of small cords (John ii. 15), in driving out of the temple so vast a multitude, overthrowing the tables and the seats, and doing other like things, which scarcely a troop of soldiers could have accomplished."

The second question is, "What is the significance of the act? Did its significance cease when the fane whose sanctity Christ thus marvellously vindicated, was for ever desecrated and cast to the ground, or has it any reference to the new state of things in the kingdom of God? To this we answer, it asserts an universal principle, that whatsoever is consecrated to the true God, be it building, or society, or body, cannot be profaned without bringing on those who desecrate it the severe anger of God. God has nowhere, in so many words, commanded that the buildings devoted to the prayers and Eucharists of the New Covenant should be dedicated with a special service. He has left such a thing to be inferred from His Word, and a certain Divine instinct has led Christians everywhere solemnly to set apart their material churches to the exclusive service of God; but when they do so God holds them to their word. They have set apart these buildings to Him, He has accepted the offering, and inasmuch as He has not ceased to be a jealous God, He will certainly regard any desecration of them as profanity and impiety. If it be asserted that the Jewish temple was of greater sanctity than a Christian Church, because so much is said in Scripture about its dedication, we answer, No. A building, however humble, set apart for the offering up of prayer in the Name of Jesus, must be greater than a temple, however magnificent, in which His Name was never invoked—a building set apart for the celebration of the Eucharist must be holier than a building set apart for the offering of bullocks and calves. And so with the Mystical Body, the Church, in all its branches. It also is defiled by heresy and false

16 And would not suffer that any man should carry *any* vessel through the temple.

17 And he taught, saying unto them, Is it not written, ¹My house shall be called ||of all nations the house of prayer? but ᵏ ye have made it a den of thieves.

¹ Is. lvi. 7.
| Or, *an house of prayer for all nations?*
ᵏ Jer. vii. 11.

---

doctrine, and traffic in holy offices ; and Christ will assuredly look upon this with more anger than He looked upon the profanation of the temple, inasmuch as a temple of living stones, built into a spiritual house, is a greater thing than a building even of marble and gold. And so with the bodies of Christians, which together with their souls, are so made the temple of God in Holy Baptism, that an inspired Apostle could ask, " Know ye not that your body is the temple of the Holy Ghost which is in you ? " and so he says, " If any man defile the temple of God, him will God destroy." Let us then cleanse our souls by prayer and thoughts about the holiest things, or Christ may suddenly visit us and cast us out of the true house of God.

With respect to our Lord's not suffering anyone to carry a vessel through the temple, Dr. South has a good remark : " We must know that the least degree of contempt weakens religion ; because it is absolutely contrary to the nature of it ; religion properly consisting of reverential esteem for things sacred." (Quoted in Ford.)

17. " And he taught, saying unto them, My house shall be called," &c. If, as is very probable, the marginal translation (" a house of prayer for all nations ") is the true one, then there may be here a tacit reference to the fact that the court of the Gentiles, as being the least sacred part of the temple, had been employed, in part at least, for the infamous traffic ; in which case the Lord's words would mean, " My house shall be called the house of prayer for all the Gentiles, but ye have driven them out and polluted their share, and made it a den of thieves."

It has been asked, Were not the future houses of God to be houses of preaching—was not, that is, preaching to be their characteristic ? No, we answer, and for this reason : preaching may be, and ought to be, everywhere ; wherever people can be congregated to hear it : Whereas the celebration of the Eucharist and also united Church prayer ought, if possible, to be in places set apart from the world,

CHAP. XI.]  THE FIG TREE WITHERED.  257

18 And ¹the scribes and chief priests heard *it*, and sought how they might destroy him : for they feared him, because ᵐ all the people was astonished at his doctrine.

19 And when even was come, he went out of the city.

20 ¶ ⁿ And in the morning, as they passed by, they saw the fig tree dried up from the roots.

21 And Peter calling to remembrance saith unto him, Master, behold, the fig tree which thou cursedst is withered away.

22 And Jesus answering saith unto them, ‖Have faith in God.

¹ Matt. xxi. 45, 46. Luke xix. 47.
ᵐ Matt. vii. 28. ch. i. 22. Luke iv. 32.
ⁿ Matt. xxi. 19.
‖ Or, *Have the faith of God*.

---

its associations, its businesses, and pleasures ; and ought to be in places, the architecture and arrangement and associations of which tend to raise the worshipper above the world. The restriction on the part of the authorities of the English Church, for nearly two centuries, of preaching to the interior of churches, has been most disastrous. It has been the real reason why she has lost so many of the working classes. Our missionaries in India preach to the heathen in thoroughfares, in bazaars, at times even in the temples, and the heathen of England require to be met in the same way.

18. " And the scribes and chief priests heard it, and sought how they might," &c. This is the first instance in the Synoptics of the " chief priests " taking serious measures to destroy Him, and the reader will notice how closely it follows upon the cleansing of the temple.

"They sought how they might destroy him." Their fears made them think that it would be no easy thing to destroy Him. They did not count upon the fleeting nature of all popularity. Three days after this the people who were astonished at His doctrine made no effort to save Him.

19, 20, 21. "And when even was come, he went out . . . . withered away." I commented on these verses above, and shall not now refer to them.

22. " And Jesus answering saith unto them, Have faith in God." We have explained the miracle of the withering of the fig tree

23 For ° verily I say unto you, That whosoever shall say unto this mountain, Be thou removed, and be thou cast into the sea; and shall not doubt in his

° Matt. xvii. 20. & xxi. 21.
Luke xvii. 6.

23. "For" omitted by ℵ, B., D., N., eight or ten Cursives, Old Latin, Vulg., Syriac (Schaaf), Armenian; retained by A., C., L., later Uncials, most Cursives, Coptic, some Syriac, Gothic.

entirely on its typical side, as setting forth the withering up of all life in nations or Churches, who, at the time of their visitation, have no fruit to show; but the Lord makes no allusion whatsoever to its spiritual import, and treats it as simply a putting forth of Divine power. But this is the case with all His miracles. He never attaches a distinct spiritual meaning to them. To us they shadow forth His action on the souls of His people, but it is impossible that they should have conveyed this lesson to those who saw them performed. It required the full light of Pentecost to teach their spiritual meaning. And especially would it have been impossible to make the disciples receive the import of the withering of the fig tree, which was, in the first place, the drying up of the spiritual life of their own nation. History alone could teach the Church this.

23. "For verily I say unto you, That whosoever shall say unto this mountain," &c. The removal of the mountain, and the casting of it into the sea was, no doubt, a proverbial expression, or would remind the Apostles of one. Thus St. Paul alludes to it: "Though I have all faith, so that I could remove mountains," and a similar figure was used by the prophets: thus, Zechariah, "Who art thou, O great mountain? before Zerubbabel thou shalt become a plain" (iv. 7). Not, of course, that anyone in his senses would ever pray to God that He would, at his word, remove an actual mountain: no one having any true conception of God would pray for such a thing; but the meaning is, that those whom God has inspired with a true faith would perform miracles, and remove obstacles requiring as great an exertion of Divine power as the removal of a mountain. But as the true significance of the Lord's illustration has been much misunderstood, it may be well to dwell somewhat upon it.

The Apostles, when the Lord was taken away from them, would have to commend His doctrine to the world by miracles. To this end it was needful that their faith in God, as the Bestower of all

CHAP. XI.]   THE POWER OF FAITH.   259

heart, but shall believe that those things which he saith shall come to pass; he shall have whatsoever he saith.

---

23. "Those things which he saith." So A., C., later Uncials, almost all Cursives; but ℵ, B., L., one or two Cursives, some Old Latin, Vulg., Coptic, Gothic, Syriac (Schaaf) read, "What he saith" in the singular.

"Shall come to pass." Properly, "Cometh to pass."

"Whatsoever he saith" omitted by ℵ, B., C., D., L., Δ, three or four Cursives, Vulg.; but A., N., later Uncials, almost all Cursives, Syriac, Gothic, Armenian retain.

---

power to do such things, should be raised. For the real doer of every miracle or sign was God, and God only. When the Apostles healed suddenly any sick person, or cast out any evil spirit, it was by the combined exercise of prayer and faith. They secretly, or openly, called upon God, and they implicitly believed that He would accompany their word with His power. Now being men totally ignorant of science, and so unable to form a conception of the kind or amount of power put forth in the performance of any miracle, they would naturally look upon it as a matter of size, or weight, or extension. They would, as a matter of course, look upon the removal of the Mount of Olives as a far greater thing, demanding far greater power, than the sudden drying-up of the life-juices of a single fig-tree; but it may not really be greater, by any means. On the contrary, the sudden touching and arresting the springs of life in the living thing may require far more knowledge of the greatest secret of all—the secret of life, and far more real power in applying that knowledge, than the removal of the most stupendous mass of dead matter. Now the Apostles, though they could not understand this, must yet act as if it were so. They must not judge by the sight of their eyes of the difficulty or easiness of anything which they felt moved by the Spirit to peform. They must think of nothing but the almighty power of God, and His pledge to accompany their prayers or words with that power.[1]

---

[1] A very distinguished scientist has somewhere said that to bring down from the clouds a single shower, or to stay its falling, would be as great a miracle as to reverse the falls of Niagara, and make the water rise upwards. And he is perfectly right, for undoubtedly the change of atmospheric influences which would bring about or stay a single shower would extend over an area vastly more extensive than a thousand Niagaras; but then we believe that scientists

p Matt. vii. 7.
Luke xi. 9.
John xiv. 13.
& xv. 7. & xvi.
24. James i.
5, 6.

24 Therefore I say unto you, ᵖ What things soever ye desire, when ye pray, believe that ye receive *them*, and ye shall have *them*.

24. "Believe that ye receive." So A., N., later Uncials, almost all Cursives, Syriac, Gothic, Armenian; but ℵ, B., C., L., Δ, Coptic, "Ye have received them." D., Old Latin, Vulg., "Ye shall receive."

Now with respect to spiritual miracles—miracles, that is, of conversion, of sudden influx of spiritual light, of sudden subjugation of evil habits or removal of evil tendencies. If the spiritual world is higher than the natural, any one of these very probably requires a higher exertion of power than any miraculous changes in the physical sphere; and yet men who have doubts and difficulties respecting physical miracles, seem willingly to accept such as these.

24. "Therefore I say unto you, What things soever ye desire, when ye pray," &c. It has been supposed that the Lord here refers to the faith of miracles, emphatically so called, because it was a certain supernatural confidence and assurance wrought by the Spirit in the soul of a man, by which he was sure he could do such or such miracles before he attempted to do them. By this supernatural confidence or impulse it was that men knew, as by a sign, when they could work wonders, and when not. (Dr. Hickes, in Ford.)

But I do not think that the Lord here alludes to this. He had considered this sort of faith in the previous verse; and now, lest His hearers should think that what He had said only referred to such acts of faith as preceded the performance of miracles, He apparently lays down in this verse a general truth.

Now, I think that we must apply to these words that principle

are not the highest beings in the universe, as, by denying the supernatural, they profess to be. We believe that there is an omnipotent, omniscient, omnipresent Intelligence, to Whom the highest science of our scientists is a very clumsy, roundabout, imperfect way of expressing the relations to one another of the various things—atoms, molecules, energies, vital forces, &c.—to which He has given existence, and of which He alone knows the real nature, and on which He has reserved to Himself the right and power of acting as He pleases.

## WHEN YE PRAY, FORGIVE.

25 And when ye stand praying, ᑫ forgive, if ye have ought against any: that your Father also which is in heaven may forgive you your trespasses.

ᑫ Matt. vi. 14.
Col. iii. 13.

---

which I have before noticed, as applying to so many of our Lord's startling sayings. He lays down with solemnity and decisiveness some great principle, and does not mention, or, for the time, makes no account of, the necessary exceptions. Thus it seems quite possible that a man may with great confidence pray for what is contrary to the will of God, or for what would be injurious to himself or to others, and an hindrance to the work of God in the world, or he may pray for some Christian grace for himself which it is well that he should have, but not at present, for he may require another grace first, which is, in the order of God, its necessary antecedent: for instance, he may pray for comfort when God sees that he requires a much deeper sense of sin. Now it seems that a man may pray with much confidence for such things, and God may not hear his prayer, at least at the time. Well, it is very necessary, on principles of common sense, to take account of such exceptions; but what our Lord here desires to impress upon us is that our *first* duty is to have faith in God, Who always hears every prayer, Who always regards it with favour, if it be offered in the least sincerity, Who always registers it in His memory, and Who will not allow one sincere prayer to be really lost, and to be as if it had not been offered to Him. In coming to God in prayer, then, the first and foremost thing is to come with confidence—to look to the promises only, and not to think of the necessary limitations or exceptions. One who is led by the grace of God to pray earnestly is most likely to pray for what God has it in His mind to grant to him. When Christ, then, bids us believe that we receive what we ask, He bids us put before ourselves the promises of God to hear prayer; He bids us put before ourselves the intercession of Christ, and the assistance of the Spirit, and the many instances which every Christian has heard of, in which God has answered the petition of those that have asked in His Son's Name, for by such endeavours we can do our part to excite in ourselves the faith here commended by the Lord.

25, 26. "And when ye stand praying, forgive, if ye have ought against any: . . . forgive your trespasses." Our Lord seems to

26 But ʳif ye do not forgive, neither will your Father which is in heaven forgive your tresspasses.

ʳ Matt. xviii. 35.
ˢ Matt. xxi. 23. Luke xx. 1.

27 ¶ And they come again to Jerusalem: ˢ and as he was walking in the temple, there come to him the chief priests, and the scribes, and the elders,

---

26. "But if ye do not forgive," &c. This verse omitted by ℵ, B., L., S., Δ, seven or eight Cursives, some Old Latin, and some versions; but retained by A., C., D., E., G., H., K., M., N., and some other Uncials, almost all Cursives, nearly all Old Latin, Vulg., Gothic, Syriac.

speak with greater earnestness respecting this matter of forgiveness of injuries than He does upon any other subject. In the Sermon on the Mount He teaches His hearers the Lord's Prayer, and He directs their attention to but one part of it, and that is the petition, "Forgive us our trespasses *as we forgive them that trespass against us.*" And none of his parables end with so very severe a warning as that of the unmerciful servant, which He concludes with: "So shall also my heavenly Father do also unto you, if ye from your hearts forgive not every one his brother their trespasses." Thus Tertullian: "The remembrance of the commandments paveth the way to heaven for prayers, of which commandments the chief is that we go not up to the altar of God before that we undo whatever quarrel or enmity we may have contracted with our brethren. For what is it to retire into the peace of God without peace? unto the remission of debts, retaining debts? How shall he appease the Father who is angry with his brother, seeing that all anger is from the beginning forbidden us? . . . How rash a thing is it either to pass a day without prayer, while thou delayest to make satisfaction to a brother, or by persisting in wrath to undo prayer!" (On Prayer, xi.)

27. "And they come again to Jerusalem: and as he was walking in the temple," &c. This was, no doubt, on the Tuesday.

As He was walking in the temple, very probably employed in works of mercy, according as St. Matthew says, "The lame and the blind came to him in the temple, and he healed them." St. Luke also adds, "As he preached the gospel."

"There come to him the chief priests," &c. This was the one public intimation which He received from these very dignified persons that His pretensions were known to them. Hitherto they

## WHO GAVE THEE THIS AUTHORITY?

28 And say unto him, By what authority doest thou these things? and who gave thee this authority to do these things?

29 And Jesus answered and said unto them, I will also ask of you one ‖ question, and answer me, and | Or, *thing*. I will tell you by what authority I do these things.

---

had simply ignored Him as a body, though individual priests or rulers may have remonstrated with Him.

28. "By what authority doest thou these things?" What is meant by "these things?" If it was the healing of the lame and the blind, such power of doing good, especially in the very temple of God, must have come from the Author of all good; and they ought to have been the very first to confess it. If they alluded to His preaching and teaching, there seems to have been among the Jews a very great liberty for preaching—the rulers of the synagogues frequently sending to strangers to ask them if they had any word of exhortation. But if, as no doubt was the case, it was because He had interfered in the management of the temple, then, as rulers of the temple, they had a perfect right to ask the question, only they must come with clean hands, which they were not doing, as their hands were defiled with the ill-gotten gains of sacrilege. They must also ask the question in sincerity, which they were not doing: for they had prejudged Him, and were watching for their opportunity to destroy Him.

But the question arises, seeing that they were the religious rulers and leaders of the Jewish nation,—how was it that they were so late in inquiring personally into His claims? They had sent a deputation to the Baptist on the banks of the Jordan to inquire who *he* was: how was it, then, that they allowed the Lord to teach and preach and perform miracles in the most open way, all over the Holy Land, for three years, and did not solemnly, and as the God-appointed leaders of Israel, require publicly and personally of Him to give account of Himself? It was surely their duty to do so. It was clearly the most cowardly dereliction of their highest functions, as judges in matters of religion, to ignore such claims. They knew well all that He had done. They knew well the resurrection of Lazarus, which had taken place but a very short time before. They had had their solemn conclave, and an animated discussion about it (John xi. 47); but all conducted with the determination of con-

264  FROM HEAVEN, OR OF MEN? [St. Mark.

30 The baptism of John, was *it* from heaven, or of men? answer me.

31 And they reasoned with themselves, saying, If we shall say, From heaven; he will say, Why then did ye not believe him?

32 But if we shall say, Of men; they feared the people: for ᵗ all *men* counted John, that he was a prophet indeed.

ᵗ Matt. iii. 5. & xiv. 5. ch. vi. 20.

---

32. Revisers, following א, A., B., C., L., N., later Uncials, almost all Cursives, Coptic, Gothic, read, "But should we say from men," or, "Shall we say from men?" No doubt the preferable reading.

---

demning Him, no matter what the signs of His Messiahship. Such was the spirit in which they approached the Lord—insincere, hypocritical, crafty, bloodthirsty. And the Lord met them—met not their words only, but the secret machinations of their hearts, and at once and effectually silenced them, not only by a simple question, but by one which, above all men, He had a right to ask. They had sent to John to ask who he was, and John had told them that he was but a forerunner—a voice to call men's minds to One Who should come after. They must have known, their emissaries must have told them, that the One Whom John pointed to was Jesus; and the Lord fulfilled in His own person all that John had foretold: for He had filled the Holy Land, and the neighbouring territories, even Jerusalem itself, with the fame of His mighty deeds. John baptized, but it was not into the belief of himself, but of One that should come after him. What was the significance of John's baptism—His Baptism, of course, including his whole mission—was it earthly or heavenly?

30. "The baptism of John, was it from heaven, or of men?" And, apparently, they were confounded by the question; and, after pausing for an answer, He, no doubt, looked them in the face, and said, "Answer me."

31. "And they reasoned with themselves, saying, If we shall say," &c. "Why then did ye not believe him?" of course, here means, Why did ye not believe him when he testified of Me? John's mission and baptism had no meaning, except as preparing for Another's. He founded no Church, no institution, no sect. He was a herald, and, so far as office was concerned, nothing more;

33 And they answered and said unto Jesus, We cannot tell. And Jesus answering saith unto them, Neither do I tell you by what authority I do these things.

---

and yet he had so stirred the religious heart of the whole people that they were persuaded that he was a prophet indeed. And the chief priests and scribes dare not shipwreck their whole influence with the people by denying this. And so they were in a dilemma. The Lord in His wisdom conducted them, with their eyes wide open, into the snare. And they were forced to say, "We cannot tell." We, the judges of the faith and worship of Israel, cannot tell whether the greatest teacher who has appeared amongst us for many centuries is from God or not.

To have to make such a confession was to seal their own condemnation as the leaders of the people of God.

And so the Lord answered them: "Neither do I tell you by what authority I do these things." If they had possessed the smallest residue of the spirit of their great and holy predecessors, Phinehas, Abiathar, Zadok, Jehoiada, Joshua, the Lord would not have answered them thus.

## CHAP. XII.

AND <sup>a</sup> he began to speak unto them by parables. A *certain* man planted a vineyard, and set <sup>a</sup> Matt. xxi. 33. Luke xx. 9.

---

1. "And he began to speak unto them by parables. A certain man planted," &c. This parable of the "wicked husbandmen" is not the first of those which the Lord now began to speak. According to St. Matthew's account, it succeeds the short parable of the Two Sons, in which the same lesson is taught.

In the parable of the vineyard let out to unthankful husbandmen, the Lord brings before us by a parable exactly the same lesson as He had taught men by the withering of the fruitless fig tree, except that, in the parable, instead of one time of visitation only, we have

an hedge about *it,* and digged *a place for* the winefat, and

many; the last and final one, however, gathering up into itself all former ones.

The "certain man," or householder (St. Matt.) is God the Father. The time of the planting was the time when God, having disciplined them and given them His law, and His ordinances of Divine service, put them in possession of the land of Canaan. Thus the Psalmist sings: "Thou hast brought a vine out of Egypt. Thou hast cast forth the heathen and planted it. Thou madest room for it, and when it had taken root it filled the land" (Ps. lxxx. 8).

"And set a hedge about it." This hedge is by some explained to be the protecting providence of God, by others the guardianship of angels; but most probably it is the Law, especially those prohibitory statutes which prevented the Israelites from mixing with the heathen, and so kept them a separate people.

"And digged a place for the winefat, and built a tower." It is uncertain whether the Lord means by the winefat and the tower any special institution of the Jews. The planting and the due ordering of the vineyard could not be described in any picturesque and striking way without bringing in such accessories. Most expositors, however, have assigned a special meaning to the "winefat," and to the "tower."

Inasmuch as the winefat is the instrument for pressing out the juice or blood of the grape, most of the ancient commentators (who, unlike the moderns, delight to see a reference to Christ in everything) believe that it means those parts of the Jewish system which set forth the Sacrifice of the Son of God. Thus Origen speaks of it as the place of Sacrifice; another as the altar; another as the word of God, which crucifies the old man, and to which the nature of the flesh is opposed. If it has any special meaning it must accord with the fact that the winefat or winepress is that which makes the very perishable fruit of the vine profitable by extracting wine from it, and so it may mean God's perpetual discipline of His people. The tower is the place in which the keeper of the vineyard dwelt, and from which he could discern the approach of enemies, and guard against them. It has been explained by Origen and Chrysostom to signify the temple in which God dwelt among His people.

CHAP. XII.] THEY CAUGHT HIM AND BEAT HIM. 267

built a tower, and let it out to husbandmen, and went into a far country.

2 And at the season he sent to the husbandmen a servant, that he might receive of the husbandmen of the fruit of the vineyard.

3 And they caught *him*, and beat him, and sent *him* away empty.

4 And again he sent unto them another servant; and at him they cast stones, and wounded *him* in the head, and sent *him* away shamefully handled.

---

4. "[At] him they cast stones, and," &c. So A., C., N., later Uncials, most Cursives, Syriac, Gothic, Armenian, Æthiopic. "Cast stones" omitted by א, B., D., L., Δ, a few Cursives, Old Latin, Vulg., Sahidic, Coptic.

"Sent him away shamefully handled." So A., C., N., later Uncials, almost all Cursives, Syriac, Gothic, Armenian, Æthiopic; but א, B., D., L., one Cursive (33), Vulg., Sahidic, Coptic read, " shamefully handled," omitting " sent him away."

"And let it out to husbandmen." That is, to the children of Abraham, Isaac, and Jacob; whom He had trained in the wilderness to keep and cultivate the religion which He gave them.

"And went into a far country." This probably means that He quickly withdrew the sensible tokens of His presence, and left them in great part to themselves. Thus Jerome: "He went into a far country, not by a change of place, for God, by Whom all things are filled, cannot be absent from any place; but He seems to be absent from the vineyard, that He may leave the vine-dressers a freedom of acting."

2. "And at the season he sent to the husbandmen a servant, that he might," &c. The season cannot be limited to any particular time of their history, but covered the whole life of the nation from Moses to Christ. Still there were particular periods when God seemed to demand an account from them of their fruits or works; the time of Samuel seems to have been one, the time of Elijah another, that of Jeremiah and Ezekiel another, and perhaps we may add that of the Maccabees, and, of course, that of the Baptist.

3, 4, 5. "And they caught him . . . . And again he sent another . . . . beating some and killing some," &c. In all the three Evangelists there seems to be three servants especially alluded to, but it is impossible to identify any of these servants with any

5 And again he sent another; and him they killed, and many others; beating some, and killing some.

6 Having yet therefore one son, his wellbeloved, he sent

---

6. "Having yet therefore one son, his well-beloved." "Therefore" read in A., C., D., N., later Uncials, almost all Cursives, Vulg., Syriac; but ℵ, B., L., Δ, and one or two Cursives omit.

"His well-beloved." "His" omitted by ℵ, B., C., D., L., Δ, some Old Latin, Vulg., Sahidic, Coptic, Syriac (Schaaf). The Revisers render, "He had yet one, a beloved son, he sent him last," &c.

messengers of God under the Old Testament, treated so as here described. The Lord may have had certain individual prophets, or messengers, in His mind; but we must remember that it was the Lord's intention to make the Jews who heard Him pass sentence upon themselves, either in their own conscience or, as St. Matthew seems to imply, openly and aloud (Matt. xxi. 41); and if He had enabled them easily to identify these servants of the householder with prophets whom their fathers had persecuted, they would have seen the drift of His parable too soon and would have been on the watch lest they should have condemned themselves. There seems, however, to have been three orders of messengers who were successively raised up by God to act on the consciences of His people: first, the Law pure and simple as represented by Moses, Joshua, and the elders who outlived Joshua; then the judges, and after that the prophets from Samuel to Malachi. That they persecuted and martyred these prophets, or servants of God is clear from the appeal of St. Stephen: "Which of the prophets have not your fathers persecuted?" and the latter part of the 11th chapter of the Epistle to the Hebrews, vv. 36, 37, seems to indicate far more severe and prolonged persecution of the true servants of God than is recorded in the Old Testament. Even Moses and Samuel were rejected by them (Exod. xxxii. 1; 1 Sam. viii. 6, 7).

6. "Having yet therefore one son, his well-beloved, . . . last unto them." But were not the prophets who bore faithful witness true sons of God? So far as mere men could be, they were, but in a very subordinate sense compared to the Lord. They were sons by adoption and by being "led by the Spirit" (Rom. viii. 12). He was the Son in the unique sense of being the only begotten—fully partaking of His Father's nature. The complement of this place is, "God so loved the world that He gave His only begotten Son."

## THEY WILL REVERENCE MY SON.

him also last unto them, saying, They will reverence my son.

7 But those husbandmen said among themselves, This is

---

"They will reverence my son." " Thus did the Almighty Father please to express Himself in the wonderful condescension of human language, as 'hoping against hope,' and though He knew that such reverence was far from them, yet did He deliver up from His bosom His well-beloved into their merciless hands: as if still looking for other treatment from them . . . . The parable is spoken of a certain *man*, a householder. But yet, nowithstanding, these words, 'They will reverence my Son,' though He knew what would follow, are not said lightly and after the manner of men, but seem to contain within them a description of all God's dealings with mankind—for even when He knows their wickedness and final impenitence, yet He mysteriously acts towards them as having hope of them. For if the words which are here used contain any apparent contradiction to the foreknowledge of God, it is precisely the same which pervades all His dealings with mankind." Jerome well remarks, " God is spoken of as being uncertain in order that freewill may be left to man."

And yet the words are true, and are a Divine prophecy; for though the mass of the chosen people rejected the Lord, yet a remnant received Him, and this remnant was the root of His Church, and made His Name reverenced throughout all nations by the obedience of faith.

7. "But those husbandmen said among themselves, This is the heir, come," &c. This is what any ignorant peasants, when the lord of the property which they farmed lived at a great distance, might do. Regardless of future consequences, and remembering how hitherto they had successfully resisted all his claims, they would think only of the gratification of their envy and greed; but could this be put into the mouths of the Jews who rejected and crucified the Lord? Of course they would not dare to say among themselves, "This is the Son of God, let us kill him;" but if ever men sinned against the truth—sinned against the plainest evidence that He Whom they persecuted came from God—the high priests and scribes and elders did: they knew the prophecies respecting the Messiah—they knew that the times were drawing to a close they had, in part, acknowledged the mission of the Baptist,

the heir; come, let us kill him, and the inheritance shall be our's.

they knew perfectly the miracles of Jesus and the extraordinary holiness of His teaching, and the blamelessness of His life; they had every means of arriving at a true and right conclusion. But they were like men who had a problem before them which they were bound to work out, and they saw as distinctly as men could do what the solution would be—that it would be against them—against their false pretensions, or self-righteousness, or covetous gains. And so they refused to take the last steps and work it out.

"And the inheritance shall be our's." In what sense could the Jews who killed the Lord be said to do so that they might have the inheritance of God—whatever that meant—to themselves? Somewhat, I think, in this way. They were then lording it over God's heritage—treating it as if it were their own; they even went to the extent of letting out the courts of the temple, as if it were their private property. In them was fulfilled the words of Ezekiel respecting the apostate shepherds: "Ye eat the fat and ye clothe you with the wool, ye kill them that are fed, but ye feed not the flock" (xxxiv. 3). Now the presence and teaching of the Lord shook their self-security. It was the earnest that God would deliver His flock out of their hands, and set shepherds over it that should feed it. It was the earnest of the fast approaching purification when He should purify the sons of Levi, and purge them as gold and silver. The thought of this was hateful to men with unclean hands. They wanted to live to themselves—to be their own—to enjoy their proud position in Israel for their own sake: but if there was one thing which all the Lord's teaching impressed upon men, it was that they were not their own. Archbishop Trench explains it thus: "They desired that the inheritance should be theirs; they desired that what God had intended should only be transient and temporary, enduring till the times of reformation, should be made permanent,—and this because they had prerogatives and privileges in the imperfect system which would cease when the more perfect scheme was brought in, or rather which, not ceasing, would yet be transformed into higher privileges, for which they had no care." But is not this to credit them with an insight into a great truth, which was especially revealed to St. Paul only among the Apostles (Ephes. iii. 3-7), and which the Christian Jews

## CHAP. XII.] THEY TOOK HIM AND KILLED HIM. 271

8 And they took him, and killed *him*, and cast *him* out of the vineyard.

9 What shall therefore the lord of the vineyard do? he will come and destroy the husbandmen, and will give the vineyard unto others.

---

9. "Therefore" omitted by B., L., and Coptic; retained by ℵ, A., C., D., N., later Uncials, all Cursives, Old Latin, Vulg., Syriac, &c. I notice this merely for the purpose of drawing attention to the way in which certain modern editors (Tischendorf and Westcott and Hort, who omit the word) throw aside the evidence of all Christendom on the authority of two MSS.

of Jerusalem would not submit to till it was bound on them by the authority of the first council (Acts xv.)?

8. "And they took him, and killed him, and cast him out of the vineyard." There can be no particular significance in the order here, for both St. Matthew and St. Luke put the "casting out of the vineyard" first. They gave Him into the hands of the heathen as a reprobate, and slew Him without the city. But Theophylact says, "not Jerusalem, but the people are called the vineyard of the Lord, so as suffering not by their own hands, but by the hands of the Gentiles He is said to be cast without the vineyard."

9. "What shall therefore the Lord of the vineyard do? He will come and destroy the husbandmen?" According to St. Mark and St. Luke the Lord answers His own question, but according to St. Matthew they first answer Him in the words, "He will miserably destroy those wicked men, and will let out his vineyard unto other husbandmen." I cannot but think that St. Matthew gives us the more correct account. The Lord here deals with them as Nathan did with David. He makes them condemn themselves, and then He reiterates what they had said and so confirms it, or it may be that St. Mark and St. Luke represent that He Himself says what He had led them to say. Thus Augustine: "Matthew indeed subjoins that they answered and said, He will miserably destroy those wicked men," which Mark says here was not their answer, but that the Lord, after putting the question, as it were, answered it Himself. But we may easily understand, either that their answer was subjoined without the insertion of "they answered," or "they said," which at the time was implied; or else that their answer being the truth, was attributed to the Lord, since He also Himself, being the Truth, gave this answer concerning them. Here those

10 And have ye not read this scripture; ᵇ The stone which
the builders rejected is become the head of the corner:

11 This was the Lord's doing, and it is marvellous in our eyes?

ᵇ Ps. cxviii. 22.

who heard Him understood that He referred to their Church and nation, and exclaimed, " God forbid " (Luke xx. 16).

10. "And have ye not read this scripture; The stone . . . . marvellous in our eyes?" Bishop Andrewes notices how very frequently Christ is prophesied of as a stone. He is Daniel's stone, " cut forth without hands " (Dan. iii. 24). In His Passion He was Zachary's stone, " graven and cut full of eyes all over " (Zech. iii. 9). In His Resurrection He was Isaiah's stone, " laid in Zion " (Is. xxviii. 16). He was the stone or rock in the wilderness, for St. Paul says, " that rock was Christ " (1 Cor. x. 4).

There is a legend which I have seen somewhere, which describes the origin of the figure in this way: That at the building of the temple a stone was cut and shaped in the quarries, of which the builders could make no use. It lay about during the period of the building, held by all to be a hindrance (a stone of stumbling), but at the very last its place was found to be at the head of the corner, binding the two sides together. And so the Fathers explain Christ the corner stone, as binding Jew and Gentile in one Church of God.

It is very remarkable how this has been repeated in the history of the Church—how great religious movements have been frowned down, if not actively opposed by those in high places, which have afterwards subdued all opposition. In our own times, in this very century, this has occurred twice. First, the great Evangelical movement in our Church was set at naught by the builders, though it was the assertion of the primary truth of personal religion—that each soul must have a personal apprehension of Christ, and look to Him with the eye of a living faith; and then the great Church movement was almost unanimously rejected by the Bishops between 1840 and 1850, though it was the assertion of the truths patent through all the New Testament, that the Church, though a visible organization, is the mystical body of Christ—that it is a supernatural system of grace, and that its Sacraments are the signs of grace actually given in and with the outward sign. Are then the

Chap. XII.] WE KNOW THAT THOU ART TRUE. 273

12 <sup>c</sup> And they sought to lay hold on him, but feared the people: for they knew that he had spoken the parable against them: and they left him, and went their way.

<sup>c</sup> Matt. xxi. 45, 46. ch. xi. 18. John vii. 25, 30, 44.

13 ¶ <sup>d</sup> And they send unto him certain of the Pharisees and of the Herodians, to catch him in his words.

<sup>d</sup> Matt. xxii. 15. Luke xx. 20.

14 And when they were come, they say unto him, Master, we know that thou art true, and carest for no man: for thou regardest not the person of men, but teachest the way

---

leaders and heads of the Church as guilty as the Jewish builders were? God forbid that we should say so, if for no other reason than this—that so much of what was human, imperfect, and extravagant, was mixed up with both these movements; but it is not the less true that in neither case did "the builders" discern the strength of the principles asserted, and foresee that they must win their way: though the formularies of the Church, of which these builders were the exponents and guardians, assert very unmistakably both these truths in conjunction, viz., spiritual apprehension of Christ, and Sacramental union in His Body.

12. "And they sought to lay hold on him, but feared the people." They seem to have retained this fear of the Lord's popularity to the last, for their bargain with Judas was, that he should betray Him unto them, "in the absence of the multitude."

13. "And they sent unto him certain of the Pharisees and of the Herodians." This was done in order that they might lay hands on Him. They must, consequently, have hoped that He would have taken the popular side, for the mass of the people hated the Roman yoke, and they knew that His whole life was opposed to the worldliness of the Herodian following, and His whole teaching to the Sadduceeism which was the only form of religion which they professed, if, indeed, they professed any at all.

14. "And when they were come, they say unto him, Master, we know that thou art true, and carest for no man." Observe the flattery and seeming fairness with which they approached Him. "Thou regardest not the person of men." This must mean: "One who trusts in God as Thou dost, and has such a message from Him

T

of God in truth: Is it lawful to give tribute to Cæsar, or not?

15 Shall we give, or shall we not give? But he, knowing their hypocrisy, said unto them, Why tempt ye me? bring me a ‖ penny, that I may see it.

16 And they brought it. And he saith unto them, Whose is this image and superscription? And they said unto him, Cæsar's.

17 And Jesus answering said unto them, Render to Cæsar the things that are Cæsar's, and to God the things that are God's. And they marvelled at him.

*margin:* ‖ *Valuing of our money seven pence halfpenny, as Matt. xviii. 28.*

---

as Thou hast, cannot be in fear of Cæsar, or of his representative. One who professes to be the Messiah, and so the true King of Israel, as Thou dost, must sooner or later assert His claims against all foreign usurpation."

14, 16. "Is it lawful to give tribute . . . . and they said unto him, Cæsar's." The courage, if one may reverently use the word, of our Lord, in thus demanding the coin, was remarkable, for they hated the Roman money, not only for its being the badge of foreign subjection, but also because it had engraven on it an image of the Emperor, a thing which they held to be utterly unlawful. In the temple they would not receive this coin because of the head engraven upon it, which seemed to them to savour of idolatry; and yet to this very hated image the Lord appealed, as witnessing to them that through the righteous judgment of God, they were not their own masters, and must submit to their conquerors.

17. "And Jesus answering said unto them, Render therefore unto Cæsar the things," &c. The best comment on this is in the words of Christ's inspired servant. "Rulers are not a terror to good works, but to the evil. Wilt thou then not be afraid of the power? Do that which is good, and thou shalt have praise of the same. For he is the minister of God to thee for good . . . wherefore ye must needs be subject, not only for wrath, but also for conscience sake. Render, therefore, to all their dues; tribute to whom tribute is due, custom to whom custom, fear to whom fear, honour to whom honour." (Rom. xiii. 3-7.)

"And to God the things that are God's." The best exposition of

18 ¶ ᵉ Then come unto him the Sadducees, ᶠ which say there is no resurrection; and they asked him, saying,

ᵉ Matt. xxii. 23. Luke xx. 27.
ᶠ Acts xxiii. 8.

this also is in the words of the same blessed Apostle, "Ye are not your own, for ye are bought with a price, therefore glorify God in your body, and in your spirit, which are God's" (1 Cor. vi. 19). "The coin of Cæsar is on gold on which his image is depicted. But the coin of God is man, on whom His image is stamped. Give therefore your money tribute to Cæsar, but preserve for God your conscience and your innocence" (Williams). In the former parable the Lord sets forth the relation of His kingdom to the ancient theocracy, here He shows its relation to the kingdoms of this world, that it in no way interferes with them, but upholds their rightful claims in the matter of tribute, as the means whereby, though imperfectly, they maintain peace and order. The reader will also perceive that the Lord's answer in no respect bears on the questions now agitated amongst us, such as the relations of the spirituality to the temporality in a professedly Christian kingdom, courts of final appeal, the position of an ecclesiastical corporation holding property as well as doctrine. The Church being in the world, and having no carnal weapons, must of necessity be at the mercy of the world, but the world itself is at the mercy of God, and under His control; so that the weapons of an aggrieved Church are prayer and faith, and passive resistance, and unity in itself; and very powerful weapons these are, as the world has found.

18. "Then come unto him the Sadducees, which say there is no resurrection." How is it that the Sadducees came to the Lord with this question? It does not seem to have been intended to entrap Him into saying something for which they might accuse Him:—it may have been for some reason of this sort. They had heard how He had raised the dead, and they knew that the doctrine of the Resurrection and future retribution was taught most explicitly in all His discourses; they had also seen how He had silenced those who questioned His authority, and those who had thought to entrap Him in the matter of the tribute. They thought then they would try Him on the point of their favourite doctrine, or rather negation, that there was no real ground for the doctrine of a Resurrection, or even of a future state, or it would have been distinctly asserted in the Law, which all Jews looked upon as the

19 Master, *Moses wrote unto us, If a man's brother die,
*Deut. xxv. 5. and leave *his* wife *behind him,* and leave no
children, that his brother should take his wife, and raise up
seed unto his brother.

20 Now there were seven brethren: and the first took a
wife, and dying left no seed.

21 And the second took her, and died, neither left he any
seed: and the third likewise.

22 And the seven had her, and left no seed: last of all
the woman died also.

---

22. " And the seven had her, and left no seed." " Had her " omitted by א, B., C., L.,
Δ, two Cursives (28, 33), Coptic, Armenian; retained by A. (virtually), most later
Uncials, almost all Cursives, Syriac (Schaaf), also, virtually, by Old Latin, Vulg., and
versions.

most sacred and the most highly inspired part of the Old Testament. They were thorough-going materialists, and could form no conception of any future state, except one which reproduced after death this miserable life, with its affections and lusts. They consequently came to Him with a question which seemed to make the idea of a future life absurd and impossible, because they assumed that it must be clogged with all the selfish and sensual conditions of this life.

19. " Master, Moses wrote unto us, If a man's brother die, and leave his wife," &c. The law alluded to is the Levirate, and is thus laid down in Deut. xxv. 5: " If brethren dwell together, and one of them die, and have no child, the wife of the dead shall not marry without unto a stranger: her husband's brother shall go in unto her, and take her to him to wife. . . . And it shall be, that the first-born which she beareth shall succeed in the name of his brother which is dead, that his name be not put out of Israel."

20, 22. " Now there were seven brethren . . . last of all the woman died also." It shows clearly the low and debased state of their minds, that they should have chosen such a case, for the sort of marriage in question was not for the sake of affection, but for the most secular of purposes; simply that the estate might not be alienated. It was not a matter of choice with the brother or brothers of the deceased—they were publicly disgraced (Deut. xxv. 7-11) if they did not comply with the law, though they would

23 In the resurrection therefore, when they shall rise, whose wife shall she be of them? for the seven had her to wife.

24 And Jesus answering said unto them, Do ye not therefore err, because ye know not the scriptures, neither the power of God?

---

23. "When they shall rise" omitted by ℵ, B., C., D., L., Δ, two or three Cursives (28, 33), Old Latin (c, k), Coptic, Syriac (Schaaf); retained by A., later Uncials, almost all Cursives, several Old Latin, Vulg., Gothic.

have in most cases wives and children of their own, and so it might affect the interests of their own children.

24. "And Jesus answering said unto them, Do ye not therefore err, because ye know not the scriptures," &c. They were, no doubt, very well acquainted with the mere letter of Scripture; but they knew not its hidden depths of meaning, its absolute truth in the expression of the spiritual and eternal relations between God and His creatures, and this because they read it and judged respecting it, as they would of any other book. They read the words, " I am the God of Abraham," and they never asked themselves how He could be the God of one long before annihilated—on their principles it meant, " I am the God of a little dust;" and so they erred upon the most vital question that can interest a human being, whether he shall live after death, and be judged for the things done in the body. And they erred also because they knew not "the power of God." They knew not and cared not to contemplate the power of God in bringing about the Resurrection of the whole man, body, soul, and spirit, and his resurrection, not to live over again the same sort of life which he lives now, but to live for ever in a far higher, because a more spiritual sphere.

These two things must go together, to know the Scripture, and to know the power of God to bring about that which is promised or implied in Scripture, which is, in fact, a belief in Scripture as being the word of Almighty God.

" Neither the power of God." Most of those who notice these words consider that they set forth the power of God in the natural world. It seems as if He said, "Ye know not, ye realize not the power of God in the world around you. As Sadducees ye profess to hold the Books of Moses, ye acknowledge God, if ye believe in Him at all, as the Creator and Upholder of all things. If, then, He has made you, and the world around you, and adapted it to your

25 For when they shall rise from the dead, they neither marry, nor are given in marriage; but ʰ are as the angels which are in heaven.

ʰ 1 Cor. xv. 42, 49, 52.

25. "As the angels which are in heaven," or, "As angels in heaven." So A., B., E., G., H., S., &c.; but א, C., D., F., K., L., M., Δ, a large number of Cursives, Coptic, Syriac, Æthiopic omit "which are." "But are as angels in heaven" (Revisers); *sed sunt sicut angeli in cœlis* (Vulg.).

wants and preservation, why can ye not believe that He can raise you into a higher state of existence in which He can reward you or punish you? which state of existence will be infinitely above this, so that ye will not be in bondage to the same wants, the same low desires, the same narrow limitations as ye are now." "Supposing man to be just such a nothing after this life as he was before it, yet as he had his being at first from nothing, so surely he may be restored to that being again from such a nothing. For it seems to be a work of greater difficulty to give a beginning to what is not, than a restoration of being to what has been. Do you believe that which is vanished from our short sight to be lost to God? For all bodies, whether dried to powder, or dissolved to water, or crumbled to ashes, or attenuated to smoke, are lost to us indeed; but God, the Almighty Guardian of the elements, has them still in reserve as much as ever. . . . . Behold how all nature is at work to comfort us with images of our future Resurrection. The sun sets and rises again, the stars glide away and return, the flowers die and revive, the trees put forth afresh after the decay of age, and 'that which thou sowest is not quickened except it die;' and just so may our bodies lie in the grave till the season of Resurrection. Why then so hasty for a resurrection in the dead of winter? We must wait with patience for the spring of human bodies" (Minucius Felix). It is to be remembered, of course, that this Christian writer cites these things as parables or images, not as analogies, much less proofs.

25. "For when they shall rise from the dead . . . in heaven." "As if He had said, 'There will be a certain heavenly and angelic restoration to life when there shall be no more decay, and we shall remain unchanged, and for this reason marriage shall cease. For marriage now exists on account of our decay, that we may be carried on by succession of our race, and not fail; but *then* we shall be as the angels which need no succession by marriage, and never come to an end.'" (Theophylact.)

26 And as touching the dead, that they rise: have ye not read in the book of Moses, how in the bush God spake unto him, saying, ¹I *am* the God of Abraham, and the ⁱ Ex. iii. 6. God of Isaac, and the God of Jacob?

27 He is not the God of the dead, but the God of the living: ye therefore do greatly err.

---

26. "How in the bush." Some suppose that this means in that section of Exodus which is called by the name of "the bush;" but the voice of God actually proceeded from the bush.

27. "But the God of the living." "The God" omitted by אּ, A., B., C., D., F., K., sixty Cursives, Old Latin, Vulg., &c. So the most probable reading is, "But of the living."

[For further remarks on this see my notes on St. Matthew.]

26, 27. "And as touching the dead, that they rise: have ye not read... do greatly err." In order to see something of the force of this, we must remember (1) that the present tense is used, "*I am* the God of Abraham," not "I was," but "I *am;*" and (2) that God, as the God of Abraham, made certain very great promises to Abraham, which promises He did not fulfil in Abraham's life-time, and which promises are clearly distinguished from the promises to Abraham's seed. Thus Abraham's sole spot of land which he could call his own when he died was the cave of Machpelah and the field in which it was situated, and yet God had said, "All the land which thou seest, to thee will I give it, and to thy seed after thee." Again the same is repeated in Gen. xv. 7, and xvii. 8. Now how God will fulfil this to Abraham is yet a mystery. God may have some means of fulfilling this to Abraham literally and personally at the day of the Resurrection; or He may fulfil it to him in some infinitely blessed way above all that Abraham can ask or think: but anyhow God, as Abraham's God, having promised to the patriarch personally certain blessings, Abraham must be yet in existence to receive the fulfilment of God's promise.

And again, as I have shown fully in my notes on St. Matthew, the Name of God to the Jews implied personal relations to them, as Father, and Saviour, and Judge, just as much as father, and saviour, and judge among men imply personal relations to the individuals who are begotten by the father, or saved by the saviour, or judged by the judge; so that, if God said, "I am the God of Abraham," Abraham must be somewhere in existence as God's

28 ¶ ᵏ And one of the scribes came, and having heard them reasoning together, and perceiving that he had answered them well, asked him, Which is the first commandment of all?

ᵏ Matt. xxii. 35.

28. "Which is the first commandment of all?" or as Revisers, "What commandment is the first of all?" The great majority of authorities, taken literally, make "all" to be neuter, "Which is the first commandment of all things?" but the questioner cannot possibly have intended to ask such a thing.

son, to be loved by Him, and God's subject, to be judged and rewarded by God for obedience to Himself, for which obedience he received no corresponding reward in his life here on earth.

Again, and far better than all. When God called Himself the God of Abraham, God in a measure gave Himself to Abraham, so that Abraham should be able to say, Because God is my God, I possess God. Well, then, as St. Hilary argues, " It should be further considered that this was said to Moses at a time when those Holy Patriarchs had gone to their rest, and so they of whom He was the God were in being, for they could have had (possessed) nothing if they had not been in being, for in the nature of things that of which somewhat else *is*, must have itself a being ; so they who have a God, must themselves be alive, since God is eternal, and it is not possible that that which is dead should possess that which is eternal. How, then, shall it be affirmed that those do not and shall not hereafter exist, of whom Eternity Itself has said that He is (theirs) ? "

28. " And one of the scribes came, and having heard them reasoning," &c. A much more favourable view of this scribe, and of his " questioning," is given in St. Mark than in St. Matthew. St. Matthew tells us that the Pharisees were gathered together, apparently in a hostile spirit ; and one of them asked Him the question, "tempting him." In St. Mark, on the contrary, the same man, called a Scribe (no mention being made of the Pharisees), was struck with admiration at the Lord's reasoning ; and, of his own accord, asked him the question. Both accounts are perfectly true to fact. The Pharisees were gathered together, no doubt, unfavourably to Him ; but there were differences among them, and one better than the rest came forward with a desire to have the question solved, " Which is the first commandment of all ? "

CHAP. XII.] THE LORD OUR GOD IS ONE LORD. 281

29 And Jesus answered him, The first of all the commandments *is,* ¹Hear, O Israel; The Lord our God is one Lord:

30 And thou shalt love the Lord thy God with all thy

¹ Deut. vi. 4.
Luke x. 27.

---

29. "The first of all the commandments is." Most probably it should be, "The first commandment of all is." So A., C., K., M., or, simply, "The first is," with אּ, B., L., Δ, Coptic ; *Primum omnium mandatum est* (Vulg.).

"The Lord our God is one Lord." This most sublime utterance is utterly spoilt and turned into something very like nonsense by the Revisers of 1881, "The Lord our God, the Lord is one." The comma they have inserted turns the sentence into two distinct propositions having no connection with one another. Their marginal reading, "The Lord is our God, the Lord is one," is still worse. There is no necessity for the smallest alteration.

29. "And Jesus answered him, The first of all the commandments is, Hear, O Israel; The Lord our God is one Lord," *i.e.,* Jehovah our God is one Jehovah, or, the Eternal One our God is one Eternal. This in no respect militates against the Athanasian formula of Catholic doctrine, in which we confess "so likewise the Father is eternal, the Son eternal, and the Holy Ghost eternal;" for we proceed to confess, "and yet they are not three eternals, but One eternal."

I have noticed all through my commentary on St. John, how the Son of God constantly maintains His unity with the Father. He does nothing apart from the Father: He does whatsoever He sees the Father do. All that He teaches men He hath heard and learned of the Father. He that hath seen Him hath seen the Father. He and the Father are One. The unity of God is the first principle of all religion, because it is the unity of power, of will, of wisdom, of goodness at the head of the universe.

30. "And thou shalt love the Lord thy God with all thy heart, and with all thy soul, and with all thy mind, and with all thy strength." Thou shalt love thy God with thy whole inner being, with thy whole self, with all thy faculties.

There is nothing tautological in this mention of heart, soul, mind, and strength. The heart signifies the will, the higher power of choice—the soul, the affections—the mind, the intellectual powers, and the strength, the intensity with which in the perfect Christian all are directed Godwards. The Fathers, however, give different meanings to "heart," "soul," "mind." Thus Augustine: "You are commanded to love God *with all thy heart,* that your whole

heart, and with all thy soul, and with all thy mind, and with all thy strength: this *is* the first commandment.

---

30. " This is the first commandment." So A., D., later Uncials, almost all Cursives, Old Latin (except a), Vulg., Syriac, Gothic, Armenian, Æthiopic; omitted by ℵ, B., E., L., Δ, Sahidic, Coptic, and Old Latin (a).

---

thoughts; *with all thy soul*, that your whole life (the word 'soul' being often translated 'life'); *with all thy mind*, that your whole understanding may be given to Him from Whom you have that which you give." But Origen somewhat differently: "With all thy *heart*—that is, in all recollection, act, thought; with all thy *soul* (or life)—to be ready, that is, to lay it down for God's religion; with all thy *mind*, thy mind bringing forth nothing but what is of God." (From " Catena Aurea.")

I cannot help adhering, however, to the distinction which I have made above, which is true to nature, that the heart signifies the higher and more spiritual power of choice, and the soul the lower and more animal: for is it not often the case that the more spiritual and moral nature fastens on God, but does not take the affections equally with it? And do not the affections, particularly in excitable persons, move Godwards, but not so much under the influence of the moral and spiritual nature as they should? Thus there is often a sort of animal love to God and Christ shown in excited feelings, where there is little or no reverence, no moral earnestness, no depth—in fact, a love hardly worthy of God.[1]

Williams has a beautiful passage on "with all thy mind." "The love of God fills 'the mind,' when knowledge gathereth all things with reference to God; when speculation ever weigheth the things of God with the things of men; when imagination compareth all

---

[1] Throughout the Old and New Testament, the words translated heart always, I think, stand for the deepest thing within us, and the soul always for one not so deep—being, in fact, interchangeable with animal life. Thus, when the Lord says, " Blessed are the pure in heart," this must mean the purity of the highest and most spiritual part, whereas St. Paul uses the adjective derived from the word soul (psychical) to indicate what is natural as opposed to spiritual. " The natural (or psychical man) receiveth not the things of the Spirit of God," &c. (1 Corinth. ii. 14).

31 And the second *is* like, *namely* this, ᵐThou shalt love thy neighbour as thyself. There is none other commandment greater than these.

ᵐ Lev. xix. 18.
Matt. xxii. 39.
Rom. xiii. 9.
Gal. v. 14.
James ii. 8.

---

31. "And the second is like, *namely* this." So A., later Uncials, most Cursives, Old Latin, Vulg., Syriac, &c.; but ℵ, B., L., D., Sahidic, Coptic omit "like." "The second is this" (Revisers).

things with the things of God; when memory storeth in her treasure things of God, new and old; when the thoughts ever turn to God as their end; when all studies are in God, and there is no study which hath not God for its end. We are always thinking of something, at all times, and in all places; we can behold no object in the earth or sky, but thought is busy with the same. The thoughts are according to the heart. If one might say it with reverence, as angelic ministrations execute God's will, so are the thoughts to the heart and soul of man ever busy traversing and returning, through earth and heaven, as the heart wills. And these, in the good man, are ever full of God."

31. "And the second is like, namely this, Thou shalt love thy neighbour as thyself." In what respect is the command to love our neighbour like the command to love God, seeing that the objects are so different? Evidently in this way. The Lord here speaks of the highest love to our neighbour, not the love of mere companionship or self-interest. Now the highest love of our neighbour is like the love of God—a holy love. We should love him because he is made in the image and likeness of God. It is the love of that in our neighbour which is from God.

"As thyself." As thou desirest the preservation and well-being of thine own life, so thou shouldest desire the preservation and well-being of thy neighbour's life. As thou wouldest that men should do to thee, so do thou to thy neighbour.

Now we must thoroughly understand in what way this commandment is the *second*. It is not the second, in that it can be dispensed with, which it often is, when men think that certain lively frames and feelings towards God absolve them from charity, consideration, purity, and even honesty towards their neighbours. To such the Apostle writes: "He that loveth not his brother whom he hath seen, how can he love God whom he hath not seen?" "He that seeth his brother have need, and shutteth up his compassion from him, how dwelleth the love of God in him?"

32 And the scribe said unto him, Well, Master, thou hast said the truth: for there is one God; and there is none other but he:

ⁿ Deut. iv. 39.
Is. xlv. 6, 14.
& xlvi. 9.

---

32. "*Well, Master, thou hast said the truth.*" This may more properly be rendered "Well spoken; Master, truly thou hast said." So Vulg., *Bene, Magister! in veritate dixisti, quia Unus est Deus.*
"*For there is one God.*" "God" omitted by א, A., B., K., L., M., other later Uncials, Vulg., [Cod. Amiat.], Syriac; retained by D., E., F., G., H., many Cursives, most Old Latin, Sahidic, Coptic, Armenian, &c.

But it is the second in this, that he only can truly and perfectly keep it who has some care and earnest desire to keep the first. The man who has begun to love God is the only man who can truly and properly love his neighbour: for he only can love that in his neighbour which is of God; he only can love his neighbour as being the image of God; and he only can earnestly desire that his neighbour should retain, or be restored to, that image. The holy man only can desire the holiness of his neighbour; the religious man only can care earnestly for the eternal well-being of his neighbour.

And now, before we leave this all-important subject, two questions have to be considered—1. Since we cannot command our affections, how is it that God asks us to love Him, seeing that He is so infinitely above and beyond us, seeing that He is an eternal, invisible, incomprehensible Spirit? Now the answer is, that God never commands men to love Him till He has made Himself known to them, and entered into relations with them, and shown His regard for them. The God who commanded the children of Israel to love Him supremely was the God of Abraham, Isaac, and Jacob, their fathers. He was the God Who had redeemed them from the slavery of Egypt by bringing them through the Red Sea, and sustaining them for forty years by a daily miracle, so that they knew Him as a God Whom they had every reason to love.

2. The second is, how can we get to love God supremely? By what process can so exalted an affection become the ruling principle within us?

Now the secret of this lies in the extraordinary fact that the first commandment of God's law is not (directly, at least) the first commandment of His Gospel. The Lord Himself distinctly lays down the first requirement of the Gospel to be belief in Himself. '* This is the work of God, that ye believe on Him Whom He hath

## MORE THAN ALL OFFERINGS.

33 And to love him with all the heart, and with all the understanding, and with all the soul, and with all the strength, and to love *his* neighbour as himself, °is more than all whole burnt offerings and sacrifices.

° 1 Sam. xv.
22. Hos. vi. 6.
Mic. vi. 6, 7, 8.

---

33. "With all the soul" omitted by ℵ, B., L., Δ, a few Cursives, Coptic, Armenian; but retained by A., D., later Uncials, most Cursives, most Old Latin, Vulg., Sahidic, Syriac, &c.

sent" (John vi. 29). And the beloved disciple, evidently speaking with reference to the two great commandments, has: "This is His commandment, that we should believe in the Name of his Son Jesus Christ, and love one another as He gave us commandment" (1 John iii. 23). It may not be in our power to command our affection towards an invisible Spirit, but it is in our power to set before our minds the Person and Work, the Life and Death, the Character and Example of the Son of God; and this, as nothing else can, will form within us the love of that Eternal and Infinite Father Who is so perfectly represented to us in His Son that that Son has said, "He that hath seen Me hath seen the Father." If, then, we would grow and increase in the love of God, we must devoutly and adoringly contemplate the sufferings of the Son of God. We must take pains to impress upon ourselves that we were the occasion of these sufferings, and that they are for us; "that He was wounded for our transgressions; that He was bruised for our iniquities; that the chastisement of our peace was upon Him; and that by His stripes we are healed."

Of course, the love of God is the gift of the Spirit; and this is our great hope, that what is not in us by nature may be in us by grace; but as God commands us to believe, He commands us to use all the means that He has given to us to strengthen and confirm our faith. And so this is the way of the Catholic Church, which, instead of setting before us an abstract Christ, the Weaver of an external robe of righteousness, would have us fasten our minds on, and adoringly contemplate, the very Son of God incarnate, in the womb of the Virgin, born, baptized, tempted, living, working, teaching, agonized, betrayed, deserted, suffering, dying, rising again, ascending, and coming again in the Spirit.

Such is the path to the love of God set before us by the Spirit both in the Scriptures and in the Church—in her year, in her

34 And when Jesus saw that he answered discreetly, he said unto him, Thou art not far from the kingdom of God.

p Matt. xxii. 46.

p And no man after that durst ask him *any question.*

q Matt. xxii. 41. Luke xx. 41.

35 ¶ q And Jesus answered and said, while he taught in the temple, How say the scribes that Christ is the son of David?

---

services, in her creeds, in her Sacraments. Let us try then in sincerity, and we shall have the humble, holy, reverential love of God within us.

"And the scribe said unto him, Well [or properly, well spoken], Master." The answer is evidently not a mere formal acknowledgment of the truth of a certain abstract proposition; but an earnest and devout expression of what was to the man a fact—that godliness and righteousness were the things to the production of which, in the souls of us His creatures, all other parts of God's religion are subordinate. By the earnest, hearty confession of this the Lord saw that the Scriptures had wrought in this man what God had intended that they should work in every one who possessed them, and so the Lord pronounced him to be "not far from the kingdom of God:" and so we cannot but hope that in less than two months after this he was amongst the number of those whom the Lord "added to the Church."

35. "And Jesus answered and said." How is it that the account of what follows begins with the words "Jesus answered"? We must turn to St. Matthew, and from him we learn that the Lord Himself *began* by asking the Pharisees, "What think ye of Christ, whose Son is He?" and when they replied "the Son of David," "He saith unto them," which words correspond with what we have in St. Mark, "He answered and said." He answered their low thoughts of the Messiah. They were quite satisfied with their answer that Christ was the Son of David; but the Lord begins to show them that they, as little as the Sadducees, understood the depth and fulness of Scripture. How say the Scribes, *i.e.*, "How say ye, who adopt the opinions of the Scribes, that Christ is the Son of David? For David himself said by the Holy Ghost, The Lord said unto my Lord, Sit thou," &c. David, therefore, himself calleth Him Lord, and whence is He then His Son?

36 For David himself said ʳ by the Holy Ghost, ˢ The LORD said to my Lord, Sit thou on my right hand, till I make thine enemies thy footstool.

ʳ 2 Sam. xxiii. 2.
ˢ Ps. cx. 1.

37 David therefore himself calleth him Lord; and whence is he *then* his son? And the common people heard him gladly.

---

There is but one answer to this question, which the Lord Himself gives in the vision in the last chapter of the Revelation, "I am the Root and the Offspring of David." Inasmuch as David calls Him Lord He is David's Root, for all things were made by Him. Each child of Adam, and David among them, though he seems to be brought into being by the law of generation, yet really receives that being from the Eternal Word, "by Whom all things were made, and without Him was not anything made that was made." So that the Root—the Author of the being of all men, and of David among the rest, was that Eternal Word Who was made flesh, and was then questioning the Pharisees and Scribes. This mystery, of course, the Lord's questioners could not then apprehend; but if they were led by the authority of their own Scriptures, they must acknowledge that the Christ when He comes must be superhuman. He must be such an One that the greatest hero and king of God's people—the real founder of their monarchy, could call Him Lord. Let them think of this—let them think of the very many words of the Psalmists and of the Prophets in which superhuman, even Divine names, attributes, and actions are ascribed to the Messiah, Whom they all expected—and they would not be startled when, shortly after this, after He had been crucified and had risen again and had ascended, they heard the Apostles, who were performing stupendous miracles by the mere invocation of His Name, proclaim Him to be the veritable Son of God, the Judge of quick and dead, the Prince of Life, the Lord of all.

" And the common people heard him gladly." And yet He spake the deepest mysteries—the highest things in the kingdom of grace. when He thus, by implication, set Himself forth as David's Son and David's Lord. And so it ever is. The common people are like children, and so do not carp and cavil and ask such questions as, How can these things be? They may be misled, misinformed, mistaken in matters of religion—but they do not reject mysteries as such, *i.e.*, as being above their comprehension. I am well aware

38 ¶ And ᵗ he said unto them in his doctrine, ᵘ Beware of the scribes, which love to go in long clothing, and ˣ *love* salutations in the marketplaces.

ᵗ ch. iv. 2.
ᵘ Matt. xxiii. 1, &c. Luke xx. 46.
ˣ Luke xi. 43.

38. "And he said unto them." So A., later Uncials, almost all Cursives, Vulg., Sahidic, Gothic, Æthiopic; but "unto them" omitted by ℵ, B., L., Δ, Cursive 33, Coptic, Syriac (Schaaf).

that very many working men who have a little knowledge, and are proud of their mechanical skill, are primed by Infidels and Socialists to cavil and question; but this is not the normal state of the common people, it is an artificial state. It is very sad to see those who have few hopes in this world flinging away the hopes of the eternal world; but how is it all to be met? Not by keeping back what is supernatural in Christianity, but by humbly and reverently bringing it forward and leaving the issue to God: for that which is Divine and Supernatural supplies the deepest wants of the human and the natural. Its devout and careful enunciation finds out those that are of God and attracts them to Him, according to the Divine sayings: "He that doeth truth cometh to the light," and " He that is of God heareth God's words."

38. "And he said unto them in his doctrine, Beware of the scribes, which love," &c. This and the following two verses are the only portions given to us by St. Mark of a discourse of considerable length occupying the whole of St. Matthew's 23rd chapter. The reason of this curtailment seems to be clear if St. Mark reproduced the preaching of St. Peter to the Roman Christians; for St. Peter, preaching to Gentiles in Rome, would not give them very much of what concerned Jews only, as a great part of our Lord's denunciation of the Pharisees in Matthew xxiii. does. St. Mark gives only three or four warnings of a general kind, which are needed by all those who have put themselves forward as teachers or leaders of religion.

First, "loving to go in long clothing." This "long clothing" was, of course, not the sacerdotal and sacrificial robes worn by the priests, which God had Himself ordained to distinguish, not the man, but the most holy service in which he was, for the time, engaged. Such things as the Lord denounced implied personal distinction, as distinguished from holy service—in fact, what tended to minister to personal display, whether of learning or social

39 And the chief seats in the synagogues, and the uppermost rooms at feasts :

---

39. "Uppermost rooms." "Seats" (Revisers); Vulg., *Primos discubitus*.

position. What answers to them in this our day would be university hoods or chaplains' scarves, or whatsoever marks the mere man and not the Divine Function.

"Salutations in the market-places." This, of course, means not the greetings—the "peace be with you" of their friends—but the deferential recognitions of those assembled in public places.

"The chief seats in the synagogues," answering to the stalls of cathedrals.

"The uppermost rooms at feasts." Answering to our taking precedence. Now, none of these things are wrong in themselves. Public teachers ought to have deference paid to them. To treat them with anything like contempt would be a very bad thing, not for themselves, but for those who did so. If people sit at tables such as ours, some must be nearer the place of honour than others. If people teach, or perform any divine service in a public assembly, they must be, in some measure, separated from the congregation. Those who make a merit of despising these things, such as Quakers and Plymouth Brethren, are as a rule pretentious and self-complacent in their religion.

But what the Lord denounces is the *love* of these things in teachers; so that those who put themselves forward to teach (as some must do) should desire that which personally exalts and distinguishes them. There must always be such a temptation amongst Christian teachers as well as amongst others, and so the Lord's warnings are general and for all time. Now let the reader particularly remark that the Lord here warns men not against the abuses of the Divine Aaronic sacerdotal succession, but against those of a teaching institution of human origin—the order of Scribes. And so it is now. The things which minister now to the self-importance and vanity of Christian ministers are their teaching functions, not their Eucharistical celebrations. It is the pulpit and the platform which feed pride and vanity, whereas at the altar the sense of the Ineffable Nearness, if men have any sense of It, humbles them to the dust.

## A CERTAIN POOR WIDOW.

40 ʸ Which devour widows' houses, and for a pretence make long prayers: these shall receive greater damnation.

41 ¶ ᶻ And Jesus sat over against the treasury, and beheld how the people cast ∥ money ᵃ into the treasury: and many that were rich cast in much.

42 And there came a certain poor widow, and she threw in two ∥ mites, which make a farthing.

*ʸ Matt. xxiii. 14.*
*ᶻ Luke xxi. 1.*
*∥ A piece of brass money: See Matt. x. 9.*
*ᵃ 2 Kings xii. 9.*
*∥ It is the seventh part of one piece of that brass money.*

---

40. "Which devour widows' houses, and for a pretence make long prayers." Under the pretence of religion they prey upon those that have lost their natural protectors. Quesnel pertinently asks, "Will widows never learn to mistrust hypocrites? Give to hospitals, to prisons, to those who are ashamed to ask, above all to poor relations: this is the way to avoid the snares of such as are only pretenders to religion."

Nothing requires greater watchfulness lest men use it for unworthy purposes than fluency of utterance. I have known habitual drunkards boast of their proficiency in pouring out floods of words, and that in public prayer to God.

41. "And Jesus sat over against the treasury, and beheld how the people cast," &c. "In that great central quadrangle, or court of the temple, that was accessible to the Jewish women." It lay in front of the sanctuary, "forming," says Thrupp, "a kind of ante-court to the rest of the inner temple." In the place near which our Saviour sat there stood thirteen brazen vessels shaped like trumpets into which those who visited the temple cast their gifts. These were labelled according to the purposes to which their contents were respectively appropriated.

"And beheld how the people cast money into the treasury." An interesting question presents itself: Did they give so as that others could see the amount? From the shape of the boxes for receiving the money it would seem that each person's offering could not be seen unless he ostentatiously allowed it. So that the Lord alone knew the amount that each threw in, and their circumstances.

42. "And there came a certain poor widow, and she threw in two mites," &c. The mention of this incident is very remarkable. It must have taken place immediately after the tremendous denun-

CHAP. XII.] SHE OF HER WANT. 291

43 And he called *unto him* his disciples, and saith unto them, Verily I say unto you, That [b] this poor widow hath cast more in, than all they which have cast into the treasury:

44 For all *they* did cast in of their abundance; but she of her want did cast in all that she had, [c] *even* all her living.

[b] 2 Cor. viii. 12.

[c] Deut. xxiv. 6. 1 John iii. 17.

---

ciations uttered by the Lord against the hypocrisy and avarice of the leaders of religion—the Scribes and Pharisees—which are given us in St. Matthew's Gospel, and which culminate in the words: "Behold, your house is left unto you desolate." The nation and the temple of which they boasted were irrevocably doomed, and yet the Lord noticed with approval this single act of liberality in a poor, unknown giver, though she gave it for the maintenance of a temple destined to speedy destruction, and of a ritual which would soon become obsolete, and pass away. "No stronger proof could have been afforded us that in the midst of the greatest national guilt each individual is still an object of His peculiar regard," and that even after the judgment has been finally decreed, no one prayer, no one act of obedience, no single mite, which is in very deed the offering of faith and love, can escape the notice of the Saviour.

43. "And he called unto him his disciples, and saith unto them," &c. The Lord measures all gifts and offerings, whether of mind, body, or estate, by the self-denial and labour and purity of intention with which they are accompanied.

44. "For all they did cast in of their abundance, but she of her want," &c. What the sense of duty was which prompted her to offer that which was to her so costly a sacrifice we are not told. She must have done it in great faith that the God of the widow would not allow her to starve. It was a real sacrifice. Mr. H. Gray gives a very apt illustration. "A rich man is much stirred up by the report of some missionary work, and exclaims, 'Well, I will give five pounds; I can give this amount and not feel it!' Suppose, my Christian brother, you should give twenty pounds, and feel it! Would you be ultimately the worse for it?"

## CHAP. XIII.

AND *as he went out of the temple, one of his disciples saith unto him, Master, see what manner of stones and what buildings *are here!*

<sup>a</sup> Matt. xxiv.
1. Luke xxi. 5.

1. "And as he went out of the temple, one of his disciples . . . what manner of stones?" So that the last thing that He did in the house of His Father was to commend the poor widow, and in her to pronounce His eternal approval of all true devotion and self-sacrifice.

He went out of the doomed sanctuary to be Himself, before a week had passed, in His own Death and Resurrection, the foundation of the true temple of God, the temple of living stones, growing up from Him, as its foundation, to Him, as its chief corner-stone.

"What manner of stones." Notice how the disciple draws attention to the stones, before he mentions the buildings : and, from all accounts, it seems that the magnitude of the stones was even more remarkable than the grandeur of the buildings. Josephus thus describes them: "So Herod took away the old foundations, and laid others, and erected the temple upon them . . . Now the temple was built of stones that were white and strong, and each of their lengths was twenty-five cubits, their height was eight, and their breadth about twelve." There seems to have been two measures of length called cubits, one nearly ten inches, the other double its length—about twenty. Even if the shorter measure is here used the stones were very large—above twenty feet in length, nearly seven feet high, and ten in depth.[1]

"What buildings are here!" It is scarcely possible to form even a remote idea of what the magnificence of these buildings must have been. The principal porch, or covered cloister, was longer,

---

[1] The reader will see in the article on Weights and Measures in Smith's "Dictionary of the Bible" the difficulties about ascertaining the length of the cubit. The two measures, and their respective lengths, I have given from two tables in one of Baxter's Bibles.

2 And Jesus answering said unto him, Seest thou these great buildings? ᵇ there shall not be left one stone upon another, that shall not be thrown down.  ᵇ Luke xix. 44.

---

2. "Answering." So A., later Uncials, almost all Cursives, Vulg.; but ℵ, B., L., four Cursives (33, 115, 237, 255), Sah., Coptic, Syriac (Schaaf) omit "answering."

broader, and higher than York Minster, our largest English cathedral. This huge erection formed one side of the square enclosure, in the midst of which was the most sacred part, the holy place, and holy of holies, all which were built on a platform of such a height that at a distance it would be seen towering over the surrounding porches by those entering Jerusalem. "Whatever the exact appearance of its details may have been, it may safely be asserted that the triple temple of Jerusalem—the lower court standing on its magnificent terraces—the inner court raised on its platform in the centre of this, and the temple itself rising out of this group and so crowning the whole—must have formed, when combined with the beauty of its situation, one of the most splendid architectural combinations of the ancient world." (From Article "Temple" in "Dictionary of the Bible," by James Fergusson.)

2. "And Jesus answering said unto him, Seest thou these great buildings," &c. How complete this destruction was! We are told by one who was not a Christian, that " it was so thoroughly laid even with the ground by those that dug it up to the foundation, that there was left nothing to make those that came thither believe it had ever been inhabited " (Josephus' "Wars," Bk. VII., chap. i.). The only things left of the ancient temple are the stones of the foundations of the terraces which were then buried. These having been covered with a mass of débris, which appeared to be the side of a considerable hill, have since been discovered by tunnellings; but of that which was above ground, to which the Lord alluded when He said, "as for these things *which ye behold*," His words were fulfilled to the letter. The whole army of Titus seems to have been employed in razing it to the ground, so that every city of the world should take warning how it rebelled against the power of Rome.

And souls also must take warning, lest they know not the time of their visitation, and reject the overtures of Christ through His Spirit. Thus Origen: "Each man being the temple of God, by

3. And as he sat upon the mount of Olives over against the temple, Peter and James and John and Andrew asked him privately,

<sup>c</sup> Matt. xxiv. 3. Luke xxi. 7.

4 <sup>c</sup> Tell us, when shall these things be? and what *shall be* the sign when all these things shall be fulfilled?

---

reason of the Spirit of God dwelling in him, is himself the cause of his being deserted, that Christ should depart from him." The same Christian writer brings out a mystical meaning from the fact that the disciples themselves call the Lord's attention to the stones and buildings. "It is worthy of note how they show Him the buildings of the temple, as if He had not seen them. We reply, that when Christ had foretold the destruction of the temple, His disciples were amazed at the thought that so magnificent buildings should be utterly ruined, and, therefore, they show them to Him, to move Him to pity, that He should not do what He had threatened. And because the constitution of human nature is wonderful, being made the temple of God, the disciples and the rest of the saints confessing the wonderful working of God, in respect of the forming of man, intercede before the face of Christ, that He would not forsake the human race for their sins, .... He who after sin has no regard for himself [so as to repent] is gradually alienated, until he has altogether forsaken the living God; and so one stone is not left upon another of God's commandments which he has not thrown down." (Quoted in "Cat. Aurea.")

3. "And as he sat upon the mount of Olives over against the temple," &c. This is the only case in which Andrew is associated with the three. "Peter, James, and John and Andrew asked him privately." It may either mean apart from the rest of the Apostles, or that they came in the name of the Apostles, apart from the multitude, some of whom were continually following Him about.

4. "Tell us, when shall these things be? and what shall be the sign .... shall be fulfilled?" The latter clause should be translated: "What shall be the sign, when all these things are about to be accomplished?" As if they asked, When shall these things be (*i.e.*, the utter overthrow of the city and temple), and what shall be the sign of the time of the impending fulfilment, that we may know it, and be prepared?

stand,) then ᵖ let them that be in Judæa flee to the mountains:   ᵖ Luke xxi. 21

was the most significant of portents to those without—*i.e.*, to the dwellers in the Holy Land, especially to the Christians, that God had finally given up His sanctuary. Now we are to remember that the Christians of Jerusalem were not sufferers by this robbery and massacre on the part of the Zealots, for they had before this quitted the doomed city. Eusebius tells us that "the whole body of the Church of Jerusalem, having been commanded by a Divine revelation given to men of approved piety there before the war, removed from the city and dwelt at a certain town beyond the Jordan, called Pella." Some suppose that this took place at the time that Cestius Gallus having invested Jerusalem, suddenly, and for no apparent reason, withdrew his army, so that all who had fears respecting the fate of the city saw their opportunity, and escaped. Such a portent, then, as the seizure of the temple by the Zealots, would be a sign to all Christians throughout Judæa that they must lose no time in seeking safety by flight. Still there seems to be several reasons against accepting this as the true meaning of "the Abomination of Desolation," as, for instance, why should those who saw or heard of this catastrophe be enjoined such extreme haste in their flight that they were not even to enter their houses to take their clothes with them? The Zealots were some time in possession of the city and temple before it was finally beleaguered by Titus; and the parallel passage in St. Luke would lead them to look for the sign in connection with the Roman armies, not with loose bands of robbers and murderers.

Dr. Morison, to whom I am under obligations for his able historical sketch of the interpretations of this passage, quotes the opinion of Grotius as referring it to the idolatrous ensigns of the Roman army. Having given a remarkable passage from the Antiquities of Josephus, xviii. 3, sec. 1, in which Pilate was threatened with a serious revolt for having introduced these ensigns into the Holy City, he gives the following account: "And now the Romans, upon the flight of the seditious into the city, and upon the burning of the Holy House itself, and of all the buildings round about it, brought their ensigns to the temple, and set them over against its eastern gate. And then did they offer sacrifices to them, and then did they make Titus Imperator with the greatest accla-

15 And let him that is on the housetop not go down into the house, neither enter *therein*, to take any thing out of his house:

16 And let him that is in the field not turn back again for to take up his garment.

<sup>q</sup> Luke xxi. 23. & xxiii. 29.

17 <sup>q</sup> But woe to them that are with child, and to them that give suck in those days!

---

mations of joy." (B. I. vi. 6, Sec. i.) If this had occurred somewhat earlier it would have been the best explanation, because connecting the portent more closely with the Roman armies, according to St. Luke's report of the Lord's words.

The words thrown in by the Lord, "Let him that readeth understand," may either refer to the words of Daniel or to the Lord's citation of those words. The Gospel of St. Matthew had been published long before this caution was required, and was, no doubt, in the hands of all leading Christians.

15, 16. "And let him that is upon the housetop . . . take anything out of his house: And let him that is in the field . . . take up his garment." If this refers to those who dwelt in the country at some distance from Jerusalem, it is difficult to explain, as I have just said. Still, the Roman armies having taken before the siege some of the principal towns, very likely scoured the country all round, plundering, burning, and destroying. If it includes those in Jerusalem, then we must suppose that there might remain some few of God's saints in the devoted city: and if so, their flight must be of the character here described if they would save themselves.

That the man, when he heard of, or saw the portent is to use such haste as not to enter his house on any account, seems to imply that, if he lived in the country, there was an outer staircase by which he might descend and flee at once. Perhaps, however, these expressions are of a proverbial nature, such as ours, that "not a moment is to be lost."

17. "But woe to them that are with child, and to them that give suck in those days!" The reader cannot fail to remember the warning words of the Lord: "Daughters of Jerusalem, weep not for Me, but weep for yourselves and for your children. For, behold, the days are coming in the which they shall say, Blessed are the barren, and the wombs that never bare, and the paps which

5 And Jesus answering them began to say, *Take heed lest any *man* deceive you:

d Jer. xxix. 8.
Eph. v. 6.
1 Thess. ii. 3.

---

5. "And Jesus answering." So A., D., later Uncials, almost all Cursives, most Old Latin, Vulg.; but ℵ, B., L., Cursive 33, and some versions omit "answering."

5. "And Jesus answering them began to say, Take heed lest any man deceive you, . . . saying," &c.

The sublime discourse which follows is the one great prophecy of the Son of Man. The accounts of it in SS. Matthew and Mark are virtually the same. In expounding the corresponding verses in St. Matthew, I drew attention to its great principles, and its leading features. I must now ask the reader's permission to repeat what I said of the gist and thread of this discourse, in my notes on St. Matthew: " Christ, in uttering this prophecy, had evidently in His mind two things. He had to hold before His Church in ALL AGES—in the first age immediately after His Ascension, as well as in the last—its one hope, the hope of His appearing: so that each generation of Christians should live in the thought and expectation of it. And yet He had to prepare one particular generation—that of His own Apostles and first followers and believing countrymen—for a catastrophe of a more temporal, but yet most fearful character, which they must, if possible, escape. Now this double purpose was effected by two things—1st. By setting forth as signs of the impending destruction of Jerusalem certain signs, which would be partially, and yet truly fulfilled then, and yet which would be far more effectually and universally fulfilled just before the Second Advent. 2nd. By a certain indistinctness respecting the termination of the wrath upon the Jews, and the treading down of their city, and their dispersion, and its attendant persecutions. In the wondrous composition of this discourse, and arrangement of the various predictions the Lord prepares His whole Catholic Church to look for His coming at any time, and at all times; and yet prepares a part of that Church—the part which, speaking after the manner of men, would be dearest to Himself, because composed of His own countrymen—to be ready to escape a particular catastrophe, which might annihilate them. But the latter must not interfere with the former. It is the express will of God that all Christians, from the time of Christ's departure on the Mount of Ascension, should be awaiting His return; and so, the moment He disappeared, two angels were

6 For many shall come in my name, saying, I am *Christ;* and shall deceive many.

---

6. "For many." So A., D., later Uncials, almost all Cursives, Old Latin, Vulg., some versions; but ℵ, B., L., and Æthiopic omit "for."

sent to warn even the Apostles that He should return in like manner as they had seen Him go into heaven; and so SS. Peter and Paul, long before the fall of Jerusalem, looked for Christ's near approach, and preached it to Christians, such as those of Corinth and Thessalonica, who were not directly interested in that fall."

5, 6. "And Jesus answering them began to say, Take heed lest any man deceive you . . . deceive many." This, though said to the Apostles, must have been intended rather for their converts and followers. We do not read of any coming in His Name. Simon Magus apparently came in his own name, giving out that he was some great one, and many gave heed to him as being "the great power of God." But very probably the Lord's words must be taken as referring to the remarkable prevalence of false teachers in the first age of the Church. We should have thought that when the Church was governed by the Apostles appointed by Christ Himself, and by St. Paul, whose commission came direct from the Risen Lord, and was so abundantly supported by miracles and signs, that no false teachers would have dared to thwart and oppose the teaching of such men. But it was not so; on the contrary, the seeds of all early heresies seem to have been sown in the Apostolic age itself. St. John says that there were in his time many Antichrists. Now that a false teacher should be an Antichrist does not at all necessitate that he should openly assume the name of Christ. It would effect Satan's purpose far better if he could undermine the truth of Christ's Holy Incarnation; and so the beloved Apostle warns us, "Every spirit that confesseth not that Jesus Christ is come in the flesh is not of God" (1 John iv. 2). It is to be carefully remarked that these false teachers come in the name of Christ, and yet say, "I am." This seems to imply that they were professedly Christian teachers, and yet taught false doctrine, which was incompatible with any true acknowledgment of Christ as the One Great Teacher. Such were both the Judaizers and the earliest Gnostics, and the deniers of the Resurrection of the Body, who were at their wicked work as early as the writing of the First Epistle to the Corinthians.

## WARS AND RUMOURS OF WARS.

**7 And when ye shall hear of wars and rumours of wars, be**

Still, as our history of the period between the Resurrection and the destruction of Jerusalem is very imperfect, there may have been actual pretenders to Messiahship not mentioned in either the Acts or in Josephus.

Again, consider how this "take heed" is required in these last days. Every man who denies the Incarnation of the Son of God, every one who denies the atoning power of His Death, and the truth of His Resurrection, by so doing sets himself against, and pronounces judgment upon, the Christ of the New Testament, as if he was His superior, at least in knowledge. Such an one virtually says, "I am he;" for upon some of the things which beyond all others interest mankind—their redemption, their future state, their judgment,—he pronounces Christ to have been mistaken.

Again, consider that in these latter days there have not been wanting pretensions to actual Messiahship, which have perverted hundreds of thousands, perhaps millions, of souls. Men may laugh at the pretensions of the Mormon prophet; but it is a very serious matter to think of what numbers of clever and religiously disposed men, of the lower middle and the labouring class, he has robbed the Church of Christ.

7, 8. "And when ye shall hear of wars and rumours of wars . . . the beginning of sorrows." These verses must be taken as referring far more to the consummation of all things than to the end of the Jewish polity by the destruction of Jerusalem.

The wars and rumours of wars between the Ascension and the war ending in the Destruction of Jerusalem, were few and insignificant. Dean Mansell, in the "Speaker's Commentary," can give but three or four. An intended war of the Romans against Aretas, hindered by the death of Tiberius (Ant. xvii. 5, sec. 8). One of Caligula against the Jews, which also came to nothing (Ant. xviii. 8, sec. 2). An insurrection against Cumanus in the reign of Claudius (Ant. xx. 5, sec. 3), and against Felix and Festus, in that of Nero (Ant. xx. 8, see 6-10). But for years before the delivery of this prophecy, the Jews had constantly revolted against the Roman power, so that the "wars and rumours of wars" in the times before this were more frequent than in those which followed it. But from the breaking up of the Roman Empire to the present, there has been a continuous state of warfare, certainly never twenty years without

ye not troubled: for *such things* must needs be; but the end *shall* not *be* yet.

8 For nation shall rise against nation, and kingdom against kingdom: and there shall be earthquakes in divers

---

7. "For such things." So A., D., L., later Uncials, all Cursives, Old Latin, Vulg., Syriac; but א, B., Sah., and Coptic omit "for." This is another glaring instance in which Tischendorf and Westcott and Hort make two MSS. and two versions outweigh the testimony of all the rest of Christendom.

one in Europe or the western parts of Asia; so that the words of the Lord seem to teach us that a state of actual or impending war is not to be looked upon as necessarily ushering in the end.

"Such things must needs be." Why? Because, as St. James teaches us, of the lusts warring in men's members. So that warfare is not so much a sign of impending judgment, as of the existence and unrestrained power of original sin.

"For nation shall rise against nation, and kingdom against kingdom." If this verse is the sequence of the previous one, then it can hardly refer to the time before the destruction of Jerusalem; for then the Roman power kept the peace of the world. It is consequently explained by many commentators as fulfilled in various local tumults between the Jews who were scattered everywhere, and the various Gentile nations amongst whom they dwelt. But this by no means answers to such expressions as, "nation against nation," and "kingdom against kingdom." They seem rather to refer to such a time as the present, when the civilized world is divided into many separate nationalities. Christianity, though it may have much mitigated the horrors of war, has left it war still, the greatest scourge that can afflict the race.

"Earthquakes in divers places." A few of these occurred in various parts of the world in Apostolic times, but most of them were insignificant, and not to be mentioned by the side of those which have devastated parts of Europe and America within the present half century.

"There shall be famines." The reader will, of course, call to mind the dearth prophesied by Agabus (Acts xi. 28), which called forth the outburst of liberality in distant churches of the Gentiles. Others also are recorded, but not apparently in greater number or severity than what is usual among mankind. One would have thought that the various means of rapid communication which

CHAP. XIII.]  THE BEGINNINGS OF SORROWS.  299

places, and there shall be famines and troubles:  <sup>e</sup> these *are*
the beginnings of ‖ sorrows.   ᵉ Matt. xxiv. 8.

9 ¶ But ᶠ take heed to yourselves: for they shall deliver you up to councils; and in the synagogues ye shall be beaten: and ye shall be brought

‖ The word in the original importeth *the pains of a woman in travail.*
ᶠ Matt. x. 17, 18. & xxiv. 9. Rev. ii. 10.

8. " Famines and troubles." So A., later Uncials, almost all Cursives, Sah., Syriac; but א, B., D., L., most Old Latin, Vulg., Coptic, Æthiopic omit " and troubles."
"Beginnings." So A., E., F., G., H., M., most Cursives. " Beginning " (singular) read in א, B., D., K., L., about forty Cursives, many Old Latin, Vulg.
9. For punctuation of this verse see below.

characterize this nineteenth century would have made famines impossible, and yet in countries traversed by railways such scourges have occurred: witness that in Ireland in 1847, and in South India but six or seven years ago.

" These things are the beginnings of sorrows," or, " These things are the beginnings of travail or birth pangs," not of sorrow generally, but of that particular birth anguish which will terminate in the new birth of all things. I gather from this, that before the final catastrophe, there will be wars, national convulsions, earthquakes in the social and physical world, famine, pestilence, and other woes, such as will make men fear how all will end. Such things may have been more frequent in the two or three decades preceding the overthrow of the Jewish state of things, than the historical records of the time lead us to believe, but they must have been on a small scale, because they were intended to warn only a small portion of the world and of the Church; but before the day of judgment they will be universal.

9-13. These verses are given with much less fulness in the corresponding part of the discourse in St. Matthew, but they are the reproduction, almost word for word, of what we find in a discourse at the first mission of the Apostles in Matthew x. 17, 18, &c. The explanation seems to be that in Matthew x., the Evangelist gives, woven into one, parts of several discourses setting forth the things which shall precede the Second Advent.

9. " Take heed to yourselves." This appears in St. Matthew as " Beware of men." It seems to mean that they must not rashly expose themselves to danger, but when persecuted in one city flee to another. These words also seem to look to the immediate rather

before rulers and kings for my sake, for a testimony against them.

<sup>g</sup> Matt. xxiv. 14. 10 And <sup>g</sup> the gospel must first be published among all nations.

---

than to the remote future. They contemplate a period when the councils (Sanhedrim) and synagogues would have power to call before them and persecute those whom they esteemed to be heretics. This state of things did not, of course, outlast the destruction of the Jewish polity. There ought, very probably, to be a different punctuation of the verse, so that we should read it, "They shall deliver you to councils and to synagogues : ye shall be beaten and ye shall be brought before rulers and kings."

"Before rulers and kings." Before Felix, Festus, Agrippa, Domitian, and perhaps Nero. "For a testimony against them." Rather, "to them," that they might hear the truth which, perhaps, owing to their high position, they would have no other means of hearing. The reader will remember how two governors, Felix and Festus, and a king, Agrippa, heard the Gospel through the persecutions of St. Paul by the Jews—heard it so that Felix "trembled," and Agrippa said, "Almost thou persuadest me to be a Christian."

10. "And the gospel must first be published among all nations." Does this refer to the preaching of the Gospel before the destruction of Jerusalem, or before the Second Advent ? Apparently to both. Before the year 70 A.D. there were missionary efforts made by the Church, through the Apostles and their companions, such as have never been known since. "Ecclesiastical historians testify that this was fulfilled, for they relate that all the Apostles, long before the desolation of the province of Judæa, were dispersed to preach the Gospel over the whole world, except James, the son of Zebedee, and James, the brother of our Lord, who had before shed their blood in Judæa." (Bede.)

I cannot help thinking that this universal publication of the Gospel, insisted upon as taking place before a particular event, the siege and fall of a particular city, was especially for the sake of the Jews dispersed among all nations, whose ecclesiastical metropolis that city was. When the Gospel was preached unto them, there would be embodied in the account of the preaching and teaching of Christ, this very discourse predicting the absolute and complete

CHAP. XIII.] TAKE NO THOUGHT BEFOREHAND. 301

11 ʰ But when they shall lead *you*, and deliver you up, take no thought beforehand what ye shall speak, neither do ye premeditate: but whatsoever shall be given you in that hour, that speak ye : for it is not ye that speak, ¹ but the Holy Ghost.

12 Now ᵏ the brother shall betray the brother to death, and the father the son; and children

ʰ Matt. x. 19.
Luke xii. 11.
& xxi. 14.

¹ Acts ii. 4.
& iv. 8, 31.

ᵏ Mic. vii. 6.
Matt. x. 21.
& xxiv. 10.
Luke xxi. 16.

---

11. "Neither do ye premeditate." So A., later Uncials, almost all Cursives, Syriac; but the words omitted by א, B., D., L., some Cursives (1, 33, 69, 157, 209), some Old Latin, Vulg., and some versions.

destruction of Jerusalem; so that the Jews everywhere would see the hand of God in fulfilling the prophecy of the Lord, and would be led to believe in Him.

11. "But when they shall lead you, and deliver you up, take no thought beforehand," &c. This, it is to be remembered, is not said of teaching and preaching generally, but simply of answering when they are examined before magistrates. They were poor men, and could not afford to hire an advocate to plead for them; their adversaries, on the contrary, could engage men like Tertullus, versed in all the arts of flattery, and well skilled in making the worse seem the better reason. The Lord here, then, engages to furnish them with an Advocate Who should speak in them, and enable them to bring before their judges just such arguments as He saw would best promote the spread of the truth.

Should not those who are thrown into the company of infidels recollect this? and rely more upon silent prayer for God's help, than upon the recollection at the moment of subtle arguments and trains of reasoning, for unbelievers, especially if proselytes, are unscrupulous, and care not what arguments they use, provided they can gain a victory, and impress upon bystanders the falsity of the religion of Jesus Christ. All who can do so should study carefully the evidences of our Holy Religion; but in the conflict they must remember that the foolishness of God is wiser than men, and the weakness of God is stronger than men, and that the words for ever hold good, "Not by power, nor by might, but by my Spirit, saith the Lord."

12. "Now the brother shall betray the brother to death . . . . cause them to be put to death." As the religion of Jesus Christ

shall rise up against *their* parents, and shall cause them to be put to death.

<sup>l</sup> Matt. xxiv. 9. Luke xxi. 17.
<sup>m</sup> Dan. xii. 12. Matt. x. 22. & xxiv. 13. Rev. ii. 10.

13 <sup>l</sup> And ye shall be hated of all *men* for my name's sake: but <sup>m</sup> he that shall endure unto the end, the same shall be saved.

---

gives birth to and cherishes the most perfect love, so it calls forth the most bitter hatred. It calls forth a love which is above nature, because it makes men love their enemies. Contrariwise it calls forth a hatred which is unnatural, for it makes men hate and betray, and, if they can, destroy their own flesh and blood. Thus we read that the Emperor Domitian, in his hatred of the Christian name, slew Flavius Clemens, and his niece, or near relation Flavia Domitilla; the Emperor Maximin martyred Artemia, his own sister, and Diocletian his own wife, and other relatives. St. Barbara also was killed by her own father, and if we had a full martyrology of obscure Christians, we should find multitudes of others similarly betrayed by their own flesh and blood. We are told also by Indian missionaries, that as soon as converts are baptized, they become objects of hatred to their nearest relatives, even their wives often desert them. Now if this be so in a country where Christianity is the religion of the rulers, what would it be if heathenism were unchecked in its power of persecution?

13. "And ye shall be hated . . . but he that shall endure unto the end, the same shall be saved." "Ye shall be hated of all men for My Name's sake, and so ye shall be under constant temptation to deny or make shipwreck of your faith, but he that shall persevere in his testimony to Me and My Gospel, the same shall be saved." What means this "saved"? It can only mean saved in soul at the last; for in the great catastrophe of the doomed city the Christians saved their lives by fleeing to Pella. It seems to be recorded for all times and all ages: and teaches that in times of persecution, as well as in times of more dangerous peace and prosperity, those who follow Christ have to maintain a lifelong struggle either against outward opposition or inward temptation. (See my note on Matthew x. 22 on the way in which popular Revival teachers and preachers ignore these words of Christ by making a man finally saved at the beginning of his Christian walk, instead of at the end of it.)

CHAP. XIII.] THE ABOMINATION OF DESOLATION. 303

14 ¶ ⁿ But when ye shall see the abomination of desolation, º spoken of by Daniel the prophet,    ⁿ Matt. xxiv. 15.   º Dan. ix. 27.

---

14. "Spoken of by Daniel the prophet." So A., later Uncials, almost all Cursives, some Old Latin and Syriac; omitted by ℵ, B., D., L., some Old Latin, Vulg., Sah., Coptic, Armenian.

14. "But when ye shall see the abomination of desolation, spoken of by Daniel the prophet, standing where it ought not." Further consideration in preparing these notes on St. Mark have not solved to my mind the difficulties surrounding this matter which I mentioned in my comment on St. Matthew. I will now more fully consider the subject, and will ask the reader to bear in mind two or three things.

1. The word translated "abomination" most usually means an idol, or something connected with idolatrous worship.

2. In the case before us it seems to mean some idolatrous thing (idol, ensign, rite) connected with desolation.

3. Its appearance would be a very marked and visible sign or portent, apparently to be known far beyond the walls of the city, for—

4. It was a sign of imminent danger, not to the Christians in Jerusalem, but to "them that were in Judæa."

5. No mention of it is made in St. Luke, but the words of the Lord, as reported in the parallel passage (Luke xxi. 20, 21), are:— "When ye shall see Jerusalem compassed with armies, then know that the desolation thereof is nigh. Then let them which are in Judæa flee to the mountains, and let them which are in the midst of it depart out, and let not them that are in the countries enter thereinto."

What then have been the interpretations of this? The Fathers usually explain it of idols or images of the Emperors set up in the temple. Thus Bede, but with evidently no clear view of the historical sequence of facts. "It may either be said simply of Antichrist, or of the statute of Cæsar which Pilate put into the temple, or of the equestrian statue of Adrian, which for a long time stood in the holy of holies itself." Theophylact explains it very generally as "the entrance of enemies into the city by violence." Chrysostom of the statue of Titus: "By abomination He meaneth the statue of him who then took the city, which he who desolated the city and temple placed within the temple; wherefore Christ

standing where it ought not, (let him that readeth under-

calleth it ' **of desolation.**'" But this, if it ever took place, would seem to come too late as a sign of warning. Louis Cappel, a considerable Hebrew scholar and critic of his day, propounded another and totally different explanation, which has found favour with many modern critics, even with two men of such different views as Bishop Wordsworth and Dean Alford. It is, that the abomination was the seizure of the temple by the party of Zealots, or, as Josephus calls them, "robbers," who committed in the sanctuary itself unheard of abominations, desolated the city by murder and massacre as long as they had possession of the temple, which they used as a fortress, and were the real cause through their mad resistance of its total destruction. They admitted the Idumeans into the temple to assist them, and so terrific was the slaughter that "the outer temple was all of it overflowed with blood, and that day, as it came on, saw eight thousand five hundred dead bodies there" (Joseph., B. I. iv. 5, sec. 1). Again: "There is nobody but hath tasted of the incursions of these profane wretches, who have proceeded to that degree of madness as not only to have transported their impudent robberies out of the country, and the remote cities into this city, but out of the city into the temple also; for that is now made their receptacle and refuge, and the fountain-head whence their preparations are made against us. And this place, which is adored by the habitable world, and honoured by such as only know it by report, as far as the ends of the earth, is trampled upon these wild beasts born among ourselves."

No doubt such a band of lawless wretches polluting such a sanctuary, might well be called the abomination of desolation. It is urged against this view that the Hebrew word abomination is almost always applied to something idolatrous, and these murderers, though they polluted the holy place with robbery and blood, did not defile it by idolatry;[1] on the contrary, they carried on their reign of terror under the cloak of being politcally, at least, the most zealous of Jews; but there can be little doubt that their seizure of the temple, and continued possession of it as a stronghold,

---

[1] By their consecrating an ignorant rustic to be high-priest they expressed the greatest contempt for the Levitical institution, but they are never accused of idolatry.

18 And pray ye that your flight be not in the winter.

19 ʳFor *in* those days shall be affliction, such as was not from the beginning of the creation

ʳ Dan. ix. 26. & xii. 1. Joel ii. 2. Matt. xxiv. 21.

---

18. "Your flight." So A., Δ, later Uncials, most Cursives, Syriac, Sah., Coptic, Gothic, Æthiopic. "Your flight" omitted by ℵ, B., D., L., a few Cursives, Old Latin, Vulg.

never gave suck." Theophylact writes: "It seems to me that in these words He foretells the eating of children, for when afflicted by famine and pestilence they laid hands on their children;" but this can hardly be the meaning; for it is implied that they were at liberty to flee, but would be in extreme danger from swiftly pursuing foes if their flight was in the least degree impeded. All this seems to imply a very swift destruction, not only of the doomed city, but of the whole country.

18. "And pray ye that your flight be not in the winter." When the bye roads and paths would be almost impassable; when there would be scanty foliage to conceal fugitives, and when there would be no ears of corn, or roadside fruit, to pluck for some sustentation on the way.

Several MSS. of the so-called Neutral Text omit "your flight," and read, "pray that it be not in the winter;" but if by this the scribes of these documents mean the siege, then severity of weather would be against the Roman army camped out in the fields rather than in its favour.

St. Matthew adds, "neither on the Sabbath day," on which day the gates of the cities would be shut, and they would be able to get no help in their flight by hiring beasts of burden. The delay in journeys occasioned by the Sabbath seems to have become proverbial all over the world. Ovid alludes to it: "nec te peregrina morentur Sabbata." This shows that the particular evils against which the Lord is now warning them were local and Judaical.

19. "For in those days shall be affliction, such as was not from the beginning . . . neither shall be." Josephus thus describes the miseries of the besieged: "Now of those who perished by famine in the city, the number was prodigious, and the miseries they went through were unspeakable: for if so much as the shadow of any kind of food did anywhere appear, a war was commenced presently, and the dearest friends fell a-fighting one with another for it, snatching one from another the most miserable supports of life.

which God created unto this time, neither shall be.

Nor would men believe that those who were dying had no food; but the robbers would search them when they were expiring, lest any one should have concealed food in their bosoms, and counterfeited dying. Nay, these robbers gaped for want, and ran about, stumbling and staggering along like mad dogs, and reeling against the doors of the houses like drunken men; they would also, in the great distress they were in, rush into the very same houses two or three times in one and the same day. Moreover, their hunger was so intolerable that it obliged them to chew everything, while they gathered such things as the filthiest animals would not touch, and endured to eat them: nor did they at length abstain from girdles and shoes, and the very leather which belonged to their shields they pulled off, and gnawed: the very wisps of old hay became food to some." (B. J. VI., iii. 8.)

Again, the historian, adding up the whole number of those slain, says that eleven hundred thousand perished by famine and the sword; and that the rest—the factions and robbers—mutually informing against each other after the capture, were put to death. Of the young men, the tallest, and those distinguished for beauty, were preserved for the triumph. Of the remaining multitude, those above seventeen were sent prisoners to labour in the mines in Egypt. But great numbers were distributed to the provinces, to be destroyed by the sword, or wild beasts in the theatres. Those under seventeen were carried away, to be sold as slaves. Of these alone there were upwards of ninety thousand.

So that the prophecy of the Lord, that the affliction was beyond anything which had ever befallen the human race, or ever would befall it, was literally fulfilled. There is nothing in history which can compare to it.

Now all this happened about forty years after the Crucifixion of the Lord; so that, of those who cried, "Crucify him, crucify him," but the merest faction could then have been alive. Did, then, all this unspeakable misery come upon them because they had crucified the Lord? No, by no means; but it came upon them because they had not accepted His Crucifixion as the atonement for their sins. The forty years between the death of Christ and the destruction of the city was a forty years' rejection of the Holy Ghost, Who witnessed to them by the presence of the Church among them, and by

20 And except that the Lord had shortened those days, no flesh should be saved: but for the elect's sake, whom he hath chosen, he hath shortened the days.

21 *And then if any man shall say to you, Lo, here is Christ; or, lo, *he is* there; believe *him* not:  * Matt. xxiv. 23. Luke xvii. 23. & xxi. 8.

---

the preaching and miracles of the Apostles, of the efficacy of the Lord's Death in putting away sin, and of the power of His Resurrection, not only in the performance of innumerable miracles, but in the present Resurrection of myriads of souls from the death of sin to the life of Righteousness. For forty years after the perpetration of their great crime they had offers of mercy and salvation, through the very Death they had inflicted on the Lord; and, because they rejected these, the long-delayed wrath came upon them to the uttermost.

20. "And except that the Lord had shortened those days . . . . he hath shortened the days." This is taken to refer to the fact that, under ordinary circumstances, the city might have held out much longer; but that, if it had, the fury of the conquerors would have been so great that the nation would have been exterminated. All flesh can here only refer to all dwellers in Jerusalem or in Palestine.

"But for the elect's sake, whom he hath chosen," &c. This means for the Christians' sake: the Church of Christ taking the place of the older Jewish election in the favour of God. But what is meant by "for the elect's sake"? It may mean that, in answer to their prayers for their country, many Jews were spared; or it may mean that many were spared and escaped the horrors of the siege, because God foresaw that this tremendous visitation would cause many of them to turn to Christ. Some have supposed that the word "elect" refers to the original election of the Jews in Abraham, and that its key is to be found in the words of St. Paul: "As touching the election, they are beloved for the fathers' sake." I do not, however, think that this is the meaning.

21. "And then if any man shall say to you, Lo, here is Christ; or, lo, he is there," &c. When Christ comes the second time it will not be as He came at the first—in poverty and obscurity—but so that all the world shall recognize Him in a moment. Certain words of St. Matthew, bringing this out with great sublimity, are omitted by St. Mark. They are: "Wherefore, if they shall say unto you,

22 For false Christs and false prophets shall rise, and

Behold, he is in the desert; go not forth: behold, he is in the secret chambers; believe it not. For as the lightning cometh out of the east, and shineth even unto the west; so shall also the coming of the Son of Man be" (xxiv. 26-8). No Messiah can be looked for except the one Who is to come in the clouds of heaven. We have now to discern His spiritual presence by faith, and this only will enable us to bear the sight of Him when He comes visibly at the end.

22. "For false Christs and false prophets shall rise, and shall shew signs and wonders." To be a false Christ, it is not needful that a man should assume the name of Christ. The office of Christ was to be the final and perfect Revealer of the Person and Will of God. Anyone, then, who asserts that the final Revelation is not made in Christ, but that Christ's Revelation must be supplemented by something which he teaches as from God, is a false Christ. Such was Mahomet. He acknowledged that Christ was a true prophet; and he did not assume the name or title of Christ, but he endeavoured to supersede Him. And through the declension of the Church—its laxity, its superstitions, its divisions—he has won nations and empires from Christ.

And ever since the commencement of Christianity there have been these pretenders to the office of Christ as the final Revealer. I do not now speak of heretics, but of pretenders to special Revelations—Montanus, and the leaders of the Anabaptists of Munster, and the Fifth Monarchy men of the Rebellion, the Mormon prophet or prophets, and others, whose names will suggest themselves to anyone who has taken even a small interest in religious history. None of these movements have been contemptible in their effects. But their importance to us seems to consist in this: they teach us what things serious and religious men are capable of asserting, and what things an immense number of serious and religious men and women are capable of believing. For these men and their movements were not heretical, or fanatical, or enthusiastic merely. They were not men who took certain Scripture statements, and rode them to death, as the saying is; or, as is the case with all heresy, made all Scripture bend to a text or two. Their speciality was that they had each of them a new revelation from God to declare the final truth— not a mission from God to bring before men's minds an old for-

shall shew signs and wonders, to seduce, if *it were* pos-

gotten truth, but a special revelation, which was to supersede all previous ones; or, what really amounts to much the same thing, to put the top stone to the temple of truth. In this, and not in any particular heresy or extravagance, they are the foreshadowing of the Antichrist.

But did these men show "signs and wonders"? Yes, most of them did, more or less. They professed to tell men what they had done in secret, or what was going on at a distance. In some cases they professed gifts of healing, in many more powers of exorcising. Mahomet and his followers appealed to their success, and with reason, for it was portentous; but it was a sign of God's wrath upon those whom they subdued, not of the truth of what they taught. Many appealed to their success in converting men, not into soberminded Christians, but into enthusiasts; and whenever fanatical men are capable of exciting great enthusiasm, sober-minded men ought to look into and watch the process, and they will probably learn something, sometimes to imitate, always to warn their flocks against.

If, however, it turns out that these men have done actual miracles, I should not be so much surprised, for I believe that there is a supernatural world; and if this supernatural world be what its name imports, then the actions of its denizens, their powers of motion, their means of acquiring knowledge, their means of imparting knowledge, must be in our eyes supernatural—natural to them, but supernatural to us, for the very reason that they are in a spiritual world, which is a world above ours. Now if a man professes to supplement the teaching of Christ, or to be a special messenger from God, to bring in some kingdom or organization over and above the Church of Christ, then it seems to me not unlikely that he has his inspiration, and active but secret assistance from the evil side of the spiritual or unseen world. That God should permit such a thing is not so difficult to me as that He should permit many other forms of evil which I see around me. I believe that every man is safe from any such delusions who consciously commits his way to God, and faithfully uses the sources of knowledge and means of grace which Christ has left amongst us.

Our Lord, having thus warned the people against false Christs, does not specifically mention the false Christ which many places of

sible, even the elect.

22. "Even." So A., C., L., later Uncials, almost all Cursives, Old Latin, Vulg., Syriac, Coptic, &c.; but ℵ, B., D., W. omit.

Scripture lead us to believe will be revealed before His coming. That he will do miracles, or what to all intents and purposes will be miracles to all who see them, is clear from St. Paul's express statement.

Now will He, or if His coming be delayed, will any other false Christ which may yet arise, be able to do miracles in the face of the advance of modern science? Most certainly, I answer; and in all probability godless scientists will be the very first to be deceived by them.

For the modern scientist rejects the Scripture miracles, because, he says, he can conceive of no higher order of things than the order made known by natural science. He is obliged to confess that there is a moral order, but he does his best to show that this springs by natural evolution from the protoplasm or bacteria or what not, from which he supposes all other forms of life are evolved. Now if, as all Christians believe, there is a God, and this God a moral Being, then the moral order is to Him an infinitely more important thing than the natural, and He has sent His Son into the world to reveal the certainty of this moral order to show to men that goodness and righteousness are in the sight of the unseen God of infinitely more importance than all else; that He has put it into the power of all men to right themselves with respect to this moral order, by the Redemption which His Son has accomplished, that He will at last make the moral order paramount by the judgment wherewith His Son will judge all men. Now if this be so, and if God accredited His Son by miracles, especially by the miracle of His own Resurrection, then God cannot be indifferent as to whether men accept the credentials of His Son or not. If they do not, it must be because they prefer the natural order to the moral, the fleshly to the spiritual, the temporal to the eternal. Not finding eternal life revealed in the crucible or in the microscope or in the solar spectrum, they hold themselves unworthy of it, and so God will turn from them. They have rejected His testimony to His Son, which is all on the side of goodness and righteousness, and their Nemesis will be that when one comes doing what they will be obliged to confess to be miracles on the side of evil, they will receive him and share his doom.

"To seduce, if possible, even the elect." It is wrong to trans-

23 ᵗ But take ye heed: behold, I have foretold you all things.

24 ¶ ᵘ But in those days, after that tribulation,

ᵗ 2 Pet. iii. 17.
ᵘ Dan. vii. 10.
Seph. i. 15.
Matt. xxiv. 29,
&c. Luke xxi. 25.

late this " if it were possible ; " such a rendering implies that it is absolutely impossible. If we render it strictly and literally to "seduce, if possible," then it rather implies that it is very difficult to seduce them. And this is in accordance with common sense, for those whom God has chosen have all of them, in consequence, chosen Him ; and, if so, they commit their way to Him, asking Him to direct and protect them from all evil ; and if they see one apparently coming with credentials from the unseen world, they will ask God for special guidance, and remember that Christ has strictly bidden them to look for none but Himself.

23. " But take ye heed : behold, I have foretold you all things." The "ye" is emphatic. Could it be that any of the Apostles were in danger from false Christs ? We cannot tell : but they represent the Church, and in them the Lord warns first the Church in the age immediately succeeding His own—then the Church in all ages. The Church of Christ has always been in danger, not only from the world without, and the flesh within, but from false teachers, even from false Christs, who come with claims of a special Revelation, and from false prophets who come with a claim of special Inspiration.

24. " But in those days, after that tribulation, the sun shall be darkened," &c. What is meant by "those days" ? Evidently the " times of the Gentiles." What is meant by " that tribulation " ? the treading down of Jerusalem by the Gentiles. (Luke xxi. 24.) Now this " treading down " is not the treading down of one city, or one province, but of the whole people. We get this from St. Luke, for the exactly corresponding passage in his Gospel is : " They shall fall by the edge of the sword, and shall be led away captive unto all nations : and Jerusalem shall be trodden down of the Gentiles, until the times of the Gentiles be fulfilled."

We now are living in these " times of the Gentiles," and at this very time there is, in all parts of the world, wrath upon this people of the Jews, for though they may be living in peace amongst us, and in a few other countries, yet we can scarcely take up a newspaper but we see accounts of the Jews being mobbed and left to the fury

the sun shall be darkened, and the moon shall not give her light,

---

of the populace, and dragged before local tribunals upon all sorts of absurd charges; and what is worse than all, the veil of unbelief is yet on their hearts. They are yet in the spiritual state described by St. Paul (Rom. xi.), of branches broken off from their own olive tree—"they abide yet in unbelief." "Blindness in part is happened unto Israel, until the fulness of the Gentiles be come in." After this tribulation, when the times of the Gentiles are fulfilled, the Lord tells us that "the sun shall be darkened, and the moon shall not give her light, and the stars," &c.

These words of the Lord may be interpreted literally or figuratively. There is no reason whatsoever why they should not be taken literally. God, by ways utterly unknown to us, brought about the obscuration of the sun at the time of the Lord's Crucifixion, and He can, by ways equally unknown, bring about the same phenomena before the time of the end. It is not for a moment to be supposed that the vast luminary is to be annihilated, or that it is to be permanently deprived of its power of giving light, or that it may not enlighten other worlds besides our own. All that is required is that it should not give light to a doomed world. A short time ago, during the year 1879, we had in this country not one quarter of the average sunshine. There are, at times, even in midday, black thunder clouds which make everywhere under their shadow a darkness which may be felt; so that we can well suppose that God has abundance of means, even in this lower sphere, of warning men, by depriving them of the light from the heavenly bodies, that they must be prepared for the worst. And I believe that when He does this He will do it in such a manner that it will manifestly appear as something portentous. It will be seen that so-called natural appearances, such as the extinction of the light of the heavenly luminaries, however brought about, does not then signify that certain natural changes are taking place upon which men may safely speculate, but that a certain moral catastrophe is impending, the thought of which will make the stoutest heart quail.

Again, when the Lord says that the stars of heaven shall fall, He does not mean that the globes themselves shall fall, but that their light shall not be seen. This would be their falling from heaven, so far as we are concerned. We must remember that if all this is

25 And the stars of heaven shall fall, and the powers that are in heaven shall be shaken.

25. "And the stars of heaven shall fall." "Stars shall be falling from heaven," Revisers, after א, A., B., C., U., about thirty Cursives, Sah., Coptic, Syriac, Æthiopic; but L., later Uncials, most Cursives, Vulg., &c., read as in Authorized.

to be fulfilled literally, it is for our sakes, that the children of men may be prepared for that which will fix their eternal destiny.

Another matter should also be noticed, that the Lord here evidently moulds His words in the form of the Hebrew Parallelism, which requires that in the sentences which compose the parallelism the idea should be repeated in different words. Thus, instead of saying the sun and the moon shall be darkened, He expresses it in strict Hebrew poetical form, "the sun *shall be darkened* and the moon shall *not give her light*." And so "the stars of heaven shall fall," is paralleled by "the powers that are in heaven shall be shaken." Now we know not what the Lord means by these "powers in heaven." The only powers or forces which we know are the forces by which the earth and planets move, and by which they are kept in their courses. Now if the Lord was at this tremendous juncture to allow this world to be shaken and in any way deflect from its axis, the fixed stars would appear to move or to fall.

We have endeavoured hitherto to give a rational and yet a thoroughly believing view of these words: but it must be remembered that what the Lord foretells will be the greatest and most visible manifestation of God to the Universe. It will manifest the glory of His moral attributes of righteousness and justice. Its issues will, for aught we know, affect the whole intelligent creation. For this world, inasmuch as it has been the scene of the Incarnation and Death of Christ, has been the theatre of events manifesting the Unseen God such as no other part of God's creation has been or can be. What marvel then if all things visible and invisible are affected by it, even to the remotest star? We know that what takes place in this little world in the development of the Church is for the benefit of "principalities and powers in heavenly places," that they by it may know "the manifold wisdom of God." (Ephes. iii. 10.)

2. Upon the figurative interpretation of these words—if they are not to be interpreted literally—the greatest differences prevail. Thus, St. Ambrose: "The moon is the Church, which will then

26 ˣ And then shall they see the Son of man

ˣ Dan. vii. 13,
14. Matt. xvi.
27. & xxiv. 30.
ch. xiv. 62.
Acts i. 11.
1 Thess. iv. 16.
2 Thess. i. 7,
10. Rev. i. 7.

borrow no light from Christ, who is her Sun, being eclipsed by the earth, *i.e.* by carnal desires. They will not be able to see the Sun, for faith will fail." St. Augustine also seems to suggest that the Church and the saints will be eclipsed, and scarcely visible on earth from the darkness of those days of Antichrist. Amongst moderns, Lightfoot explains that the Jewish heaven shall perish, and the sun and moon of its glory and happiness shall be darkened and brought to nothing." "The sun is the religion of the Church; the moon is the government of the state; and the stars are the judges and doctors of both." (Lightfoot's Exercitations from Dr. Morison's St. Matthew.) Such an interpretation seems absurd: but we are to remember that in the Hebrew Prophets the judgments of God upon various kingdoms are attended by the obscuration of the light of the sun and moon, which seems to point to the kingly or chief powers in these kingdoms being destroyed or weakened. [So Isaiah xiii. 10, spoken of Babylon, and Ezekiel xxxii. 7, of Egypt.] Still, I do not see how such signs as the dethronement of kings or the weakening of governments can be that universal sign seen by all, and striking terror and amazement into all that see it, which the words of the Lord seem to set forth.

26. " And then shall they see the Son of man coming in the clouds with great power and glory." "Then shall they see." Who shall see? St. Matthew tells us, " all the tribes of the earth when they see Him" shall mourn. St. Luke also tells us the same. The hearts of men are "failing them for fear, and for looking after those things which are coming on the earth." And then shall they—these men whose hearts quail—these shall see Him: so that all men alike, good and bad, believers and unbelievers, Christians and heathen, all alike shall see Him. Now men see Him only by faith. Then they shall see Him Whom they have pierced. With what eyes? The living with the eyes of their present bodies before they are changed; the dead with the eyes of the Resurrection Body.

" They shall see the Son of Man coming in the clouds." It must be for some purpose that the Lord is so frequently and emphatically said to come with clouds. Thus here, and in the parallel place of

coming in the clouds with great power and glory.

---

St. Matthew, "The Son of Man coming in the clouds:" and again, each Evangelist represents Him as saying before Caiaphas, "Ye shall see the Son of Man sitting on the right hand of power, and coming in the clouds of heaven." Again, the beloved disciples in the Revelation says, "Behold, He cometh with clouds, and every eye shall see Him." Now by this the Lord claims to be the Son of Man of whom the Prophet Daniel speaks: "I saw in the night visions, and behold, one like the Son of Man came with the clouds of heaven, and came to the Ancient of Days, and they brought Him near before Him." To those who had the smallest knowledge of the contents of the Book of Daniel the Lord's saying that He would come with clouds in power and great glory could mean nothing else but that He would come from the presence of the Ancient of Days to judge us as before He had returned to the bosom of the Ancient of Days on His Ascension.

But there is another reason of infinite importance. By saying that He will come in the clouds of heaven, He declares that He will come visibly, openly, manifestly, in the greatest possible contrast to His first coming, when He came in a stable and was laid in a manger, and was known only by special revelation—to the shepherds, the Magi, Simeon, and Hannah.

And He has now various ways of coming to individual souls or to Churches. He comes spiritually to the soul at the time of its true enlightning, "When the day dawns, and when the daystar arises in the heart." (2. Pet. i.) Or He comes sacramentally, when as the true Priest and Pastor He feeds the soul at the altar with the spiritual food of His most precious Body and Blood, so that He may henceforth dwell in that soul, and that soul dwell in Him. And He comes to a Church, as to the Church of Laodicea, to "remove her candlestick out of her place unless she repent."

Now His coming in the clouds is in contrast to all these. By no possible straining of language can this coming in the clouds of heaven—this coming with myriads of attendant angels—this coming like the lightning, lighting up the heavens from one end to the other—the coming so that every eye should see Him, both of those that rejoice and those that wail,—by no perversion of language can this be made to mean a spiritual coming—a coming by

27 And then shall he send his angels, and shall gather together his elect from the four winds, from the uttermost part of the earth to the uttermost part of heaven.

---

27. "His angels." So ℵ, A., C., later Uncials, almost all Cursives, some Old Latin, Vulg., and some versions; but B., D., L., some Old Latin read, "the angels."
"His elect." So ℵ, A., B., C., later Uncials, almost all Cursives and versions; but D., L., four or five Cursives, and some Old Latin read, "the elect."

Gospel preaching, a coming in conversion, a coming in consecrated elements, a coming in mysterious providences. It can only mean what every little child will understand by it. And it is only right and fitting that this Son of Man, Who in the sight of this visible world endured such unspeakable humiliation, should in the sight of the same visible world be manifested in such unspeakable glory.

27. "And then shall he send his angels, and shall gather together his elect," &c. It is to be remarked that the angels are always associated with the proceedings of the last day. They are not only the retinue of the Judge to add to the pomp and glory of the assize, but they take part in the work of the judgment; they sever the wicked from the just, they gather the elect from the four winds. How can they do this with unerring certainty? Does the Judge give them some special mark by which in a moment they can tell who are His and who are not? Or have they powers of spiritual discernment whereby they can look into souls and see their state at a glance? I think it must be the latter. Such beings would scarcely be employed mechanically, as it were, on such a day, and for such a purpose. What they do they must do intelligently. Humanly speaking, such a work may tax their highest faculties to the uttermost; but we may be sure that an omnipresent and omniscient Guidance will be with them that they fail not in any one case—that they lose not one grain of the wheat of Christ. "And shall gather together His elect," *i.e.* those who have made their calling and election sure—those who have endured to the end—those who have watched and prayed that they might stand before the Son of Man—those that have done good—those, above all, who answer to the character of those who in the great vision of judgment are set on the right hand; that is, those who have fed Christ in His hungry brethren, visited Him in His sick brethren, clad Him in His naked brethren.

"His elect." In the procedure of such a Judge on such a day,

CHAP. XIII.]     KNOW THAT IT IS NIGH.     319

28 ʸ Now learn a parable of the fig tree; When her branch is yet tender, and putteth forth leaves, ye know that summer is near: ʸ Matt. xxiv. 32. Luke xxi. 29, &c.

29 So ye in like manner, when ye shall see these things come to pass, know that it is nigh, *even* at the doors.

---

28. Revisers translate this, "Now from the fig tree learn her parable; when her branch has now become tender, and putteth forth its leaves," &c. *Cum jam ramus ejus tener fuerit, et nata fuerint folia,* Vulg. The word "yet" in our translation confuses the sense.

it seems absolutely blasphemous to suppose that His elect are His mere favourites, chosen for no other reason than His mere will.

This day, then, will be the manifestation, not only of God, and of his Son, but of the great unseen and spiritual universe—of the innumerable company of angels, of their ranks and orders, thrones, dominions, principalities, and powers—of the whole assembly and Church of the first-born, for "Then shall the righteous shine forth as the sun in the kingdom of their Father." Then it will be manifested once and for ever that the visible and material universe, with all its order and beauty, and contrivances, and forces and laws, is as nothing to the invisible and spiritual. Then will be manifest the wisdom of faith, in that it has discerned the unseen, and prepared for its unveiling.

May God in His mercy grant to him who writes and to all who read these words, that when the veil is rent and all this breaks upon us, we may be ready!

28. "Now learn a parable of the fig tree; When her branch is yet tender, and putteth forth," &c. This means, now from the fig tree learn her parabolic or mystical lesson.

In St. Luke we read that the Lord said, "Behold the fig tree and all the trees." The shooting forth of tender twigs and buds in spring is the surest pledge of the coming of summer.

If a man were alone in the world and had lost all reckoning of time, yet he would know the near approach of summer from the shooting forth of the tender branches and young leaves in spring; and so from the signs which I have foretold, ye yourselves may gather the swift approach of the doom of Jerusalem, and of the world. The sequences of nature are not more certain than the sequences of the spiritual world.

30 Verily I say unto you, that this generation shall not pass, till all these things be done.

---

30. "Verily I say unto you, that this generation shall not pass, till all these things be done." A great difficulty has been made of this place, but I do not see that there is any special difficulty in it, over and above what we find in the rest of this discourse. For throughout this prophecy there is no distinct line drawn between the signs which precede the downfall of Jerusalem, and those which harbinger the end of all things; and, as I have shown, it was the Lord's intention that there should not be, because it was His will that His second coming should be expected from the moment that He left. We have to explain His words on principles of common sense, not taking them so absolutely as to make them mean what the discourse itself forbids that they should mean.

Now, taking a generation to signify, what it is always assumed to do, some thirty or forty years, what the Lord evidently means is that one or both of the events with which His prophecy has been occupied should take place within the lifetime of those then living or of most of them, which the destruction of Jerusalem actually did. One or both, I repeat: for the second coming might take place at any moment at or after the fall of Jerusalem. There is but one note of time, and that a perfectly indefinite one, which we have in St. Luke's report of the discourse, and it is, "Jerusalem shall be trodden down of the Gentiles until the times of the Gentiles be fulfilled." Does then the Lord mean that that generation should not pass till the times of the Gentiles be fulfilled? The event shows that He cannot have meant this. We must then confine the words "all these things" to the events which precede the destruction of Jerusalem, unless we adopt a way of getting over the difficulty, which has found favour with Alford and others, that "generation" means, not the lifetime of a man, but of the Jewish race. Now that would be a very short-lived race which should exist one thousand years. The Jews had already existed two thousand, and might exist two thousand more, so that, on this hypothesis, our Lord by "this generation," instead of meaning a limited and definite period of the greatest interest to those who heard Him, because it was *their* period, really meant an indefinite one, which I need not say is exceedingly unlikely, considering the way in which He emphasizes His words.

31 Heaven and earth shall pass away: but ᶻ my words shall not pass away. ᶻ Is. xl. 8.

32 ¶ But of that day and *that* hour knoweth no man, no,

---

The real key to these words, as I have shown in my notes on St. Matthew, is the declaration of the Lord in St. Matthew xxiii. 36. He had been denouncing woes upon the Scribes and Pharisees, and concluded with the words, "Upon you shall come all the righteous blood shed upon the earth, from the blood of righteous Abel unto the blood of Zacharias, son of Barachias. Verily I say unto you, All these things shall come upon this generation." "These things" most closely affected the persons for whose especial guidance as regards their *near* fulfilment the whole discourse was spoken. So that it seems making a gratuitous difficulty to include among "these things" the day and the hour, which no man knew, which was not to be till after the times of the Gentiles had been fulfilled.

31. "Heaven and earth shall pass away, but my words shall not pass away." "For heaven and earth have in their constitution no necessity of existence, but Christ's words, derived from eternity, have in them such virtue that they must needs abide." (Hilary.) Let us remember that this saying of Christ is true not only of His words respecting the coming desolation, or His own second coming, but of all His words: even of those which men are most slow to receive. So that such words of His as, "Blessed are the merciful, for they shall obtain mercy; blessed are the peacemakers, for they shall be called the children of God," "He that eateth My Flesh and drinketh My Blood, hath everlasting life, and I will raise him up at the last day," and if there be any other of His words at which even many religious men stumble, let them know that such words, no matter what their hardness, no matter what their contrariety to the world's thoughts and the world's maxims—such words, if once uttered by Him, shall surely be fulfilled.

32. "But of that day and that hour knoweth no man ... neither the Son, but the Father." The words "neither the Son," no matter how they are interpreted, contain a very great difficulty, but we must thoroughly understand in what the difficulty consists. It does not consist in reconciling them with the creeds and doctrines of the Catholic Church, but with the statements of Christ Himself, and of His Spirit through His servants respecting His own omniscience, and particularly that that omniscience includes

not the angels which are in heaven, neither the Son, but the Father.

the perfect knowledge of His Father. Thus He declares, in words which cannot be mistaken, that the knowledge of the Father and of the Son of One Another is the same. "No one knoweth the Son but the Father, neither knoweth any one the Father save the Son;" and again, "As the Father knoweth Me and I know the Father." "I am in the Father, and the Father is in Me." Again, "I and the Father are one." Now the difficulty is that One Who thus knoweth all that is in the Father, should not know the day and hour of the great crisis of the universe. But the difficulty is a Scripture difficulty, not a Church or ecclesiastical one. It has been explained by some of the Fathers as meaning that He does not know the day so as to reveal it. Thus Hilary: "If there are in Him all the treasures of knowledge, He is not ignorant of this day; rather we ought to remember that the treasures of wisdom in Him are hidden; His ignorance, therefore, must be connected with the hiding of the treasures of wisdom, which are in Him. For in all cases in which God declares Himself ignorant, He is not under the power of ignorance, but it is not a fit time for speaking." (Hilary, quoted in Cat. Aurea.) Lightfoot, who has written an exercitation on this passage, seems to come to the same conclusion. "The Son (in the sense of the Messias) knoweth not, *i.e.*, it is not revealed to Him from the Father, to reveal to the Church." But notwithstanding the high authority for this interpretation, it seems to me unlikely.

Again, reference has been made to the passage that "He increased in wisdom and stature," which can only be said of His human nature; and so here some divines interpret that it is said of Him simply as the Son of Man; but the Lord here speaks as the Eternal Son, not as made a little lower than the angels, but as above them, for He says, "No, not the angels which are in heaven, neither the Son."

I cannot help thinking that this ignorance of the Lord on this matter must be connected with His "emptying Himself." In the very same breath in which St. Paul intimates the Lord's equality with His Father he says that He "emptied Himself," but of what? Of His glory; but of what did His glory consist? Surely in the glory of Omniscience, as well as of the other attributes of God. The Son of God then, in some way of which it is not lawful to

CHAP. XIII.] WATCH AND PRAY. 323

33 <sup>a</sup> Take ye heed, watch and pray: for ye know not when the time is.

<sup>a</sup> Matt. xxiv. 42. & xxv. 13.
Luke xii. 40. & xxi. 34.
Rom. xiii. 11.
1 Thess. v. 6.

---

33. "And pray." So ℵ, A., C., L., later Uncials, almost all Cursives, many Old Latin, Vulg., and most versions; omitted by B., D., Old Latin (a, e, k).

think, exercised power over His Infinite knowledge, so that it should be in abeyance, as it were, at least on this matter. Olshausen has a good remark: "If, however, the Son of God is here referred to, the ignorance of the 'day and hour' predicated of Him cannot be absolute, because the consubstantiality of the Father and the Son does not permit a specific separation between the knowledge of the Father and that of the Son; on the contrary, it must be understood of the 'emptying Himself' on the part of the Lord in His position of humiliation."

"Of that day and that hour." Is this to be understood as referring to the time of the Second Advent in a general way, as if the time of His coming was wholly hidden from the Lord, or does it refer to the knowledge of the exact time? I think the latter; for the Lord prophesies, as if He saw them, of events immediately preceding His Advent. He is sitting ready, but He awaits the signal from His Father.

33. "Take ye heed, watch and pray: for ye know not when the time is." The Lord finishes this prophecy with three different parables of warning, all of which must be taken together if one would realize the full lesson. First, we may take the Lord's words in St. Luke, which teach us what will hinder us from being ready: "Take heed to yourselves, lest at any time your hearts be overcharged with surfeiting and drunkenness and cares of this life, and so that day come upon you unawares;" also what will enable us to be ready: "Watch ye, therefore, and pray always, that ye may be accounted worthy," &c. The parable in St. Matthew teaches us that we are to watch as we would against a thief whom we know to be in the neighbourhood, and who was on the watch to force an entrance into our own house. Now this implies something more than ordinary vigilance. It seems a step beyond what is required in the Lord's words in St. Luke—more, that is, than taking heed against intemperance and worldly cares. It is a watching combined with fear, lest we be robbed of our future by remissness.

34 ᵇ *For the Son of man is* as a man taking a far journey,
who left his house, and gave authority to his servants, and to every man his work, and commanded
the porter to watch.

ᵇ Matt. xxiv. 45. & xxv. 14.

34. "And to every man his work." "And" omitted by ℵ, B., C., D., L., two or three Cursives, most Old Latin, Vulg.; retained by A., later Uncials, almost all Cursives and versions.

But the parable in St. Mark is beyond this. It is watching for the return of a Master, whilst we are doing the task He has assigned to us. The Son of Man is represented as a man taking a far journey, who left his house. This He did on His Ascension. "And gave authority to his servants, and to every man his work." This does not mean, I think, that He gave some servants authority over others, though He has done this; but it should rather be: "He left His house, and gave to His servants the authority which He had Himself exercised, or He gave them authority in the sense of the warrant and permission to work His work in His absence."

"To every man his work, and commanded the porter to watch." It would seem, then, that one was to watch for the rest, and the members of the Christian ministry have, in a sense, to watch for all: but then immediately after this come the words, "Watch ye, therefore, for ye know not when the master of the house cometh." Does He here speak to them as being porters? Only a few can be porters, or gate-keepers. No; He does not assume that they are all porters; but they are each one, when at his task, to watch as if they were. Among servants it is the duty of the porter to watch, but in regard of the return of the Lord everyone is to behave as if he were the porter, for he is to do his work and to watch. And so He concludes with "What I say unto you I say unto all, Watch."

Now what is this watching? It is certainly some act of the soul towards Christ which, though it is united with others, is distinct from them. It is something, for instance, distinct from what is commonly understood as "faith." Faith in Jesus Christ is almost always concentrated on His atoning Death. It is believing that Christ made a full, perfect, and sufficient sacrifice, oblation, and satisfaction for the sins of the whole world, and pleading this Sacrifice, and claiming constantly our part in it, and believing that through

35 ᶜ Watch ye therefore: for ye know not when the master of the house cometh, at even, or at midnight, or ᶜ Matt. xxiv. 42, 44. at the cock-crowing, or in the morning:

---

it we both are and shall be accepted by God. It is, above all, believing that "He Himself bare our sins in His Own Body on the tree, that we, being dead to sin, should live unto righteousness." But watching for Christ is believing that this Christ once crucified will, at a moment known only to the Father, appear again in the clouds of heaven, and then suddenly, in a moment, cut short the present state of things; and it is the constant acting as if this were true; and so being in a state of spiritual wakefulness and expectancy. Take two religious men. One believes that the world will last thousands upon thousands of years longer, and that he and those who succeed him will be, one by one, draughted out of it by death, and taken up to a heaven of such glory that it is scarcely conceivable that anything should be added to it by the resurrection of the vile body. Such an one cannot well be said to watch for Christ's coming; all his religious notions prevent it. All that he does is to watch against the possible suddenness of death. Such a man may have certain lively feelings towards Christ, but not that particular feeling which is demanded by Christ in His discourse—not the attitude of mind contemplated in this parable, or in the parable of the Ten Virgins. But take another religious man who, by God's grace and Holy Spirit, has been taught habitually to look for, not the hour of death, but the Second Coming. See what will be the difference. Take his views of the world. He will look upon it as a condemned world awaiting its execution. The fashion of it may be grand and beautiful, but "the fashion of it passeth away." "The world passeth away and the lusts thereof." In fact, his views of all temporal things are best described by the words of the Apostle: "The time is short: it remaineth, that both they that have wives be as though they had none; and they that weep, as though they wept not; and they that rejoice, as though they rejoiced not; and they that buy, as though they possessed not; and they that use this world, as not abusing it: for the fashion of this world passeth away" (1 Cor. vii. 29). Again, take his view of his duty. He will regard it as assigned to him by his Master, but with no time absolutely allotted to

36 Lest coming suddenly he find you sleeping.
37 And what I say unto you I say unto all, Watch.

him in which he must do it; consequently he must be ready to submit it at any moment to his Master's inspection. He cannot lay it down and take it up as he pleases, because his Master may at any moment demand not only to see it, but whether he is at work at it.

Again, take such a man's view of Christ Himself. The man who realizes the suddenness of the Personal Coming of the Lord in the clouds of heaven, is the only one who realizes the Saviour as a Judge: and the man who does not realize Him fully and heartily in this capacity does not realize the Christ of the New Testament. For in the Christ of the New Testament, the Judge is never lost sight of in the Saviour, just as the Saviour is never lost sight of in the Judge. If any men ever enjoyed the personal love of Christ they were the Apostles. And yet the Lord never treats them as His mere favourites. He always speaks to them as men who will have to give account, and who are to live in the fear of His Father (Luke xii. 4), as well as to abide in His love, and who will not do so as a matter of course. All these warnings respecting watching and praying for the unknown day are given primarily to the Apostles as if they, each one for himself, had need of them, and if the Apostles had need of such warnings, who now can say that he has not?

## CHAP. XIV.

AFTER ᵃtwo days was *the feast of* the passover, and of unleavened bread: and the chief priests and the

ᵃ Matt. xxvi.
2. Luke xxii.
1. John xi. 55.
& xiii. 1.

We now enter on the account of the Lord's Passion. As I noticed in my work on St. Matthew, the Evangelists seem to take pains to connect the Redeeming work of the Lord with the Passover. In St. Matthew, "When Jesus had finished all these sayings, He said

scribes sought how they might take him by craft, and put *him* to death.

———

unto His disciples, Ye know that after two days is the feast of the Passover." St. Mark, " After two days was the feast of the Passover and of unleavened bread." St. Luke, " Now the feast of unleavened bread drew nigh, which is called the Passover."

1. "After two days was the feast of the passover, and of unleavened bread," &c. Properly, after two days was the Passover and the Azuma or Leavenless feast. The two, though inseparably united, being quite distinct. The Passover was the slain Lamb (as God said to Moses, "Ye shall eat it in haste, it is the Lord's Passover"). The unleavened bread, the Azuma, was the accompaniment. The spiritual significance of the two, as distinct and yet united, is well expressed in the words of St. Paul, "Christ our Passover is sacrificed for us, therefore let us keep the feast . . . with the unleavened bread of sincerity and truth."

Of all the sacrifices of the Jews the Passover was the most national and the most individual. It was the annual commemoration of the redemption from bondage of the nation, and as the nation and Church were conterminous, it was the commemoration of the redemption of the Church; and it was also the most individual, for (in the original form) the blood had to be sprinkled on every doorpost, and the body of the victim to be partaken of by every individual in the household. It was thus the annual renewal of the covenant by the whole people and church of Israel. So that the fact that so much stress is laid in the Evangelists on the Lamb of God suffering at the time of this festival of the slain Lamb is very significant indeed.

"And the chief priests and the scribes sought how they might take him by craft," &c. The events of the last three days had thoroughly alarmed them. The entry into Jerusalem, the Hosannahs penetrating even into the temple; the cleansing of that temple; the parable of the labourers in the vineyard, evidently directed against themselves; the denunciation of the Scribes and Pharisees, recorded in St. Matthew; the moral and intellectual power displayed in His answers to their ensnaring questions; the physical power wielded by an unarmed man on the side of God's honour against the polluters of the Sanctuary—all this convinced them that the crisis was come. But the popularity of the Lord,

2 But they said, Not on the feast *day*, lest there be an uproar of the people.

3 ¶ ᵇ And being in Bethany in the house of Simon the leper, as he sat at meat, there came a woman having an alabaster box of ointment of || spikenard very precious; and she brake the box, and poured *it* on his head.

ᵇ Matt. xxvi. 6. John xii. 1, 3. See Luke vii. 37.
|| Or, *pure nard*, or, *liquid nard*.

---

2. "But they said." So A., C²., later Uncials, almost all Cursives and versions; but ℵ, B., C., D., L., Old Latin, Vulg. [Cod. Amiat.], Coptic read, "for they said."

3. "Alabaster box." Properly, "An alabaster," there being no mention of "box." It would more probably be a small bottle or cruse.

"Of ointment of spikenard." The Greek is "pistic nard," "pistic" being supposed to mean "pure." Some, however, think that it means "liquid."

---

evinced by the shouts of the multitude, and the crowds that were very attentive to hear him, made them fear to take the Lord openly; there would be a dangerous riot and an attempt at rescue, if it was done in broad daylight; so they must take Him in secret in the absence of the multitude, and not when the city was crowded to excess at the feast so rapidly approaching. Every hour made it more dangerous, for Galileans and Pereans were trooping in who thoroughly believed in the mission from God of the Man Who had wrought such miracles in their borders. So we read:

2. "But they said, Not on the feast day, lest there be an uproar of the people." They did not say, "Not on the feast day, lest the most holy feast of the redemption of Israel be defiled by the worst of crimes, the shedding of innocent blood, deliberately out of malice and envy, but—lest there be an uproar of the people."

3. "And being in Bethany in the house of Simon the leper, as he sat at meat," &c. We learn from the account in St. John that this woman was Mary, the sister of Lazarus and of Martha. It is very singular that some of the Fathers—Origen, Jerome, and others—should have supposed that, because there are certain differences between this account (together, of course, with that of St. Matthew) and St. John's account, that there were two women who thus anointed the Lord: One, Mary, the sister of Lazarus, who anointed His feet six days before the Passover, another, an unknown woman, who anointed His head two days before. But the events are manifestly the same. Why may she not have anointed both His head and

4 And there were some that had indignation within

---

4. "Within themselves." Revisers, "Among themselves."

His feet, but one narrator taking more notice of one, the other of the other? And as regards the time, this is perfectly explained by the fact that SS. Matthew and Mark do not relate it with the view of accurately fixing its time, but in regard of the sequence of thought; for Judas being disappointed of making money out of what seemed so utterly wasted, thereupon determined to make money in another way, by betraying the Lord; or perhaps they may have inserted it because of the Lord's claiming it as the anointing of His most sacred Body, the anointing of which after death was prevented by His Resurrection. Anyhow, it seems impossible to suppose that on two separate occasions there was the same substance used in anointing, the same murmuring, the same mention of three hundred pence, the same mention of the poor, the same claim on the Lord's part that it was done for His burial.

It is, to my mind, another instance of the truth of the threefold narrative on account of its independence. The Evangelists are not careful to make everything in one narrative tally with everything in another. No two men would give exactly the same account of the same transaction unless they had compared their experiences together.

4, 5, 6. "There were some that had indignation within themselves, and said, Why was this waste? . . . She hath wrought a good work on Me." This verse, together with the parallel one in St. Matthew, seems to show that Judas, who, no doubt, spoke confidently, and, as we may say, in the interests of charity, carried some of the twelve along with him in his remonstrance. Now we must remember that if the Lord had been an ordinary prophet sent by God with substantially the same message as other prophets, it would have been waste, but inasmuch as He was the "Word made flesh," "God manifest in the flesh," it was not waste, because it was adoration. It was not waste, just as the frankincense and myrrh of the Magi were not waste but sacred offerings. It was not, perhaps, the conscious adoration of the Lord as Divine, but it was a long step in that direction: anyhow, it was accepted by Him in a sense beyond that in which she meant it. It was given with a

themselves, and said, Why was this waste of the ointment made?

---

true and right instinct that He Who had raised her brother from the dead, and had set Himself forth to her sister as the Resurrection and the Life, and the Object of Life-giving faith, must be very near to God indeed.

Now there is a great principle involved in her offering, or rather, in our Lord's acceptance of it—which is this, that we may give that which is costly to adorn and beautify the sanctuary of God and His worship. God Himself enjoined on the Jews that they should make a tabernacle of worship of such materials as gold, and purple, and fine linen, and precious stones, and the man after God's own heart collected a vast treasure of gold and costly materials to build and beautify a temple which was to be "exceeding magnifical." But since then a new dispensation has been given which had its foundations in the deepest humiliation—in the manger of Bethlehem—in the journeying of a poor, homeless man, with the simple peasants His companions—ending in the cross and in the sepulchre. Is there place in such a kingdom for generous men and women to lavish precious things on His sanctuaries and the accompaniments of His worship? Now this incident at the end of the Lord's life, taken together with that at its beginning, when God-directed men offered to Him gifts of gold, frankincense, and myrrh, teaches us that there is. Just as this woman was led by a Divine instinct to lavish upon His Person what was costly and fragrant, so the Church has, by the same Divine instinct, been led to pour at His feet the richest treasures of the nations she has subdued to His faith. The Church has done what she could. At least her faithful sons and daughters have. At first, in her days of persecution, she could worship only in catacombs, and in her days of poverty she could only offer what was rude; but when she subdued her persecutors and emerged from her poverty, then also she did what she could. The grandest efforts of architectural skill have been raised to the honour of Christ, the greater part built in the form of the cross on which He hung to redeem us. The noblest paintings are of His acts and sufferings; and the most elevating strains of music are accompaniments of His worship. It is too true that many have taken part in these offices who have not, like Mary, sat at His feet, and chosen the good part, but what we are now concerned with is, whether this incident

CHAP. XIV.]  LET HER ALONE.  331

5 For it might have been sold for more than three hundred ‖ pence, and have been given to the poor. And they murmured against her. *See Matt. xviii. 28.*

6 And Jesus said, Let her alone; why trouble ye her? she hath wrought a good work on me.

7 For ᶜ ye have the poor with you always, and whensoever ye will ye may do them good: but me ye have not always. ᶜ *Deut. xv. 11.*

---

warrants those who have first given themselves to Him to offer in and for His worship what has cost labour and treasure and skill.

5. "It might have been sold for more than three hundred pence, and have been given to the poor," &c. But for what purpose would it have been sold? Most likely to some rich, vain, luxurious woman—some daughter of Herodias, perhaps to some harlot. Now it had been used for a purpose unutterably sacred. It was pronounced by the Lord to be a good work done upon Him, and who but a Judas would grudge a good work upon Him Who during the whole time of His ministry had been living for the poor?

7. "Ye have the poor with you always . . . . do them good. Me ye have not always." "Ye have the poor," &c. Here the Lord emphatically declares the truth laid down in the Law: "The poor shall never cease out of the land. Therefore I command thee saying, Thou shalt open thy hand wide unto thy brother, to thy poor, and thy needy in thy land."

"Me ye have not always." It may be well to dwell a little on the question, How can this be true, seeing that the Lord is now with us—with His Church—far more effectually than He was with the Jews of Jerusalem and Galilee in the days of His Flesh? These are the days in which the saying is true: "I will not leave you comfortless, I will come to you . . . the world seeth Me no more, but ye see Me." The sense in which we must receive it is this: "Me ye have not always, so that ye should acknowledge and honour Me in My state of humiliation." *Now* Christ is in a state of glory: and they who honour Him at all do this with the same Divine honour which they accord to the Father. But *then* it was not so: it was a special grace of God to discern His Divine Greatness, when He was in such lowly guise, "despised and rejected of

8 She hath done what she could: she is come aforehand to anoint my body to the burying.

9 Verily I say unto you, Wheresoever this gospel shall be preached throughout the whole world, *this* also that she hath done shall be spoken of for a memorial of her.

---

9. " This Gospel." So A., C., later Uncials, most Cursives, some Old Latin, Vulg., Sah., Coptic, Syriac, &c.; but א, B., D., L., and three or four Cursives read, " The " Gospel.

men." Verily and indeed it was no flesh and blood which revealed to St. Peter that the Man Who had sojourned in his house was the Son of the Living God. It was given to men in that day that they should succour Christ, assist Him, shelter Him, and pay honour to His Human Person, as in the nature of things they cannot do now. We may honour Him in what is in some respects a better way, but not in this way.

8. " She hath done what she could : . . . my body to the burying." If the very and eternal Son of God sojourned amongst us, no event relating to Him could be a common passing event—all must be significant of things pertaining to salvation. But especially must this have been so when the end was so fast approaching. Now this anointing on the part of Mary was ordered so as to signify His coming Death and Burial. It signified her deep devotion and love; but it signified far more—it set forth that, in love to us, He would give His life for us; and that with the surrender of His life His humiliation should be ended. He should be "with the rich in His Death." Preparatory to His Body being enclosed in the costly new tomb, hewn out of the solid rock, it should be anointed with an unguent of extraordinary value and fragrance, betokening how not only His Soul, His Spirit, His teaching, His example, but His very Body, the lower part of His adorable human Person, should be had in the deepest reverence in all ages.

9. "Verily I say unto you, Wheresoever this gospel shall be preached . . . memorial of her." " Who then proclaimed it, and caused it to be spread abroad ? It was the power of Him Who is speaking these words. And while of countless kings and generals, the noble exploits (even of those whose memorials remain) have sunk into silence ; and having overthrown cities, and encompassed them with walls, and set up trophies, and enslaved many nations,

CHAP. XIV.]  ONE OF THE TWELVE.  333

10 ¶ ᵈ And Judas Iscariot, one of the twelve, went unto the chief priests, to betray him unto them.  ᵈ Matt. xxvi. 14. Luke xxii.
11 And when they heard *it*, they were glad, 3, 4.

---

they are not known so much as by hearsay, nor by name, though they have both set up statues, and established laws; yet that a woman who was a harlot[1] (?) poured out oil in the house of some leper, in the presence of ten men, this all men celebrate throughout the world; and so great a time has passed, and yet the memory of that which was done hath not faded away; but alike Persians and Indians, Scythians and Thracians, and Sarmatians, and the race of the Moors, and they that dwell in the British Islands, spread abroad that which was done secretly."

And since this eloquent Bishop wrote this, continents have been added to the Christian world, in which the book which contains this account is extensively circulated; so that, to adopt the words of St. John, "the world is filled with the odour of this deed of grace."

10, 11. "And Judas Iscariot, one of the twelve, went unto the chief priests," &c. For remarks on the steps which led to the fall of Judas, see my notes on St. John (xii. 6).

"One of the twelve," *i.e.* one of those who had companied with the Lord and His Apostles all the time that He went in and out among them: consequently, one of those very few who had opportunities such as no other men had of observing closely the private life of the Word made flesh. During all this time he had an example before him of the highest goodness and holiness, of the most exalted piety towards God, of the greatest possible kindness and considerateness and patience and forbearance towards men. During this time he had seen stupendous miracles of healing done by the Lord daily; and had heard such denunciations of the two vices of covetousness and hypocrisy as must have, at the first, at least, made his heart quail and his ears tingle. And yet this man goes to the bitter enemies of the Lord to betray Him unto them—*i.e.* he undertook to watch all the Lord's movements, so that, if He went to some of His

---

[1] He identifies this Mary who anointed the Lord's head and feet with the woman mentioned in Luke vii. 37, but I believe this to be impossible.

and promised to give him money. And he sought how he might conveniently betray him.

<sup>a</sup> Matt. xxvi. 17. Luke xxii. 7.

12 ¶ <sup>a</sup> And the first day of unleavened bread,

accustomed resorts for the purpose of secret prayer, he might let the Lord's enemies know where they might seize upon Him without danger of a tumult. Of him Quesnel says: "An apostle of Jesus Christ gives himself up to the devil, betrays his Master into the hands of His enemies, and thinks of nothing but of that which he had engaged to do for the love of money. Who can forbear trembling when he reflects upon this league and conspiracy betwixt an apostle of the Christian Church and the chief priests to destroy its Founder and Head? Christ sees, and permits it, to teach the faithful not to be greatly troubled at the desertion and treachery even of pastors, when it happens in the Church."

"And he sought how he might conveniently betray him." Very probably they impressed upon him that it must be done with the greatest possible despatch, so that, if possible, it should be done before, and not after, the feast day—*i.e.* He must be delivered into their hands before the Friday evening.

12-16. "And the first day of unleavened bread, when . . . made ready the Passover." It is very important to remember that the word "killed" means sacrificed—the Passover was the great national and federal sacrifice of the Jews. The Paschal Lamb was slain at the place of sacrifice, and its blood poured at the bottom of the altar. So vast was the number of lambs to be slain that the priests were obliged to form two rows from the gate of the court (beyond which the lay Israelite could not pass) to the altar, and to hand the vessel which contained the blood of each lamb from one to another, as rapidly as possible; and even with these, and perhaps many other contrivances which have not come down to us, it is impossible to imagine how they got through the week in the time. I give in a note an extract from Josephus,[1] with a calculation

---

[1] "That this city could contain so many people in it is manifest by that number of them, which was taken under Cestius, who being desirous of informing Nero of the flower of the city, who otherwise was disposed to contemn that nation, entreated the high priests, if the thing were possible, to take the number of their whole multi-

when they || killed the passover, his disciples said ¹ Or, *sacrificed*.

founded upon it, by which the reader will perceive that it is very difficult, indeed impossible, to suppose that the killing of all the lambs required could be accomplished in one day; so that, in all probability, very many partook of the sacrifice before, as did also very many after, the very short time which was laid down in the Law of Moses for the slaying and sprinkling of the blood.

tude. So these high priests, upon the coming of their feast, which is called the Passover, when they slay their sacrifices, from the ninth hour to the eleventh, but so that a company not less than ten belong to every sacrifice (for it is not lawful for them to feast singly by themselves)—and many of us are twenty in a company, found the number of sacrifices 256,500, which, upon the allowance of no more than ten that feast together, amounts to two millions seven hundred thousand and two hundred persons " [the reckoning is that of the historian]. ("Wars of the Jews," bk. vi. ch. ix. § 3.)

Now supposing that we reduce this number of lambs to 200,000, and seeing that there are 7,200 seconds in the two sacrificial hours mentioned by Josephus, this would require that the blood of twenty-seven lambs should be poured at the foot of the altar every second—a thing apparently incredible; and, in addition to this, all these lambs had to be previously slaughtered within the temple precincts. But take the pouring out of the blood. We are told that there were two rows of priests, who handed the vessel containing the blood of each lamb from one to another—the first receiving it at the gate of the court, the last pouring it at the foot of the altar. But if the reader considers for a moment he will see that it would require more than twenty rows of priests to get through the work in the time allotted; for no man, however expeditious, could take a basin into his hands, empty it of its contents, and relieve his hands of it by passing it back again, in less than three or four seconds. The slightest hitch in the arrangements might make it minutes instead of seconds. Now why do I dwell upon all this? Simply to show that it is impossible to say that this, that, or the other rule or rubric *must* have been observed when you have to prepare sacrificially a sacred meal for between one and two millions of persons. I firmly believe that the exigencies of such a festival required that very large

unto him, Where wilt thou that we go and prepare that thou mayest eat the passover?

13 And he sendeth forth two of his disciples, and saith unto them, Go ye into the city, and there shall meet you a man bearing a pitcher of water: follow him.

---

"Where wilt thou that we go and prepare that thou mayest eat the passover?" Taking these words, together with the account in St. Luke, where we read that it was the Lord who began with the words, "Go and prepare us the passover," and also taking into account other words of His, "With desire I have desired to eat this passover with you before I suffer," I think that there can be no doubt that the Lord intended to eat, and therefore sent His disciples to prepare an actual passover. If He had intended them to prepare merely a makeshift passover such as the Jews observe now, He could not have said, "Go and prepare us the *passover*," for the Passover did not mean a meal of unleavened bread and wine, but a lamb slain and roasted after its blood had been sacrificially presented. I have not the slightest doubt but that He so timed His command that all the requirements of the ceremonial law that in His day needed to be fulfilled were fulfilled, and that the day before the great day of the sacrificing, He ate an anticipatory passover which His sovereign will, always in accord with the will of His Father, combined with the necessities of the case, made to be a true and valid one. In my note on St. Matthew xxvi., I mentioned a number of the features of the original institution which had dis-

---

numbers had their Passover lambs prepared, killed, presented, roasted, and eaten, both before and after the strictly legal time.

Exception may be taken to Josephus's account; but such exceptions are taken by those who live 1,800 years after the time when all this took place; and he was a contemporary of the greater part of the Apostles, and had probably attended at the Passover every year of his life. The ruins of the cities of ancient Palestine are so numerous, especially in Galilee, that the population must have been immense, and every Jew was bound to present himself, with as many of his family as he could bring, at this festival especially; so that it is not at all improbable that one or, perhaps, nearly two millions of people were at that time in, or camping about, Jerusalem.

## WHERE IS THE GUESTCHAMBER?

14 And wheresoever he shall go in, say ye to the goodman of the house, The Master saith, Where is the guestchamber, where I shall eat the passover with my disciples?

15 And he will shew you a large upper room furnished *and* prepared: there make ready for us.

---

14. "The guestchamber." So A., later Uncials, almost all Cursives; but א, B., C., D., L., several Cursives, some Old Latin, Vulg., and versions read, "Where is *my* guestchamber?"

appeared altogether in our Lord's time, so that the only parts which then remained seem to have been the slaying and eating of the lamb, and the use of the unleavened bread. Certainly the part which we hold to be by far the most significant, the sprinkling of the blood on the lintel of the door, had been discontinued for ages.[1]

14. "Wheresoever he shall go in . . . say ye." This action of the Lord seems to be the same as that mentioned a little before this, when He sent the disciples to procure Him the colt. It has been conjectured that the man was a believer, and had had a previous intimation; but is it not quite as likely that he was one who had a room prepared for those who, like the Lord, had need to keep the feast a little earlier?

15, 16. "And he will shew you . . . they made ready the passover." It has been conjectured that the name of the man was not mentioned, to conceal the matter from Judas, who was on the watch to show to His enemies where the Lord was to be found; but I think it is much more likely that the Lord sent them to this

---

[1] Archdeacon Farrar, endeavouring to prove that the Lord only ate a quasi-passover, writes, "We have not a word about the Lamb, the mazzoth or unleavened bread, the merorim, or bitter herbs, the sauce charoseth," &c; but why should we if it was, as far as possible, a true passover? If it was a true passover the Evangelists would take for granted that all was, as far as could be, in order, and make no mention of particulars; but if it had been a substitute I think they would have mentioned the circumstance. Again he writes: "The Paschal meat could now have no significance for Him," &c. . . . But it would certainly have the significance of obedience. (Matt. iii. 15.)

16 And his disciples went forth, and came into the city, and found as he had said unto them: and they made ready the passover.

[f Matt. xxvi. 20, &c.] 17 ᶠ And in the evening he cometh with the twelve.

18 And as they sat and did eat, Jesus said, Verily I say unto you, One of you which eateth with me shall betray me.

19 And they began to be sorrowful, and to say unto him one by one, *Is* it I? and another *said*, *Is* it I?

---

19. "And another said, Is it I?" omitted by אֵ, B., C., L., about twenty Cursives, Vulg., Sah., and some versions; retained by A., D., later Uncials, most Cursives, and some Old Latin.

man as having a room ready to be used by any party who desired it.

16-18. "And in the evening ... one of you which eateth with me shall betray me." St. Mark gives as the words, "One of you *that eateth with me* shall betray me." St. Matthew and St. Luke not mentioning that He said "One that eateth with me." It would be the greatest aggravation of treachery, to the Oriental mind, that one who had partaken food with any man should then and there meditate to do him an injury. This peculiar aggravation of the sin of Judas is foretold in Psalm xli., "Yea, mine own familiar friend in whom I trusted, which did eat of my bread, hath lifted up his heel against me." There is a story told of one who had slain a man in the heat of passion, and was fleeing from his pursuers, that he took refuge with a gardener, and described to him his danger, and the cause of it. The gardener said nothing, but offered him half a peach, which the fugitive ate, he eating the other half. As soon as this was done the gardener said to him, "From your account of him whom you slew, I believe that he was my son, but you killed him not in malice, so I invited you to take a morsel of food with me, and I can now do you no harm. If you flee that way you will be secure. I will see to it that your pursuers take another road."

19. "And they began to be sorrowful, and to say unto him one by one, Is it I?" &c. Notice how each one suspected himself, none looked at his neighbour, not one looked at Judas. "It is

20 And he answered and said unto them, *It is* one of the twelve, that dippeth with me in the dish.

21 ᵍ The Son of man indeed goeth, as it is written of him: but woe to that man by whom the Son of man is betrayed! good were it for that man if he had never been born.

ᵍ Matt. xxvi. 24. Luke xxii. 22.

---

21. "The Son of Man." So A., C., D., later Uncials, almost all Cursives. "Because the Son of man" read by א, B., L., Sah., Coptic, Vulg. Some Old Latin, Syriac, &c. read, *Et filius hominis*.

natural to the just to fear lest some sin should lie hidden in their hearts, without their knowing it. A man ought always to think himself more subject to fall than others; because every one best knows his own weakness, and has reason to apprehend everything from his own infidelity." (Quesnel.)

20. "It is one of the twelve, that dippeth with me in the dish." The Orientals, instead of bringing the meat in various dishes, arrange it in one large dish, into which everyone dips his fingers. Thus the repast is much more like a *common* meal, more like eating *together* than in our meals. We eat, as far as we can, separately, even when dining together; they eat, as far as is possible, together.

21. "The Son of man indeed goeth, as it is written of him." He goeth to death by the way of betrayal, agony, apprehension, denial, insult, mocking, scourging, crucifixion, all these things are written of Him, but though foreseen, they are not the less the actions of willing, and self-conscious, and so guilty agents. God foresaw all this excess of guilt, and decreed that it should bring in everlasting righteousness: but the sin was the same.

"Good were it for that man if he had never been born." Dr. Pusey has some very deep remarks upon these words as showing that they are absolutely incompatible with the doctrine of the universal restoration of all sinners, for if after ever so long a punishment Judas was restored, in ever so small a degree, to the favour of God, he would be an eternity in that favour, and so it would be impossible to say of him, that it would have been better for him if he had never come into existence. Judas made himself, by his persistence in sin, irredeemable. After he had fallen into sin, and deliberately continued in it, in spite of the example, the teaching,

22 ¶ ʰAnd as they did eat, Jesus took bread,

*ʰ Matt. xxvi. 26. Luke xxii. 19. 1 Cor. xi. 23.*

the mighty works, the warnings and threatenings of the Son of God, it is impossible to conceive of any action of God which could turn him to God, and yet preserve to him his freewill.

22. "And as they did eat, Jesus took bread, and blessed, and brake it," &c. We now come to the institution of the Eucharist. I have commented very fully upon this in my notes on St. Matthew, and must refer the reader to those notes upon this point especially, the bearing of the Essential Godhead of Him Who instituted the Eucharist upon what He instituted, and also upon the words in which He instituted it. If the Lord was a mere man, then the Eucharist is one of many merely human memorials. His Flesh and Blood being in this case no more than any other man's flesh and blood, we must apply to the words in which He gave it to us the same rules of interpretation by which we should explain (or explain away) similar words spoken to us by any other mere man. If any mere human being had offered to us on his death-bed bread and wine, calling it his body and his blood, and then departed out of this world without explaining his meaning, we should have thought it a very strange way of speaking, for we should have said to ourselves, Why need we partake of his body and his blood in order to remember him? Remembering him is an act of our minds quite unconnected with his body. When we think of our friends we think of their minds and souls, of their conversation, of their example, not of their body and blood. We should never think of expressing a loving act of memory towards any departed friend by saying that we eat his flesh and drink his blood; and so we should at once proceed to divest the dying man's words of all mystery. We should make excuses for their strangeness by calling to mind that our friend sometimes spoke figuratively, but we should be very hard pressed if we were obliged to explain how he could have used so extraordinary a figure to set forth so commonplace a reality as remembering him after he was gone. Such would be undoubtedly our view of the matter, if we considered our friend to have been in all respects the same as ourselves, and such have been the views of those who held Christ to be nothing more than a man, as Socinus and his followers.

But supposing that any Christian firmly and thoroughly grasped the truth of the Lord's Godhead, must not his view of the meaning

and blessed, and brake *it*, and gave to them, and said,

---

of such a rite, instituted in such words, be altogether different? He must plainly put this to himself: "These are the words of One Who is perfect God and perfect man. They are the words of the tender, loving Son of man, but must they not partake of the eternity and infinity of the Godhead of the Speaker? They are the words of God Incarnate; must they not have to do with the deep and unfathomable mystery of His holy Incarnation? They are the words of One Who could offer His Body a sacrifice for all men; must they not embody and set forth the mystery of that Sacrificial Body? They are the words of One Who rose from the dead in a Spiritual Body, having faculties and properties far above those of the natural body; must they not have to do with the profound mystery of the existence of a Spiritual Body, in which dwells all the fulness of the Godhead? They are the words of One Who was able to make Himself the Second Adam of the human race, so as to enable all men to partake of His pure and holy human nature, to counteract the effects of their having partaken of the impure and unholy nature of the first Adam. Must not such words of necessity be linked with such a mystery?"

We must then approach the institution and the words which set it forth in the firm faith that He is the God-man, the Word made flesh, God manifest in the flesh. If we do not do this we are in danger of judging of it as of any other memorial ordained by men. If we do this—if we approach the consideration of it in the faith of His Godhead and Incarnation, then God will open out to us the mystery as we are able to bear it.

The Lord in the institution of the Eucharist fulfilled three things:—

1. He fulfilled the prophecy of the 110th Psalm, "Thou art a priest for ever, after the order of Melchizedek."

2. He fulfilled the Passover by making Himself the Paschal Lamb, and ordaining a means by which, till He comes again, His Church should partake of Him as that Lamb.

3. He fulfilled the promises which He had given in the synagogue of Capernaum, that He would give Himself as the true Manna, the Living Bread which came down from heaven.

(1.) First He claimed to be the priest after the order of Melchizedek, and acted as such. Melchizedek is the most mysterious

Take, eat: this is my body.

---

22. "Take, eat." The word "eat" omitted by א, A., B., C., D., K., L., M., several Cursives, most Old Latin, Vulg., Sah., Coptic, Syriac, &c.; retained by E., F., H., some other later Uncials, and most Cursives.

character of the Old Testament. He appears for a moment on the scene, and then disappears as if he were a visitant from another world. He is declared to be greater than Abraham, for he pronounced a blessing upon that greatest of Patriarchs, and "without all contradiction, the less is blessed of the greater." (Heb. vii. 7). Of the way in which he exercised his priesthood, but two things are said—that he brought forth bread and wine, and that he blessed the Father of the faithful. What he did with this bread and wine we know not, but of one thing we may be most certain, that its significance could not end with the temporary refreshment with which it recruited Abraham. In the 110th Psalm, which the Lord claims as referring to Himself, the Messiah is said to be ordained by God with an oath : " Thou art a priest for ever after the manner of Melchizedek ;" not so much after the order, in the sense of succession, but rather after the manner, which is the way of exercising his functions, and which is in extreme contrast with that of Aaron, Aaron slaying animals and offering their blood, of which, in respect of Melchizedek we are told nothing. Well, the Lord on the night before His crucifixion did this thing which His great forerunner and type did, He brought forth bread and wine. But what had this to do with His priesthood? It was His most characteristic act in His capacity as Priest, as distinguished from His suffering as a Victim, for by this voluntary act on His part He, as the Priest, surrendered Himself to be the Victim. By breaking the bread, and saying over it, "This is my body," He gave up His Body to be wounded and pierced, that is, broken. By saying, "This is my blood," He gave His Blood to be separated from His Body in death. This was His formal surrender of Himself as the Priest-Victim. He offered His Body and Blood as the Priest; He, by anticipation, surrendered His Life as the Victim. In it He fulfilled His own words, " No man taketh my life from Me, but I lay it down of Myself. I have power to lay it down, and I have power to take it again " (John x. 18). In this way the bringing forth of bread and wine by Melchizedek betokened the action by which the Eternal Son formally offered Himself. As the offerer had to lay his hand upon the

23 And he took the cup, and when he had given thanks,

---

23. "The cup." So A., later Uncials, almost all Cursives. "A cup" read by ℵ, B., C., D., L., and some Cursives.

victim, and so parted with all power over it and all ownership in it, and gave it up to be dealt with according to the Sacrificial Law, so the Son of God did that which corresponded to this when He brake the bread and took the cup, which betokened the separation of His Blood from His Body in death. Wherefore there follows: "And as they did eat, Jesus took bread;" that is, in order to show that He Himself is that Person to whom the Lord swore, "Thou art a priest for ever after the order of Melchizedek. ... He Himself also breaks the bread, which He gives to His disciples to show that the breaking of His Body was to take place, not against His will, nor without His intervention; He also blessed it, because He, with the Father and the Holy Spirit, filled His human nature, which He took upon Him in order to suffer, with the grace of Divine power. (Bede, Cat. Aurea.)

(2.) But, in the second place, the Lord in the institution fulfilled the Passover by making Himself the Paschal Lamb. He most earnestly desired to eat the Jewish Passover with His disciples before He suffered, in order that He might regenerate it, as it were, and give it a new form, and invest it with new grace and power. For the Jewish Passover was the feeding upon tens of thousands of lambs, whereas the Christian Passover is the One Lamb once for all slain, Whose Blood must be sprinkled on every heart, and Whose Body must be partaken of by every believer. The Eucharistic Rite which He instituted, He instituted for the purpose of making men everywhere and at all times partakers of the Flesh of the Lamb of God once for all slain upon the Cross. The event on Calvary was hidden from the comprehension of man, the offering was dishonoured, without partakers, without public testimony to its dignity and power. The Christian Passover—the Eucharist, remedies this. It honours the One Offering, it enables men to partake of it publicly before God and before His Church, and to show forth the Lord's Death. All this is involved in certain words of St. Paul. To Gentile Christians, who had no interest in Jewish feasts, he writes, "Christ our Passover is sacrificed for us, therefore let us keep the feast." The feast on what? He himself

he gave *it* to them: and they all drank of it.

---

tells us in the same epistle, " The cup of blessing which we bless, is it not the partaking of the Blood of Christ? the bread which we break, is it not the partaking of the Body of Christ? " (1 Corinth. x. 7, 8; x. 16.)

(8.) But, in the third place, the Lord here institutes a means of grace by which men are enabled to lay hold of His promise respecting the reception of His Body and Blood to be our spiritual food and sustenance, which He gave in the discourse in the synagogue at Capernaum. He there sets forth the most astonishing benefits as coming from the believing reception of His Body and Blood: but He makes no mention of the form under which, or the means by which, this reception can be brought about. The words of that discourse, as I have shown in my notes on St. John, certainly demand something more than a mere mental or spiritual manducation. What is this "something more"? The words of the Institution teach us this. It is the receiving of the elements of bread and wine, accompanied by a special act of faith, by which we discern in them an Inward Part, even His Body and Blood.

It is clear that such words as "Take, eat; this is my body," must be addressed to faith, and to very special faith too. But how was this faith excited? What teaching of the Lord would enable the Apostles to hear and receive the words of Institution, and the rite they instituted, in a spirit worthy of Himself, and of the occasion, for it was the eve of His own Sacrifice? Evidently the words uttered in the synagogue of Capernaum, " Verily, verily, I say unto you, except ye eat the flesh of the Son of man, and drink His Blood, ye have no life in you. Whoso eateth My flesh and drinketh My blood hath eternal life, and I will raise him up at the last day. For My flesh is meat indeed, and My blood is drink indeed. He that eateth My flesh and drinketh My blood hath eternal life, and I will raise him up at the last day." Unless these words were spoken by the Lord to prepare them for the believing reception of the Eucharist, then they received that Eucharist without a word from Christ to prepare them for it: unless the Eucharist be the means whereby we receive what is promised in these words, then the most extraordinary promise was given by the Lord, with no means for our receiving that promise in a way at all corresponding to the

## THIS IS MY BLOOD.

24 And he said unto them, This is my blood of the new

---

24. "Of the new testament." So A., later Uncials, almost all Cursives, most Old Latin, Vulg., Syriac, and some versions. "New" omitted by ℵ, B., C., D., L., Sah., Coptic.

terms of the promise: for the terms of the promise are not merely spiritual, but also bodily terms; they refer not to spirit only but to flesh—they refer not to acts of the mind, such as thinking, reflecting, dwelling upon something, but to an act of the body: they seem in fact to demand an outward act of eating, not of mere carnal eating, but of eating in such a way that the highest and most submissive faith can be simultaneously exercised with the bodily act, and these things we have combined in the right and faithful use of what the Lord now ordained.[1]

---

[1] They had learned before that His Flesh and Blood are the true cause of eternal life; that this they are not by the bare force of their own substance, but through the dignity and worth of His Person which offered them up by way of sacrifice for the life of the whole world, and doth make them still effectual thereunto; finally that to us they are life in particular, by being particularly received. This much they knew, although as yet they understood not perfectly to what effect or issue the same would come, till, at length, being assembled for no other cause which they could imagine, but to have eaten the Passover only that Moses appointeth, when they saw their Lord and Master with hands and eyes lifted up to heaven, first bless and consecrate for the endless good of all generations till the world's end the chosen elements of bread and wine, which elements made for ever the instruments of life by virtue of His Divine benediction, they being the first that were commanded to receive from Him, the first which were warranted by His promise that not only unto them at the present time, but to whomsoever they and their successors after them did duly administer the same, those mysteries should serve as conduits of Life and conveyance of His Body and Blood unto them, was it possible they should hear that voice, "Take, eat, this is My Body; Drink ye all of this, this is My Blood;" possible that doing what was required, and believing what was promised, the same should have present effect in them, and not fill them with a kind of fearful admiration at the heaven which they saw in themselves (Hooker "Eccles. Pol." v. lxvii. 4).

testament, which is shed for many.

---

We now proceed to say a few words apart from the general subject, on the Lord's words as set forth in St. Mark's Gospel.

22. "And as they did eat, Jesus took bread." This "taking of bread" is mentioned in all the four accounts, *i.e.*, in the Gospels, and in St. Paul's first Epistle to the Corinthians (chap. xi. 23). He took it, and, no doubt, raised it up in His hands with peculiar solemnity. It must have formed a prominent feature in this first celebration, or it would not have been specially mentioned.

"Bread." Augustine has a remark worth reproducing. "The Lord committed His Body and Blood to substances which are formed an homogeneous compound out of many. Bread is made of many grains, wine is produced out of many berries. Herein the Lord Jesus signified us and hallowed in His own table the mystery of our peace and unity."

"And blessed." What the words of this blessing were we know not, only we are sure of this, that inasmuch as He, the Great Institutor, was celebrating, therefore His blessing reached not merely the elements then on the table, but all future ones: so that when His ministers bless in His Name they fulfil His Institution. For He, as the Great Priest, accompanies each blessing, *i.e.*, each prayer of consecration pronounced in His Name with His power, so that this Sacrament is to the end of time what it was at the first.

"And brake." On this account the Sacrament is called the "breaking of bread." I have looked into many Liturgies, and have found none in which the breaking of the bread is in such prominence as it is in the office of the Church of England, where it is embodied in the Consecration Prayer itself. In many offices, notably in that of the Church of Rome, the actual breaking takes place long after the recital of the words of Institution, *i.e.*, the words, "This is my body," whereas in the case of the institution by the Lord the breaking and the saying, "This is my body," went together.

"And gave to them, and said, Take [eat] this is my Body." By these words He made the bread to be the Sacrament of His Body, so that it is now a mystery containing two parts, an outward of bread, and an Inward Part, the Body of Christ, which, in the words of the Church, is given to us to be our spiritual food and sustenance, and which, in our communion office, is given to the faithful with the words: "The Body of our Lord Jesus Christ,

**25** Verily I say unto you, I will drink no more of the fruit

---

which was given for thee, preserve thy body and soul to everlasting life." Respecting the mode in which all this is brought about, I desire to repeat what I wrote in my note on St. Matthew xxvi. 28, p. 412: "The Lord has here enshrined a thing, which, being a Mystery, never can be explained, never can be made clear, never can be made simple, never can be so expressed as not to require very humble faith in those who would accept it in Christ's own terms."

23. "The cup," *i.e.*, of mingled wine and water—for wine was always drunk mingled with water.

"When he had given thanks." Apparently the same as the "blessing." Thus St. Paul (in 1 Cor. x. 16) speaks of the *cup* being blessed. "The cup of blessing which we bless."

"He gave it to them, and they all drank of it." These words are different from those recorded in St. Matthew, but exactly correspond to them. For in St. Matthew we read that the Lord said: "Drink ye all of it," and St. Mark, without giving these words, tells us that "they *all* drank of it." Bishop Butler thinks ("Anal." pl. ii. chap. 3) that it might possibly be intended that events as they come to pass, should open and ascertain the meaning of several parts of Scripture. "We can understand, in this view, the emphasis laid on the term ' all,' as a timely protest against the denial of the cup to the laity " (Ford).

24. "And He said unto them, This is my blood of the new testament." The Lord, in instituting His Sacrament in the element of wine, or of the mixed cup, further fulfils the promise in John vi.: "He that eateth my Flesh, *and drinketh my blood* hath everlasting Life." The Blood especially points to the violent Death of the Lord—for a man's blood is only separated from his body by a violent death. The blood is especially the sign of the ratification of a covenant. Thus we read in Hebrews ix. 19: "When Moses had spoken every precept to all the people according to the law, he took the blood of calves and of goats, with water, and scarlet wool, and hyssop, and sprinkled both the book, and all the people, saying, This is the blood of the Covenant, which God hath enjoined to you" (quoting Exod. xxiv. 8).

The Lord's Blood actually shed on the cross is the ratification of the New or Christian Covenant to the world and the

of the vine, until that day that I drink it new in the kingdom of God.

---

Church, and the same Blood sacramentally applied ratifies the covenant individually to each Christian.

Of the consecration of the cup, the same must be said as of the consecration of the bread. The Lord, by His word of power, made it a Sacrament, so it also is a twofold mystery, having an outward, and an Inward Part.

"Which is shed," rather is "being shed." This is not merely said in anticipation of the Death the next day, but it implies the absolute certainty of that shedding. The Lord Who said it, is at once the Lamb " foreordained before the foundation of the world "— "the Lamb slain from the foundation of the world," and now at this present time He appears in heaven, "the Lamb standing as slain" (1 Pet. i. 20; Rev. xiii. 8; Rev. v. 6). Bengel remarks: "Such is the Divine efficacy in the Holy Supper, as if, at the same moment of time, the Body of Jesus was ever being crucified, and His Blood being shed."

25. "Verily I say unto you, I will drink no more of the fruit of the vine," &c. The Lord here calls what He had consecrated the "fruit of the vine," by this showing that it was yet the same in its natural substance as before. And by the unusual character of the expression, "fruit of the vine" He seems to emphasize this. Dr. Pusey, in his "Presence of Christ in the Holy Eucharist," in the Notes, vol. i. page 67, Note 8, discusses this matter very fully and acutely.

"Until that day that I drink it new in the kingdom of God." This place, as I remarked, on St. Matthew, is a very difficult one indeed. I now give Chrysostom's explanation as being, perhaps, the best. "And having spoken of the Passion and Cross He proceeds to speak of His Resurrection: 'I say unto you, I will not drink henceforth,' &c. By the kingdom He means His Resurrection. And He speaks thus of His Resurrection, because He would then drink with the Apostles, that none might suppose His Resurrection a phantasy. Thus when they would convince any of His Resurrection they said: 'We did eat and drink with Him after He rose from the dead.' This tells them that they shall see Him after He is risen, and that He will be again with them. That He says 'New,' is plainly to be understood, after a new manner, He no

26 ¶ ¹And when they had sung an ‖ hymn, they went out into the mount of Olives.

27 ᵏ And Jesus saith unto them, All ye shall be offended because of me this night: for it is written, ¹I will smite the shepherd, and the sheep shall be scattered.

¹ Matt. xxvi. 30.
‖ Or, *psalm*.
ᵏ Matt. xxvi. 31.
¹ Zech. xiii. 7.

---

27. "Because of me this night." So A., E., F., K., M., N., and a few more later Uncials, most Cursives, and some versions; omitted by אּ, B., C., D., H., L., and some other later Uncials and Cursives.

longer having a passible body, or needing food. For after His Resurrection He did not eat as needing food, but to evidence the reality of the Resurrection."

"And when they had sung an hymn." Probably certain Psalms from the 115th to the 118th. And so we also, at the conclusion of our Eucharistic service, sing one of the most ancient, if not the most ancient of Christian hymns, the "Gloria in Excelsis."

"They went out into the mount of Olives." The Lord, in the Sacrament just instituted, had formally surrendered His life for us; now instead of withdrawing Himself, as He had done aforetime, before His hour was come, He went forward to the place where He knew that they would take Him.

27. "And Jesus said unto them, All ye shall be offended," &c. That is, because of My apprehension, ye shall be afraid for yourselves, and desert Me, and so commit sin.

"For it is written." They did not forsake the Lord and so sin grievously in order to bring about the fulfilment of the prophecy, but God, Who foresaw their defection now, had caused it to be written in the prophecy of Zechariah, so that when it came to pass, and they repented and looked back with shame at their cowardice they might see that He, in Whose desertion, and betrayal, and humiliation, all these things were fulfilled to the letter was the true "Shepherd;" even the "Man that was God's Fellow," for the whole prophecy runs: "And one shall say, What are these wounds in thine hands? Then He shall answer, Those with which I was wounded in the house of my friends. Awake, O sword, against my shepherd, and against the man that is my fellow, saith the Lord of hosts: smite the shepherd, and the sheep shall be scattered" (Zech. xiii. 6, 7).

28 But ᵐafter that I am risen, I will go before you into Galilee.

29 ⁿBut Peter said unto him, Although all shall be offended, yet *will* not I.

30 And Jesus saith unto him, Verily I say

ᵐ ch. xvi, 7.
ⁿ Matt. xxvi. 33, 34. Luke xxii. 33, 34. John xiii. 37, 38.

---

28. "But after that I am risen I will go before you into Galilee." There is a difficulty about these words which none of the commentators seem to be able to clear up. It seems to be an intimation, first of His own Resurrection, then of their restoration after their fall to be again His flock. "I will smite the shepherd, and the sheep shall be scattered." But that smiting, though He was smitten to death, was to be followed by His Resurrection, and as before He had preceded them to Jerusalem, the place where He was smitten, so now He would go before them to Galilee, their home, and the scene of His and their most successful labours. But this does not remove the difficulty, which is, that He appeared to them twice in Jerusalem before He appeared in Galilee. Very probably there was some circumstance which has not come down to us connected with the appearance in Galilee, which made it of such importance. One thing is certain, that it was the only meeting by appointment. At all other manifestations of Himself He appeared suddenly when not expected by them. At the appearance in Galilee He made the appointment with them, and gave them their commission to evangelize the world.

29. "But Peter said unto him, Although all shall be offended, yet will not I." This presumptuous answer, we must remember, was given after the Lord had given Him the special warning mentioned in Luke xxii. 31, 32. Dean Alford remarks:—"Nothing can bear a greater impress of exactitude than this reply. Peter had been before warned (Luke xxii. 31, 34), and still remaining in the same spirit of self-confident attachment, now that he is included in the 'all,' not specially addressed, breaks out into this asseveration, which carries completely with it the testimony that it was not the first. Men do not bring themselves out so strongly . . . unless their fidelity had been previously attainted."

30, 31. "And Jesus saith unto Him, Verily, I say unto thee . . . Likewise also said they all." "What the One affirms by His power of foreknowledge, the other denies through love. Whence we may

unto thee, That this day, *even* in this night, before the cock crow twice, thou shalt deny me thrice.

31 But he spake the more vehemently, If I should die with thee, I will not deny thee in any wise. Likewise also said they all.

32 °And they came to a place which was

° Matt. xxvi. 36. Luke xxii. 39. John xviii. 1.

30. "Crow twice." So A., B., L., N., later Uncials, almost all Cursives, Vulg., Sah., Coptic, Syriac; but ℵ, C., D., some Old Latin, and one or two versions omit.

take a practical lesson, that in proportion as we are confident of the warmth of our faith, we should be in fear of the weakness of our flesh. Peter seems culpable, first because he contradicted the Lord's words; secondly, because he set himself before the rest; and thirdly, because he attributed everything to himself, as though he had power to persevere strenuously. His fall, then, was permitted to heal this in him, not that he was driven to deny, but left to himself, and so convinced of the frailty of his human nature." [Remigius (adapted from Chrysostom) in Cat. Aurea.]

32. "And they came to a place which was named Gethsemane." A small orchard or farm, named from its having contained a press to extract oil out of the olives (literally, wine-press of oil). Its locality is pretty well ascertained. Dean Stanley writes :—"A few words, and perhaps the fewer the better, must be devoted to the Garden of Gethsemane. That the tradition reaches back to the age of Constantine is certain. How far it agrees with the slight indication of its position in the Gospel narrative will be judged by the impression of each individual traveller. Some will think it too public, others will see an argument in its favour from its close proximity to the brook Kedron. . . . But in spite of all the doubts that can be raised against their antiquity, or the genuineness of their site, the eight aged olive trees, if only by their manifest differences from all others on the mountain, have always struck even the most indifferent observer. They are now, indeed, less striking in the modern garden enclosure, built round them by the Franciscan monks, than when they stood free and unprotected in the rough hill-side; but they will remain, so long as their already protracted life is spared, the most venerable of their race on the surface of the earth; their gnarled trunks and scanty foliage will always be regarded as the most affecting of the sacred memorials in

named Gethsemane: and he saith to his disciples, Sit ye here, while I shall pray.

33 And he taketh with him Peter and James, and John,

---

or about Jerusalem; the most nearly approaching to the everlasting hills themselves in the force with which they carry us back to the event of the Gospel history."

"And he saith unto his disciples, Sit ye here, whilst I shall pray." The Lord seems always to have retired for prayer, as He bid us to do. "When thou prayest enter into thy closet." "It was His practice to pray apart from them, therein teaching us to study quiet and retirement for our prayers." (Chrysostom.)

33. "And he taketh with him Peter and James, and John." The three who were witnesses of the short gleam of heavenly glory which shone from Him on the Mount of Transfiguration were now the chosen witnesses of His deepest sorrow and distress; for with the exception of the utterance of the words, "My God, my God, why hast Thou forsaken Me?" He seems to have exhibited no mental agony on the cross equal to that which He endured in the Garden. And so though the Cross was the time of His agonizing pain of body, this scene in the Garden was emphatically His "Agony."

33. "And began to be sore amazed, and to be very heavy." How is it that it is said He began to be? Because He now, as He had perhaps not done before, set before His strictly human consciousness the sufferings which He was about to undergo, and the fearful sins of envy, malice, treachery, falsehood, and resistance to the light of God's truth in the chief actors, as well as the coarse brutality and blasphemy of the subordinate ones, all which were the immediate instruments by which His Passion was brought about, as well as the world's sin and wickedness, which was in some mysterious sense to be laid upon Him, and which if borne in any real way must have crushed any merely created nature. Besides this, He may have had the unutterable woes present to His mind which the Father would bring upon the people of the Jews—the Jerusalem over which he wept such bitter tears a few days before, because, having shed His Blood, they refused to have that Blood sprinkled upon them by His Spirit.

For the expansion of these thoughts, as approaches to the solution of this very bitter agony which the Lord now suffered, I must

and began to be sore amazed, and to be very heavy;

---

refer the reader to my exposition of St. Matthew. But I would now bestow a little consideration upon a point noticed by many of the Fathers, as well as by modern writers, with regard to our Lord's Agony in the Garden. Many ancient and modern Christian writers are anxious that we should not think that our Saviour suffered so bitterly through any fear of death. They appeal to the heroic heathen who met death calmly and resolutely, and to Christian martyrs, who courted it, and if we may say so, joyfully embraced it. But is a stoical indifference to death a Christian thing? I think not. For in the first place, how must a Christian regard the death of the body? He cannot but regard it as the remaining penalty of sin, which in his own person he must pay. By the death of Christ its sting is removed, but death itself remains to all, except to those who shall be alive when the Lord comes. Again, it is the closing of a man's state of probation, and the sealing him for judgment, that he should be judged for the deeds done in the body. And surely, if any Christian regards Christ as a Judge, *i.e.*, if he realizes the plainest statements of Scripture, that Christ will judge all, good and bad alike, if he remembers how such a saint as St. Paul lived in the expectation that the Searcher of hearts would judge him, he must regard that with awe, to say the least, which will terminate his accepted time, his day of salvation. If he has done as much as the angel of the Church of Ephesus—if Christ the Judge, has "known his works, his labour, his patience, for His name sake," yet, it is quite possible that He may have "somewhat against him." If, as the angel of the Church of Pergamos, he has held fast Christ's name, and has not denied the faith even under persecution, yet the Searcher of the hearts and reins may "have a few things against him" (Rev. ii. 3, 4, 13, 14). So that so far from the fear of death being a proof that a man has no saving hold of Christ, those whom we should account very good Christians may at times be permitted by God to feel it.

But in such fear can they have any part in the sympathy of Christ? Now it is in the highest degree probable that a feeling akin in many respects to our fear of death, contributed to the Lord's Agony; for there is a Psalm (lv.) of His great ancestor, David, in which we seem to have a greater than David speaking: "My heart is disquieted within me, and the fear of death is fallen

34 And saith unto them, ᴾ My soul is exceeding

*p John xii. 27.*

upon me. Fearfulness and trembling are come upon me, and an horrible dread hath overwhelmed me." This seems to have its fulfilment in nothing short of the Lord's Agony, and this appears certain when a few verses further on we hear the Psalmist complaining of a treachery which can be no other than that of Judas: "It is not an open enemy that hath done me this dishonour, for then I could have borne it . . . But it was even thou, my companion, my guide, and mine own familiar friend." [1]

Now seeing that anything akin to the fear of death in the Lord could not arise from the same feelings from which it can exist in Christians, such as the sense of searching judgment, can we reverently surmise respecting any view which He may have had of death, which we cannot have, which may have contributed to this (I will not say fear of death), but profound and intense shrinking from it? I think we can, for the Lord alone knew the real mystery of death—He alone knew its mysterious connection with sin, so that in us men, sin and death should be as cause and effect. Now if God be life, death must be most abhorrent to Him, because the opposite of His life, just as sin is the opposite of His righteousness. It is remarkable, as bearing upon this, that in the Levitical Law, God treated death as if it defiled and polluted, so that if a man touched a corpse, he was for a time rendered unfit to enter the Church or Temple of God, or to partake of any consecrated food in religious worship. Now Christ, as the Son of God, knew the reality of all this. He knew the loathsomeness of that which in a few hours turns the image of God into a mass of corruption, so that we must bury our dead out of our sight. And the Lord had to undergo this death. It did not come upon Him as an evil thing to which He must, of necessity, submit, as all His brethren have to do. He had voluntarily to surrender Himself into the dread keeping of him whom all His brethren accounted as the King of Terrors. And I believe that His pure human consciousness, knowing its fearful mystery, shrunk from it with intense horror, so that He could learn from experience what His poor, weak, feeble brethren

---

[1] That there are imprecatory passages in the Psalm in no degree affects its Messianic character. The 69th contains similar imprecations, and yet no one would deny that it is Messianic.

sorrowful unto death: tarry ye here, and watch.

---

felt at the prospect, so that by means of this Agony it comes to pass that "we have not an High Priest which cannot be touched with the feeling of our infirmities," even in the prospect of death, "but was in all points"—even in the point of the fear of death—"tempted like as we are, yet without sin."

34. "My soul is exceeding sorrowful [even] unto death," &c. "My soul is exceeding sorrowful." His human soul, of course, was the seat of sorrow, and all other affections as ours are. As Peter Lombard well expresses it: "The sufferings of the soul were the soul of His sufferings. The Divine nature did rest (*i.e.*, was in a manner quiescent) that the human might suffer; but it upheld the human in its agonies that it might overcome."

The Godhead did not suffer, because Its Nature is above suffering, as it is above death; but the Son of God had so knit the human nature to Himself—so taken it into the unity of His Person—that the Son of God truly suffered in His lower nature; so that not the man Christ Jesus, but the Son of God, can truly enter into the feeling of all our sufferings, and truly sympathize with us. "It is, to my mind, a most gracious instance of our Lord's exceeding love to us that He Himself drank the cup of human suffering to the very bottom; that no servant of Christ can fear his death so painfully, or feel himself so forsaken and miserable, whilst actually undergoing it, as his Master did before him" (Dr. Arnold).

"Even unto death." This seems to mean, "so bitter and so intense, as to be able to cause death at once, unless I be sustained to bear it:" but Origen explains it, "As much as to say, 'Sorrow is begun in Me, but not to endure for ever, but only till the hour of death: that when I shall die for sin, I shall die also to all sorrow, whose beginnings only are in Me.'" The former seems much preferable.

"Tarry ye here, and watch." This was said not merely because He desired their sympathies and, no doubt, their prayers along with His—for it would be some consolation to Him to think that in such an hour He was not absolutely alone, altogether friendless; but because he desired their deliverance from the peril to which He foresaw they would be exposed of forsaking and denying Him, through lack of watchfulness and prayer. "The rest I bade sit yonder as weak, removing them from this struggle, but you I have

**356**   TAKE AWAY THIS CUP FROM ME.   [St. Mark.

35 And he went forward a little, and fell on the ground, and prayed that, if it were possible, the hour might pass from him.

<sup>q</sup> Rom. viii. 15.
Gal. iv. 6.
<sup>r</sup> Heb. v. 7.

36 And he said, <sup>q</sup> Abba, Father, <sup>r</sup> all things *are* possible unto thee; take away this cup from me:

---

35. "Went forward." So ℵ, B., F., K., M., N., most Old Latin, Vulg., Coptic; but A., C., D., E., G., H., L., some other later Uncials, most Cursives, and Syriac read, "drew near."

brought hithes as being stronger, that ye may toil with Me in watching and prayer" (Origen).

35. "And he went forward a little." So as to be but a little way removed from the three: so that He might not feel absolutely alone, and yet be in some degree apart and retired, as all who pray earnestly desire to be.

"And fell on the ground." With His face to the earth—a posture betokening far more abasement and far more earnestness than even kneeling. That the Son of God should have prayed in such a posture, teaches us the fearful darkness of that shadow of death which He had resolved to pass through on our account; that the Son of God should have prayed in such a posture teaches us that we must worship God with the worship of the body. What a reproof to those who would fain make a show of prayer, sitting at ease, to see the Holy One of God prostrated on the ground!

"That, if it were possible." That is, if God could be glorified in Redemption, and man saved from sin and death without it.

"The hour might pass from him." The hour called by Himself the hour of "the power of darkness," and of evil men who had cast in their lot with that power (Luke xxii. 53).

"And he said, Abba, Father." Did He only use the word which would be used by his countrymen, the Syriac Abba, or did He speak to God in both words? The one, the word which the chosen race would use, the other the Gentile word, betokening that He was about to bring all men into the true family of God. We would fain believe that He spake both words. And it seems consonant with His deep distress of spirit to use more than one name in His pleading.

"All things are possible unto thee." This seems to imply that Redemption might have been brought about in some other way

"nevertheless not what I will, but what thou wilt. *John v. 30. & vi. 38.

37 And he cometh, and findeth them sleeping, and saith unto Peter, Simon, sleepest thou? couldest not thou watch one hour?

---

than by the Son of God drinking the cup of agony: otherwise, how could the Lord have said, "All things are possible," "Take away this cup"? This is a matter upon which it is utterly unlawful to speculate, but this we may assert on the warrant of inspiration, that the drinking of this cup was necessary if the Lord was to "learn obedience by the things which He suffered;" and to be made perfect as an High Priest Who is able to sympathize with us to the uttermost (Heb. ii. 10, 16, 17; iv. 14, 15). Whatever depth of misery lies before the Christian, Christ has, in His agony, passed through a deeper.

"Not what I will, but what thou wilt." "He was heard in that He feared," or rather for His piety, for His submission to His Father· for such is the meaning of the words. The cup did not pass from Him, but He was strengthened to drink it; and, by drinking it, He achieved greater glory, for by draining it to the dregs He was perfected as the One Mediator. The Captain of our salvation is now "made perfect through sufferings." The shrinking of His human soul from this hour—this cup—was that which made the obedience more meritorious, for it cost Him more to submit under such a shrinking of soul than if He had steeled Himself to lay aside all natural human feeling, and to bear it all stoically as one insensible to ignominy and torture.

37. "And he cometh," &c. Earnestly desiring their sympathy, wanting to know if *they* felt for Him in His distress, as He was anxious for *them* in the view of their coming danger.

"And findeth them sleeping." "We are but too ready to lose our sleep, when it is to watch with the world, and to share in the pleasures and diversions thereof during the night; but what pain, what sluggishness seizes us, when we should watch one hour with Christ, either by way of mortification, or out of love towards a sick person, or to praise God in the great solemnities, or to adore Jesus Christ in His sufferings" (Quesnel).

"And saith unto Peter, Simon, sleepest thou?" The three were alike asleep, but Peter had made by far the loudest profession; and

38 Watch ye and pray, lest ye enter into temptation. ˢThe spirit truly *is* ready, but the flesh *is* weak.

ˢ Rom. vii. 23.
Gal. v. 17.

---

so the Lord speaks to Him alone, " Simon,-thou who saidst, 'If I should die with thee, yet will I not deny thee;' 'Though all shall be offended, yet will not I,'—sleepest thou?" The other two, James and John, when He asked them, " Can ye drink of my cup?" had said, "We are able." But if these chosen ones did not watch, which of us would have watched with the Lord?

38. "Watch ye and pray." We have to watch against sin and Satan; we have to watch over ourselves; we have to watch for our Lord's coming; but we have also to watch *with* the Lord. We cannot now watch with Him in His agony. Mortal men could only do that once, and they failed to do it, and we failed in them: but the nearest thing to watching with the Lord seems to be to watch lest we lose the sense of His presence. They fail to watch with the Lord who spend time in needless sleep which ought to be given to prayer.

"Watch ye and pray, lest ye enter," &c. It may be that through too much self-confidence and neglect of the Lord's warnings they did not strive to pray, perhaps they did not put themselves into a posture of prayer. They could hardly have done so with anything like a will, if He found them asleep. " Christian vigilance and humble prayer are the source of all our strength. The former renders the vigilance of the devil ineffectual; the latter procures the vigilance and protection of God."

"The spirit truly is ready, but the flesh is weak." As if He said, "The spirit truly is ready to go with Me to prison and to death: for the spirit has apprehended My mission from God; but the flesh, in which are the lower affections, fear, cowardice, sloth, love of ease, shrinking from the cross—the flesh is weak, and weighs down the spirit, and lusteth against it, so that ye cannot of yourselves do the things which ye would."

Tertullian pertinently remarks: " We read that the flesh is weak, and hence occasionally we flatter ourselves. But we also read that the Spirit (*i.e.*, the Spirit of God) is strong; one being an earthly, the other a heavenly quality. Why then, in our proneness to excuse ourselves, do we object our weaknesses, and disregard our means of strength?"

## CHAP. XIV.]  HE COMETH THE THIRD TIME.  359

39 And again he went away, and prayed, and spake the same words.

40 And when he returned, he found them asleep again, (for their eyes were heavy,) neither wist they what to answer him.

41 And he cometh the third time, and saith unto them, Sleep on now, and take *your* rest : it is enough, ⁿ the hour is come ; behold, the Son of man is betrayed into the hands of sinners.

ⁿ John xiii. 1.

---

40. "And when he returned, he found them asleep again." So A., C., N., later Uncials, almost all Cursives, Vulg., Syriac, Armenian, Æthiopic ; but א, B., L., read, "He came again, and found them asleep."

39. "And again he went away, and prayed, and spake the same words." St. Matthew alone gives us the second words. In spirit they are the same, but their form seems to betoken more clearly the acceptance of the cup : "O my Father, if this cup may not pass away from Me, except I drink it, thy will be done."

40. "And when he returned, he found them asleep again." How is it that the Lord again broke off His prayer, and returned? Must it not have been through anxiety about His poor disciples, whose only safety from a most grievous fall lay in their watchfulness and prayer ? The good Shepherd, even in the hour of His agony, cannot forget His sheep, cannot leave them to themselves. He cannot pray for Himself without thinking of them. One says, " Our prayers are most perfect when intermixed with an anxious concern for the welfare of others."

"Neither wist they what to answer him." As men would not be able to do who were not half awake. St. Peter's memory calls this to mind, as if ashamed to think they were so overcome as not to have a word of sympathy for Him, or a word of prayer to Him to forgive them their unwatchfulness.

41. "And he cometh the third time, and saith unto them, Sleep on now . . . it is enough, &c. In my notes on St. Matthew on the difficulty of this verse, inasmuch as the Lord bids them sleep and take rest, and then immediately arouses them, I ventured the explanation that between the words, "Sleep on now," and "It is enough," a short time intervened, sufficient for their needful bodily refreshment. I find Augustine takes some such view : "We must

42 ˣ Rise up, let us go; lo, he that betrayeth me is at hand.

43 ¶ ʸ And immediately, while he yet spake, cometh Judas, one of the twelve, and with him a great multitude with swords and staves, from the chief priests and the scribes and the elders.

ˣ Matt. xxvi. 46. John xviii. 1, 2.
ʸ Matt. xxvi. 47. Luke xxii. 47. John xviii. 3.

---

43. "Judas." A., D., K., M., other later Uncials, and some Cursives read, "Iscariot;" omitted by א, B., C., E., G., H., L., N., most Cursives, Vulg. [Cod. Amiat.], Sah., Coptic, Gothic.

"A great multitude." "Great" omitted by א, B., L., two or three Cursives, some versions; inserted by A., C., D., N., later Uncials, most Cursives, Vulg., Syriac.

understand, then, that after saying, 'Sleep on now, and take your rest,' our Lord remained silent for a short time, to give space for that to happen, which He had permitted ; and then that He added, 'The hour is come,' and therefore He puts in between, 'It is enough,' that is, your rest has been long enough."

42. "Rise up, let us go; lo, he that betrayeth me is at hand." Notice the alacrity with which the Lord would meet and surrender Himself to those who were coming to apprehend Him. This reminds us of His stepping forth in front of the disciples when they came up to Jerusalem for the last time, as related by the Evangelist (x. 32). Till His hour was come He hid Himself from His enemies, now that His hour was come, He seems almost in haste to surrender Himself. "I have a baptism to be baptized with, and how am I straitened till it is accomplished."

43. "And immediately, while he yet spake, cometh Judas, one of the twelve." Notice here, first, how all the accounts mention the alacrity and shameless effrontery of this most wicked of men. St. Matthew and St. Mark speak of Judas "coming," and the multitude "with him." St. Luke, that "he that was called Judas went before them."

Notice, also, that in each case he is characterized as "one of the twelve"—*i.e.* one of the Lord's constant companions, one of His own familiar friends, who "eateth bread with him."

"A great multitude." Why a great multitude? Evidently because they remembered what multitudes had, four days before, attended His triumphal entrance. If the report of His capture got abroad, there were multitudes of disciples or adherents who might,

## THE TOKEN.

44 And he that betrayed him had given them a token, saying, Whomsoever I shall kiss, that same is he; take him, and lead *him* away safely.

45 And as soon as he was come, he goeth straightway to him, and saith, Master, master; and kissed him.

46 ¶ And they laid their hands on him, and took him.

---

45. "Master, master." Second "Master" omitted by א, B., C., D., L., M., some versions; but retained by A., E., F., G., H., other later Uncials, most Cursives, Syriac, &c.

as they thought, attempt to rescue Him. St. John speaks of their coming with "lanterns and torches and weapons."

44, 45. "And he that betrayed him had given them a token, saying," &c. But was not the countenance of the Lord sufficiently known? Had He not daily taught in the temple? Had He not entered Jerusalem publicly, so that the whole city was moved? Why did they require a special token to distinguish him? A curious tradition is mentioned by Origen, that the Lord did not appear to all alike, but that "He appeared to each man in such a degree as the beholder was worthy." But this is conjecture.

45. "And as soon as he was come, he goeth straightway," &c. As if he was afraid that even then the Lord might escape. And so he stipulated that after he had given the sign he had earned the money. Their part was then to hold Him fast, and lead Him away safely. If any mischance occurred after the giving of the kiss it was not the fault of Judas.

"And kissed him." The compound word signifies not merely to kiss, but to kiss affectionately or eagerly—a further proof of the hypocrisy and degradation of the traitor.

46. "And they laid their hands on him, and took him." Between the kiss of betrayal and the apprehension here mentioned there occurred the incident which St. John mentions, that the Lord stepped forward, and asked, "Whom seek ye?" And when they answered, "Jesus of Nazareth," and He replied, "I am [He]," "they went backward, and fell to the ground."

I commented on this fully in my notes on St. John, showing that it was probably miraculous, being incapable, on principles of common sense, of explanation on any other hypothesis—that it took place as a sign that the Lord delivered Himself up of His own free

ONE OF THEM DREW A SWORD.

47 And one of them that stood by drew a sword, and smote a servant of the high priest, and cut off his ear.

48 ᶻ And Jesus answered and said unto them, Are ye come out, as against a thief, with swords and *with* staves to take me?

ᶻ Matt. xxvi. 55. Luke xxii. 52.

---

will, for they had an overwhelming proof that they could not have touched Him without His own permission, and also to overawe them so that they should obey His words, "Let these go their way." If the Lord had not thus exhibited His power, they would most probably have seized the Apostles.

47. "And one of them that stood by drew a sword, and smote a servant," &c. St. Mark mentions this incident in the barest and most cursory manner. St. Matthew appends the words, "Put up thy sword into his sheath," &c. St. Luke alone gives the miracle of healing with which it was accompanied. St. John alone mentions St. Peter as the one who stood by and drew the sword, and also the name of the servant.

It has been conjectured that St. Mark's account is the briefest, because the incident exhibits the zeal of St. Peter, and brings him somewhat into prominence; and so, at the suggestion of St. Peter, St. Mark passes over the incident as briefly as possible. Others have suggested that St. John, who wrote when all the other actors had passed from the scene, mentions that it was St. Peter, as there would be then no danger to him from his name being known; but surely this is unlikely, as the man had received no permanent injury. As I have observed several times, it is impossible to account for the omission of this, and the insertion of that, in the narratives of the four Evangelists, on any principles derived from merely human motives. The only explanation in vast numbers of cases is the control of the Spirit, Who "divideth to every man severally as He will."

48. "And Jesus answered and said unto them, Are ye come out," &c. Rather as against a robber, the head of a band, having weapons, who could defend themselves. The Lord seems to have felt deeply this indignity. He had spent all His life in doing good to others, in preaching the holiest doctrines, and performing the most beneficent acts of power; and they treat Him as if He had been a Barabbas.

49 I was daily with you in the temple teaching, and ye took me not: but ᵃ the scriptures must be fulfilled.

50 ᵇ And they all forsook him, and fled.

51 And there followed him a certain young man, having a linen cloth cast about *his* naked *body;* and the young men laid hold on him:

ᵃ Ps. xxii. 6.
Is. liii. 7, &c.
Luke xxii. 37.
& xxiv. 44.
ᵇ Ps. lxxxviii.
8. ver. 27.

---

49. "But the scriptures must be fulfilled." Revisers translate more accurately, "But *this is done* that the scripture might be fulfilled."

51. "The young men laid hold on him." So A., N., later Uncials, most Cursives, Gothic, Armenian, Æthiopic; but א, B., C., D., L., Δ, Old Latin, Vulg., Coptic, Syriac (Schaaf) read, "They laid hold on him."

49. "I was daily with you in the temple teaching, and ye took me not . . . fulfilled." If they had taken Him in the temple, He would have suffered death by stoning, as they would have inflicted summary punishment upon Him. Only at this special juncture could He be taken, so as to suffer crucifixion at the hands of Pilate, and so that particular form of death be inflicted upon Him in which His hands and feet would be pierced. Only at this juncture, also, could He have suffered as the Paschal Lamb. I have brought this out fully in my notes on the parallel passage in St. Matthew, to which I refer the reader.

50. "And they all forsook him, and fled." This was the fulfilment of prophecy: "Smite the shepherd, and the sheep shall be scattered" (Zech. xiii. 7); also of Psalm lxxxviii., "Thou hast put away mine acquaintance far from me, and made me to be abhorred of them." It was also the fulfilment of the Lord's prediction: "All ye shall be offended because of Me this night." It was also the fulfilment of the Lord's request, or rather command: "Let these go their way;" but it was not the less their sin, though it was foreseen by God, and worked out His purpose, that His Son should be alone in His sufferings.

51. "And there followed him a certain young man, having a linen cloth," &c. As if he had been suddenly aroused from sleep in some neighbouring house by the tumult, and had come forth with only his night-clothes around him; and, seeing that they were apprehending the Lord, of Whom he was a disciple, followed Him. From the expression, "there followed him" I cannot think that he

## 364 HE LEFT THE LINEN CLOTH. [St. Mark.

52 And he left the linen cloth, and fled from them naked.

53 ¶ ᶜ And they led Jesus away to the high priest: and with him were assembled all the chief priests and the elders and the scribes.

ᶜ Matt. xxvi. 57. Luke xxii. 54. John xviii. 13.

---

was some indifferent person, who was following after mere curiosity: he must have been attached to the Lord, and on this account he was seized by the soldiers.

Very many conjectures have been hazarded respecting his name. Many of the Fathers suppose that it was St. John; but the one sole reason given for this is that he is called "a young man," and St. John was then young; but St. John's name would have been mentioned. Others, with greater probability, suppose that it was St. Mark himself; and the extreme simplicity of the incident, almost amounting to the ludicrous, makes us ask why was it mentioned at all, except that it was St. Mark who desires to record that he was once in the presence of the Lord. My own opinion is, that the account was inserted for a purpose—to show that the Apostles had escaped being taken, not because they were too insignificant, but simply because of the power which accompanied the words of Christ, "Let these go their way." How is it that Peter, who had aimed a deadly blow at one of the servants of the high priest, and had all but taken his life, was allowed to escape unpursued, and this young man, who was only following, seized hold of? It is narrated to show us how, in the matter of the escape of the Apostles, the Lord's word was with power.

53. "And they led Jesus away to the high priest: and with him were," &c. This, though only a preliminary meeting, must have been a very important one indeed, if it could be said that, at that time of night, under the presidency of the high priest, all the chief priests and the elders and the scribes were assembled. It shows how thoroughly they were in earnest about the Lord's condemnation. This, too, was the night before the Passover.

The high priest here is Caiaphas. They had led the Lord to the house of Annas first; but as I showed in my notes on St. John, that was in all probability a mere matter of form, though a necessary one, for the succession to the high priesthood really centred in Annas." "Jesus appears as a criminal before the ecclesiastical tribunal. How different are things to the eyes of faith from what

54 And Peter followed him afar off, even into the palace of the high priest: and he sat with the servants, and warmed himself at the fire.

55 ᵈ And the chief priests and all the council sought for witness against Jesus to put him to death; and found none.

ᵈ Matt. xxvi. 59.

---

54. "At the fire." Properly, "At the light." Probably it is called "the light" because through its light Peter was recognised by the maid.

they appear to the eyes of the world! There can be nothing more august than this assembly, if we judge of it by the state and profession of those who compose it. Here holiness, authority, and learning seem to be united and consulting together; and yet, in reality, it is no better than a sacrilegious meeting, and a cabal of murderers. The criminals usurp the place of the judge, and the judge is arraigned and condemned as a criminal." (Quesnel.)

54. "And Peter followed him afar off, even into the palace of the high priest . . . at the fire." We have in Peter a type of the inconsistency of human nature. He had a most sincere love of the Lord, and so he followed Him; but he was afraid for himself, and so he followed Him afar off.

"And he sat with the servants, and warmed himself at the fire." Not the place for one called by Christ to be His representative. Remembering the character of Caiaphas, a worldly, ambitious, unscrupulous man, his household was not likely to be God-fearing, nor his servants such as a follower of Christ should even sit with.

55. "And the chief priests and all the council sought for witness against Jesus," &c. It is singular, and deserves notice, that they did not bring against Him some of the words which he spake in the temple, for which their adherents had accused Him of blasphemy, and attempted to stone Him. Was it that evidence of such sayings was not at hand, or was it that they were afraid of His power of asking them questions in return, and of showing their ignorance and disregard of Scripture? They remembered, perhaps, their discomfiture when He asked them, "What think ye of Christ, whose son is he?" or "The Baptism of John, whence was it?"

56 For many bare false witness against him, but their witness agreed not together.

57 And there arose certain, and bare false witness against him, saying,

e ch. xv. 29. John ii. 19.

58 We heard him say, *I will destroy this temple that is made with hands, and within three days I will build another made without hands.

59 But neither so did their witness agree together.

f Matt. xxvi. 62.

60 ᶠAnd the high priest stood up in the midst,

---

56. "For many bare false witness against him, but their witness agreed not together." It seems, then, that some show of cross-examination was kept up. Was this out of respect for the forms of justice, or were there men amongst their number who, like Nicodemus, and Joseph of Arimathea, and others (John xii. 42), made some feeble stand for fairness and decency?

57, 58, 59. "And there arose certain, and bare false witness . . . witness agree together." The witnesses distort the Lord's words at the first cleansing of the temple. And the perversion deserves notice. They made the Lord to say, " I will destroy this temple," whereas He said to them, " Destroy (ye) this temple." They made Him to say, " In three days I will build another," whereas speaking of the temple of His body, He had said, " I will raise it," that is, " I will raise the same temple again."

To judge of the force of this accusation, we must remember that the Jews idolized the temple. Thus the accusation against Stephen was, " We have heard him say that this Jesus of Nazareth shall destroy this place." Again, Jeremiah speaks of the self-deceivers among them, exclaiming, " The temple of the Lord, the temple of the Lord, the temple of the Lord," so that any accusation against Him that He had cast a slight on the temple, would be the most invidious of any which they could allege.

60. "And the high priest stood up in the midst, and asked Jesus," &c. Some suppose that he stood up to overawe the Lord, some that it was in anger at being foiled by the contradiction of the witnesses. But probably he desired to take the trial entirely into his own hands.

and asked Jesus, saying, Answerest thou nothing? what *is it which* these witness against thee?

61 But ᵍhe held his peace, and answered nothing. ʰAgain the high priest asked him, and said unto him, Art thou the Christ, the Son of the Blessed?

62 And Jesus said, I am: ⁱand ye shall see

ᵍ Is. liii. 7.

ʰ Matt. xxvi. 63.

ⁱ Matt. xxiv. 30. & xxvi. 64. Luke xxii 69.

---

"Answerest thou nothing? what is it which these witness against thee?" What justice was there in demanding of the Lord that He should take notice of accusations which, when the evidence was sifted, turned out to be false? and so it is said, "He held his peace and answered nothing." It was then that the high priest adjured Him, that is, put Him on His oath. The form of adjuration is not in St. Mark, but it is given in full in St. Matthew: "I adjure thee by the living God that Thou tell us whether Thou be the Christ, the Son of the Blessed."

62. "And Jesus said: I am, and ye shall see the Son of man sitting on the right hand," &c. Why did the Lord when thus adjured break his silence? Some have thought that it was out of respect to the office of the high priest, as the representative of God, and the spiritual ruler of the people, and if we can separate the office from the character of him who held it, no more fitting opportunity could have presented itself. For here was the head of the nation, considered as a Theocracy, demanding of One whose credentials showed that He came direct from God, Who He was. This was the first time that Jesus was face to face with the chief minister of His Father's religion. It ought not to have been so. His claims ought long ago to have been investigated as to whether He really fulfilled the prophecies of the Messiah. But long ere this they had prejudged His case. Long ere this they had condemned Him. And now they sought not for the truth, but for that which might enable them to carry out their evil will against Him. He might consequently, I think, if He had only looked to the motive of Caiaphas in putting such a question, have declined to answer, but the crisis had come. He must assert Who He was, though He knew it would lead to His crucifixion, and His answer was one which became the Son of God in His character of Supreme Ruler

the Son of man sitting on the right hand of power, and coming in the clouds of heaven.

63 Then the high priest rent his clothes, and saith, What need we any further witnesses?

---

and Judge. "I am the Christ, the Son of the blessed God, and whereas I now seem to be in your power, and to be judged by you, yet ye shall see Me, the Son of man, sitting on the right hand of power, and coming in the clouds of heaven."

"Ye shall see the Son of man sitting on the right hand of power," &c. From the expressions used by St. Matthew, "*from henceforth* ye shall see," &c., many have thought the Lord meant that from the day of His Ascension, they should see the manifestation of His power in the Pentecostal miracles and the irresistible spread of the Truth. This would be His sitting at the right hand of power, and that at the great day they should see Him visibly manifested as coming in the clouds of heaven. It seems doubtful, however, whether their experience of His power, whilst they refused to acknowledge it, could be expressed by seeing Him "sitting on the right hand of power." When the Lord comes in the clouds of heaven, He will not the less sit on the right hand of power; for He will come in the glory of His Father, as well as in His own glory. The glory or Schekinah of the Father will appear at the great day to do honour to the Eternal Son as Judge of all.

The high priest adjures Him to tell them whether He be the Christ, the Son of God, and He answers rather as the Son of man, "I am, and ye shall see the Son of man," &c. By this He claimed as referring to Himself the most exalted prophecy of the Messiah in all the Scriptures—that in Daniel—where "One like the Son of man came with the clouds of heaven, and came to the Ancient of days, and they brought Him near before Him. And there was given to Him dominion, and glory, and a kingdom, that all people, nations, and languages should serve Him: His dominion is an everlasting dominion, which shall not pass away " (Dan. viii. 13, 14).

63. "Then the high priest rent his clothes." Considering his opinions as a Sadducee, and his character as a man, it is evident that this was a piece of hypocritical acting. The Fathers, I think with reason, account it as symbolical. Thus Theophylact and Bede: "The high priest does after the manner of the Jews; for

64 Ye have heard the blasphemy: what think ye? And they all condemned him to be guilty of death.

65 And some began to spit on him, and to cover his face, and to buffet him, and to say unto him, Prophesy: and the servants did strike him with the palms of their hands.

---

65. "The servants did strike him." So E., H., M., some later Uncials, and most Cursives; but ℵ, A., B., C., I., K., L., N., some other later Uncials, and some Cursives read "The servants received him with blows of their hands."

whenever anything intolerable or sad occurred to them, they used to rend their clothes. . . . But it was also with a higher mystery that in the Passion of our Lord the Jewish priest rent his own clothes . . . whilst the garment of the Lord could not be rent, even by the soldiers who crucified Him. For it was a figure that the Jewish priesthood should be rent on account of the wickedness of the Priests themselves." If the rending of the garment of Samuel by Saul was pronounced to be symbolical of the rending of the kingdom from him, must not such a rending by so typical a person as the high priest, and in the very presence of the Son of God, and at the crisis of the greatest conflict which ever took place in the universe between good and evil, be also accounted symbolical?

64. " Ye have heard the blasphemy : what think ye? " In what sense blasphemy ? It could not have been blasphemy if the Lord, when He said, "I am," claimed no more than every Jew did for himself when he called himself the son of God, because adopted into God's Church and family. It must have been asserted by the Lord, and accepted by them in that special unique sense which he had used once before in their hearing, when He had said that "God was His Father, making Himself equal with God" (John v. 18).

65. " And some began to spit on him, and to cover his face, and to buffet him, and say unto him, Prophesy : and the servants," &c. In all this, like the heathen soldiers, they knew not what they did, and yet they were verily guilty, for they must have noticed the calmness ond gentleness of His demeanour; they must have known that He worked miracles. Some of them must have seen Him heal by His touch the ear of Malchus, and yet none of these things softened them. They treated Him with more indignity than if He had been some degraded and blood-stained criminal, for they knew

66 ¶ ᵏ And as Peter was beneath in the palace, there cometh one of the maids of the high priest:

ᵏ Matt. xxvi. 58, 69. Luke xxii. 55. John xviii. 16.

67 And when she saw Peter warming himself,

---

66. "In the palace." Rather, "In the court"—the same court at which at its higher end the Lord was.

that such an one would retaliate and return curse with curse, and gesture with gesture, but they saw that the Lord was patient and unoffending, and in cowardice as well as in malice, they thus abused Him. But was it not to be expected that the retainers and servants of such an one as Caiaphas should be as their master?

66. "And as Peter was beneath in the palace [or court] there cometh one of the maids." I have entered so circumstantially into the examination and (as far as may be consistent with the entire independence of the four narratives) into the reconciliation of the four accounts of St. Peter's denials in my notes on St. John, that I must refer the reader to these notes for the fullest treatment of this matter which I am able to give. In the following notes I shall, as far as I can, confine myself to St. Mark's account.

"And as Peter was beneath." "Beneath" does not mean that he was in a lower story, or in a room on a lower level, for he must have been in the same court as the Lord, or the Lord could not have turned and looked upon him; but it signifies that the trial was going on in a raised part of the hall farthest from the door, near which was the fire.

"There cometh one of the maids of the high priest." After she had, at the request of St. John, who was known to the high priest, opened the door and let in Peter, she came up to him, as the light of the fire gleamed on his features, and said, "And thou, also, wast with Jesus of Nazareth." The word "also" is given in each of the four accounts, but St. John alone who gives the account of himself being there, and using his influence to get Peter admitted, gives us the reason for it. It means, "Thou also as well as John, who asked me to let thee in, wast with Jesus." This is very important, for if John could have been in safety in such a place why not Peter? The cowardice in this instance in denying the Lord to this maid seems to have been gratuitous.

"Thou also wast with Jesus of Nazareth." These words are the same as those reported in St. Matthew's Gospel. In St. Luke she

she looked upon him, and said, And thou also wast with Jesus of Nazareth.

68 But he denied, saying, I know not, neither understand I what thou sayest. And he went out into the porch; and the cock crew.

69 ¹And a maid saw him again, and began to say to them that stood by, This is *one* of them.

¹ Matt. xxvi. 71. Luke xxii. 58. John xviii. 25.

---

67. "With Jesus of Nazareth." So א, A., D., later Uncials, most Cursives, Old Latin, Vulg., &c.; but B., C., L. (followed by Revisers) read, " Thou also wast with the Nazarene, even Jesus."

68. "And the cock crew." So A., C., D., N., later Uncials, almost all Cursives, some Old Latin, Vulg., and versions; omitted by א, B., L., and Coptic.

69. "Saw him again, and began to say." So A., later Uncials, almost all Cursives, but א, C., D., L., "Saw him, and began again to say."

is said to have addressed the bystanders, "This man was also with him." In St. John's account she prefaced the remark with a question, "Art not thou also one of this Man's disciples?" But is it not most probable and true to nature that she should have uttered more than one sentence? As she looked at his features in the light of the fire, she asked him the question, "Art not thou?" &c.; then she would express her certainty, and say, "Thou also wast with Jesus." Then she would turn to the bystanders, and exclaim, "This man, too, was with Him."

68. "But he denied, saying, I know not, neither understand I what thou sayest." It is very unlikely that in this denial St. Peter confined himself to one sentence. Taking the four accounts together, he would say, "Woman" (St. Luke), "I am not" (St. John), "I know him not" (St. Luke), "I know not, neither understand I what thou sayest."

"And he went out into the porch," *i.e.*, probably the wide archway leading from without into the court, rendered by the Revisers "the forecourt."

"And the cock crew." This was the first crowing, not probably so loud and clear, but distinctly heard by Peter, who yet did not take warning by it. It is only mentioned by St. Mark, who alone of the four reports that the Lord had said (v. 80), "Before the cock crow twice, thou shalt deny Me thrice."

69. "And a maid saw him again." This was also whilst he was in the porch. Others apparently joined with the maid in this accu-

70 And he denied it again. ᵐ And a little after, they that stood by said again to Peter, Surely thou art one of them: ⁿ for thou art a Galilæan, and thy speech agreeth *thereto*.

71 But he began to curse and to swear, *saying*, I know not this man of whom ye speak.

ᵐ Matt. xxvi. 73. Luke xxii. 59. John xviii. 26.
ⁿ Acts ii. 7.

---

70. "And thy speech agreeth thereto." So A., N., later Uncials, almost all Cursives, Syriac, and some versions; omitted by א, B., C., D., L., some Cursives, most Old Latin, Vulg., Sah., Coptic.

sation, as St. John says, "they said therefore unto him." According to St. Matthew another maid, according to St. Luke a man-servant also. St. Mark says merely that he denied it again. St. Matthew that he denied with an oath, "I do not know the Man." St. Luke that he particularly denied to the man-servant, "Man, I am not." All this is true to nature. The maid who at the first let him in, and first accused him, for some reason resented his presence, and so naturally took with her the second time she attacked him, two others, a maid and a man-servant, who set upon him and roused him, so that he denied with an oath, and particularly addressing the man-servant said, "Man, I am not."

70. "And he denied it again. And a little after, they that stood by said again to Peter, Surely thou art one of them." According to St. Luke, this was after an interval of about an hour. Surely during this hour Peter had time for reflection, and should have seen that the longer he remained in such company, the more danger he incurred. In the matter of this third denial, St. Luke notices that one put himself forward with the words, "Of a truth this fellow also was with Him, for he is a Galilæan;" St. John, that the kinsman of Malchus, whose ear Peter had cut off, joined in the accusation; and St. Matthew and St. Mark merely mention that the accusation was taken up by "them that stood by," who doubtless simply re-echoed what the man in St. Luke's narrative stated when they said, "Thou art a Galilæan, and thy speech agreeth thereto." Then came the third denial.

71. "But he began to curse and to swear, saying, I know not," &c. Peter would say to the man who was the first in asserting that he was with the Lord because he was a Galilæan, "Man, I

72 ° And the second time the cock crew. And Peter called to mind the word that Jesus said unto him, <sup>o</sup> Matt. xxvi. 75.

---

72. *"And the second time."* So A., C., later Uncials, almost all Cursives, and some versions. ℵ, B., L., D., G., some Cursives, Old Latin, Vulg., Syriac read, *"And immediately the second time."*

know not what thou sayest," and to the rest, "I know not the Man—this Man of whom ye speak."

The difficulties of reconciling the various narratives of the denials have been indefinitely increased by adhering to the absurd and unnatural supposition, that in a crowd of menials only one spoke at a time—that they spoke only to Peter, or must all be assumed to speak only to him—that each denial on the part of St. Peter consisted of but one sentence. Whereas we have only to imagine a scene in which a single person is beset and worried by perhaps a dozen others, to be convinced how true the account is to nature, and how impossible it would be for any two bystanders, if afterwards examined, to give an exactly coherent account of all that was said and done.

For the lessons to be drawn from this fall of the Apostle, and his restoration, I refer the reader to my notes on St. Matthew. I will add two or three now from the Fathers.

First, Augustine writes: "I boldly assert that it is a useful thing for the proud and self-sufficient sometimes to fall into an open and apparent sin, by means of which they who were supplanted by an over great liking of themselves, may be brought to a salutary self-abhorrence, just as Peter was more benefited by his self-condemnation, when he wept bitterly, than by his self-complacency, when he presumed." ("De Civ. Dei," Lib. ii. chap. 14. Ford.)

Again, Ambrose: "More happily did Peter fall, than others stand upright. The very miscarriages of holy men are useful. I was nothing hurt by Peter's denial; I am much the better for his repentance. It has taught me to avoid bad company." (Ford.)

So Leo: "Blessed tears, O holy Apostle, which had the virtue of Holy Baptism in washing off the sin of thy denial. The Right Hand of the Lord Jesus was with thee to uphold thee before thou wast quite thrown down, and in the midst of thy perilous fall, thou receivedst strength to stand. The rock quickly returned to its stability, recovering so great fortitude, that he who in Christ's

**374** THOU SHALT DENY ME THRICE. [St. Mark.

Before the cock crow twice, thou shalt deny me thrice. And
when he thought thereon, he wept.

Or, *he wept abundantly,* or, *he began to weep.*

"Crow twice." So A., L., N., later Uncials, almost all Cursives, Vulg., Syriac, &c.
"Twice" omitted by ℵ, C., some Old Latin, Æthiopic.

Passion had quailed, should endure his own subsequent sufferings with fearlessness and constancy." (Cat. Aurea.)

And Theophylact: "For tears brought Peter by penitence to Christ. Confounded then be those who say, that he who sins after Baptism, is not received to the remission of his sins. For behold Peter, who had also received the Body and Blood of the Lord, is received by penitence, for the failings of saints are written, that if we fall by want of caution, we also may be able to run back through their example, and hope to be relieved by penitence." (Cat. Aurea.)

## CHAP. XV.

AND ᵃ straightway in the morning the chief priests held a consultation with the elders and scribes, and the whole council, and bound Jesus, and carried *him* away, and delivered *him* to Pilate.

ᵃ Ps. ii. 2.
Matt. xxvii. 1.
Luke xxii. 66.
& xxiii. 1.
John xviii. 28.
Act iii. 13. &
iv. 26.

1. "And straightway in the morning, the chief priests," &c. This was a more formal meeting of the Sanhedrim : the meeting in the night being only a preparatory one to collect evidence.

St. Luke alone gives the account of what took place at this Sanhedrim (Luke xxii. 66-71). The examination of the Lord and His answers are so similar, that some have thought that St. Luke is recording the examination of the previous night. But at a second meeting there would be necessarily a repetition of what had taken place at the previous one, as its object was not to collect new evidence, but to record and confirm, as it were, the evidence taken previously.

2 ᵇAnd Pilate asked him, Art thou the King    ᵇ Matt. xxvii. 11.

"And bound Jesus." He had been previously bound, but was, probably, partially unbound when He stood before the high priest.

"And carried him away, and delivered him to Pilate." Pontius Pilate was the Procurator, or deputy of the Governor of Syria, of which latter province Judæa formed a part.

Why was the Lord thus brought before Pilate? Of course the ready answer is, that the Jews had no power to put any man to death, and this they urged against Pilate when he had said, "Take ye him, and judge him according to your law." But they had, on several other occasions taken up stones to stone Him—they also stoned Stephen, apparently with impunity; and if they had excited the people to stone the Lord for blasphemy, it would, probobly, have been winked at. It would have been represented to the governor that this Man had insulted their religion in its holiest place, and that the people could not be restrained from taking summary vengeance upon Him.

But their real reason was that they might put an end for ever to His pretensions by procuring that a form of death should be inflicted upon Him which was not only cruel and ignominious, but was accounted cursed, so that anyone who suffered by it must be held to be under the ban of the Almighty. Thus in Deut. xxi. 23: "He that is hanged is accursed of God;" and the Apostle cites this as fulfilled in the case of the Lord: "Christ hath redeemed us from the curse of the Law, being made a curse for us: for it is written, Cursed is every one that hangeth on a tree" (Gal. iii. 13).

Now it is clear from the whole narrative that they were determined that He should suffer by this death, and no other. If He had suffered by any other, He might have been held to be a martyr, and His doctrine might have spread after His death; but not if He was hung on a tree, or crucified. And so far as the unbelieving Jews were concerned they were right in their assumption. The name of ignonimy, by which the Saviour of the World is known amongst His unbelieving countrymen, is the One Who was hung, the Taloi. The mere fact that He was thus suspended in death is sufficient to discredit His claims to have been in the favour of God.

2. "And Pilate asked him, Art thou the King of the Jews?" What suggested this question to Pilate? for at the two examinations before the Sanhedrim not a word was said about His kingly claims.

of the Jews? And he answering said unto him, Thou sayest *it*.

All turned upon the unique sense in which He asserted that He was the Son of God. Neither in St. Matthew's, St. Mark's, or St. John's Gospel is there a word of accusation on the part of the Jews that He had made Himself a King, at least at this stage of the proceedings; but the missing link is to be found in St. Luke, who alone tells us that when He was first brought to Pilate " they began to accuse Him, saying, We found this fellow perverting the nation, and forbidding to give tribute to Cæsar, saying that He Himself is Christ a King" (Luke xxiii. 2).

From this we learn how completely independent the four narratives are, and yet that they supplement one another, and that God intended that they should be read and compared together.

The accusation that the Lord made Himself a King was the only one which Pilate could understand. Any matter respecting the Messiahship, or the Sonship, or of breaking the Sabbath, or of forgiving sins, or destroying the temple, he would have dismissed with contempt as being a " question of their own superstition." Again, it was the only one which they thought Pilate must enter into—it was the only one which touched his own fears: as was proved by the impression made upon him by their exclamation, " If thou let this man go, thou art not Cæsar's friend." Again, it was the only one of which they could get public proof, for a vast multitude had attended the Lord when He rode a few days before into Jerusalem; which multitude shouted: " Blessed be the King that cometh in the name of the Lord." So that they had the shameless effrontery to condemn Him for blasphemy at their own assembly, and to bring Him before Pilate on a totally different charge.

" Thou sayest it." Notwithstanding that Theophylact, a Greek Father, says: " His answer is doubtful, since it may mean : ' *Thou* sayest, but *I* say not so,' it is agreed by almost all that the words are a decided affirmation : ' Thou sayest the fact,' or 'It is as thou sayest.' " Before this stage of the proceedings the things occurred which are mentioned in St. John's Gospel—that Pilate went out to them—that he bid them take Jesus and judge Him according to their law— that Pilate asked the Lord whether He were the King of the Jews, and received the answer, " My kingdom is not of this world," by which Pilate understood that the Lord claimed only a mystical or

3 And the chief priests accused him of many things: but he answered nothing.

4 ᶜAnd Pilate asked him again, saying, Answerest thou nothing? behold how many things they witness against thee.

ᶜ Matt. xxvii. 13.

5 ᵈBut Jesus yet answered nothing; so that Pilate marvelled.

ᵈ Is. liii. 7. John xix. 9.

---

3. "But he answered nothing," omitted by א, A., B., C., D., later Uncials, almost all Cursives, some Old Latin, Vulg.; retained by some Cursives, Old Latin (a, e), some versions.

4. "They witness against thee." So A., E., G., H., K., M., N., other later Uncials, most Cursives, some versions; but א, B., C., D. read, "They accuse thee of."

spiritual empire, and that the weapon by which He asserted His kingship was His witness to the truth.

3. "And the chief priests accused him of many things: but he answered nothing."

4. "And Pilate asked him again . . . Pilate marvelled." Why did not the Lord answer these accusations? Very probably, not only because they were palpably false, but because the leading allegations were respecting points which involved His Messiahship. He could not answer accusations respecting His universal Empire—His being the supreme Judge—His being the Lord of the Sabbath, by denying them; and yet He could not make the sense in which these things were to be understood plain to a sceptical and unspiritual heathen like Pilate.

"Pilate marvelled." On this Calvin sensibly remarks: "The integrity of Christ was such that the judge saw it plainly without any defence. But Pilate wished that Christ might not neglect His own cause, and might thus be acquitted without giving offence to many people. And up to this point the integrity of Pilate is worthy of commendation, because from a favourable regard to the innocence of Christ, he urges Him to defend Himself;" and he further remarks: "Christ, therefore, was at that time silent, that He may now be our Advocate and by His intercession may deliver us from condemnation."

The reader will remember how this silence of the Lord before His accusers was the subject of one very distinct prophecy: "He is brought as a lamb to the slaughter, and as a sheep before her shearers is dumb, so He openeth not His mouth."

6 Now <sup>a</sup> at *that* feast he released unto them one prisoner, whomsoever they desired.

<sup>a</sup> Matt. xxvii. 15. Luke xxiii. 17. John xviii. 39.

7 And there was *one* named Barabbas, *which lay* bound with them that had made insurrection with him, who had committed murder in the insurrection.

---

7. "That had made insurrection with him." So A., G., H., N., &c.; but ℵ, B., C., D., K., and a few Cursives, and Sah. read simply, "made insurrection."

One of the accusations directed against Him at this time contained the word "Galilee." The chief priests said, "He stirreth up the people, teaching throughout all Jewry, beginning from Galilee." Pilate eagerly caught at this word, and hoping to get rid of the foul business he sent the Lord to the Tetrarch of Galilee, who was then in Jerusalem, but Herod sent Him back mocked and insulted, and without a word on which a charge of death could be preferred against Him.

6. "Now at that feast he released unto them one prisoner, whomsoever they desired." From St. John's account we should gather that Pilate first suggested to them the custom, in order that he might release the Lord (John xviii. 39).

The custom of having one of the prisoners released by the governor on the festival to gratify the people was "an open abuse of the worship of God; for nothing could be more unreasonable than that festivals should be honoured by allowing crimes to go unpunished."

7. "And there was one named Barabbas, which lay bound with them that had," &c. As nothing is said in Josephus of this man's insurrection, it is not at all probable that it was more than a dangerous riot attended with murder and plunder, though, no doubt, the insurrection was directed against the Roman authority.

It is exceedingly improbable that, as some suppose, it was in the remotest degree connected with Messianic claims on the part of the leader. For the remarkable variety of readings supported by one or two later MSS., and known to Origen, see the note in St. Matthew, xxvii. 16. That he was a common, vulgar ruffian, with no redeeming features in his character, seems evident from St. Peter's reproach: "Ye denied the Holy One and the Just, and desired a murderer to be granted unto you" (Acts iii. 14).

8. "And the multitude crying aloud began to desire him to do as he had ever," &c. This is peculiar to St. Mark. It seems at

CHAP. XV.] THE MULTITUDE CRYING ALOUD. 379

8 And the multitude crying aloud began to desire *him to do* as he had ever done unto them.

9 But Pilate answered them, saying, Will ye that I release unto you the King of the Jews?

10 For he knew that the chief priests had delivered him for envy.

11 But ᶠthe chief priests moved the people, that he should rather release Barabbas unto them.

ᶠ Matt. xxvii. 20. Acts iii. 14.

---

8. "Crying aloud." So A., C., N., later Uncials, almost all Cursives, Syriac, and Armenian; but ℵ, B., D., some Old Latin, Vulg., Sah., Coptic, Gothic read, "went up." So Revisers. "Went up and began to ask him," &c.

"Ever done unto them." So A., C., D., N., later Uncials, most Cursives, Vulg.; but ℵ, B., Δ, Copt., Sah. omit "ever."

first not in full accordance with what St. John says—that Pilate himself suggested that he should himself observe the custom of the feast. It may be explained thus: that they had noticed some hesitation on the part of the governor to observe the custom unless it would result in the release of Jesus.

9, 10. "But Pilate answered them, saying, Will ye . . . delivered him for envy." This saying, "He knew that they had delivered him for envy," distinctly implies that Pilate must have known much of the character and works of Jesus which excited the envy of the chief priests. He must have known the favour in which Jesus was with the common people, and the reasons for it. In appealing to the people he trusted that they would go against those in authority, and demand the release of Him Who had done so many miracles of healing amongst them, and Whom they had so lately welcomed into Jerusalem with shouts of triumph.

11. "But the chief priests moved the people." With what arguments did they thus "move the people?" Very probably with appeals to their disappointment in that Jesus was not in the least degree the Messiah which the mass of the people expected. Very probably they would urge against Him blasphemy, sabbath-breaking, too great strictness in the upholding of the marriage vow. But it is likely that the crowd collected at the prætorium consisted mainly of their own creatures—those whom their emissaries had beaten up. And, as Williams well remarks, those who were really

12 And Pilate answered and said again unto them, What will ye then that I shall do *unto him* whom ye call the King of the Jews?

13 And they cried out again, Crucify him.

---

12. "Pilate answered and said again." So A., F., G., H., K., M., N., most Cursives; but א, B., C., Vulg., and Sah. read, "Pilate again answered."

"What will ye that I shall do unto him whom ye call the King of the Jews?" Great variation of readings here, none of any importance. Vulg., *Quid ergo vultis faciam regi Judæorum?* Revisers, "What then shall I do unto him whom ye call the King of the Jews?"

deeply moved by His doctrine, would have been the least loud and prominent in such a multitude, being more in secret; and in large bodies of men and popular assemblies good is smothered: the bad predominate; good principle is despised by the wicked, and the weak are ashamed of it. Moreover, on this subject of Barabbas they were seditiously excited, and, perhaps, nationally; his insurrection, or riot, having been, in all probability, against some display of Roman authority.

12. "And Pilate answered and said again unto them, What will ye then . . . . King of the Jews?" Comparing together the accounts in St. Matthew and our Evangelist, he said: "What shall I do then with Jesus which is called Christ, whom ye call the King of the Jews?"

It is to be noticed how in all the accounts Pilate seems either determined in himself or led by a higher Power to impose on the Jews the kingship of our Lord. If this was wholly, or in part, from himself, it came of his utter contempt for the Jewish race. He delighted to call a poor, down-trodden, persecuted, manacled prisoner their King. But, no doubt, in doing this he "prophesied," as Caiaphas had done. He spoke and acted under the inspiration of a higher Power. What he taunted them with was the truth. And when he wrote the title, and when he refused to alter it, he adhered to the truth of God, that the despised Nazarene was the King of the Jews, the King of Israel, the King of kings.

13. "And they cried out again, Crucify him." That means, "Kill him by torture. Put Him to the foulest and the most cruel death thou knowest of." Did the people shout for this of themselves, or were they stirred to it by the chief priests? No doubt the latter is the truth. For the chief priests of that time, particularly those of the family

14 Then Pilate said unto them, Why, what evil hath he

---

of Annas, were men who excelled in wickedness. They had bought their dignity of the Romans. They were Sadducees, and so alien in heart from the system which they administered. They were guardians of the Temple, and yet profaned it by making it a den of thieves. They were men who could suborn witnesses—who could seek out false witnesses. Such men had sold themselves to do evil. No wonder, then, that they hated Jesus with perfect hatred. They hated Him for the claims He made to be a spiritual, unworldly Messiah, for His extreme reverence for His Father's house, for His assertion of the doctrine of the Resurrection, and for the proof He had given of it by having Himself raised to life a dead body. They hated Him for His influence with the best and most simple-minded of the people, for His purity and goodness. And so being given over to the spirit of envy and cruelty, they scrupled not to move the professing people of God to demand that the worst of Gentile punishments should be inflicted on their Victim. And no doubt, as I said at the outset, they insisted on this punishment as that most akin to the hanging on a tree, which their law pronounced accursed. And so they hoped to extinguish His claims by His death.[1]

14. "Then Pilate said unto them, Why, what evil hath he done?" Pilate says this not once, but over and over again, "I find no fault in this man." "I find in Him no fault at all. Behold I, having examined Him before you, have found no fault in this Man; no, nor yet Herod." "I am innocent of the blood of this just Person." I bring Him forth to you that ye may know that I find no fault in Him. "Take ye Him, and crucify Him, for I find no fault in Him." Perhaps it was partly on account of these reiterated assertions on the part of His judge that He was innocent, that His common designation amongst the Christian Jews was, "the Just One," "The Holy One and the Just."

---

[1] Thus Justin Martyr makes Trypho, the unconverted Jew, say: "This so-called Christ of yours was dishonourable and inglorious; so much so, that the last curse contained in the law of God fell upon Him, for He was crucified." (Ch. xxxii.)

done? And they cried out the more exceedingly, Crucify him.

<sup>e</sup> Matt. xxvii. 26. John xix. 1, 16.

15 ¶ <sup>e</sup> And *so* Pilate, willing to content the people, released Barabbas unto them, and delivered Jesus, when he had scourged *him*, to be crucified.

---

14. " They cried out the more exceedingly." So E., N., some other later Uncials, most Cursives; but א, A., B., C., D., G., H., K., M., and some Cursives read, "exceedingly."

"They cried out the more exceedingly, Crucify him." As if this appetite for blood was sharpened by the delay. Bede quotes very appositely: "Mine heritage is unto me as a lion of the forest, it crieth out against me." (Jerem. xii. 8.)

15. "And so Pilate, willing to content the people, released Barabbas unto them," &c. How was it that the representative of the Roman power, that crushing iron despotism which had subdued the world, would not abide by his convictions, but desired to "content" them? St. John tells us what enables us to understand this. The Jews had said to him, when they saw him vacillating and hesitating, "If thou let this Man go, thou art not Cæsar's friend; whosoever maketh himself a King speaketh against Cæsar." It would have gone hard with Pilate at Rome if a report had been sent up that he had allowed a Man to escape without punishment, indeed, without due investigation, Who had a few days before entered the turbulent city at the head of an immense multitude, who hailed him as King, and as the successor of the founder of the Jewish monarchy. "Hosanna to the Son of David."

"Released Barabbas unto them." In the almost ironical words of St. Luke, "he released unto them him who for sedition and murder was cast into prison." But how astonishing was the retribution! At the time of the siege of Jerusalem, the city which had thus rejected the Lord, suffered unheard of calamities through the tyranny of a band of murderers and robbers of the very type of Barabbas, who got possession of their temple, destroyed their store of provision (which occasioned the fearful famine), and exercised the greatest profanity and cruelty.[1] This Barabbas represents ourselves delivered from eternal death by the rejection and crucifixion of the Lord.

---

[1] See notes on Chap. xiii., pp. 304, 305.

## CHAP. XV.] THE HALL CALLED PRÆTORIUM. 383

16 [h] And the soldiers led him away into the hall, called Prætorium; and they call together the whole band.

[h] Matt. xxvii. 27.

"And when He had scourged Jesus." A fearful punishment. The whole back of the victim becoming a mass of raw bleeding flesh through the infliction. This was written in prophecy, "I gave my back to the smiters," and its saving effects were also written in the same prophet, "He was wounded for our transgressions, He was bruised for our iniquities, the chastisement of our peace was upon him, and with his stripes we are healed."

"To be crucified." A faint idea of the extreme indignity of all this inflicted on the Son of God may be got from Cicero's invective against Verres: "To bind Roman citizens, 'tis a thing unlawful; to scourge them 'tis a great crime; to put them to death, 'tis almost a parricide; but what shall I say of *crucifying* them? It is impossible to find any word of weight and significancy, so as to express a thing so abominable.". And to all this the King of Glory submitted for our sakes. Verily, sin must be an evil which we can very faintly realize, if the Son of God condescended to such igno- miny to save us from it. It is supposed that Pilate scourged the Lord, in order to excite the pity of the Jews. "Surely," he thought to himself, "it will satiate their malice to see Him all torn and bleeding. After this they cannot clamour for His crucifixion."

16. "And the soldiers led him away into the hall (or court or court-yard), called Prætorium." He had been standing without with Pilate, who had come out to hear the accusation of the chief priests, who were afraid to enter within the heathen precincts, lest they should be defiled. Now the soldiers took him within, into the large open court, surrounded by the buildings of the palace.

"And they called together the whole band." There may have been several hundred. If so many, it was to add to the mockery. The word signifies the tenth of a legion, *i.e.*, about 460 men; but it may have been only those on duty, or they may have been gathered together to see the sport. A nation whose chief public spectacle was gladiatorial shows, must have been given over to the spirit of cruelty.

How was it that Roman soldiers, who could have known nothing of our Lord, evidently delighted in inflicting upon Him this mockery and cruelty? It is absurd to suppose that it was from

17 And they clothed him with purple, and platted a crown of thorns, and put it about his *head*,

---

hatred of spiritual religion, such as that which our Lord preached, for such a thing was unimaginable by them. I cannot help thinking that it was because our Lord was a Jew, belonging to a race which they both despised and hated. They would probably have inflicted it upon any other Jew who was given over to their brutality. They would probably also take more seriously the term "King of the Jews," which they had heard applied to Him. Anyhow, their extraordinary malice against One of Whom they knew nothing, requires to be accounted for. All they do is in mockery of His supposed kingly pretensions, as the next verses tell us.

17. "And they clothed him with purple." "Purple (porphura) is vaguely used to signify different shades of red, and is especially convertible with crimson. Perhaps they may have first put on again the white dress in which Herod had caused Him to be clothed, to mark Him out as a candidate for Royal honours, and then taken it off in order to invest Him with the scarlet robe, the sign of His having attained to kingly dignity. The drama would thus be complete. They accordingly again stripped off His outer garment, and instead of it put on a scarlet military cloak (sagum), which was intended to represent the imperial purple." (Lange.)

What a reproof to those who call themselves by the name of Christ, and yet deck themselves in "gay clothing!" That which ministers to their pride, ministered to their Lord's most bitter humiliation.

"And platted a crown of thorns, and put it about his head." They crown with thorns the Head which St. John sees in vision wearing many diadems. What a lesson are we taught by this, no less than that patience and endurance are the crown of virtue! In mockery they crowned Him with thorns, and in the eye of faith His crown of thorns has turned all other crowns into tinsel. "What sort of garland, I pray you," asked Tertullian, "did he Who is both the Head of the man and the glory of the woman, Jesus Christ, the Husband of the Church, submit to? . . . Of thorns, I think, and thistles, a figure of the sins which the soil of the flesh brought forth for us, but the power of the Cross removed, blending

CHAP. XV.]   HAIL, KING OF THE JEWS!   385

18. And began to salute him, Hail, King of the Jews!
19. And they smote him on the head with a reed, and did spit upon him, and bowing *their* knees worshipped him.

---

in its endurance by the head of our Lord Death's every sting. Yes, and besides the figure, there is contumely with ready lip, and dishonour and infamy, and the ferocity involved in the cruel things which then disfigured and lacerated the temples of the Lord. . . . If for these things you owe your own head to Him, repay it if you can, such as He presented His for yours. . . . Keep for God His own property untainted. He will crown it if He choose. Nay, then, He does even choose. He calls us to it. To Him who conquers He says, ' I will give thee a crown of life.'"

18. "And began to salute him, Hail, King of the Jews!" As I noticed before, I cannot help believing that they thought in their ignorance, that the assertion of our Lord's claim to be a temporal King of the Jews had been serious. So that they supposed that they were mocking One Who was not only called a King in derision, but Who had really in some way pretended to be one. Perhaps some of them had been witnesses of His entry into Jerusalem, and understood nothing of its spiritual significance, but regarded Him as a fanatical pretender.

19. "And they smote him on the head with a reed." St. Matthew tells us that they put a reed in His right hand as a mock sceptre. It was, doubtless, with this reed that they smote Him.

"And did spit upon him." The verb being in the imperfect, implies that they thus insulted Him over and over again.

"And bowing their knees worshipped him." That is, fell down before Him as men do before an earthly sovereign. It does not, I think, imply the mockery of adoration as to God.

Such were the insults endured by the Son of God. What an untold amount of misery, short of bodily anguish, human beings inflict upon one another by ridicule, mockery, and insult. There seems to be, if it could be added up, far more misery in this evil world from these things, than from blows or tortures, or injuries to persons or property through malice and revenge. And the Son of God, Who was made sin for us, in that He submitted to endure all the miseries which sin brings upon us, bore patiently all this mockery and insult. So it was written, "He is despised and rejected of men, a man of sorrows and acquainted with grief. He was despised and

20 And when they had mocked him, they took off the purple from him, and put his own clothes on him, and led him out to crucify him.

21 [1] And they compel one Simon a Cyrenian,

[1] Matt. xxvii. 32. Luke xxiii. 26.

---

we esteemed Him not." "I gave my back to the smiters, and my cheeks to them that plucked off the hair. I hid not my face from shame and spitting." So that alike in pain of body and in distress of soul, He is One with us.

At this time the events happened related only by St. John. Pilate brought forth the Lord, Who had suffered these things within the court of the Palace, and showed Him to the people with the words, "Behold the Man." After this he was awed by the words, "He made Himself the Son of God," and apparently brought Jesus into the hall, and further questioned Him. But at last, after again seeking to release Him, he was decided by their cry, "If thou let this Man go, thou art not Cæsar's friend." Then after sitting down on the judgment seat, and making one more appeal, "Shall I crucify your King?" and hearing their response, "We have no King but Cæsar," "He delivered Him to them to be crucified."

20. "And when they had mocked him, they took off the purple from him, and put his own clothes on him." Why did they do this? Why did they not continue their insults by leading Him on the Via Dolorosa clad with the mock robe of royalty? Because, if so, the prophecy would not have been fulfilled, "They parted my garments among them, and cast lots upon my vesture." Part of his own clothes was the seamless robe, for the possession of which they must cast lots, and so fulfil the prophecy.

"And led him out to crucify him." And this also, as the reader knows, was to fulfil that which was written, that "He must suffer without the gate." "Jesus, that He might sanctify the people with His own blood, suffered without the gate. Let us go forth, therefore, unto Him, without the camp, bearing his reproach" (Hebrews xiii. 12, 13).

21. "And they compel one Simon a Cyrenian, who passed by, coming out of the country, the father," &c. The Lord, after the protracted watching and sleeplessness of twenty-four hours, the exhaustion of His agony and bloody sweat, the fatigue of being

who passed by, coming out of the country, the father of Alexander and Rufus, to bear his cross.

22 ᵏ And they bring him unto the place Gol- gotha, which is, being interpreted, The place of a skull.

ᵏ Matt. xxvii. 33. Luke xxiii. 33. John xix. 17.

hurried to and fro from the courts of three judges, the loss of blood through the scourging, and the weakness of body which in every human being must occur through the harassing of the mind by insults and humiliation which He deeply felt, was unable to bear His cross but a short way, perhaps only just beyond the gate. Here His persecutors met one who was probably known to some in the crowd as one who favoured His teaching, and as the soldiers were on military duty, they had power to press men to assist them. And they compelled this man to bear the Cross, so that the Lord might not expire under its weight, but be reserved to the torture of being nailed to it. By thus treating him, they thought to do Simon a deep dishonour, but instead of this they enshrined his name in the very Gospel of the Cross, so that wherever "this Gospel is preached," his name is recorded as the Lord's cross-bearer.

"And who was that man of Cyrene? What good deed of faith had he done to Christ, or to Christ's little ones, that he, of all the sons of Adam, should have been deemed worthy to be admitted to this the first and greatest of all earthly honours? Who he was, excepting the name, we know not, nor what he had done; for God withdraws from the sight of men and hides, in His own presence, those whom He most delights to honour."

He is called in St. Mark alone the "father of Alexander and Rufus." Being so mentioned, his two sons were probably of note in the early Church. As St. Mark wrote in Rome, it has been conjectured that one was the Rufus living there to whom St. Paul sent a salutation. (Rom. xvi. 13.)

22. "They bring him unto the place Golgotha," &c. "They bring him." They do not now lead Him, He was probably too weak, but half carry or drag Him.

"Unto the place Golgotha." No doubt the place of death for the worst criminals. This was also a part of the Lord's humiliation, that He should suffer in the accursed place of public executions. As is natural, all sorts of conjectures have been hazarded respecting the place and its name, as, for instance, that it was the place where

23 ¹And they gave him to drink wine mingled with
myrrh: but he received *it* not.

¹ Matt. xxvii. 34.

---

23. "Gave him to drink." So A., D., later Uncials, almost all Cursives, some Old Latin, Vulg., Sah., Syriac, Æthiopic, Gothic; but ℵ, B., C., L., Δ, Coptic, and Armenian omit " to drink."

Adam was buried, that it was the place where Abraham laid Isaac on the altar, that it was the centre of the earth. Respecting its identification, there seems little doubt but that it was a small knoll, insignificant in height (a mediæval traveller calls it monticulus), very near the place of the Holy Sepulchre.[1] As each of the four Evangelists expressly connects it with a skull, I cannot but think that it was a place polluted by the skulls and bones of criminals; perhaps some one skull was retained there to mark it as accursed. The Jews, from their close association of death with ceremonial pollution, must have had some place set apart for the death of criminals: such could not be put to death anywhere near the Holy City.

23. "And they gave him to drink wine mingled with myrrh: but he received it not." St. Matthew calls this potion "vinegar mingled with gall:" but both Evangelists evidently mean the same thing. This wine would be the sour wine, tasting like vinegar, which was the ordinary drink of the Roman soldiers, and the myrrh being exceedingly bitter (bitter as gall) would naturally be called gall. It may have had other stupefying ingredients mixed with it. It was, of course, given as an anodyne.[2] "He tastes a little (Matth. xxvii. 34) of this bitter, intoxicating, and strengthening liquor, that He may suffer from its acrid quality: he refuses the rest, to show that He was resolved to endure all the pains of the Cross, to offer His sacrifice with a perfect freedom of mind. How wonderful, O Jesus, is the whole œconomy of Thy sufferings! It is peculiar to Thee alone to suffer with this clear state of mind, this strict conformity to the will of Thy Father, and this determinate choice of sufferings, out of love to us sinners and for our salvation." (Quesnel.)

24. "And when they had crucified him, they parted his garments,

---

[1] See note in Speaker's Commentary at the end of Matth. xxvii.
[2] According to the Talmud it was provided by the humanity of the ladies of Jerusalem, for all criminals about to be crucified.

24 And when they had crucified him, ᵐthey  ᵐ Ps. xxii. 18.
Luke xxiii. 34.
John xix. 23.

casting lots upon them." None of the four Evangelists attempt to describe the fearful circumstances of the Crucifixion itself. Three, Matthew, Luke, and John say, "They crucified Him." St. Mark, "When they had crucified Him." The punishment was too well known to require description. We will (God helping, and, we trust, pardoning any mistake or shortcoming) say a few words first upon the instrument of this punishment, then upon the infliction. The Cross on which the Lord suffered the all-reconciling Death was, no doubt, the Latin Cross, the Cross of the figure with which we are most familiar: only we are to remember that it was much lower than what it is usually represented in pictures. The body of the sufferer was not raised far aloft, his feet almost above the heads of the surrounding spectators, but only a little above them, so that they could come close to him to gibe at him, to threaten him with their gestures, even to strike him. There was also a projection in front, not seen in pictures, on which the principal weight of the body rested, as the hands would not be equal to the strain of the whole weight. Such a cross is repeatedly found on the coins and columns of Constantine, who abolished its use throughout the empire.

The infliction is thus described: "Enough remained to preserve the pre-eminence of torture to the cross. The process of nailing was exquisite torment, and yet worse in what ensued than in the actual infliction. The spikes rankled, the wounds inflamed, the local injury produced a general fever, the fever a most intolerable thirst; but the misery of miseries to the sufferer was, while racked with agony, to be fastened in a position which did not permit him to writhe. Every attempt to relieve the muscles, every instinctive movement of anguish, only served to drag the lacerated flesh, and wake up new and acuter pangs, and this torture, which must have been continually aggravated until advancing death began to lay it to sleep, lasted on an average two or three days." (Timbs.)

The endurance of this horrible punishment was the lowest depth of the Lord's humiliation. "Being found in fashion as a man, He humbled Himself, and became obedient unto death, even the death of the cross."

Two inferences from the Lord's endurance of this death are certain.

1st. The atoning virtue of such a Death endured in His human nature by the Son of God must reach to the lowest depths of human

parted his garments, casting lots upon them, what every man should take.

---

sin. The Second Adam endured no ordinary death, but the Death which men well versed in contriving tortures had invented for the lowest, the meanest, the most degraded. Such a Sacrifice endured by the Son of God must be all sufficient. So far as an innocent Being could be, He was "made sin for us." In writing this, I do not for a moment broach the doctrine that the Atonement wrought on the Cross is a matter of equivalence, of exact measure, of so much pain for so much sin—I regard this as a perversion of the truth; but in the counsels of God, the Son of God must suffer, and He endured the extremity of human pain, so that we may be sure that if such an One thus suffered, no sin can be out of the reach of the virtue and power of His expiation.

And, in the second place, by such a form of death the Lord in His own Person sounded the lowest depth of human anguish and distress.

Is any Christian, for instance, called upon to suffer a public execution, accompanied with torture and attended with every circumstance of ignominy and disgrace, and to suffer all this iniquitously, the forms of justice having been outraged to bring him under the punishment? A worse case of human suffering cannot be conceived, and yet the Lord explored before him even this bottomless pit of misery. As in His agony in the garden the Lord explored the depths of mental suffering, so on the Cross He experienced the sharpest bodily anguish, and hereby we are assured of the perfect sympathy of our High Priest in all we are called upon to endure.

"They parted his garments, casting lots upon them, what every man should take." This fulfilment of a minute particular prophesied of by David above a thousand years before, identifies to the believer this Crucifixion and Death as those by which God intended to redeem the world. The sufferings as depicted in the former part of this Psalm cannot be imagined to meet in any other death than that of crucifixion. They are not the sufferings of one dying in battle, or in prison, or by poison, or by being burnt to death, or by being strangled, or by being beheaded, or by being stoned. They are the sufferings of one "lifted up," surrounded by an enraged mob of enemies heaping upon Him all manner of taunts and insults, but not attacking Him with weapons: the bones of the Sufferer were out of joint, His strength dried up, His tongue, through thirst, cleaving to the gums,

CHAP. XV.]   IT WAS THE THIRD HOUR.   391

25 And ⁿ it was the third hour, and they cruci-fied him.

26 And ᵒ the superscription of his accusation was written over, THE KING OF THE JEWS,

ⁿ See Matt. xxvii. 45. Luke xxiii. 44. John xix. 14.
ᵒ Matt. xxvii. 37.

---

His hands and feet pierced. Such were the sufferings of those crucified, those dying by a death unknown to David, a purely Gentile punishment. But amidst these inflictions the Psalmist prophesies that they should part His garments among them and cast lots for His vesture: this was a circumstance which would not occur in one crucifixion out of ten thousand: the crucifiers might part the garments, but why cast lots for one of these garments? The solution of the ænigma is, that the sufferer had a coat woven without seam throughout, and they said among themselves, "Let us not rend it, but cast lots for it;" and so they did, and by doing this they fulfilled the prophecy. But the Psalm is one continued prophecy respecting One particular Man Whom, in the extremity of His sufferings, God hears, so that He escapes out of the hands of His enemies by what is to all appearances a Resurrection; and the consequences of His restoration are, "All the ends of the world shall remember themselves and be turned unto the Lord, and all the kindreds of the nations shall worship before Him." It may seem strange to the unbeliever that the parting of the garments of the Crucified should be mentioned in one breath, as it were, with the Crucifixion, but to the believer it speaks of the One atoning Death, and the Life from the dead, and the Eternal Glory and Reign.

25. "And it was the third hour, and they crucified him." For the reconciliation of this with the statement of St. John that He was finally led out by Pilate to the Jews about the sixth hour, see note on John xix. 14. The third hour of St. Mark would be nine o'clock, but any time between nine and twelve would be reckoned under the third hour. Augustine considers that the third hour refers to the time when they cried, "Crucify Him, crucify Him," but this seems impossible.

26. "And the superscription of his accusation was written over, THE KING OF THE JEWS." This is the shortest and most concise of the three titles. In all probability it was that which was written in Latin. St. Luke's "This is the King of the Jews," is evidently the same. The angel had prophesied, "The Lord God shall give unto

27 And ᵖ with him they crucify two thieves; the one on his right hand, and the other on his left.

28 And the scripture was fulfilled, which saith, ᵠ And he was numbered with the transgressors.

ᵖ Matt. xxvii. 38.
ᵠ Is. liii. 12. Luke xxii. 37.

27. "Two thieves;" rather, "two robbers." *Latrones*, Vulg.
28. This verse omitted by ℵ, A., B., C., and a good many Cursives; but inserted by most later Uncials, E., F., G., H., K., L., M., some Old Latin, Vulg., &c.

Him the throne of His Father David, and He shall reign over the House of Jacob for ever." In fact, we may say that the leading idea of the Messiah in the Hebrew Scriptures is that He should be first King of Israel, and then an Universal King [thus Psalm lxxii., lxxxix., cxxxii., Isaiah ix. 7, Jerem., xxiii. 5, 6]. So that in the eyes of the Priests and Pharisees, who knew at least the letter of Scripture, it was exactly as if Pilate had written, " This is the Messiah, the King Whom you look for." To us who confess Him to be the Only Begotten Son of God, and God of God, the " King of the Jews " is the lowest of His titles ; but though the lowest, yet if He be the veritable King of the Jews in the sense of the Psalmist and of the Prophets then He is infinitely more—He is all that He claimed to be, the Only Begotten of the Father.

27. "And with him they crucify two thieves; the one on his right hand, and the other," &c. I have noticed that each Evangelist particularly mentions that He was crucified between these two, and that one was set on His right hand, and the other on His left. Remembering that one of these repented and the other died in impenitence, we cannot but look upon this as typical and prophetical. As Augustine observes : " The very cross was the tribunal of Christ, for the Judge was placed in the middle : one thief who believed was set free, the other, who reviled, was condemned ; which signified what he was already about to do with the quick and dead." So also Hilary and Leo.

28. " And the scripture was fulfilled, which saith, And he was numbered," &c. The reader will see from the critical note that there is some doubt whether this verse was originally written by the Evangelist. Many suppose that it was a very ancient gloss which crept into the text. But that it contains the Truth of God is as certain as possible : for the whole chapter contains a number of places of Scripture cited as having reference throughout to Christ's

29 And ʳ they that passed by railed on him, wagging their heads, and saying, Ah, ˢ thou that destroyest the temple, and buildest *it* in three days,

ʳ Ps. xxii. 7.
ˢ ch. xiv. 58.
John ii. 19.

30 Save thyself, and come down from the cross.

31 Likewise also the chief priests mocking said among

---

sufferings and Death, and one of the leading features of the humiliation of His Death was, that He being innocent, was crucified with two robbers, as if He were Himself a malefactor worthy of such a fate—which, no doubt, by very many of those who passed by, He was accounted to be. In the company of malefactors of the worst type He died the death of a malefactor.

29. "And they that passed by railed on him, ... Ah, thou that destroyed the temple, ... Save thyself." Surely if they had possessed the common feelings of humanity the knowledge of the agonizing pain which Jesus was then enduring would have moved even their hard hearts to some pity and restained their reproaches.

"Ah, thou that destroyest the temple and buildest it in three days," &c. How is it that this accusation, brought forward only in the dead of the night before, could have found its way into the mouths of the "passers by"? It seems as if to please the chief priests, or at their instigation, some of those who had heard it went to and fro before the Crucified, jeering the Sufferer, Who, so far from compassing the destruction of the temple, had cleansed it from the pollutions of their unholy traffic. Surely such a reproach must have come from the lips of those whom the Lord had driven ignominiously out of it!

31. "Likewise also the chief priests mocking said among themselves with the scribes." That any of the heads of the twenty-four courses should have so demeaned themselves—should have been so lost to all sense of the holiness of their office, as to take part on such a solemn day in insulting One Whom they knew to be innocent, is the most striking vindication possible of the justice of God's dealings in rooting them out utterly and destroying every vestige of the temple they had polluted, and the worship by which they had profaned His Name. But there is a greater depth of wickedness still, for they were conscious that the Man Whom they were crucifying was in some sense a Saviour—they actually proceed to throw

themselves with the scribes, **He saved others**; himself he cannot save.

32 Let Christ the King of Israel descend now from the cross, that we may see and believe. And ᵗthey that were crucified with him reviled him.

33 And ᵘwhen the sixth hour was come, there

<small>ᵗ Matt. xxvii. 44. Luke xxiii. 39.</small>
<small>ᵘ Matt. xxvii. 45. Luke xxiii. 44.</small>

---

in His teeth His acts of healing, of restoration of sight, even of restoration to life, for they exclaim:

"He saved others: himself he cannot save." What *others* had He saved? They knew that He had saved the man born blind, for they had made a show of investigating it (John ix.). They knew that He had raised Lazarus from the dead; they knew that during this very week the blind and the lame had come to Him in the temple, and He had healed them (Matt. xxi. 14). By whose power had He performed such miracles? Had any prophet ever performed greater? He saved from disease, from blindness, even from death, and yet these hardened men could exclaim, "He saved others, himself he cannot save." Surely this was perilously akin to the sin against the Holy Ghost, by Whose power He had done His benevolent acts!

32. "Let Christ the King of Israel descend now from the cross, that," &c. He came not down from the Cross, for if He had, the offer of salvation could not have been made, even to these His crucifiers, as it was: but He gave them a far greater sign. He came out from the tomb which they had sealed, and which they had guarded with soldiers, but as He had foretold, "they were not persuaded, though He rose from the dead."

"And they that were crucified with him reviled him." From the accounts of St. Matthew and St. Mark we should gather that both robbers at the first reviled Him, but that one—struck, perhaps, by the meekness and patience of the Sufferer, and overawed by the gathering darkness, repented and confessed Him. Augustine, however, suggests that Matthew and Mark, who touch but lightly on this place, put the plural for the singular. The repentance of one of the thieves does not seem from the first to have had a place in the tradition of the Lord's life and acts, but was afterwards ascertained by St. Luke.

33. "And when the sixth hour was come, there was darkness over

CHAP. XV.] ELOI, ELOI, LAMA SABACHTHANI? 395

was darkness over the whole land until the ninth hour.

34 And at the ninth hour Jesus cried with a loud voice, saying, *x* Eloi, Eloi, lama sabachthani? which is, being interpreted, My God, my God, why hast thou forsaken me?

*x* Ps. xxii. 1. Matt. xxvii. 46.

---

33. " Land." Probably, "earth." See below.
34. " Lama." This word variously spelt. " Lema " in א, C., L.; " lima," A., K., M., U.; " lama " in B., D.; " lemono," Syriac.

---

the whole land," &c. By what physical means God brought about this darkness, it is impossible to conjecture. It was not an eclipse, for it was the time of full moon, and the darkness of an eclipse could not have lasted above a few minutes. It seems to have been very distinctly referred to by a Gentile chronicler, Phlegon, who lived under the Emperor Hadrian. Eusebius quotes the very words under the date of the fourth year of the 202nd Olympiad: " Then occurred the greatest darkening of the sun which had ever been known; it became night at midday, so that the stars shone in the heavens. A great earthquake in Bithynia, which destroyed a part of Nicæa." Phlegon refers it to an eclipse, in which he was manifestly wrong, as it is computed that no eclipse then occurred; but though he was wrong about the cause, the fact remains that he mentioned the extraordinary darkness. Tertullian, also, in his Apology addressed to the heathen, appeals to their own annals. The passage deserves to be given in full: " At length being nailed to the Cross, He showed many special signs to mark that Death. Of Himself He with a word gave up the ghost, preventing the office of the executioner. At the same moment the light of midday was withdrawn, the sun veiling his orb. They thought it, forsooth, an eclipse, who knew not that this also had been foretold concerning Christ; when they discovered not its cause, they denied it; and yet ye have this event, that befell the world, related in your own records." From these passages we cannot but gather that this darkness extended far beyond the confines of the Holy Land. Seeing that the Son of God was then expiating the sins of a world, it seems but a small thing that physical nature should, at God's bidding, testify to the unutterable moment in His sight of what was then being accomplished.

34. " And at the ninth hour [that is, at three o'clock] Jesus cried with a loud voice, saying, Eloi . . . forsaken me?" This is not the cry of despair, as some say, who desire to prove that our

35 And some of them that stood by, when they heard it, said, Behold, he calleth Elias.

Lord suffered all the torments of the lost. Such seems an impious opinion, and the words of the Lord confute it, for in this lowest depth of distress He claims God as His God, "My God, My God." It is rather the cry of One Who, holding fast by God, is yet deprived of all sensible consolation, even at the near approach of death. If it be lawful to dwell on these words, we may best illustrate them by the language of the Psalm of which they form the first words. There the Psalmist is inspired, as it were, to remonstrate with God. "Why art thou so far from my health [saving me] and from the words of my complaint? I cry in the day time, but Thou hearest not. I am a worm and no man, a very scorn of men and the outcast of the people. Go not from me, for trouble is hard at hand, and there is none to help me." Again, in the 69th, also a purely Messianic Psalm: "Thy rebuke hath broken my heart, I am full of heaviness . . . neither found I any to comfort me." Again in Psalm lxxxviii.: "Lord, why abhorrest Thou my soul, and hidest Thou Thy face from me?" So that here is the cry of one cast down—deserted utterly by man and forsaken by God, in the only way in which God can possibly forsake the good, by hiding the light of His countenance from them for a brief season. We learn from this that depression of mind and spiritual desertion are no proofs of rejection by God; but rather, like bodily sufferings, form part of that resemblance to His Son, which render us on that account the more acceptable to our Heavenly Father. Bengel considers that the words really mean, "Why didst Thou forsake me?" the bitterness of the being forsaken, endured in darkness and silence, being then past and over.

Quesnel remarks: "How many things does this 'why' comprehend? It is a question which cannot be fully answered, but by explaining the fall of Adam, and of his posterity in him, the design of God's mercy in their recovery, the nature and rigour of His justice, the necessity of a Sacrifice worthy of God, and all the incomprehensible designs of His wisdom in the establishment of the Christian religion and in the work of eternal salvation."

35. "And some of them that stood by, when they heard it, said, Behold," &c. The word for Elias in the Syriac is Elēyo. If the Lord's words were pronounced as written in St. Matthew and were

36 And ⁷ one ran and filled a spunge full of vinegar, and put *it* on a reed, and ᶻ gave him to drink, saying, let alone; Let us see whether Elias will come to take him down.

⁷ Matt. xxvii. 48. John xix. 29.
ᶻ Ps. lxix. 21.

---

heard somewhat indistinctly, then we can account for their supposing that He called for Elias, or Elijah. If they were pronounced, as they are written in St. Mark, then the Lord must have laid great stress upon the first syllable, which is not unlikely.

Two explanations have been given of the mistake. First, that it was a wilful mistake, and so was the last of the insults heaped on the Lord. The second, that it was said seriously, but ignorantly. Men's minds were full of the coming of Elias about that time as the precursor of the Messiah, and the supernatural darkness made some think that Jesus was the Messiah, and was invoking the aid of His forerunner.

36. "And one ran and filled a spunge full of vinegar, and put it on a reed," &c. This followed on the Lord's saying, "I thirst," as we learn from St. John's Gospel. It was done out of humanity. The vinegar not being given because it was nauseous, but because very sour wine was the common drink of the Roman soldiers. It was done also in fulfilment of prophecy. One sign had yet to be fulfilled before He could expire. All had now been accomplished except the words of the Psalmist, "When I was thirsty they gave me vinegar to drink," and so the Lord, that this one prophecy which remained might be fulfilled, exclaimed, "I thirst." In order that it might reach His mouth it was put on a reed, or stalk of some plant of hyssop which was at hand.

Those who were standing by, apparently Jews, remembering the first word of his cry, said tauntingly, "Let alone; let us see whether Elias will come to take him down."

"And Jesus cried with a loud voice." By this loud cry of the Lord the moment before He expired we are taught that of His own accord, and by an act of His Own will, He surrendered His Life. The strength of His body, evinced by this "cry with a loud voice," showed that in the natural course of things (if it be right to use such an expression of Him) He would have retained His life for hours, perhaps for a day or more longer; for it was no uncommon thing for those crucified to live till the third day. So that now at this

## 398   JESUS GAVE UP THE GHOST.   [ST. MARK.

<sup>a</sup> Matt. xxvii. 50. Luke xxiii. 46. John xix. 30.

37 <sup>a</sup> And Jesus cried with a loud voice, and gave up the ghost.

---

moment His own words were fulfilled: "No man taketh My life from Me, but I lay it down of Myself; I have power to lay it down, and I have power to take it again" (John x. 18).

"Gave up the Ghost." By one word (for in the Greek "He gave up the ghost" is one word, ἐξέπνευσεν) the Evangelist records the greatest event which has taken place in the history of all worlds, the greatest in itself, for it was the Son of God, Who is the Life, submitting to that which is the negation and opposite of life, even to death. "Being in the form of God," and "equal with God," "He became obedient unto death, even the death of the cross." And also an event the greatest in its issues, for having made peace by the Blood shed on this cross, God has by Him Who hung upon it, reconciled all things to Himself, both things on earth and things in heaven, so that by this Death not only men but even the angelic spirits are brought nearer to God.

Astonishing truth, that the greatest putting forth of God's power is the Divine nature, in the Person of the Son, submitting to the extremity of weakness in death!

I know no words which better express the Evangelical meaning of this death, than some preached by Cyril, Bishop of Jerusalem, within a stone's throw of the place where the atoning Death took place. "These things the Saviour endured, making peace through the Blood of His Cross for things in heaven and things in earth. For we were enemies of God through sin, and God had appointed the sinner to die. There must needs, therefore, have happened one of two things: either that God, keeping His word, should destroy all men, or that in His loving-kindness, He should cancel the sentence. But behold the wisdom of God; He preserved both to His sentence its truth, and to His loving-kindness its exercise. Christ took our sins in His own body on the tree, that we being dead to sin, should live to righteousness. Of no small account was He Who died for us. He was not a literal sheep; He was not a mere man; He was more than an angel; He was God made man. The transgression of sinners was not so great as the righteousness of Him Who died for them. We have not committed so much sin as He hath wrought righteousness, Who laid down His Life for us."

38 And ᵇthe veil of the temple was rent in twain   ᵇ Matt. xxvii.
from the top to the bottom.                          51. Luke xxiii. 45.

And with respect to the pleading of His Death with a just and righteous God, I know no words fitter than those of the great Archbishop of Canterbury, St. Anselm, in a tract written for the use of priests in dealing with men on their death-beds. "See that, while life remains in thee, thou repose thy confidence only in the Death of Christ; trusting in nothing else; commit thyself wholly to this Death; cover thyself wholly with this alone. And if the Lord will judge thee, say, 'Lord, I cast the Death of my Lord Jesus Christ between me and Thy judgment: otherwise I will not engage in judgment with Thee.' And if He shall say to thee, that thou art a sinner, say, 'I place the Death of my Lord Jesus Christ between me and my sins.' If He shall say to thee that thou hast deserved damnation, say, 'I cast the Death of my Lord Jesus Christ between me and my evil deserts, and I offer His merits for that merit which I ought to have, and have not.' If He shall say that He is angry with thee, say, 'Lord, I cast the Death of the Lord Jesus Christ between me and Thy displeasure.'"

38. "And the veil of the temple was rent in twain," &c. This was the inner veil, the veil between the Holy Place and the Holy of Holies. It was of immense thickness, and hanging loosely from the top could not have been rent by the earthquake, but must have been torn asunder by angel hands. I have commented upon its most intimate connection with the surrender of the Lord's Life in my notes on St. Matthnw at such length, that I cannot do more than say that it was the most significant of signs, betokening that every obstacle between the soul, and the immediate presence and favour of God, was once and for ever removed by the Death of Christ.

But it has a sacramental significance, which we gather from the application made of it by the writer of the Epistle to the Hebrews (x. 19). "Having therefore, brethren, boldness to enter into the holiest by the blood of Jesus, by a new and living way, which He hath consecrated for us, through the veil, that is to say, his flesh; and having an high priest over the House of God, let us draw near with a true heart, in full assurance of faith," &c. Here the sacred writer teaches us that, perhaps thirty, perhaps forty years after the rending of the veil of the Lord's Flesh, there was a

39 ¶ And ᵉwhen the centurion, which stood over against him, saw that he so cried out, and gave up the

ᵉ Matt. xxvii. 54. Luke xxiii. 47.

39. "He so cried out, and gave up," &c. So A., C., later Uncials, almost all Cursives, Vulg., Syriac, Gothic, Æthiopic; but "cried out, and " omitted by ℵ, B., L., Coptic.

way of access to God through the veil, *i.e.*, through that Flesh. The way of access through the body of Christ was and is always open, and we must in all sincerity and in all confidence avail ourselves of it. Every time we sincerely and faithfully communicate in the Sacrament of His Body, we draw near to the very presence of God through the rent veil—the bruised and torn Flesh of the Son of God.

39. "And when the centurion, which stood over against him, saw that he so cried out," &c. There is a noticeable difference between the narratives of St. Matthew and St. Mark here. St. Matthew tells us that "When the centurion and they that were with him saw the earthquake and those things which were done, they said, Truly this was the Son of God;" but St. Mark, who only mentions the centurion as making the confession, tells us that he was mostly influenced by the manner in which the Lord voluntarily surrendered His Spirit,—"saw that He so cried out and gave up the ghost"—cried as if He yet retained bodily strength to keep Him alive much longer. There can be no doubt that the Death of the Lord was a supernatural act. What puts it beyond all doubt that He died not by the failing of nature is, that "He gave up the ghost, crying with a loud voice." A thing so extraordinary, as the Evangelist reports, that when the centurion who stood over against Him, and so was accurately observing all that took place, saw that He so cried out and gave up the ghost, he said, "Truly this man was the Son of God." So that Bourdaloue says eloquently and truly, "His death, if we consider it thoroughly, is itself the greatest of all miracles, inasmuch as, far from dying like other men, through loss of spirit, He dies, on the contrary, through an effort of His omnipotence." And this will not seem an exaggerated way of representing the matter, if we consider that the Lord Jesus being the Life, and having Life in Himself, for Him to submit to death was to submit to what was most opposite to His nature, whilst to rise again was to do that which was most natural to Him—most in accordance with His nature as the Life.

ghost, he said, Truly this man was the Son of God.

40 <sup>d</sup> There were also women looking on <sup>e</sup> afar off: among whom was Mary Magdalene, and Mary the mother of James the less and of Joses, and Salome;

<sup>d</sup> Matt. xxvii. 55. Luke xxiii. 49.
<sup>e</sup> Ps. xxxviii. 11.

"The Son of God" without definite article—" a Son of God."
40. "James the less." So called, perhaps, on account of his stature—"James the little."

"This man was the Son of God." Of course he could not have used these words in the sense of the Catholic creed. He had, however, heard that the chief priests had come to Pilate with the words, "We have a law, and by our law He ought to die, because He made Himself the Son of God." Remembering this, he considered that the signs and wonders which attended the Lord's Death, showed that the Lord was just and good, and that His persecutors were utterly unjust and wicked in condemning Him, and so in some very high way He was the Son of God, in the sense in which they had accused Him of making Himself. No doubt he said together, and as with one breath, "Certainly this was a righteous man—truly He was the Son of God."

40. "There were also women looking on afar off: among whom was Mary Magdalene," &c. The presence of these women, though afar off, seems to be particularly recorded, as in constrast with the absence of the disciples. They showed more love and regard for the Lord in His extreme agony, than those who were emphatically His own, His chosen. With respect to these names, one must observe first, that it is extremely unlikely, if not impossible, that the Mary named as Magdalene should be Mary, the sister of Lazarus. She would certainly have been called such, or the sister of Martha; and Mary, who the second time anointed the Lord's feet, and who is all but named as the sister of Lazarus and Martha (John xii. 23), is never identified with the Magdalen. The Magdalen is most probably not the woman mentioned in Luke vii. 37, though some of the fathers think so. Besides, these women had followed Him when He was in Galilee, and came up with Him to Jerusalem, which seems to exclude Mary of Bethany.

2. "Mary the mother of James the less and of Joses." Seeing that James and Joses (together with Judas and Simon) are mentioned in both Matthew and Mark as the nearest relatives of the

D D

41 (Who also, when he was in Galilee, ᶠfollowed him, and ministered unto him;) and many other women which came up with him unto Jerusalem.

42 ¶ ᵍAnd now when the even was come, because it was the preparation, that is, the day before the sabbath,

ᶠ Luke viii. 2, 3.
ᵍ Matt. xxvii. 57. Luke xxiii. 50. John xix. 38.

---

Lord who could properly be called His brethren, it seems certain that this Mary, who was their mother, must have been the sister, or some very near relative of the Blessed Virgin; but this we shall consider more fully in an excursus on the Lord's brethren.

3. "Salome." She is called in the parallel place in St. Matthew, "the mother of Zebedee's children." She has been supposed, on the ground of a peculiar reading of John xix. 25, to have been the sister of the Virgin.

It may be asked, Where was the Virgin herself? St John, in xix. 27, seems to imply that at the time that the Lord committed her to his care he took her to his own home, perhaps in a fainting state, or distracted, or otherwise totally unable to bear the scene of horror. The other women, or two of them, were with her and St. John when she was committed to his care, but very probably all were driven to a distance by the mob or by the soldiers.

41. "Who also, when he was in Galilee ... with him unto Jerusalem." Here we are told how the Lord had lived. He was sustained by the kindness and piety of his followers. So in St. Luke, viii. 2, we read of "certain women which had been healed of evil spirits and infirmities, Mary called Magdalene, out of whom went seven devils. And Joanna, the wife of Chuza, Herod's steward, and Susanna, and many others who ministered unto Him of their substance." These also, or some of them, would doubtless be amongst the many others who came up with Him. It has been remarked that no woman is to be found amongst the number of those who opposed or persecuted Christ.

42. "And now when the even was come, because it was the preparation, that is," &c. This Sabbath was one of very peculiar solemnity, being at once Sabbath and Passover. The preparation would be Friday afternoon before sunset, at which time the Sabbath would begin, and they would naturally hasten to take Him down before it began. The Jews also, for the same reason, lest the Sab-

43 Joseph of Arimathæa, an honourable counsellor, which also ʰ waited for the kingdom of God, came, and went in boldly unto Pilate, and craved the body of Jesus.  ʰ Luke ii. 25, 38.

44 And Pilate marvelled if he were already dead : and calling *unto him* the centurion, he asked him whether he had been any while dead.

---

43. "Which also waited for." Rather, as Revisers, "Who also himself was looking for."

44. "Had been any while dead." So ℵ, A., C., E., G., K., L., M., S., &c., and almost all Cursives; but B. and D. read, "If He were already dead."

bath should be polluted by the corpses hanging on the crosses on that day, were anxious that they should be despatched and taken down as soon as possible (John xix. 31).

43. "Joseph of Arimathæa, an honourable counsellor, which also waited for the kingdom." St. Matthew describes this man as Jesus' disciple. St. Mark calls him an honourable counsellor, St. Luke's addition to this, that he "had not consented to the counsel and deed of them," *i.e.*, of course, of the great majority, shows that he was in all probability a member of the Sanhedrim. St. Mark and St. Luke mention that "he waited for the kingdom of God." St. John that he was a disciple, but "secretly for fear of the Jews."

"Came, and went in boldly unto Pilate." This bold confession of his regard for the Crucified One, must be put by the side of St. John's word, "secretly." The Death of Christ seems to have made him ashamed of his former cowardice, and inspired him with courage to confess that he had the greatest regard for One Whom his fellow-rulers had treated with such cruelty and ignominy. When all the world had opposed the Lord, and thought that they had made an end of Him, when even His own had deserted Him, then this good man came forward to save His Dead Body from further dishonour. This, and the centurion's confession, were thus the first fruits of the Death of Christ.

44. "And Pilate marvelled if he were already dead," &c. This is peculiar to St. Mark. It is an additional confirmation of the fact that the Lord's Death had that in it which no other man's decease ever had.

"And calling unto him the centurion, he asked him," &c. The

45 And when he knew *it* of the centurion, he gave the body to Joseph.

46 [1] And he bought fine linen, and took him down, and wrapped him in the linen, and laid him in a sepulchre which was hewn out of a rock, and rolled a stone unto the door of the sepulchre.

[1] Matt. xxvii. 59, 60. Luke xxiii. 53. John xix. 40.

---

45. " **He gave** the body " (*soma*). So A., C., E., G., K., M., other later Uncials, almost all Cursives, Old Latin, Vulg., Coptic, &c. ; but ℵ, B., D., L. read, " the corpse " (*ptoma*).

centurion who had been so struck with the manner of the Lord's Death and the signs attending it, that he had made the confession that He was the Son of God, would have given Pilate an account of what had occurred very unlike that of an enemy. This, no doubt, would revive Pilate's awe of the Lord as One altogether different from any other prisoner he had ever had before him; and probably from a desire of making some reparation for his criminal weakness, he apparently gave the body very willingly to Joseph.

46. " And he bought fine linen, and took him down, and wrapped him in the linen," &c. St. John tells us that in this he was assisted by his fellow ruler Nicodemus, who brought a mixture of myrrh and aloes.

They " wrapped him in the linen, and laid him in a sepulchre," because the sabbath had already come. and the embalming was reserved till early on the first day.

" In a sepulchre which was hewn out of a rock," &c. All the three Synoptics particularly mention that the sepulchre was hewn out of a rock. So that the sepulchre having but one entrance, there would be no undermining it, no possibility of entering by chiselling through the sides to make a new entrance, and so by no human means could the body emerge except through the door, which was, as we know from St. Matthew, both sealed and closely guarded. Such was the Burial of the Lord. The reader will remember the words of the hymn for Easter Eve :

> " Let me hew Thee, Lord, a shrine,
> In this rocky heart of mine,
> Where in pure embalmèd cell
> None but Thou may ever dwell.

47 And Mary Magdalene and Mary *the mother* of Joses beheld where he was laid.

---

> Myrrh and spices will I bring,
>    True affection's offering:
> Close the door from sight and sound
>    Of the busy world around,
> And in patient watch remain
>    Till my Lord appears again."

**47.** " And Mary Magdalene and Mary the mother of Joses," &c. In St. Matthew she is called "the other Mary;" as one of those standing by the Cross she is called " Mary the mother of James the less and of Joses." This is important. It identifies her as beyond all doubt the real mother of those who in chap. vi. 3 are called the brethren of the Lord. She must then have been in the closest relationship with the Virgin, who very probably was too weak and prostrate to move, and had sent this Mary to represent her. " Seest thou," says Chrysostom, "women's courage? seest thou their affection? seest thou their noble spirit in (bestowing) money? their noble spirit even unto death. Let us men imitate these women; let us not forsake Jesus in temptations. For they for Him even when dead spent so much and exposed their lives, but we neither feed Him when hungry, nor clothe Him when naked, but seeing Him in want [in His poor members] we pass Him by."

## CHAP. XVI.

AND <sup>a</sup> when the sabbath was past, Mary Magdalene, and Mary the *mother* of James, 

<sup>a</sup> Matt. xxviii. 1. Luke xxiv. 1. John xx. 1.

---

**1.** " And when the sabbath was past, Mary Magdalene, and Mary the mother of James," &c. They purchased these on Saturday night, the Sabbath ending at six o'clock.

and Salome, [b] had bought sweet spices, that they might come and anoint him.

[b] Luke xxiii. 56.

[c] Luke xxiv. 1. John xx. 1.

2 [c] And very early in the morning the first *day* of the week, they came unto the sepulchre at the rising of the sun.

3 And they said among themselves, Who shall roll us away the stone from the door of the sepulchre?

---

2. "At the rising of the sun." Revisers, "When the sun was risen." Vulg., *Orto jam sole*.

"That they might come and anoint him." They did this to ward off corruption for as long a time as possible from the body of Him Whom they loved. They had, seemingly, no idea of His Resurrection. The thought never crossed their minds that in Him was fulfilled the words of the Psalmist, "Thou wilt not suffer Thy Holy One to see corruption."

2. "And very early in the morning the first day of the week," &c. When they set off it was yet dark (John xx, 1), but it began to dawn (Matth. xxviii. 1), and when they neared the sepulchre the sun was rising and they could see all things clearly. Mary Magdalene, and Mary the mother of James and Salome are mentioned; but were there not others? St. Luke seems to imply that there were, for he speaks of the women also who came with Him from Galilee (xxiii. 55), that they came very early in the morning "and certain others with them:" but this latter reading is doubtful.

It is conjectured, not without some show of probability, that there were two companies of women: the first that mentioned by St. Mark, who had purchased their spices the night before, *i.e.*, on Saturday evening after six o'clock, when the Sabbath was past; and another consisting, among others, of Joanna and the women who came up with him from Galilee, who had prepared the spices and ointments before the Sabbath, *i.e.*, on Friday evening (Luke xxiii. 55, 56; xxiv. 10).

3. "And they said among themselves, Who shall roll us away the stone from the door," &c. It is impossible to say whether the Lord arose and the angel descended and the earth shook before this, or whilst they were on their way. I should think before. The appearance of the angel, his countenance as lightning, his raiment

4 And when they looked, they saw that the stone was rolled away: for it was very great.

5 <sup>d</sup> And entering into the sepulchre, they saw a    <sup>d</sup> Luke xxiv. 3. John xx. 11, 12.

---

4. "Was rolled away." So A., C., later Uncials, all Cursives, &c. ; but א, B., L. read, "rolled back."

glistering, seems more in accordance with a bright vision in the obscurity of the earliest hours.

St. Mark says nothing of the things which St. Matthew relates about the earthquake, and the appearance of the angel to the soldiers, and his sitting on the stone when, apparently, the women came up, and yet St. Mark must have learnt what he relates from one of the party, no doubt through St. Peter; for he mentions how before they reached the tomb, they said among themselves "Who shall roll us away the stone?" The relation of such a circumstance is eminently characteristic of the manner of St. Mark in noticing little incidents.

4. "And when they looked, they saw that the stone was rolled away; for it was very great." This also must have been received from one of the group. As Lange says, "These are all accurate statements which are characteristic of St. Mark's clear view of things. The stone was lying in the hollow cut deep into the rock, so as to form the door, and must accordingly be rolled forth from this recess outwards; hence 'rolled away.' The rock tomb, however, itself lay upon a height (a very slight elevation) ; hence the women saw the stone when they looked *up;* and because the stone was very great they could, even from a great distance, see it lying." Williams, however, supposes that they saw that the stone was rolled away, not from seeing the stone, but the wide-open aperture which would form the entrance.

At this moment it was that Mary Magdalene seeing the sepulchre open, hastens back at once to the Apostles, Peter and John, with the words, "They have taken away the Lord out of the sepulchre, and we know not where they have laid Him."

5. "And entering into the sepulchre, they saw a young man sitting on the right side," &c. St. Matthew seems to say that the angel was sitting on the stone which was rolled to the outside. From St. Mark, on the contrary, we seem to learn that they saw the angel as they entered into the hollow chamber of the tomb sit-

young man sitting on the right side, clothed in a long white garment; and they were affrighted.

<sup>e</sup> Matt. xxviii. 5, 6, 7.

6 <sup>e</sup> And he saith unto them, Be not affrighted: Ye seek Jesus of Nazareth, which was crucified:

---

ting there; but there need be no discrepancy whatsoever, for St. Matthew speaks of the angel immediately on his having descended, and of his position as he appeard to the keepers, from which place when the women came up he may have moved, and gone further in: St. Matthew not telling us that he was sitting on the stone when he appeared to the women, but merely recording what he said to them wherever he was. St. Mark's account is, however, quite consistent with the fact that he was sitting on the stone on one side of the doorway, for he speaks of their seeing the angel as they were entering in, not before; the angel not being permanently visible, but showing himself to them according as he had had instructions as to what he should do. One thing, however, is clear, that whatever slight discrepancy there may be, we are not to imagine two appearances of angels recorded, one by St. Matthew, another by St. Mark, as it is clear from their delivering, almost verbatim, the same message, that they were one and the same.

"They were affrighted." The last thing which they expected was to see either the Lord Himself or any supernatural messenger from Him about His tomb. They came to embalm the Body—to wind it in linen clothes as the manner of the Jews was to bury; believing that the rock-hewn sepulchre would hold it till the day of judgment.

6. "And he saith unto them, Be not affrighted: Ye seek Jesus of Nazareth, which was," &c. God accepted their love to His Son as crucified in lieu of their faith in Him as risen. These words are capable of the widest Evangelical application. If we seek Jesus Who was crucified, nothing in the visible or in the invisible world—nothing in heaven, or earth, or hell, can harm us.

"He is risen; he is not here." Such is the announcement of the Gospel of the Resurrection, such are the few plain, simple words which teach mankind that death is swallowed up in victory.

"He is risen." All the gospel of the grace of God is contained in these words, "He is risen."

"He is risen." Therefore He is the Only-begotten Son of God,

he is risen; he is not here: behold the place where they laid him.

7 But go your way, tell his disciples and Peter that he goeth before you into Galilee: there shall ye see him, ᶠ as he said unto you.

ᶠ Matt. xxvi. 32. ch. xiv. 28.

for God would not have raised One from the Dead Who claimed to be His Son when He was not.

"He is risen." Therefore His Death was a full and perfect atonement for our sins, for He died not for His own sins, but for ours; and God would not have raised Him from the dead if He had not done them away by His Sacrifice.

"He is risen." Therefore we can now partake of His Life—of His risen Life. He is risen as the Second Adam. By His Resurrection Life, imparted to us in baptism, we can now walk in newness of life. By His Resurrection He is able to feed us with the Living Bread, even His Flesh.

"He is risen." And so we shall rise again, according to His own words, "I am the Resurrection and the Life." "Because I live ye shall live also."

"Behold the place where they laid him." This is very properly said to those women who according to the last verse of the last chapter, "beheld where he was laid."

They had had the love and the courage to witness His burial, and were rewarded with the sight of the Empty Sepulchre shown to them by an angel of God to assure them of His Resurrection.

7. "But go your way, tell his disciples and Peter," &c. No doubt the Divine message is sent to Peter for his reassurance. He had fallen deeply and had wept bitterly, and lest he should despair his name is expressly mentioned as having a part in the Lord's favour.

"That he goeth before you into Galilee." The reason why the Lord by His angel, and afterwards Himself personally, reminds them so particularly that He went before them into Galilee, and that there they were to meet Him, has not been clearly revealed. The difficulty is, that on the evening of that very day He intended to meet them before they could possibly set out to meet Him in Galilee, and would there give them the power of remitting and retaining sins. The reason must be something intimately connected

8 And they went out quickly, and fled from the sepulchre;

8. "Quickly" omitted by ℵ, A., B., C., D., most later Uncials, a very large number of Cursives, Old Latin, &c.

with His former work in Galilee, but the words seem to express that they were to set out at once, which, apparently with His own sanction, they did not do, but lingered in Jerusalem eight days. The appearance in Galilee, or one of them, if it is that alluded to by St. Paul as the one in which He was seen by above five hundred brethren at once (1 Cor. xv. 6), was, in one sense, the most important of all, as it was the only great public appearance.

8. "And they went out quickly, and fled from the sepulchre; for they trembled," &c. St. Matthew tells us that they departed quickly from the sepulchre, "with fear and great joy." St. Mark, without denying the undercurrent of joy, lays most stress upon the fear. The words, literally translated, would be, "Trembling and ecstasy took possession of them." The trembling, or agitation, would naturally arise from the visible presence of a denizen of the unseen world.

"Neither said they any thing to any man; for they were afraid." That is, they said not a word to anyone by the way, but ran off as quickly as possible to carry the message to the disciples.

Whilst they were making their way to the body of the disciples, Peter and John, having heard from Mary Magdalene that the sepulchre was empty, ran thither, and shortly after this the Lord Himself appeared to these women, or to some of them, as narrated in Matth. xxviii. 9. It is wrong to say that St. Mark takes no notice of this, for his mode of narration undergoes a marked change at this point.

This change of the mode of narration, I shall now proceed to examine. The reader will have noticed two things: 1st, That up to this point, *i.e.*, up to the end of the eighth verse, St. Mark follows the course of events as given by St. Matthew. He does not follow it minutely, for he omits several things which St. Matthew notices, particularly the appearance of the angel to the keepers; and he adds several of those minutiæ which are characteristic of him, as, for instance, the anxiety of the women about the removal of the stone—their looking and seeing that the stone was removed—the appearance of the angel as that of a young man—the place where he sat, *i.e.*, on the right side—the length of his garment—their first seeing him as they entered in—their fright at seeing him,—all these cir-

## CHAP. XVI.] THEY TREMBLED AND WERE AMAZED. 411

for they trembled and were amazed: <sup>f</sup> neither said they any thing to any *man*; for they were afraid.

9 ¶ Now when *Jesus* was risen early the first

<small>f See Matt. xxviii. 8. Luke xxiv. 9.</small>

---

cumstantials are peculiar to St. Mark, and the noticing of such things forms the characteristic of his Gospel, as we have abundantly shown. It is on this account (combined with the direct testimony of early Church history) that his Gospel is allowed to be mainly that of St. Peter. But now his narrative and that of St. Matthew diverge altogether: and this is the more noticeable because St. Mark, along with St. Matthew, mentions the message of the angel to the disciples, that the Lord would go before them into Galilee. St. Mark, in company with St. Matthew, alone had recorded the Lord's promise on the way to Gethsemane that He would thus go before them. In company with St. Matthew alone, he tells us that the angel reiterated this promise. One might say, then, that, in the ordinary course of circumstances, he was bound to follow St. Matthew's narrative on this matter, and give us his own version of the Lord's appearance in Galilee as narrated in Matth. xxviii. 16-18. But he does not, and at this point his mode of narrating events undergoes a marked change. Instead of being minutely circumstantial, his narrative becomes epitomizing. It is more like a résumé, or a few recollections somewhat hastily put together.

Learned men have put forth several ways of accounting for this change. One is that at, or after, the writing of the eighth verse, St. Mark's source of information for some reason suddenly failed him, and for the finishing of his narrative he had to fall back upon his own resources. In other words, as he was writing this last chapter of his Gospel, he was deprived of the companionship of St. Peter, or for some reason had omitted to take down what he had heard from St. Peter, and so had hastily to finish his Gospel from what he had learnt from other sources.

Another conjecture is that the last leaf of the Gospel containing these twelve verses was accidentally lost or destroyed; and so the Gospel was finished by some person or persons unknown. I trust to show the impossibility of accounting for the difficulty in any such a way.

I shall again take up the subject of the authorship of these last twelve verses in an excursus at the end of this volume.

9. "Now when Jesus was risen early the first day of the week,

## FIRST TO MARY MAGDALENE. [St. Mark.

day of the week, ʰ he appeared first to Mary Magdalene, ⁱ out of whom he had cast seven devils.

10 ᵏ And she went and told them that had been with him, as they mourned and wept.

11 ˡ And they, when they had heard that he was alive, and had been seen of her, believed not.

ʰ John xx. 14.
ⁱ Luke viii. 2.
ᵏ Luke xxiv. 10. John xx. 18.
ˡ Luke xxiv. 11.

---

he appeared," &c.[1] This is a very short notice indeed of that which is given in full in John xx. 14-18. As we have it reported in St. John's Gospel, it is one of the most interesting accounts in the New Testament; as we find it recorded here it is the merest reference. St. Luke, who gives the account of the visit of other women to the sepulchre, among whom apparently was Mary Magdalene, omits all notice of the separate appearance to her, but agrees with St. Mark in this, that when the news of the Resurrection was told to the Apostles they received it as "idle tales." It is, consequently, impossible to suppose that the writer of these three verses followed the account in St. Luke, even if he knew of its existence.

10. "And she went and told them that had been with him, as they mourned and wept." St. John, in his account of the Magdalen telling what she had seen to the Apostles, says nothing of their "mourning and weeping," and nothing of their unbelief. St. Luke also says nothing of the mourning and weeping.

11. "And they, when they had heard that he was alive, and had been seen of her, believed not." Now, in looking over these three short verses (9, 10, 11), we must ask ourselves the question "for what purpose were they written?" The answer, of course, would seem to be to tell the Church that the Lord's first appearance was to Mary Magdalene alone, and so, perhaps, to correct the impression that might have been received from St. Matthew's account, that He appeared first to several women.

But is it not clear that there is another purpose equally important, viz., that the report of the person who first saw Him was rejected by those to whom she told it, that is, by the Apostles?

---

[1] For the supposed discrepancy between St. Matthew and St. Mark respecting the time of the Lord's Resurrection see note in St. Matthew.

12 ¶ After that he appeared in another form ᵐ unto two of them, as they walked, and went into the country. <small>ᵐ Luke xxiv. 13.</small>

13 And they went and told *it* unto the residue: neither believed they them.

---

This certainly seems to be *the* purpose for which the Magdalene and her testimony is brought in; not simply to emphasize the fact that He first appeared to this woman, but that when she told the fact of His Resurrection to those who ought to have been expecting it, they believed her not.

12. "After that he appeared in another form unto two of them, as they walked," &c. There cannot be the least doubt but that this is the same appearance as that to the two disciples (one of whom was named Cleopas) on the way to Emmaus.

"In another form," that is, of course, a form or appearance in which He was not recognized by them at the first. He was recognized by the Magdalen as soon as He called to her by name: but not so with the two. He walked some time and conversed with them, and not till the moment when He vanished did they know Him. He must, consequently, have presented to them an appearance different from that in which He was usually known.

13. "And they went and told it unto the residue: neither believed they them." There is a real, though not absolutely irreconcilable discrepancy between this and St. Luke's account. For, from the latter account, we gather that, when the two joined the company of the disciples, "and of them that were with them," they were met with the exclamation: "The Lord is risen indeed, and hath appeared unto Simon." A very great number of devices for reconciling the two accounts have been proposed, as that the meetings of the disciples were different, or that the two to whom the Lord had appeared were not the same couple in the two Evangelists: or that they were in a state of bewilderment, and so fluctuating between a state of belief and unbelief. But is it not most likely that while some believed, the rest, perhaps the majority, withheld their hearty assent, and the person from whom the author of these verses received the account was more struck with the unbelief manifested by the larger number than with the assent of the few? We must remember that the Apostles present would be ten in number, and there were others expressly mentioned as present (Luke

## 414 HE APPEARED UNTO THE ELEVEN. [St. Mark.

14 ¶ ⁿ Afterward he appeared unto the eleven as they sat at meat, and upbraided them with their unbelief and hardness of heart, because they believed not them which had seen him after he was risen.

n Luke xxiv. 36. John xx. 19. 1 Cor. xv. 5.
| Or, *together*.

---

xxiv. 38), so that it is not improbable that eighteen or twenty persons were present. Among these there would certainly be many degrees, or shades, of assent, or dissent, as, for instance, at the Lord's last appearance, as recorded in St. Matthew, it is significantly said: "They worshipped Him, but some doubted."

Now again I ask (as I did with reference to the notice of the appearance to the Magdalen) why is this appearance to the two, and their report of it to the rest, inserted in this very brief account of the Lord's manifestations? Nothing whatsoever is said respecting the conversation with the two on the way, nor of their "constraining" Him to stop with them, and of His being known in the breaking of bread. The notice in St. Mark is evidently inserted for one purpose, and for one only—to show that the Apostles and those with them rejected the second account of the Lord's appearances, which was told them by two eye-witnesses.

14. "Afterwards he appeared unto the eleven as they sat at meat," &c. This appears to be, in fact must be, a notice of the meeting recorded in John xx. 19, and Luke xxiv. 36, but in St. John's account nothing whatsoever is said of their sitting together at meat: and from St. Luke's account we should gather that if they had had a meal together it had been finished, for He asked, "Have ye here any meat? And they gave him a piece of a broiled fish, and of an honeycomb." He could scarcely have asked them if they had any meat if they had been sitting together eating a meal. There is also another noteworthy difference between St. Luke's account and this notice. In St. Luke's narrative the Lord very gently reproaches them with their terror and fright, as supposing that He was a spirit, and proves to them by his allowing them to feel Him and by His eating before them, that He was not a mere disembodied spirit; but in St. Mark's notice He upbraids them, or reproaches them with their unbelief in the testimony of others who had seen Him. So that the one purpose for which this most important appearance is recorded in this Gospel

15 ° And he said unto them, Go ye into all the world, ᵖ and preach the gospel to every creature.

° Matt. xxviii. 19. John xv. 16.
ᵖ Col. i. 23.

is to bring out more strongly the unbelief of the Apostles. So that, strange as it may appear, it is most certainly true that the three recorded instances of the Lord's appearance, as given here, are given to prove not the reality of the Lord's resurrection (that of course is involved in all), but the slowness of the Apostles to receive it.

15. "And he said unto them, Go ye into all the world, and preach the Gospel," &c. Two questions suggest themselves respecting this commission, which though they cannot be answered should both be stated. Are they sayings which were spoken on several occasions and are here placed together, just as three appearances of the Lord occurring apart from one another have been placed together, each one illustrating the slowness of belief on the part of the Apostles ? Or are these words a parting commission delivered as a whole to the Apostles just before the Ascension ? If so, their chronological place in the narrative would be after Luke xxiv., verse 50, and between Acts i. and verses 8 and 9. This is quite possible, and the mention of the Ascension, in verse 19, as apparently coming immediately after, is in favour of their being such a final word. In this case they would be the one teaching of this chapter for which we are indebted to St. Mark alone. The Lord appears to have several times repeated His commission in different words. At His first appearance to the assembled Apostles He delivered to them a very full commission which seems to comprehend all: "As My Father sent Me, so send I you. Receive ye the Holy Ghost. Whose soever sins ye remit, they are remitted unto them." Then, after this, Peter was reinstated in the words, "Feed my lambs." Feed, or pasture, My sheep. Then there was the commission on the mountain in Galilee, which seems final, though it could not have been the Lord's last charge.

Of these verses the 15th and 16th seem part of a final charge, and verses 17th and 18th not. We can scarcely think that the Lord's very last words were contained in these verses, so that, upon the whole, I incline to think that the two pairs of verses were spoken at different times.

"Go ye into all the world, and preach the gospel to every creature." "To all the world," *i.e.*, penetrate into every country where

16 ⁹ He that believeth and is baptized shall be

*q* John iii. 18, 36. Acts ii. 38, & xvi. 30, 31, 32. Rom. x. 9. 1 Pet. iii. 21.

---

men dwell, no matter what the distance, climate, or dangers of the way.

"Preach the gospel to every creature." No matter how ignorant the races to which ye come, no matter how superstitious, how besotted, how low in the scale of civilization, or how hardened and demonized by the vices of cruelty and unnatural lust, preach to all that I have died for them all, and that they can be saved.

"Preach the gospel." What is the gospel? It is the message of the Incarnation, Life, Death, Resurrection, and Ascension of the Son of Man, and of His coming again to raise the dead and to judge all men. This is the gospel (Rom. i. 2, 3, 4; 1 Cor. xv. 1, 10), all other things which men preach, such as God's willingness to accept the vilest, His saving them by grace through faith, His fully and freely pardoning, His loving His own to the end,—all are deductions from this gospel of the Death and Resurrection of the Eternal Son.

"He that believeth and is baptized shall be saved." He that believeth with the heart, he that receiveth into his spirit the truths of the Lord Incarnate, Crucified, Risen, and Ascended; he that embraceth these great things of God, because he feels that they answer to his needs, and reconcile all within him to God.

"And is baptized." He that seeks admission into the mystical Body which Christ came upon earth to found, or having been admitted into it seeks continuance in it, and strives to abide in Him as a living member of His Church.

"Shall be saved"—now and hereafter. He shall be saved now from the power of sin and from this present evil world, and hereafter at the Great Day, he shall stand before the Son of Man.

By joining, "believing," and "being baptized," as both necessary to salvation, did the Lord mean to put on an equality the highest action of the soul in embracing the truth of God and of Christ, and the reception of an outward rite? Certainly not. For He did not consider that the Baptism which He ordained was an outward rite. It is, according to His own words, a new birth of Water and of the Spirit into His Kingdom. According to the teaching of His great servant, it is a death and burial with Him to

saved; ʳbut he that believeth not shall be  ʳ John xii. 48.
damned.

sin, and a rising again with Him to newness of life (Rom. vi. 1-4), so that the baptized man must, no matter what the difficulty, count himself to be in a new state, born anew into the Second Adam, grafted into the True Vine, endued with a new life from Christ, and gifted, if he will faithfully strive to use them, with new powers against sin and on the side of holiness of life.

It was the Lord's intention by His Death and Resurrection, not only to deliver men from sin as individuals, but to incorporate them into His mystical Body, *i.e.*, His Holy Catholic Church, so that in the unity of that Church, in the unity of its faith, its hope, its charity, they might grow up, not singly, but together, in the fellowship of the One Body. And so the reception of His baptism being the outward sign of this, and the means for bringing it to each one, was worthy to be put side by side with believing.

"He that believeth not shall be damned." This ought rather to be translated "condemned." We have no right to say that God can inflict no condemnation or punishment short of the extremest final one.

Why is there no mention of baptism in the second clause? Simply because a man, no matter how validly baptized, will not be saved unless he heartily believes, and continues to believe in, the gospel.

These words have been held to be harsh; and so it has actually been made a matter of exultation, even by some in the Church of England, that, owing to the assumed doubtfulness of the whole passage, the terrible alternative contained in them is uncertain; but are not these words the exact reproduction of many universally acknowledged sayings of Christ? Such as "He that believeth not is condemned already, because he hath not believed in the name of the only begotten Son of God." "If ye believe not that I am He, ye shall die in your sins." "No man cometh unto the Father but by Me." God, we firmly believe, will make all allowances for the effects of evil education, bad example, the distortion of the truth by superstition on the one side, and by human logic perversely applied on the other, the want of unity in the Church, and the worldliness and shortcomings of the preachers of the truth—God, we may be sure, will take all this and every other

E E

17 And these signs shall follow them that believe; *In my name shall they cast out devils; ᵗ they shall speak with new tongues;

18 ᵘ They shall take up serpents; and if they drink any deadly thing, it shall not hurt them;

* Luke x. 17. Acts v. 16. & viii. 7. & xvi. 18. & xix. 12.
ᵗ Acts ii. 4, & x. 46. & xix. 6. 1 Cor. xii. 10, 28.
ᵘ Luke x. 19. Acts xxviii. 5.

---

17. "New tongues." "New" omitted by C., L., Δ., Coptic, Armenian; retained by A., Vulg.

mitigating circumstance into account, but if we are faithful to Christ, we must hold to His words, "He that believeth and is baptized, shall be saved, but he that believeth not shall be condemned."

17. "And these signs shall follow them that believe; In my name shall they cast out devils." The mention of this sign as the first is in accordance with all St. Mark's Gospel, in which the expulsion of demons occupies a more prominent place than in any other of the Gospels.

"They shall speak with new tongues." New tongues, *i.e.* tongues new to them, which they had not learnt before. It has been remarked that this is the only prophecy in all the gospel narrative of the great Pentecostal sign.

18. "They shall take up serpents." The only instance of this in the New Testament is in Acts xxviii. 3, 5, when St. Paul shook off the viper which had fastened on his hand, having received no hurt from its fangs.

"And if they drink any deadly thing, it shall not hurt them." The reader will remember the apocryphal (but it may be true) account of St. John having drunk a cup of poison and received no hurt. Eusebius gives another instance in his Eccles. Hist., book iii. ch. 39 (taken from Papias): "Another wonderful event happened respecting Justus, surnamed Barsabas, who though he drank a deadly poison experienced nothing injurious, through the grace of the Lord."

"They shall lay hands on the sick, and they shall recover." The gifts of healing together with "tongues," are mentioned amongst the manifestations of the Spirit, in 1 Cor. xii. 9, 10.

These signs were to "follow them that believe," and there is no limitation to the first ages of the Church, from which some have

they shall lay hands on the sick, and they shall recover.

<sup>x</sup> Acts v. 15, 16, & ix. 17. & xxviii. 8. James v. 14, 15.

understood that if there was a like faith now, there would be like signs. But if these signs were to be the attendants on faith to the end, then God's providential dealings would have been entirely different from what they have been for the last 1800 years. The power of healing each and every disease by miracle would have left little or no room for the thousand forms which Christian benevolence has assumed, in healing, tending, nursing the sick, and alleviating the poverty which follows so closely and almost universally on long-continued disease. Thus St. Gregory: "Are we then without faith because we cannot do these things? Nay, but these things were necessary in the beginning of the Church, for the faith of believers was to be nourished by miracles, that it might increase. Thus we also when we plant groves pour water upon them, until we see that they have grown strong in the earth, but when once they have firmly fixed their roots, we leave off irrigating them."

Again, though these signs, as miraculous or supernatural attestations of the faith, seem to have been suspended (for a time at least), yet they may be said to have been transfigured and to survive in another shape. In Christ's name, *i.e.*, by the influence of His gospel, the demons of avarice, and pride, and hatred, and vindictiveness, have been cast out of those who were once held in bondage by these evil spirits. Again, the "speaking with new tongues," was for the purpose of commending Christianity to all, and now one of the most wonderful signs of the times is the multiplicity of languages into which the Bible, and not only the Bible, but the Prayer-Book, has been translated.

Again, those who are Christ's in deed and in truth can work freely amongst the most deadly forms of evil, and be unpolluted and unharmed. Their hearts being purified by faith, in them is fulfilled the truth of the Apostolic saying, "To the pure all things are pure." And though believers cannot now lay hands on the sick for their recovery, yet in nothing has the spirit of Christianity been more apparent than in the treatment of the sick. The latest discoveries of medical science are in our great hospitals and infirmaries, immediately on their discovery, applied to the benefit of the poorest and meanest who have been taken to these places.

19 ¶ So then ʸafter the Lord had spoken unto them, he was ᶻreceived up into heaven, and ᵃsat on the right hand of God.

20 And they went forth, and preached every where, the Lord working with *them*, ᵇand confirming the word with signs following. Amen.

y Acts i. 2, 3.
z Luke xxiv. 51.
a Ps. cx. 1. Acts vii. 55.
b Acts v. 12. & xiv. 3. 1 Cor. ii. 4, 5. Heb. ii. 4.

19. "After the Lord." So A., E., G., M., Vulg. (Cod. Amiat.), &c.; but C., K., L., Δ, a few Cursives and versions read, "The Lord Jesus."

"Amen" omitted by A., but read by C. E., F. G., K., L., M., and almost all Cursives.

19. "So then after the Lord had spoken unto them . . . . signs following." The reader will see that these two verses are not an account of the Ascension, but merely a notice of it. Nothing can be more brief and succinct than "He was received up into heaven, and sat on the right hand of God." We shall reserve, then, to future occasions, remarks on the Ascension of the Lord.

20. "And they went forth, and preached every where." This must have been appended after the final dispersion of the Apostles.

"The Lord working with them." This corresponds with the promise, "Lo I am with you alway."

"And confirming the word with signs following." The reader will remember how St. Peter when he healed Æneas said unto him, "Æneas, Jesus Christ maketh thee whole;" and how St. Paul speaks of the power of Christ resting upon him.

"The Lord working with them." This is the secret of all success in the Christian religion, the power of an ever-present Christ. Theophylact ends his exposition, and we will adopt it as ours, with this prayer: "Grant then, O Christ, that the good words which we speak may be confirmed by works and deeds, so that at the last, Thou working with us in word and in deed, we may be perfect; for Thine, as is fitting, is the glory both of work and deed. Amen."

## EXCURSUS I.

### ON DEMONIACAL POSSESSION.

Many persons who accept in good faith the Gospel Narrative as containing a true account of the Life and Miracles of our Blessed Lord have a certain difficulty in receiving the statements which we find in the Gospels of men being possessed by devils or evil spirits, and of our Lord casting them out by His word. Such persons suggest that our Lord in these cases accommodated Himself to the ignorance, or even to the superstition, of the times; or that the prejudices of the Evangelists coloured their reports, and so they have represented the Lord as acting in accordance with the general opinion respecting certain cases of madness or lunacy, whereas, if we had an exact account of His proceedings, we should have seen that He avoided so committing Himself.

Now inasmuch as in the Gospel according to St. Mark, the casting out of evil spirits is much more prominent than in the other gospels, it may be well to devote a little space to the consideration of it.

The whole analogy of the natural world would lead us to believe that, as there is a descending scale of animated beings below man, reaching down to the lowest forms of life, so there may be an ascending scale above man, between him and God.

They who believe in any Being worthy of being called the Supreme Intelligence must acknowledge that such an idea is a reasonable one. Otherwise they would commit themselves to the astounding notion that there are, in all this wide universe, no beings between man—weak, short-lived, finite man—and the Infinite God: in fact, that the human intelligence is the highest in existence.

Now the Scriptures support the inference which we draw from the analogy of the natural world, and teach us that, just as in this visible state of things there are gradations of beings between ourselves and the lowest forms of life, so in the spiritual, to which we through our own spirits in part belong, there are gradations of beings between us and the God Who made all things.

The Scriptures would lead us to believe that these beings are intelligent free agents, and, like ourselves, have had their time of probation; that some fell under this trial, and are now the enemies of God, as wicked men are, though, of course, hating Him more intensely; and that others stood firm in the time of trial, and are His willing servants.

The Scriptures reveal that good angels act as good men do— they endeavour to confirm others in goodness, and to succour them in distress; and that evil spirits act as evil men do—they endeavour to seduce others, and involve them in their own condemnation.

The Scripture writers say nothing to satisfy our mere curiosity respecting this great spiritual universe. They simply describe the good denizens of it as sent on errands of mercy from God, and the evil as also acting under a leader against God. The mystery of the fall of some of these angels, and their consequent opposition to God, is analogous to what takes place amongst ourselves—some men falling from, and others abiding in, virtue and goodness. It has no special difficulty in itself, but is simply the oldest form of that which is, to those who believe in the reality of the goodness and holiness of God, the great problem of the universe, the origin and continuance of evil.

It is the counterpart in a world of free agents above us of what takes place amongst ourselves.

That evil angels can tempt the spirits of men, and in some cases injure their bodies and animal souls, is not a whit more difficult than that evil men can do the same under the government of a God who exerts so universal a providence as is described in the Bible.

I cannot understand the difficulty which some Christian writers evidently feel respecting the existence of such a thing as demoniacal *possession*, whilst they seem to feel, or at least they express, no difficulty respecting demoniacal *temptation*. Demoniacal possession is the infliction of a physical evil (at least, not a moral one), for which the person possessed is not accountable; but demoniacal *temptation* is an attempt to deprive a man of that for the keeping of which he is accountable—his own belief or his own innocence. Demoniacal possession, as represented in Scripture, is a temporal evil, whilst the yielding to demoniacal temptation may cast a man out of the favour of God for ever. And yet demoniacal temptation is perfectly analogous to human temptation. A human seducer has it in his power, if his suggestions are received, to corrupt innocence, render life miserable, undermine faith in God and in Christ, and

## DEMONIACAL POSSESSION. 423

destroy the hopes of eternity; and a diabolical seducer can do no more.

Again, the Scriptures seem to teach us that these wicked spirits are the authors of certain temporal evils; and I do not see that there is anything unreasonable in this, if it be granted that there are spirits which exist independent of bodies, or at least of such bodies as we have; that these spirits are free agents, and have different characters, and act according to their characters; and also that within the limitations, and according to the laws of their nature, they have power to act upon those below them in the scale of being, just as we can act upon the creatures below us, within the limitations, and according to the laws of our nature. We are, in our way, able to inflict evil, or to ward off evil from our fellow creatures, under the limitations which a Higher Power has set over us; and the Scriptures teach us that there are other beings in the great spiritual kingdom of God who are able to do us good or mischief, under the conditions which the same Supreme Power has imposed on their action. So that the one thing which the Scriptures reveal to us is that there is a far vaster spiritual kingdom of God than the human race.

With respect to demoniacal possession our difficulties arise from two things—from our ignorance of the nature and real causes of mental diseases, and from our ignorance of the way in which incorporeal intelligences can act upon beings such as ourselves, inasmuch as we ordinarily receive impressions only through our bodily organs. We know not, for instance, how God Himself acts upon our spirits; and yet, if He cannot, He has less power over us than we have over one another.

But there is another difficulty respecting demoniacal possession which requires notice. It is assumed that it is altogether a thing of the past—that no such cases exist at the present time; and from this sceptical minds infer that the malady has disappeared before the advance of accurate scientific knowledge.

But this is said in utter disregard of facts. There are now in this nineteenth century numbers of instances of persons afflicted exactly in the same way as those with whom our Lord is recorded in the Gospels to have come in contact. They may not have lost the use of their reason—on the contrary, at times their mental faculties seem perfectly unimpaired—but they have all the appearance of being at other times under the influence of another personality, who has so taken possession of the place of command within them that he thinks, speaks, and acts through them—through their organs.

I have memoranda of a number of such instances. I will give two or three.

(A.) A father, mother, and daughter—very ordinary persons, not in the least degree excitable or superstitious, and absolutely disbelieving in spirit manifestations and things of that sort—go into a new house. Some short time afterwards the daughter, who had given no signs of failing health, was taken with what seemed to be a fit, and, whilst in this state, lost the use of her voice, and could only make herself understood and her wants known by signs like the deaf and dumb alphabet. This state, however, was not continuous, but came on at certain intervals, and between the intervals she had no memory whatsoever of what had occurred whilst the fit was upon her. By degrees, however, when she was under the influence of these attacks, whatever they were, a voice totally unlike her natural voice proceeded from her. This voice and its utterances had all the appearance of proceeding from another personality, and an evil one, which for the time had complete dominion over her, compelling her to go, or desire to go, to low places of amusement, from which, when mistress of herself, she would have shrunk; compelling her to dress altogether differently, and to use language and express desires altogether foreign to her better self. This second personality spoke to the bystanders, reminding them of passages in their past lives which were, as they thought, secret to all save themselves, and of which the young person who was under this malignant influence could not possibly have known anything whatsoever; so that some who had their secret iniquities thus brought to light hurried out of the house. But as soon as the interval of possession came to a close, the person seemed as if she resumed her former self, and as if she awoke out of sleep, and remembered nothing of what had occurred. In the book from which I have epitomized the above (where it occupies several pages), all particulars are given, such as the name of the town and street, the name, age, and occupation of the father, &c. (From "The Gadarene," by J. O. Barrett and J. W. Peebles, Boston.)

(B.) A second case is of a person who was attacked every two or three days, and in the intervals between the attacks was perfectly well. They commenced with pains, palpitation, anxiety, and exhaustion. The patient became perfectly apathetic, and there was manifested, as a mental anomaly (these are the words of the physician narrating the case), an internal contradiction against her own thoughts and conclusions, a constant, immediate opposition against all which she thought and did. An inward "voice," which she, however, did not hear with her ear, opposed everything which she herself would do, especially did it set itself against any elevation of the sentiments, praying, &c. The voice is always wicked when the patient would do good; and sometimes calls to her, but without being heard externally: "Take a knife, and kill yourself." The attack lasted from twenty-four to forty-eight hours.[1]

(C.) A third case is from the same work as the former. A young person, without having been previously ill, was seized with convulsive attacks, in which she spoke with two voices, neither of them her natural voice: one seemed to come from a good personality, and exhorted to prayer (kept repeating, "I pray earnestly for you"). Another voice afterwards commenced to speak in a tone distinctly different from the fore-mentioned bass voice. This voice spoke almost without intermission, as long as the crisis lasted—that is, for half hours, hours, or even longer,—and was only occasionally interrupted by the bass voice, which still repeated the fore-mentioned words. In a moment this voice would represent a person different from that of the patient, and perfectly distinct from her, speaking of her always objectively, and in the third person. There was no confusion or incoherence in the words of the voice; but great consistency was shown in answering all the questions logically, or in skilfully evading them. But that which principally distinguished these sayings was their moral, or rather their immoral, character. They expressed pride, arrogance, mockery, or hatred of truth. The voice would say, "I am the Son of God, the Saviour of the world; you must adore me;" and immediately afterwards rail against everything holy, blaspheme against God, against Christ, and against the Bible; express a violent dislike against all who follow what is good; give vent to the most violent maledictions, a thousand times repeated, and furiously rage on perceiving anyone engaged in prayer, or merely folding their hands.

---

[1] From "Mental Pathology," by Dr. W. Griesinger, Professor of Clinical Medicine and of Mental Science in the University of Berlin: translated by Robertson and Rutherford, p. 242.

This evil consciousness was apparently not driven out by any medical treatment, but by the voice of the better personality commanding it to depart.

When this girl came to herself she felt tired and exhausted. She was perfectly unconscious of what had passed, and merely said that she had been dreaming.[1]

(D.) Another case investigated by two German physicians is that of a woman in good health who was possessed by the evil spirit of one long dead, who described crimes which he had committed of which the woman could not possibly have known anything, and what is more, made excuses for crimes which the woman, when herself, promptly disallowed. This case the reader will find given at great length in "Temple Bar" for January, 1862, and what is more, carefully criticized by one who, though not an unbeliever in Christianity, professed himself exceedingly sceptical as regards all present manifestations of good or evil spiritual influence.[2]

Now, of course I am well aware of all the exceptions that can be taken to these accounts. An objector may say they occurred at a distance, in other countries, and assuming himself to be the centre of truth, the further off they took place from the sphere of his ex-

---

[1] Dr. Griesinger's "Mental Pathology," pp. 243-4.

[2] There are other cases much more akin in their symptoms to possession than to ordinary lunacy or mania, in Dr. Griesinger's book. Such are to be found in pages 220 and 242 (example xvi.), 251, 257, 266, 282 (paragraph beginning, "scarcely it is necessary to remark"), 294, 295, 297. The justly celebrated work of Brierre de Boismont, a leading physician of mental diseases in Paris, contains also a number of similar instances well worthy of notice, particularly the following:—Case iii., p. 47; case vi., pp. 50, 51; case xxviii., p. 77; case xxxvii., p. 90; case xxxix., p. 97: case xlv., p. 114; case l., p. 122; case li.; case lx., p. 144; case lxi., p. 148; case lxxxviii. This last, from an incident in the life of Talleyrand, seems like a case of temporary possession rather than ordinary lunacy.

I have also now before me five other cases, all occurring in Germany, in each of which there are all the evidences of a personality wholly different from that of the person under the influence, but do not give them because I am not able to refer to the works of the physicians from which they are extracted.

perience the more unlikely they are to be true. If he had had the investigation of them, he would have been able to show that they were fraudulent, or mere ordinary cases of lunacy, and so on. Or he may object to the evidence, for in no case have we the results of legal investigation with the attestation of public notaries, and the seal of the mayor or parochial magistrate appended; it also, in its turn, duly attested. But if we happened to have such attestation, the case so attested would lie under still greater suspicion, for if the facts were true, why such pains to prove them: does not anxiety to prove the truth, betray consciousness of falsehood?

I give no opinion upon the foregoing instances. I simply cite them as showing that we have credible evidence that, in this nineteenth century, we have numbers of instances in the works of men of eminence, of persons afflicted with symptoms precisely similar to those of the persons of whom we have accounts in the Gospel narrative. The miraculous cure of demoniacal possession presents, I need hardly say, less physical difficulty than any other cure performed by our Lord. Assuming the presence of an evil spiritual intelligence in the possessed person coming face to face with the most exalted Spiritual Power and Goodness in the Person of our Lord, the natural result is, that the one quails before the Other.

But, in truth, all the difficulties respecting possession arise, not so much from our ignorance, as from our dogmatism. We assert the dogma, or at least we quietly assume its truth, that there are no spiritual or intellectual beings higher than ourselves, or in any other sphere than our own: or if we shrink from an assertion which so nearly implies our own omniscience, we lay down that these superior beings, of whose laws or limitations we know nothing, can only act upon us in ways precisely similar to those in which we act upon one another.

In the above excursus I have made much use of the contents of a chapter on Demoniacal Possession in a work entitled "The Lost Gospel," which I wrote a few years ago.

## EXCURSUS II.

### ON THE BRETHREN OF OUR LORD.

The most important notice of any "brethren of the Lord" is in Matthew xiii. 54, 55, "Is not this the carpenter's son? is not his mother called Mary? and his brethren James, and Joses, and Simon, and Judas? And his sisters, are they not all with us? whence, then, hath this man all these things? And they were offended in Him." This is part of the original tradition of the Lord's life and works, for it is repeated, almost verbatim, in Mark vi. 3: "Is not this the carpenter, the son of Mary, the brother of James and Joses, and of Judas and Simon? And are not his sisters here with us? And they were offended at him."

His brethren are also mentioned in John vii. 3, 5: "His brethren, therefore, said unto him, Depart hence," &c. "For neither did his brethren believe in him." And also in Matthew xii. 47: "His mother and His brethren stood without desiring to speak with Him." But from neither of these places do we learn anything of their names or of the degree of their relationship to Him. It seems almost certain, however, that they were the same persons mentioned in Matthew xiii. 55 and Mark vi. 3.

Now, from this notice of His brethren in the first two Synoptics we gather with almost absolute certainty two things.

1. That these four persons were the relatives nearest to our Lord who could with any propriety be called His brethren. The Nazarenes were offended at him, because they considered that by His teaching and His miracles, He set up pretensions to be some great prophet or messenger of God, and so exalted Himself above themselves, His neighbours and His equals. "Whence hath this man," they asked, "all these things?" He is but one of us, for we have His brethren and sisters dwelling here amongst us, and they are no better than ourselves. This would have lost much, if not all its point, if He had had other brethren more nearly related to Him. Being also his townsmen, some the near neighbours of His mother, and living, perhaps, in the same street, they must have known all that mere men could know about His family. It is

## THE BRETHREN OF OUR LORD. 429

absolutely impossible to suppose that He could have had nearer relatives than these unknown to the Nazarenes.

2. Then, in the next place, it seems perfectly clear that if we had only these two parallel notices (Matt. xiii. 55, and Mark vi. 3), and could put out of our minds all considerations of the extreme sacredness of even His earthly relationships derived from His Incarnation, we should gather from them that these four were His uterine brothers, sons of Mary and Joseph after the Lord's birth.

The next notice, however, entirely and for ever dispels any such idea, for in Matt. xxvii. 55, 56, we read that "many women were there, beholding (the crucifixion) afar off, among which was Mary Magdalene, and Mary the mother of James and Joses," and in the corresponding passage in Mark xv. 40, "There were also women looking on afar off, among whom was Mary Magdalene and Mary the mother of James the less and of Joses." This is decisive as to the fact that the two brethren mentioned as first of the four in Matthew xiii. 55, and Mark vi. 3, were not the Lord's uterine brothers, for they are said to be the children of another woman, and if the two first were not, neither can the two last have been, for it is absurd to suppose that the Nazarenes, in speaking of the brethren of the Lord, would place his cousins, or putative half-brothers first, and His own natural uterine brothers last.[1]

There are three other references to this Mary: one in Luke xxiv. 10, as the mother of James, another in Mark xvii, as the mother of James, and in the verse before this (Mark xv. 47) as the mother of Joses, the

---

[1] The James and Joses of the latter two passages (Matt. xxvii. 55 and Mark xv. 40) must have been the same as those of the former (Matt. xiii. 56 and Mark vi. 3), for in each Evangelist they are cited as persons well known; or, at least, as persons before mentioned; which they could not have been if, in each case, they had been a different pair of brothers. That two names should have been mentioned in conjunction by two writers, and the same two names mentioned afterwards by the same writers also in conjunction, and not denote the same persons, seems incredible. There can be no imaginable reason for mentioning this Mary as the mother of these two sons, except they were the two already alluded to. If they were two different pairs of brothers, the latter reference seems gratuitously misleading.

second of the four. These notices seem to have been written to show that the mother of the James who afterwards occupied so high a place in the Church, was not only a near relative of the Lord, but very deeply attached to Him. May I hazard the conjecture that it was in reward of the deep devotion of this woman that her children became believers?

There is another reference to James as the Lord's brother in Galatians i. 19: " Other of the Apostles saw I none, save James, the Lord's brother." This is no proof that James was one of the twelve, for Paul and Barnabas were both called Apostles.

There are two other references to the Lord's brethren. One in Acts i. 14: "These all [*i.e.* all the eleven Apostles] continued with one accord in prayer and supplication with the women, and Mary the mother of Jesus, and with his brethren." Another, in 1 Cor. ix. 5: " Have we not power to lead about a sister, a wife, as well as other apostles, and as the brethren of the Lord, and Cephas?" Both these places are important as distinguishing between the Apostles and "the brethren of the Lord."

Lastly, Jude, the writer of the Epistle, calls himself " Jude, the servant of Jesus Christ and brother of James." Now, this James must have been a person of the greatest eminence in the Church if one like Jude distinguishes himself from all others bearing the same very common Jewish name as "the brother of James." He could only be the James the brother of the Lord, and the first-named of the four brethren of Matthew xiii. 57, and so Jude naturally calls himself his brother, as he appears to be in the two notices of the Lord's brethren in the Synoptics.

These are all the places in the New Testament in which the Lord's brethren are mentioned.

If we take Biblical considerations only into account there seems to be no room for doubt as to their parentage on the mother's side. Those who from their being the nearest neighbours of the Holy Family must have known all about the Lord's belongings, name four persons from among His nearest relatives who could properly be called the Lord's brethren. A certain Mary (not the Virgin) is expressly mentioned in the same Gospels in which the names of these brethren are recounted, as the mother of two—the two first; and a third distinguishes himself from all others, bearing a very common Jewish name, as the brother of the first, and most famous of the four (Jude i.).

## THE BRETHREN OF OUR LORD.

No difficulties respecting the tracing out of the relationship of these four brethren to other persons named in the sacred narrative can, as far as I can see, affect, much less upset, the fact that all the persons called the brethren of the Lord were the sons of one mother—a Mary who stood at some distance from the cross, and afterwards with other women attended at the sepulchre.

Now of the four persons called the Lord's brethren, unquestionably the one who has most claim to the title—indeed, the only individual who is designated by name as the Lord's brother—is the first of the four, viz., James; and this Mary is four times said to be the mother of James (Matt. xxvii. 56; Mark xv. 40; Mark xvi. 1; Luke xxiv. 10). The parentage, then, of this James (and, if of him, of his three brethren), on the mother's side, is as certain as any Scripture fact can well be, and, I need hardly say, is totally unaffected by the question as to his father, who he was.

There are either two or three Apostolic or quasi-Apostolic persons of the name of James; and this is not at all strange, for the name is one of the most common of Jewish names.

One of these is the son of Zebedee, called afterwards by Church writers, but not in Scripture, James the Great. In the account of his martyrdom he is called James, the brother of John (Acts xii. 2).

Another James is designated in each of the four lists of the Apostles (Matt. x. 3; Mark iii. 18; Luke vi. 15; Acts i. 13) as the son of Alphæus. In St. John's account of the crucifixion, one of the Maries cited, who stood at the first by the cross, is Mary, the wife of Clopas [1] (not Cleophas); and it is supposed that Alphæus is the Grecized name of Clopas (in Aramaic it would be pronounced Chalphai, or Cholphai), in which case James, the second Apostle of the name, and James the Lord's brother and bishop of Jerusalem, would be the same person.

But the difficulties in the way of this identification are exceedingly great:—

1. James, the son of Alphæus, was, from the first selection of the Apostles, one of the twelve, and so was ever after that in the company of the Lord: whereas the Nazarenes speak of the James,

---

[1] It is very probable that four persons rather than three are mentioned as standing by the cross in John xix. 25—1, His mother; 2, His mother's sister (name not mentioned); 3, Mary (the wife) of Clopas; 4, Mary Magdalene.

whose name they mentioned, as if he were one of four who were with them, not with the Lord.

It would have been directly contrary to their purpose in naming the brethren of the Lord, if one or more of them had espoused His cause, and were now His companions and disciples, doing miracles and casting out devils in His Name: their allegation being that those who were nearest to Him were no different from themselves.

2. Then, in the next place, how is it that the Apostle James, the son of Alphæus, is never once distinguished by his relationship to the Lord, and the James who afterwards held so unique a place in the Church of Jerusalem, is never mentioned as the son of Alphæus?

3. Again, in two places (Acts i. 14 and 1 Cor. ix. 5) the brethren of the Lord are clearly distinguished from the Apostles. And of these brethren James was unquestionably the leading one.

4. Again, from all the accounts which we have of the Apostles, it seems to have been contrary to their original commission that they should ever become local bishops.

5. Again, how is it that, in the Synoptics, the Mary who was at the sepulchre in company with Mary Magdalene is four times called the mother of James, and twice (apparently) "the other Mary," but never once the wife of Alphæus?

These considerations seem to go very far towards showing that James the Apostle, the son of Alphæus, and James the Lord's brother, were different persons. If they were the same, then the brethren of the Lord, and unquestionably the first-named of the four, were not the sons of the Lord's mother by Joseph, nor were they the children of Joseph by a former wife.

Again, a moment's consideration will serve to show the reader that the degree of relationship of Mary, the mother of these brethren, to Mary, the Lord's mother, in no way affects the fact that, in the inspired narrative, they are called the brethren of the Lord, and yet are said to be the children of another Mary, not the Lord's mother. If this Mary was the cousin of the Virgin, or her half-sister, or any other near relative, then it affects the propriety, or the strict accuracy of the people of Nazareth, in calling her children the brothers of Jesus; but it does not take away her children from her, and assign them to another woman. It merely shows that in the time of our Lord, and in the language then spoken,

## THE BRETHREN OF OUR LORD.

the term brethren was used in a wider or looser sense than that in which we use it.

Two other considerations are important—

(A.) In the accounts of the infancy of the Lord in St. Matthew and St. Luke there is no word or hint of any other children than the Lord in the household of Joseph. From St. Luke's account, which reaches to the twelfth year of His age, the Holy Family would seem to consist of only three persons—the Lord, the Virgin, and St. Joseph.

(B.) But the second is of far deeper and more certain significance. The Lord on the cross commits His mother to the care of St. John, which He could not have done if she had children of her own, whose duty it was to take care of her; which children, be it remembered, though some time before this they were not believers, had certainly accepted Him as the Christ before the day of Pentecost.

An objection also requires notice. It has been asked: " If these persons were the cousins of the Lord, why should they not be called so ? " To which the answer is, that there was no word for cousins in either the Hebrew or Aramaic. These languages have very few words to express degrees of consanguinity; and any word answering to our term "cousin" is certainly not among them. Thus, in Luke i. 36 and 58, the word " cousin " is the translation of one signifying kinsman or relative generally, and not specifically cousin. It is translated into the Aramaic by a word, " achīn," also signifying kinsman in the wider sense. It would not have suited the purpose of the Nazarenes to call the Lord's brethren "kinsmen;" their aim was to bring Him down to their own level, and to discredit His claims : and for this purpose they would naturally bring forward the names of those who were of the same generation, and so might be assumed to be His equals, and so furnish a standard of comparison whereby to disparage Him.

The fact, then, that these brethren of the Lord have a mother assigned to them other than the Virgin, and one who also survived St. Joseph, seems to preclude the idea that they were children of Joseph by a former wife.

This latter hypothesis, however, requires some further notice, because it was adopted by many eminent Fathers—as Clement of Alexandria and Origen—and has been accepted by a biblical critic of the highest eminence amongst us, the present Bishop of Durham, in his Excursus on the Lord's Brethren, in his Commentary on the Epistle to the Galatians.

In the latter part of the Bishop's essay the reader will find the opinions of Apocryphal writers, and of a few Fathers. It appears to me that many of his citations are uncertain and indirect in their reference to the matter in hand. Some of the Fathers, however, are very explicit in favour of the view that the brethren of the Lord were children of Joseph by a former wife; the foremost of those who held this opinion being Clement of Alexandria, Origen, Hilary, Gregory Nyssen, and Epiphanius. I would, however, desire the reader to notice particularly that neither the Bishop nor any of the Fathers who uphold what he calls the Epiphanian view (i.e, that the Lord's brethren were children of Joseph), attempt to give any explanation of the fact that the persons mentioned in the Gospels as the Lord's brethren are expressly said to be the children of a woman who was certainly not the Lord's mother, and was certainly not the former wife of Joseph, for she survived him. I mean, of course, any explanation worth serious consideration, for Gregory Nyssen puts forward a view which seems absurd, viz., that the mother of James and Joses was no other than the mother of the Lord; but that the Evangelists, for no earthly reason, go out of the way to sink her more honourable appellation, and on this occasion only distinguish her as the mother of these two stepsons of hers because she undertook their education.

The Bishop summarily dismisses such a view; but as far as I can gather from an attentive reading of his essay, nowhere tells us how it can be that these four brethren are said to be the sons of a mother who cannot have been St. Joseph's deceased wife. The only hypothesis on which they can be accounted the children of Joseph, viz., that they were the sons of some deceased brother of his by this Mary, and were adopted by him (Joseph), being also dismissed by the Bishop as untenable.

I have little doubt, however, that the reason why the Epiphanian view was adopted by so many Fathers is that which is tacitly suggested by Gregory Nyssen. They could not bear to think that the Virgin did not stand by the cross till the last, and that she was not present at the sepulchre.[1] It never seems to have

---

[1] Helvidius, the denier of the perpetual virginity of St. Mary, whom St. Jerome answered, puts this argument most impudently.

occurred to them that she was most probably led from the cross in a distracted state, or perhaps more dead than alive; and so they invented the extraordinary figment that this Mary, the mother of James and Joses, was the Virgin herself, called for no assignable reason, the mother of James and Joses, rather than the mother of the Lord.

With respect to the bearing of all on the perpetual virginity of St. Mary, the reader must, of course, remember that the fact that these four were not her children does not prove the doctrine, it only removes that which would be incompatible with it. The perpetual virginity of the mother of our Lord and God is an opinion which seems to be forced upon the Catholic mind by the unutterable sacredness of that of which she was the means of bringing amongst us, the manifestation of God in the flesh. The union of the Holy Virgin with St. Joseph is unique amongst human marriages. It was not for that purpose for which all other marriages are. It was to provide protection and a home for the Only Begotten during His Infancy; so that we cannot think of it as we do of any other marriage.

Besides this, the Incarnation of the Eternal Son was designed to bring about a change in the condition of the race, so that it should be raised to a state above the necessity of marriage—in which they will neither marry nor be given in marriage, but will be the children of God, being the children of the resurrection.

And there is a truth even beyond this, for the Eternal Son was to enter into a spiritual marriage and unity betwixt himself and His Church. The Catholic mind instinctively turns to the earthly home of the Lord, as containing a foreshadowing of this highest spiritual relationship.

---

He is thus quoted in Jerome, "Adversus Helvidium," ch. xii.: " Et utique ait. Quam miserum erit et impium de Maria hoc sentire, ut quum aliæ feminæ curam sepulturæ Jesu habuerint, matrem ejus dicamus absentem: aut alteram esse Mariam, nescio quam, confingamus: præsertim quum Evangelium Joannis testetur presentem eam illic fuisse."

## EXCURSUS III.

### ON THE AUTHORSHIP OF THE LAST TWELVE VERSES OF MARK XVI.

The problem presented by the last twelve verses of this Gospel requires separate notice. The external evidence for, or against, its genuineness, as contained in Manuscripts, Versions, citations in Fathers, &c., seems to me very subordinate to certain internal considerations, the true significance of which I cannot but think has been very seriously misunderstood. First and foremost amongst these is the coherence of what comes after verse 8 with what goes before it.

The question of the discontinuity of this latter part (beginning with verse 9) with the former part, seems to me altogether independent of its authorship, for if one were absolutely assured that St. Mark was the writer (and I, for one, believe that there are overwhelming considerations in favour of his being so), still it would leave untouched the singular fact that, up to verse 8, he follows very strictly in his narrative one line of tradition which is common to him and to St. Matthew, and then he breaks off, and follows another line, or rather makes a somewhat abrupt ending, with incidents apparently derived from some other source altogether.

The following observations will, I hope, make my meaning clear. Taking as our starting point the beginning of the twenty-sixth chapter of St. Matthew, and the fourteenth of St. Mark, the reader will find that the narratives not only run parallel, but are very frequently for many verses together verbatim the same. They both begin with a reference to the coming feast of the Passover, they both relate the anointing at Bethany *out of its chronological order* (to me a very significant fact indeed). Their accounts of the Passover, of the Institution of the Eucharist, of the Lord's words of warning on the way to Gethsemane, of the Agony, of the Apprehension, of the trial before the High Priest, of the denials by St. Peter, of the leading to Pilate, of the trial before Pilate, of the Crucifixion, are virtually the same—in many cases word for word the same. It is true that some incidents are peculiar to each, as, for instance, in St. Matthew alone we have the remorse and suicide of Judas, and in St. Mark alone the account of the young man in

## THE LAST TWELVE VERSES. 437

the linen garment who attempted to follow the Lord ; but whenever they have matter in common, it is produced in almost the same words. They each record but one of the seven words said by the Lord on the Cross, and in each it is the same.

After the Lord's Death the former agreement continues. They both notice the presence of the same women—first standing at some distance from the Cross, then coming to the sepulchre.

The only difference is, that St. Mark notices the wonder of Pilate that the Lord was already dead, and St. Matthew the granting of the watch by Pilate.

We now come to the morning of the Resurrection. With one exception—that, of course, an important one—they give the same account, the exception being that St. Matthew records the account of the earthquake, and the descent of the angel, which St. Mark does not notice; but this brings out more prominently the fact that they each begin their account of the great forty days with the visit of the same women, who see one and the same angel, who gives them the same message that the Lord is risen, and that they are to go at once and bear this particular message to the disciples, that He goeth before them into Galilee, and that there they are to meet Him.

Now these two Evangelists, and these only, had recorded the words of the Lord said just before the Agony, "After that I am risen I will go before you into Galilee" (Matt. xxvi. 32 ; Mark xiv. 28), and both tell us that the angel refers to these words, and bids them go to Galilee.

So that, if we had not known the actual conclusion of St. Mark, we should have said, with almost absolute certainty, that he would have finished his Gospel with some account of the meeting in Galilee, following up the same line of tradition as St. Matthew.

So that the break of continuity is not merely the snapping of the thread of a short narration, but of a long traditional account of the Lord, occupying, one may say, the whole of this Gospel. Now this appears to me to dispose altogether of the notion that the last part of the Gospel was accidentally lost, as (according to Alford's conjecture), by the last leaf having been torn out and destroyed, for by this hypothesis we are landed in some extraordinary difficulties; for instance, the leaf must have been torn out not only before any copy had been made of it, but before anybody had even seen it; and unknown to the Evangelist, who for some extraordinary reason was never asked to make it good. For let the reader remember that the conjecture of the leaf torn out implies that the Evangelist actually finished the Gospel in the way in which all men would have expected from his strict adherence to the same line of tradition as that in St. Matthew. The torn-out leaf is a conjecture to account for the difference of the conclusion from what men, on natural principles, would have expected.

If the last leaf had been destroyed some one must have known, in a general way at least, its contents, and in these contents there must have been the fulfilment of the Lord's promise, first by Himself, then by the mouth of the angel, to meet the disciples in Galilee.

If then any person, who, from his position in the Church at Rome could, with any show of propriety, have been called upon to finish the Gospel, was requested to do so, surely his first inquiry must have been, "Has anyone seen the missing leaf?" and if it was found that no one had seen it—that it seemed to have been lost almost before the ink was dry, and the Evangelist was also not to be found, then the person must have said, "We are not left entirely to ourselves in this dilemma. We have often heard the blessed Peter deliver the tradition, how that the Lord, first by His own lips, then by His angel, promised to meet them in Galilee, and fulfilled His promise, and we must at least mention, as well as we can, what we remember that he preached respecting this meeting."[1]

The same reasoning applies to the Evangelist leaving his Gospel

---

[1] We may illustrate the reasonableness of this by the following. Supposing that instead of the leaf containing the last twelve verses, some other leaf, say that which contains the Institution of the Eucharist, had been lost, and some of the Church had met together to supply the deficiency, would they not have said, We know the traditionary account of this, which was brought to us from Palestine, and which the Blessed Peter expounded to us. Most of his words are retained in the memory of at least some or other of us. Let us see if we can put them together, assisted by a copy of the tradition which we have received from Palestine. They would do so, and they would reproduce mainly what was to be found in St. Matthew's Gospel. Afterwards if the missing part were recovered, then they would find that what they had

intentionally unfinished. The more we think of it, the more impossible this seems, not merely from the incongruity of concluding a Gospel of Salvation with the words, " They were afraid ; " but because what he had previously mentioned bound him, if I may reverently use the expression, at least to notice the fulolment of the Lord's twice repeated promise, to meet the Apostles in Galilee.

Did he leave it, then, unintentionally unfinished ? If so, it must have been because he was suddenly obliged to flee, or suddenly cut off by martyrdom, or his connection with St. Peter suddenly severed. But all historical notices of him forbid the former, for, after leaving Rome, he preached the Gospel in Alexandria, and founded the Church there, so that we have no reason whatsoever to suppose that the writing of this Gospel was the last act of his life. Again, supposing that he was suddenly deprived of the guidance of St. Peter, yet one who had been so long in the company of the Apostle, must have heard him speak of the appearance of the Lord in Galilee, and, having recorded the promise of the Lord, and having heard something of its fulfilment, he would have at least made some allusion to it, inasmuch as he had put on record the promise of the Lord by His own mouth and by the angel.

And now let us look to the contents of this, the only paragraph which has come down to us in the least degree worthy of being considered the conclusion of this Gospel, and see whether it is possible for a moment to ascribe it to anyone except an Apostle, or to one who, like St. Mark, having been the companion of two Apostles, might be considered an Apostle in the sense that Barnabas was.

For in the first place, the first six verses (9-14), are the most derogatory to the character of the Apostles as believers, of any in all Scripture. Can we possibly suppose that anyone not an Apostle, or not writing under the immediate influence or dictation of an Apostle, would have noticed two appearances of the Lord, not apparently for the purpose of showing (primarily) that the Lord had risen, but that the Apostles did not believe those who had seen Him after He was risen ; and a third to the assembled Apostles, apparently

---

reproduced was virtually, if not verbatim the same : as the reader may see if he compares Matthew xxvi. 20-32, with Mark xiv. 17-29, in each case twelve verses.

to "upbraid them with their unbelief and hardness of heart, because they believed not those which had seen Him after He was risen." The leading teaching of these six verses is not so much the Resurrection of the Lord, as the slowness of heart of His chosen ones to credit those who announced to them a Resurrection, which He Himself had so distinctly foretold. I have thought long and carefully about these verses, and I cannot imagine anyone not an Apostle, or not under the strong influence of an Apostle, giving to posterity in so short a space so much to the discredit of the Apostolic body. The few scattered notices of unbelief, or rather slowness of belief, in the three other Gospel narratives seem concentrated in these few verses.

It is to me a matter of great surprise that so many commentators have not observed this. Thus in "Notes on Select Readings," by Drs. Westcott and Hort, we have the following way of accounting for these verses: "(1) That the true intended continuation of vv. 1-8 was either very early lost by the detachment of a leaf, or was never written down; and (2) that a scribe, or editor, unwilling to change the words of the text before him, or to add words of his own, was willing to furnish the Gospel with what seemed a worthy conclusion, by incorporating with it unchanged a narrative of Christ's appearances after the Resurrection which he found in some secondary record (!) then surviving from a previous generation."

But this 'secondary record' could not have been a narrative of Christ's *appearances*. It takes no notice of the two in St. Matthew, and of two out of the four in St. John, and of, at least, three alluded to by St. Paul. It must rather have been a record of Apostolic unbelief, for the prominence is undoubtedly given to that, not to the proof of the reality of the Lord's Body.

So far for the first part of the conclusion to the Gospel.

There follows upon this a commission of the Lord of the most universal scope and character, to which is added a promise of supernatural assistance. This is by much the longest of any of the sayings of the Lord during the great forty days. It is quite independent, and cannot be identified with the commission in St. Matthew as being another version of the latter, and it covers different ground. If one may utter such a thing with the greatest reverence, it equals in authority, in simplicity, in comprehensiveness, in decisiveness any other saying of the Lord.

Of this (considered as an integral part of the whole conclusion)

# THE LAST TWELVE VERSES. 441

Drs. Westcott and Hort write: "It manifestly cannot claim any Apostolical authority, but it is doubtless founded upon some tradition of the Apostolic age."

But why "manifestly"? Is there such a difference between these words and other words of the great forty days, that on the face of them they could not have come through any Apostle, and are not worthy to be considered part of the original tradition? Is there any marked contrast between them and the words of the commission in St. Matthew, or any similar words of the Lord in St. Luke? I cannot think that there is. If any words can have the marks of being an utterance of Christ these seem to have.

They must be either the words of Christ, or an impudently wicked forgery.

Assuming them to be the latter, some one must have composed them who had an astonishing power of imitating the Lord's language in its combined authority and simplicity. He has put into the Lord's mouth words by which holy men, from the time of Irenæus downwards, have been deceived, as being His when they are not; and this for the very secondary purpose of making a decent finish to another man's book. And how could he have ventured to do so? For it surely must have occurred to him that some of his Christian brethren would ask, "Where did you get these words? Who told you that the Lord said this? We have never heard any such words ascribed to the Lord."

But now, assuming that they were the genuine words of the Lord, why should we go about to conjecture that they were founded upon some tradition of the Apostolic age, when the earliest notices of the production of the books of the New Testament assure us that there was a close connection between the writer of this Gospel, and one who, if the Lord ever said them, must have heard these words from His lips; even St. Peter himself? It seems absurd to suppose that there was any trustworthy record of one of the principal sayings of the Lord after His Resurrection which would have perished unless some "scribe," or "editor" had routed it up, and made it serve for a fit conclusion which he thought that it was not presumptuous to append to a Gospel always accounted to embody the teaching of the principal companion of the Lord.

But it has been objected that these words are unworthy of the Lord, particularly because He here says, "He that believeth not shall be damned." "If it be acknowledged," writes Dean Stanley, "that the passage has a harsh sound, unlike the usual utterances of Him Who came not to condemn but to save, the discoveries of later times have shown, almost beyond doubt, that it is not a part of St. Mark's Gospel, but an addition by another hand; of which the weakness in the external evidence coincides with the internal evidence in proving its later origin."

Notice here the word "usual." Of course the Lord *usually* utters words of encouragement and peace, but sometimes, ought we not to say frequently, He utters words of terrible significance in the way of warning, and particularly in respect of this matter of belief in Himself. "He that believeth not is condemned already, because he hath not believed in the name of the only begotten Son of God" (John iii. 18). "If ye believe not that I am He, ye shall die in your sins." "Ye do the deeds of your father." "Ye are of your father the devil." "He that is of God heareth God's words; ye therefore hear them not because ye are not of God." "Ye believe not because ye are not of My sheep" (John viii. 24, 41, 44, 47; ix. 26). "No man cometh unto the Father, but by Me." (John xiv. 6.)

What are these words in Mark, but an echo of those in St. John: "He that believeth on the Son hath everlasting life, and he that believeth not the Son shall not see life?"

So that this saying, putting in such close juxtaposition Salvation and condemnation—Salvation through belief, and condemnation through unbelief, is in the very style and manner of the Lord Himself, and is an additional proof that it is the very utterance of the Saviour and Judge.

And now before noticing the external evidence for, or against, the genuineness of these twelve verses, let us look a little to the internal in the matter of style and phraseology. Here we can do little more than refer the reader to the very exhaustive chapter (the ninth) on these points in Dean Burgon's "Last Twelve Verses of St. Mark's Gospel Vindicated." I never remember to have seen the tables so turned against gainsayers as in this chapter. In case after case of supposed unlikelihood from the employment, or non-employment, of particular words, he shows that what has been cited as against the Markian authorship is in its favour.

First as regards the style. It is quite true that the style of these verses does not show the peculiarity of St. Mark in the way of

THE LAST TWELVE VERSES. 443

graphic delineation, and the noticing of minute circumstantials, but it is to be remembered that St. Mark has another style besides this, which is a compressed narrative style, and Dean Burgon takes chap. i. 8-20, as an example of this shorter and more compressed style, and shows how exactly it corresponds with the composition of xvi. 8-20. In both these St. Mark (to adopt the words of Dean Alford) appears as an abridger of previously well-known facts. "It is a mistake to speak as if 'graphic, detailed description,' invariably characterizes the Second Gospel. St. Mark is quite as remarkable for occasionally exhibiting a considerable transaction in a highly abridged form. The opening of his Gospel is singularly concise and altogether *sudden*. His account of John's preaching (i. 1-8) is the shortest of all. Very concise is his account of our Saviour's baptism (vv. 9-11). The brevity of his description of our Lord's temptation is even extraordinary " (p. 144).

With respect to the employment or non-employment of particular words, Dean Burgon examines seriatim no less than twenty-six words or phrases which occur in (or are absent from, as $εὐθέως$ and $πάλιν$) these twelve verses, and shows, I think conclusively, that, in no case, do they make against, but rather for, the Markian origin.

It would far exceed the limits I am obliged to assign to this excursus to put down even a résumé of the Dean's remarks on these twenty-six instances, and they cannot well be compressed. I will mention one, however, which has, on examination, struck me much, and to which I trust I can add something. It has been noticed that in these twelve verses only is the word $θεᾶσθαι$ used by St. Mark—in verse 11 "had been seen of her," and in verse 14, "them which had seen him;" whereas in St. Matthew, whose phraseology is very much the same as that of St. Mark, it is used four times in the body of his Gospel. But on turning to these instances in St. Matthew, I was surprised to find that not one of them is in the least to the point, because they all occur in places to which there are no corresponding passages in St. Mark. The first is in Matthew vi. 1: "Take heed that ye do not your alms before men, *to be seen* of them." This being a part of the Sermon on the Mount is not reproduced in St. Mark. The second is in Matt. xi. 7: "What went ye out into the wilderness *to see*? To this passage there is no corresponding place in St. Mark. The third is Matt. xxii. 11: "When the king came in *to see* the guests." This parable has no place in St. Mark. And the fourth, xxiii. 5: "All their works they do *to be seen* of men." To which also the second Gospel has no corresponding passage. So that to cite the use of θεᾶσθαι in these verses as contrary to the usage of Mark betrays a plain disregard of facts or a most culpable carelessness.

Again, I will take another case out of these twenty-six exhibiting the extraordinary want of either carefulness or good faith on the part of objectors. It has been noticed, as casting doubt on the authenticity of these verses, that the adverb εὐθέως is nowhere to be found in them, though it is a very favourite one with St. Mark, being used no less than twelve times in chapter i., and six times in chapter v.; but what can the reader think of the employment of such an argument when he learns that this word εὐθέως, is not once used from chapter xi. 3 to chapter xiv. 43, *i.e.*, in a space of 154 verses? If the Evangelist writes 154 verses without it, why can he not have written 12?

We now come to the external evidence of Manuscripts, Versions, quotations from Fathers, &c., for the genuineness or authenticity of these verses. It seems a matter embarrassed with some peculiar complications, and I cannot pretend to give more than its leading features. The reader who desires to enter into its mazes is referred to Dean Burgon's volume of 320 pages, all which, however, is interesting; to Dr. Scrivener's shorter and more condensed notice in his Introduction to the "Criticism of the New Testament," 3rd edition, pp. 583-590; to Canon Cook's "Critical Notes" on the authenticity of these verses in the Speaker's Commentary, pp. 301-308. These three are in favour of the authenticity of these verses. And to Dr. Hort's "elaborate and very able counter-plea," in "Notes on Select Readings," pp. 29-51, which is against the authorship by the Evangelist.

The evidence in favour, is that of all the Uncials preserved to us, except B. and ℵ (the evidence of B., however, being decidedly against the fact that St. Mark's Gospel ended with xvi. 8). The MSS. then in favour are A., C., D., and of the later Uncials E., F., G., H., K., L, (see below), M., S., U., V., X., Γ, Δ, Σ, in fact all the Uncials which are available, *i.e.*, which contain the Gospels entire (L, N., O., P., R., T., W., Y., containing only fragments of the Gospels). All the cursives contain it, even those which frequently support B., or the Neutral Text, as 33.

It is supported by the oldest versions, all the Old Lat. available

## THE LAST TWELVE VERSES. 445

(except k.), viz. c, ff, g, l, n, o, q (a, b, e, and f, all being unavailable), the Vulgate, the three Syriacs, the Memphitic and Gothic.

B., though it does not contain these verses, witnesses to the fact that St. Mark does not end here, by leaving a column blank, which it does nowhere else, as well as by leaving the rest of the column, containing verse 8, blank also. So that the scribe of B. must have found in the MS. which he was copying a somewhat long ending which, for some reason, he did not reproduce, or when he wrote ἐφοβοῦντο γάρ he must have known that in many copies the Gospel did not so end; and so he left sufficient space for the well-known conclusion, if someone should wish to conclude the Gospel with it. Codex L. gives two alternative endings, the first introduced by the words: "Something to this effect is also met with: 'All that was commanded them they immediately rehearsed unto Jesus and the rest. And after these things, from East even unto West, did Jesus Himself send forth by their means the holy and incorruptible message of eternal salvation.'" After this, this MS. gives the words of our present ending, introduced by "But this also is met with after the words, 'For they were afraid.'"

As regards the Fathers, it is in all probability quoted by Justin Martyr [A.D. 140]. He is showing that the 110th Psalm, in the words, "He shall send forth the rod of thy power from Jerusalem," was a prophecy of the mighty word which, when the Apostles went forth from Jerusalem, they preached everywhere, ὃν ἀπὸ Ἱερουσαλὴμ οἱ ἀπόστολοι αὐτοῦ ἐξελθόντες πανταχοῦ ἐκήρυξαν. Evidently the same as ἐκεῖνοι δὲ εξελθόντες ἐκήρυξαν πανταχοῦ, in Mark xv. 20. The quotation of these verses in Irenæus [A.D. 180] is unmistakable. "In the end of his Gospel Mark saith, 'And the Lord Jesus, after He had spoken unto them, was received into heaven, and sitteth at the right hand of God.'" (Adv. Hær. iii. 10.)

Such is a short résumé of the evidence in its favour.

It appears that there is only one Greek MS. from which it is absolutely excluded, i.e., ℵ, which not only does not contain the words, but, unlike B., leaves no space in which they might afterwards be supplied. It is not found in the Old Lat. k., which concludes with the short ending found in L. It is also absent from some old Armenian MSS.

So that so far as MSS. and Versions are concerned, there is no reason whatsoever to doubt its authenticity.

But there can be little doubt, but that in the time of Eusebius, its reception was not general, as in discussing a difficulty arising out of the reconciliation of verse 9 with St. Matthew's account, he supposes that an unscrupulous objector, who wished to get rid of the whole passage, "might say that it is not in all the manuscripts of St. Mark's Gospel:" again, "Those MSS. which are most accurate terminate the Gospel with the words 'for they were afraid.'" Again, "In nearly all the copies of St. Mark's Gospel, the end comes with these words [they were afraid] : but the following words extant rarely in some, but not in all, may be regarded as superfluous, and especially if they should contain a contradiction to the other Evangelists : this one might say, declining controversy," &c. Dean Burgon has shown that this passage has been copied without acknowledgment by Jerome, Hesychius of Jerusalem, and Victor of Antioch, the last, however, giving his testimony to the verses in the words, "We, at all events, inasmuch as in very many we have discovered it to exist, have out of accurate copies subjoined also the account of our Lord's ascension (following the words 'for they were afraid'), in conformity with the Palestinian Exemplar of St. Mark which exhibits the Gospel Verity ; that is to say, from the words, 'Now when Jesus was risen early the first day of the week,' &c., down to 'With signs following. Amen.'"

It is difficult not to believe that Eusebius exaggerates when he speaks of so many copies being without the 12 verses, for, if so, how is it that there is so universal a consent of MSS. and Versions now remaining for the genuineness of these verses : how is it that all the Uncials, except in point of fact one, all the Cursives, all the Lectionaries, all the Versions, except one, which have survived are in their favour ?

And now let us review what I have written, and show its bearing.

1. The first point of all is the break in the traditional narrative common to both St. Matthew and St. Mark. This is not by any means a want of continuity in a short paragraph, but the snapping of a chain of traditionary matter from which St. Mark has scarcely ever departed (p. 436).

2. This break or discontinuity is the more extraordinary, because owing to his having mentioned the Lord's promise to meet the Apostles in Galilee, and the reiteration of that promise by the angel, St. Mark seems almost pledged to conclude his Gospel on the same lines as Matthew had done (p. 437).

## THE LAST TWELVE VERSES. 447

3. His not having done so, appears decisive against several hypotheses—as that the leaf containing the last 12 verses was destroyed before it had been copied, or that he left his Gospel unfinished, either intentionally or unintentionally (p. 488-9).

4. If, as all ecclesiastical history agrees in telling us, St. Mark wrote his Gospel from what he heard of the preaching of St. Peter, and that it was published with his approval (and, in fact, if the circumstances were at all what they are related to have been by Eusebius and others, it could hardly have been published without), then it seems to me that this break in the traditional narrative must have been by the authority of the Apostle himself (p. 440).

5. This is confirmed by the contents of the concluding part: none but an Apostle would have written them, or declared them to another, for if there be one characteristic of the Apostolic writings more than another, it is this, that they conceal or palliate nothing which is to their own discredit. They seem to have been holy and humble men of heart, who would rejoice in their own abasement, provided it was to the furtherance of their Master's Gospel. And, on the other hand, all notices of them in post-Apostolic ages are laudatory, excusing or casting a veil over their faults, and not unfrequently honouring them above what is written. So that it seems impossible to conceive that verses 9-14 could have been written under any influence except that of a present Apostle. I do not think that St. Mark himself, left to himself, would have written them.

6. The authority, majesty, and simplicity of the Apostolic Commission in verses 15 and 16 seem to make it worthy to be accounted the saying of the Lord. The short decisive juxtaposition of faith in its saving and unbelief in its condemnatory effects is in exact accordance with many other words of the Lord recorded in St. John, especially John iii. 18, 36 (p. 441). It is also in strict accordance with that manner of the Lord to which I have so frequently directed attention, of laying down very strongly some great principle unreservedly without any mention of the necessary reservations or limitations, but leaving them to be inferred. (See notes on chap. xi. v. 24.)

The reproduction of this commission can only, as far as I can see, be accounted for by the presence of one who heard it, and on whose memory it was indelibly written, viz., St. Peter. It seems absurd to suppose that one of the most striking sayings of the great forty days could be floating loosely by itself down the stream of oral tradition, and picked out by some "scribe" or "editor," who thought it would make a good finish to a truncated Gospel. The idea that such a saying is a forgery or invention, seems to me exceedingly improbable, and attended with overwhelming moral difficulties.

7. The style is exactly that of parts of St. Mark, where he compresses the account of the transactions of many months, or even years, into a short space, as for instance Mark i. 1-20 (p. 443).

The phraseology has been shown, by competent critical scholars, to be, to say the least, as agreeable to the usage of St. Mark as the phraseology of any short extract from any other writer is agreeable to the usage of the writer (p. 443).

Particularly the argument from the use of the words not elsewhere used by the Evangelist, and the omission of words, such as εὐθέως, frequently used by him, has been shown to be worthless. I believe then that the chain of tradition ending in verse 8, was broken by the authority of St. Peter himself, that the words so derogatory to the character of the Apostles in the matter of their faith were written down at the command of Peter, for no one else would have ventured to do so, and that the Lord's Commission, as here stated, came out of the memory of the Apostle himself.

But how does the omission in two MSS. and one Version, and the testimony of Eusebius bear upon the authorship? I believe not at all.

We are here obliged to fall back upon conjecture, and to me the most likely conjecture seems to be that after the writing of the eighth verse there was some delay in finishing the Gospel, and that consequently copies were made of the unfinished Gospel, which became the parents of others.

But this does not in the least degree affect the authorship. That anyone should have written these verses except St. Mark, at the dictation of St. Peter, or at least under his strong influence, is to me as incredible as that some unknown person should have invented the first words on the Cross, and put them into the Lord's mouth.

In estimating the force of the testimony of Eusebius, it is quite clear that for some reason he disliked the passage, perhaps because he could not harmonize it with others; and so in speaking of the number of MSS. which did contain it, he would unconsciously exaggerate. And it is to be remembered that he would do this with no unbelieving predilections—indeed, without any doctrinal bias of any sort, for the passage contains no appearance of the Risen Lord which is not to be found elsewhere ; and with respect to the Lord's words respecting belief and unbelief, the doctrine of the saving nature of the one, and the damning nature of the other was far too deeply rooted in the mind of the Church to be affected by the loss or retention of one passage.

It has not been till this nineteenth century that the all-seeing wisdom of the Providence which guided—which rather overruled the mind of the sacred writer to insert this whole passage, has become apparent, for the popular argument against the Lord's Resurrection is now the Vision Theory, that the loving hearts of the disciples led them to dwell in thought upon the dead Christ so much, that at last they thought they saw Him, and they went forth and lived lives of poverty and self-denial, and braved deaths of ignominy and torture, and founded the greatest institution which the world has ever seen, all on the strength of this phantom of their imagination. Now the accounts of the Resurrection in all the Gospels give the lie to this, for with one voice they tell us that the Apostles themselves neither expected the Resurrection nor believed in its reality when they were told of it.

And above all, these closing words of St. Mark teach us that the belief in the Risen Lord was forced upon them.

So that by the good providence of God their unbelief makes our assurance doubly sure.

THE END.

www.ingramcontent.com/pod-product-compliance
Lightning Source LLC
Chambersburg PA
CBHW070837020526
44114CB00041B/1420